Investing in St Petersburg

Investing in
St PETERSBURG

A Guide to Business & Investment

Consultant editor:
Dr Marat Terterov

Published with the support of Adaptec Company (Russia):

Distributed by:

KOGAN
PAGE

Published in association with:

SAINT-PETERSBURG
OPEN CITY

Published in association with:
The City Government of St Petersburg

GMB

This first edition first published in Great Britain and in the USA in 2005 by
GMB Publishing Limited.

GMB Publishing Ltd
120 Pentonville Road
London N1 9JN
UK
www.globalmarketbriefings.com

Distributed by Kogan Page Ltd
120 Pentonville Road   22883 Quicksilver Drive
London N1 9JN   Sterling VA 20166–2012
UK   USA

© GMB Publishing and Contributors 2005

ISBN 1-905050-16-X

British Library Cataloguing-in-Publication Data

A CIP record for this book is available from the British Library

---

Library of Congress Cataloguing-in-Publication Data
Investing in St. Petersburg : a guide to business & investment/consultant
editor, Marat Terterov.– 1st ed.
    p. cm.
  ISBN 1-905050-16-X
  1. Investments, Foreign–Russia (Federation)–Saint Petersburg.
2. Saint Petersburg (Russia)–Economic conditions. I. Title: Investing in
Saint Petersburg. II. Terterov, Marat.
  HG5580.2.S25T47 2005
  330.947′21–dc22
                        2005021494

Typeset by Digital Publishing Solutions
Printed in the United Kingdom at the University Press, Cambridge

Contents

Services

Company Profiles and Investor Experiences

PART FOUR: COMMERCIAL LEGISLATION FOR ST PETERSBURG – THE TAXATION AND LEGAL ENVIRONMENT

Preface

I am convinced that in its most genuine historical mission, St Petersburg is the natural connection between Russia and Europe. It is with utmost pleasure that I want to say to you now: Welcome.

V.I. Matvienko, Governor of St Petersburg

Foreword

The relationship between the UK and St Petersburg goes back 300 years to Peter the Great's time. This great city was founded in 1703, and stands now as testimony to Peter's vision and determination. Many of his closest advisors were British and, from those links, bilateral trade began. Russia remains as fascinating a country now as I'm sure it was 300 years ago.

In these early years of the 21st century, British companies continue to be interested in forming business relationships with partners in St Petersburg. Investment opportunities regularly present themselves, and good practical advice on how to be successful with their investment is often sought by potential investors.

I am therefore delighted, in my capacity as Head of UK Trade & Investment in St Petersburg, to be able to offer a contribution to this practical guide to investing in the city.

Russia has been very successful in rebuilding its economy in the period following the economic crisis of the late 1990s. Its success has encouraged many foreign businesses, from the largest multinationals to modest small and medium-sized enterprises, to look seriously at Russia as an export market and a destination for investment.

It is undoubtedly a country of great business opportunity and potential. Any country of 140 million people with increasing economic stability and an improving business climate needs to be taken seriously. However, it is clearly not for investors in search of an easy-win or a fast buck. It is only for those with patience and a realistic medium- to long-term strategy for achieving a return on their investment. Most of the international companies currently finding success in Russia would, I expect, admit that they have suffered a few 'interesting' moments at some stage.

In St Petersburg and its surrounding region, British companies such as Cadbury Schweppes, Unilever and British American Tobacco have established a manufacturing presence and continue to expand their business. They would, I'm sure, confirm if asked that it has not been all plain sailing.

And this is why the availability of good advice is vital. Russia is all about prior preparation and local knowledge. The advice must be informed, comprehensive and, above all, realistic.

International business in St Petersburg is on the up. The number of British companies represented in St Petersburg has risen by around 35 per cent since 2002. Under the leadership of Governor Matvienko, large strides have been taken towards removing the obstacles that traditionally served as a disincentive to potential investors. Her economic policy makers have mainly come from business backgrounds and therefore understand what is needed to attract international business. They are professional and committed to maximizing St Petersburg's economic potential. They recognize the importance of foreign investment and want to make it easier for companies to start doing business here.

I wish this publication success. I am sure that it will prove extremely useful to anyone thinking about St Petersburg as a potential market or investment location. The UKTI team at the British Consulate-General would be very happy to see many more well-prepared British companies enter the market and build a successful business. We stand ready to deliver UK Trade & Investment's services to help ensure that success.

Peter Langham
Head of UK Trade & Investment
British Consulate-General
St Petersburg

Doing Business with St Petersburg

Message from Maria Chernobrovkina,
Executive Director, St Petersburg Chapter,
American Chamber of Commerce in Russia

St Petersburg enjoys a number of advantages that cannot go unnoticed by international business. Its geographic location, developed land, air and maritime international transport infrastructure, large population second only to that of Moscow region, highly educated workforce, large number of manufacturing enterprises in different sectors, and world-class tourism potential are all factors that reinforce the natural competitive advantages of the region. Obviously, the city has suffered from some of the problems that plagued Russia as a whole in the 1990s, including industrial downturn, lack of infrastructure modernization and maintenance, legislative and regulatory obstacles to trade and investment, red tape and corruption. However, the local authorities clearly understand these issues and, working together with the private sector, are taking the necessary steps to improve the situation.

In 2004, these efforts coupled with nationwide economic growth contributed greatly to growth in trade and investment in the region. We are very encouraged that United States is one of the major commercial partners of St Petersburg, with trade growing by 10 per cent in 2004 to $629.6 million, while exports also grew by 10 per cent to $172.1 million and imports surged by 22 per cent to $457.5 million. In 2004, the United States became St Petersburg's leading investor with 24 per cent of all foreign investments, or $236.5 million. Export–import deals with the United States cover ferrous and non-ferrous metals, wood, aluminium and aluminium products, foodstuffs, tobacco, fast-moving consumer goods

(FMGCs), machinery, electrical equipment, and chemical and organic products.

Investment projects with American capital span many sectors, including FMCGs, IT and telecommunications, electronic equipment, foodstuffs, tobacco, tourism and hospitality. Members of the American Chamber of Commerce's (AmCham) St Petersburg Chapter are building on their commercial success to date and continue to expand their operations. British-American Tobacco, Caterpillar, Citibank, Coca-Cola, Electrolux, Ford, Gillette, Heineken, Henkel, Hewlett-Packard, IKEA, Intel, International Paper, JTI, KFC, Lucent, Merloni, Motorola, Otis, Pepsi, Peterstar, Philip Morris, Pizza Hut, Subway, Sun Microsystems and Wrigley are among the many AmCham members that are operating successfully and expanding in the region.

AmCham and its St Petersburg Chapter work closely with regional authorities on a wide range of regulatory issues in a continuous effort to further improve the business environment in the region. After adopting the Tax Code, St Petersburg changed its legislation on incentives for investors to bring them into line with the federal law. AmCham had actively participated in drafting the amendments, and our members' input was appreciated by the administration. Although there are still questions left, we are closely cooperating with regional and federal authorities on the issues of concern.

In 2004, the highlight of this private–public sector dialogue was the meeting of AmCham members with St Petersburg Governor Valentina Matvienko. Outlining the city administration's strategy to promote trade and investment in St Petersburg, the governor addressed more than 100 business leaders and fielded numerous questions from the audience on government initiatives and business projects, and a range of specific issues. The governor praised the local AmCham Chapter's activities and encouraged members to continue offering new and innovative ideas to enhance the city. She pledged to further improve city transportation, increase transparency, and reduce red tape and corruption. She encouraged foreign investment and welcomed specific proposals from the international business community for improving the city's tender and auction process and for overhauling long-term municipal development strategies and planning, declaring that:

> We fully understand that such authoritative organizations as the American Chamber of Commerce can greatly impact

the reputation of our country and its 'Northern Capital' –
St Petersburg – in the world markets, and influence the
decision-making of American and multinational companies
to develop business in our city.

The St Petersburg government's interest in attracting more investment, and its practical steps to improve the city's investment climate, have borne fruit: overall foreign investment is expected to
reach $1.2 billion in 2005. Re-invigorated privatization, infrastruc-
ture development, modernization of customs service, and simplified
business registration and reporting procedures give us solid
grounds for optimism. The city has developed a 'strategic investor'
concept under which projects bringing high volumes of investment
to the city, creating many new jobs and improving the city infrastructure are to be considered 'strategic' and receive special attention and treatment from the government. Following this concept,
the city government has signed an agreement with Chinese companies for a residential area development and Toyota announced
its new car factory project.

A particular area where we expect progress is the hi-tech
sector. Following President Vladimir Putin's endorsement of
the 'technoparks' concept in January 2005, St Petersburg and
Leningrad Oblast stand to benefit from a special regulatory, tax and
infrastructure regime to promote the development of a knowledge-
based economy in the region. The decision was welcomed by the
whole IT community. If the federal government keeps its promise
to reduce the tax burden on IT companies, St Petersburg with its
highly educated labour force is likely to become Russia's 'Silicon
Valley'. However, AmCham members involved in IT activities
believe that the idea can be effective only if the 'technopark' participants are required to invest in research, education, training and
technical libraries. Many AmCham members (especially the larger
IT companies) are supporting higher education and actively cooperating with leading universities: St Petersburg State University,
the Technical University, University of Precision Mechanics and
Optics, University of Telecommunications and Electrotechnical
University.

However, the first thing that comes to mind when speaking of
St Petersburg is of course its tourism potential, and development
of this requires the appropriate infrastructure. The city authorities
have constantly focused on the lack of hotel capacity and tourist
infrastructure, and developed a strategy to solve the problem.
The City Committee for Investments and Strategic Projects has

launched a Website, www.hotelinvest.ru, where potential investors can find up-to-date information on the hotel market and investment opportunities, and participated in a number of AmCham events to increase the awareness of the foreign business community. In 2004, a number of city-owned hotels were sold, and still more will be coming on the market in due course. Overall, the city government offers 170 locations (existing hotels as well as other buildings and land lots) for hotel development. AmCham is joining the city government's efforts to develop a specific programme for St Petersburg's image development.

The continued growth in AmCham St Petersburg Chapter's membership, which reached a remarkable 18 per cent in 2004, is a clear demonstration of the effectiveness of AmCham's business model, which is geared towards providing returns on membership fee investment in tangible, bottom-line terms. The backbone of this ROI model includes working with regional authorities to reduce barriers to normal business operations, representing members' interests to Russian federal and regional agencies, and providing valuable networking and business development opportunities. With the pro-business leadership of St Petersburg, we expect further progress in enhancing the region's position as a prime foreign investment destination.

List of Contributors

Adaptec Company, Russia is a well-established Russian consulting company, offering a range of services to foreign companies and Russian firms including: strategic planning for foreign companies approaching the Russian market; marketing, promotional services, public relations; organization of international exhibitions (both in Russia and abroad), publishing in Russian of English and American fiction and non-fiction literature.

The General Director of Adaptec Company is **Alexander M. Krivtsov, D.Sc (Econ)**, who is the author of many published works in the field of administration and management, and socio-economic problems relating to organizational development. Many of these works have also been translated into foreign languages outside of Russia.

Association of Joint Ventures Details of the services provided by AJV can be found in Chapter 3.15.

Baker & McKenzie provides sophisticated legal advice and services to the world's most dynamic global enterprises, and has done so for more than 50 years. Active in the USSR and the Commonwealth of Independent States (CIS) for over 40 years, and the first Western law firm to be registered with the then Soviet authorities, its Moscow office was opened in 1989, followed by the opening of its St Petersburg and Kyiv offices in 1992, Almaty in 1995 and Baku in 1998. It now has one of the largest practices in the CIS, offering expertise (in close cooperation with its offices worldwide) on all aspects of investment in the region.

The 76 professionals of its Moscow and St Petersburg offices are experienced advisors to leading Russian enterprises, multinational corporations and major international agencies and organizations. Regularly recognized (by both Chambers Global and European Legal 500) as market leaders in corporate and commercial law, dispute resolution, employment law, intellectual property, real estate and tax, it acts for major domestic and international clients in a range of industries including banking and finance, capital markets and securities, oil and gas, manufacturing, pharmaceuticals, IT and telecommunications and others.

Beiten Burkhardt is one of the largest German law firms with 15 offices in six countries. With 250 lawyers and tax advisors, the firm has a strong chain of offices located in Western and Eastern Europe, the Russian Federation, Ukraine, and the Far East. Beiten Burkhardt is the only German law firm permanently operating in Moscow (since 1992) and St Petersburg (since 1996) with an orientation towards regional legislation and international aspects focusing mainly on legal support and legal and tax structuring of foreign industrial investments in Russia.

Among others, the firm's services include: establishment of Russian subsidiaries and branch offices; legal analysis of and recommendations on acquisitions of existing Russian businesses; structuring financing and corporate governance; developing recommendations on operational activity schemes; day-to-day support for investors. The firm's specialists use the unique know-how they have developed, as well as the firm's extensive international experience, in order to provide comprehensive, high-quality legal advice and overall solutions elaborated on an interdisciplinary basis.

Throughout the recent years, the firm has focused its efforts on investments in the real estate sector. In 2005, the firm continued publishing comprehensive overviews in the spheres of investments in the Russian Federation, Russian real estate law etc, as well as various articles devoted to Russian Law developments and new legal aspects, which have been immensely popular since their initial distribution (for further details, please visit www.bblaw.ru).

BISNIS fosters US exports and other new US business activities in Eurasia, providing market information and related services to US and Eurasian firms, particularly small and medium-sized companies. BISNIS helps its clients identify, evaluate, prepare for, and successfully achieve new business activities.

Countries covered include 12 countries of the former Soviet Union: Russia, Ukraine, Moldova, Belarus, Kazakhstan, Kyrgyzstan, Tajikistan, Turkmenistan, Uzbekistan, Armenia, Azerbaijan, Georgia. It has 13 US-based representatives and 20 representatives in 10 Eurasian countries.

BISNIS has facilitated more than US$4 billion in US exports and BISNIS benefits US economic interests as well as US strategic interests abroad by facilitating new US exports and other business partnerships in Eurasia.

No other public or private source provides the range of information, geographic coverage, and services offered by BISNIS. BISNIS assists an extensive number of US manufacturers and service firms, particularly SMEs. Numerous trade associations, state offices, US government agencies and programme rely heavily on BISNIS support to achieve their own projects and activities. In a 2002 TPCC study, BISNIS was the USG programme most frequently cited as a best practice, particularly for market information, lead dissemination, and follow-up.

Services offered to both US and Eurasian Companies include:

- BISNIS Counselling & Resource Matchmaking. BISNIS trade specialists provide individual market guidance and referrals;

- BISNIS Events. Dozens of events live and by video for firms across the US each year;

- BISNIS Search for Partners. Partner leads from Eurasia;

- BISNIS Trades & Tenders. US export leads for Eurasia;

- BISNIS FinanceLink. Transactions seeking finance are distributed to more than 600 financiers;

- BISNIS ExpoLink Eurasia. Russian-language promotion tool for US firms to Eurasian firms.

Services for US companies (English-language) include:

- Market Reporting. BISNIS industry reports and guidance prepared by local and US experts;

- BISNIS Email Updates. Market updates, analysis, resources, leads, events sent by email;

- BISNIS Online (website). Forbes rated it a 'Best of the Web' (twice), www.bisnis.doc.gov

- BISNIS Bulletin. Monthly English-language newsletter on Eurasian market developments.

Services for Eurasian companies (Russian-language) include:

- BISNIS Eurasia Online. Russian-language practical and educational site for Eurasian needs;

- BISNIS *Vestnik*. Quarterly Russian-language newsletter for Eurasian business needs.

Igor Yegorov has been the representative of BISNIS in Northwest Russia out of St Petersburg, Russia since 2000. During that time he has written several dozens of regional overviews, industry reports and commercial news updates on topics ranging from real estate development, financing and investment to transportation, certification, healthcare and engineering services. His prior career was in the financial sector (since 1994). He graduated from St Petersburg State University, Department of Economics, and received his PhD in the area of international economics from St Petersburg State University of Economics and Finance. He is also a managing editor of *Vestnik*, BISNIS' quarterly Russian-language publication distributed throughout Eurasia (current circulation of 11,500 copies in addition to the pdf version available online and through email distribution).

Pavel A. Brusser was born in 1978 and graduated from St Petersburg State University, Department of Economics in 2000. In 2003, he obtained his Masters Degree in Development Economics from Oslo University, Norway. Pavel Brusser now heads the Economic Appraisal Department of the Committee for Investments and Strategic Projects in the Government of St Petersburg and is working on his PhD thesis dedicated to the issue of risk management in investment banking.

City Realty Ltd is a Western-owned and managed real estate company headquartered in St Petersburg, Russia. Areas of expertise include real estate sales and purchases, long-term rentals, serviced apartments, holiday apartments, project management and consulting. City Realty is a member of the American Chamber of Commerce and the American Society of Travel Agents (ASTA). The firm's clients range from private individuals and investors to Fortune 500 companies. City Realty is also the owner of the travel portals Express to Russia and Best Hotels Russia (www.express torussia.com and www.besthotelsrussia.com) offering visa support, tours and discount accommodation throughout Russia.

Paul May, a native of New Jersey, the Garden State, has been living and working in Russia for the past 13 years. Paul has an MBA from Columbia Business School and previously worked as a senior manager for ABB and as a consultant with McKinsey & Company.

Paul loves St Petersburg, especially the city's architecture and canals.

CMS Cameron McKenna is a leading international law firm and a market leader. The firm has been recognized in several prestigious awards including British Consultant of the Year – British Consultants Bureau in 2000 – for work on a water treatment project in Sofia, and the same award in 1999 for work on an airport project in Africa. CMS Cameron McKenna has practices in Central and Eastern Europe with offices in Moscow, Warsaw, Budapest, Prague and Bucharest and affiliated offices in Belgrade and Bratislava. CMS is a transnational legal services organization with member firms in the UK, Germany, France, Austria, Belgium, the Netherlands and Switzerland, and with 44 offices in 19 different countries.

DLA Piper Rudnick Gray Cary is a global legal services organization with offices across Europe, Asia and the United States. It has over 2,800 lawyers across 50 offices and 18 countries and provides a broad range of legal services through its global practice groups. In July 2005, EY Law's practices in Russia and the CIS joined DLA Piper, creating one of the largest legal practices in the region. DLA Piper in St Petersburg is a full service legal practice, with two partners and 23 specialist lawyers. It is a recognized leader in the Russian Northwest region and is active in the areas of corporate law, M&A, tax, real estate and utilities, litigation, customs, labour, intellectual property and information protection.

Victor Naumov is a Senior Associate at DLA Piper Rudnick Gray Cary, has a PhD in Law, and is Head of Intellectual Property/ Information Technology Protection Group. Victor deals with civil law, information law and intellectual property and specializes in intellectual property protection and management, telecoms and IT regulation, e-commerce and internet regulation, legal support in advertising and media business. Victor holds three higher education degrees: in engineering, legal sciences, and applied mathematics; he defended his thesis on 'Regulation of Internet Data Distribution'. As an Associate Professor of the St Petersburg State University, he gives lectures to the law and economics departments. Victor is a member of the Expert Council on intellectual property legal regulation and protection attached to the Committee for Economic Policy, Entrepreneurship and Tourism of the RF State Duma. Since 2002, Victor has been a member of the Federal

Programme 'Electronic Russia' developers' team and member of task groups of a range of the RF State Duma committees. He took part in drafting a number of laws on IT regulation, using information resources and systems, and intellectual property. He was the author of the 'Guidelines on Individual Internet Commerce in the Russian Federation' approved by the Committee for Economic Policy and Entrepreneurship of the RF State Duma in 2000. Victor is a fellow of the Russian Internet Academy; author of *Law and Internet: Theory and Practice* (2002) – the first in Russian monographic research into the problems of legal regulation of the internet. He is author of over 70 scientific papers.

Ernst & Young was one of the first international professional services firms to establish its practice in St Petersburg in 1992 and since then has worked to successfully integrate itself with the local and international business communities, rightfully earning its reputation by offering quality, client-driven services to top international and local businesses in the Northwest region. The Ernst & Young office in St Petersburg now employs more than 100 professionals, many of whom have accumulated unique experience in providing audit, and various consulting services to manufacturing, telecommunication, pharmaceutical, pulp and paper companies as well as companies from the hospitality and food and beverage industries. Its practice in the Northwest is currently notable not only for being the largest in terms of the number of professionals, but also for the variety of their specialization in types of services and industries. Ernst & Young provide professional services to leading Russian and international companies in such areas as assurance and advisory business services, business consulting services, tax, customs consulting, real estate consulting and seminars for professional education. It serves the Northwest market locally, and its approach is multidisciplinary, looking beyond the immediate project to each client's long-term business interests.

Having joined the company in 2001, **Vladislav Miagkov**, the Head of Ernst and Young's Real Estate Consulting Group in St Petersburg, has an extensive background in all types of property income analysis and valuation techniques in Russia, including title research, site inspection, appraisal, marketing and feasibility studies. He has worked in Russian and American companies specializing in land and property valuation and consulting. Vladislav served as executive manager and senior real estate appraiser for a private American company created to serve specialized commercial and income property needs of the investment community in St Petersburg.

He was senior appraisal consultant to the Russian Federal government (1998–99) in analysis and evaluation of 15 real estate properties owned abroad in Central and Northern Europe. In 1998, he made evaluations and analyses of 30 industrial sites in the St Petersburg region for a large multinational industrial firm. During the last six years he estimated the market value of 44 real properties on orders of international and Russian companies. He also provides market analysis and feasibility studies for all kinds of property income including hotel development.

Having served as country manager in Russia for several multinational corporations since 1995, **Gilbert Doctorow** is today the owner-manager of **Eurologos**, St Petersburg, where he supervises a team of translators/editors producing translations into Russian. The St Petersburg office cooperates closely with the worldwide Eurologos Group based in Brussels, Belgium to offer nearly all the world's commercially significant languages to its clientele, drawing on the resources of more than 30 offices around the globe, from Buenos Aires to Tokyo. In keeping with the Group's business model, translations are performed and edited in countries where the target language of any given assignment is spoken. This assures access to large pools of talent and competitive, moderate pricing. Further information is available by visiting www.eurologos-spb.com or contact info@eurologos-spb.com.

Victoria A. Kovaleva was born in 1977. Victoria is a graduate of Saratov State University, Department of Philology (2000) and Oslo University, Department of Economics and Social Sciences (2004), and is currently working for one of the HansaBank Group branches in St Petersburg.

The Institute for Entrepreneurial Issues (IEI), founded in 1992, is a full service certified public accounting and consulting company offering a full range of comprehensive legal, valuation, financial and other high-quality consulting services, market and industry studies. The detailed knowledge of local and industry issues and trends, and the value-creating activities of IEI have been properly evaluated by the business community. According to leading business magazines' industry ratings, IEI has been No. 1 among consulting companies in St Petersburg and Northwestern Russia since 1997. Of all Russian consulting companies outside Moscow, IEI is the leader in the market. The major and competitive benefit of IEI is the availability of specific expertise from a multi-disciplinary team of more than 350 locally-qualified professional employees that provide a greater depth of consideration in valuation, auditing, legal and financial analysis, tax consulting and marketing. This broad-based perspective is hard to find elsewhere.

The dynamic and highly competitive professionals of IEI, with past careers in government, banking, academia and Russian and Western consulting companies, possess in-depth knowledge of the local market, extensive experience and qualifications, and the insight and creative judgement needed to provide a wide variety of business/real estate-related professional services. The experts in its valuation department are able to estimate the value of business or real estate for sale/acquisition, restructuring, financing, joint venture, litigation, governance or statutory purposes, legal disputes and development decisions. IEI have provided sophisticated legal advice and services to many of the most dynamic and successful national companies. Since 2004, IEI has been a member of the 'Kreston International' network. With its head office in St Petersburg and an office in Moscow, IEI serves its clients all over the country and in various fields – dealing with Siberian energy giants and federal properties in Moscow, major retailers and suburban development, the hospitality industry and brownfield redevelopment.

Alexei I. Shaskolsky, PhD, was a college professor for 20 years, then worked for five years for the Administration of St Petersburg/Committee for the Management of City Property. Since 2000, he has worked for Gamma Group and Colliers International, and joined IEI in 2002.

KPMG is the global network of professional services firms of KPMG International. Its member firms provide audit, tax, and advisory services on an industry-focused basis. With nearly 100,000 people worldwide, KPMG member firms provide professional services from offices in 715 cities in 148 countries. KPMG in Russia has offices in Moscow, St Petersburg, Nizhny Novgorod and Ekaterinburg, with staff in excess of 700. KPMG in Russia offers, among other services, a full range of tax and legal services. This includes both corporate and personal tax advice, tax optimization and structuring, legal consulting support for new investors and existing businesses in Russia, mergers and acquisitions services, and due diligence and litigation support.

Peter Arnett is a Partner and Head of KPMG St Petersburg Tax department. Peter specializes in international and Russian taxation, including tax planning and tax optimization issues. Peter is both a qualified chartered accountant and a chartered tax advisor.

He has represented the interests of businesses in Russia in discussions with the Russian Government on tax reform, particularly regarding profits tax, VAT, tax administration and transfer pricing.

Stanislav Denisenko is a Senior Manager and Head of KPMG St Petersburg's Legal Group. Stanislav has considerable legal experience in mergers and acquisitions, joint ventures and other corporate matters, as well as in cross-border transactions, real estate and construction projects and litigation.

Alisa Melkonian is a Tax Manager and member of the Association of Certified Chartered Accountants. Alisa advises Russian and foreign companies on Russian and international taxation. She is also responsible for advising on tax aspects during the audits of financial statements and is experienced in representing clients' interests in tax disputes in courts.

Nina Goulis is a Tax Consultant of KPMG St Petersburg Tax Department. Nina advises Russian and foreign companies on Russian and international taxation, tax planning and tax optimization. Nina is also responsible for advising on tax aspects during the audits of financial statements.

Lenenergo's Larissa Semenova was born in St Petersburg in 1972. Ms Semenova graduated from the journalism faculty of St Petersburg University. After graduation, she worked in the media business. In 2001, she joined JSC Lenenergo and occupied the position of PR Director.

Gregory Kharenko was born in St Petersburg in 1975. Mr Kharenko graduated from the economics faculty of the St Petersburg Institute of Commerce and Economics and, in 2001, he defended his PhD degree in Economics (St Petersburg State University). After graduation, Mr Kharenko worked in banks, consulting companies and SUE 'Inpredservice'. In 2004, he joined the Investor Relations Department of Lenenergo.

The lawyers of **Pepeliaev, Goltsblat & Partners** provide assistance in regulating rights to land plots and other real estate assets and in solving other legal and tax problems. They specialize in:

- land and real estate due diligence, including examination of title documents for land and property;

- privatization of land and real estate;

- legal support for land and real estate transactions (purchase and sale, lease, mortgage, etc);

- drawing up contracts and negotiating contractual terms with counteragents;

- arranging an independent appraisal of land and real estate;

- acquisition of rights to land plots intended for commercial use;

- acquisition of rights to existing manufacturing facilities for setting up production;

- real estate mortgages as security for obligations under commercial contracts.

PeterStar is one of the leaders in the telecommunications market of the Northwest Region; specializing in the provision of telephony, internet and data services. During over 10 years of operation, the company has invested circa US$150 million in its network, thus significantly contributing to the development of tele-coms infrastructure in St Petersburg. PeterStar owns the largest digital fibre network (over 2,000 km) and maintains a 70 per cent market share of the business telephony market among alternative operators in St Petersburg. The company's activities have included the modernization of approximately 35,000 phone lines for residents of Vasilievsky Island. PeterStar employs about 500 people and in 2004 the company had revenues of approximately US$80 million.

PeterStar operates in seven regions outside St Petersburg. In 2003, PeterStar launched its branch in Moscow and during 2004, with the help of certain acquisitions or 'green-field' project developments, PeterStar established a presence in the following Russian regional markets: Pskov, Veliky Novgorod, Petrozavodsk, Murmansk, Vyborg and Kaliningrad. PeterStar holds 100 per cent of the shares of Baltic Communications Ltd (BCL) and Comset, 90 per cent of the shares of the Pskov city telephone network, 100 per cent of the shares of Pskovintercom, ADM-Murmansk and Telecom Zapadnoye Parokhodstvo. PeterStar was given an award by the RF State Committee of Communications: 'Contest Winner in the Field of Communications'. Based on the results of 2003, PeterStar became a laureate of the VII Russian Competition 'Best Russian Enterprises' in the nomination 'For the highest financial efficiency'.

In 2004, PeterStar was recognized as one of the top ten largest Russian internet providers and obtained the status 'Large' with RIP NCC (one of four worldwide organizations distributing the inter-net's address space in Europe). The company was the country's third-largest Wi-Fi Internet service provider, according to Dow Jones, and among the best 20 taxpayers in the city, announced by local government. PeterStar's capital expenditure programme for 2005 is anticipated to be approximately US$15 million, which will be used principally for the further development of its enterprise-wide network infrastructure. Throughout the year, PeterStar continued its sponsorship activities, including participation in International Jazz festivals, the Early Music festival, and the St Petersburg Open international tennis tournament. In 2004, PeterStar was added to the Gold Book of the Nation and honoured by the International Fund 'Maecenas of Russia' for its charity actions.

Anastassia Bogatikova was born in 1977 in Murmansk. In 1999, she graduated from the State Pedagogical University, Foreign Languages Department (English and German) in Petrozavodsk (Diploma of Higher Education). In 2001, she graduated from the International Banking Institute in St Petersburg, with the specialization in Finance and Credit (Diploma). In 2003, she graduated from the St Petersburg State University, Economics Department, specializing in Finance and Credit (Diploma of Higher Education). At the same time, in 2003, she graduated from the Open Business School in St Petersburg, where she specialized in Marketing (Diploma). In 2000, she started to work for Vana Public Relations, a Swedish marketing research company, as a specialist in research. In 2001, she joined PeterStar company, as a Marketing Specialist. In 2004, she became a Senior Marketing Specialist in PeterStar Marketing Department (Analytical Group).

The Research and Design Institute of Regional Development and Transportation (RDIRDT) was established in 1999 with the purpose of carrying out scientific, design and engineering activities in the field of transport infrastructure and urban transit systems. Expanding its initial specialization, continually enhancing techniques, and using state-of-the-art software technologies, RDIRDT has advanced to the leading position in the Northwest of Russia, operated in the Central, Southern and Siberian regions of Russia, and developed cooperation with a number of international companies. Over the years of its activity, RDIRDT has become one of the leading institutes in Russia that provides research, project design and engineering services for mass transit systems, solving issues of efficiency improvement in infrastructure management, and developing systematic technical, economic, sociological and environmental studies. Over recent years, commissioned by government agencies, RDIRDT has developed a number of integrated transport schemes for major Russian cities. The Institute's staff has completed over 250 projects on improvement and development of transit infrastructure, over 100 research projects and published over 400 scientific articles and reports, and 11 monographs and manuals.

The major activities of RDIRDT include:

- regional development programmes for transit systems and road maintenance, integrated transport schemes for cities;

- projects of construction/reconstruction of roads and bridges;

- feasibility studies, business plans for construction/reconstruction of road and bridge facilities with the involvement of private investors;

- programmes and projects on improvement of administrative and economic management tools in the transport and road sector;

- auditing transport and road companies;

- technical and economic manuals and software for transportation systems and road maintenance management using GIS-technologies;

- survey procedures, computer models for forecasting mobility and distribution of freight, passenger, traffic, and pedestrian flows;

- traffic management schemes;

- schemes for operation conditions monitoring on roads and bridge facilities based on diagnosis and system surveys;

- assessment of transportation and road facilities' impacts on the environment and environment protection plans;

- independent expertise, project support, supervising construction, reconstruction, repairs, and maintenance works; quality control of road and bridge works.

RDIRDT has been working for the Russian authorities at all levels, as well as for international clients from Canada, France, Denmark, Germany, the UK etc, on a variety of projects on: development of transport corridors, UPT management improvement, introduction of state-of-the-art traffic management systems, and development of rapid mass transportation services in St Petersburg. At present, RDIRDT employs over 100 specialists in various fields (road engineers, bridge engineers, economists, town-planners, project designers, environment managers, software developers, mathematicians, sociologists, etc.). To perform the above research, design and engineering services, RDIRDT has all the required certificates, highly-qualified staff, advanced equipment, software and techniques. Projects by RDIRDT on improvement and development of the transit system in St Petersburg were awarded diplomas of the Governor of St Petersburg. For its achievements in transport and road industries development and scientific support to projects and programmes, RDIRDT was awarded diplomas of the Ministry of Transport, Government Road Agency, and local administrations of Russian Federation.

Svetlana Vorontsova, Cand. of Economics is Senior Deputy Director and the Head of the Department of Transport Economy of RDIRDT and Assistant Professor at the St Petersburg State University of Economics and Finance.

Raiffeisenbank Austria, ZAO is a universal bank with operations equally focused on commercial, retail and investment banking activities. The bank is ranked 11th, both in terms of assets and profitability, among top Russian banks based on the 2004 results (CEA Interfax). The bank's corporate loan portfolio has exceeded US$1.8 billion, with its corporate customer base showing substantial growth and numbering more than 3000 clients. In 1999, Raiffeisenbank entered the retail banking market and now ranks among Top 10 Russian retail banks. Raiffeisenbank is also the fourth largest bank in Russia in terms of consumer lending and seventh in terms of private deposits, based on 2004 results (CEA Interfax). Raiffeisenbank's Northern Capital branch in St Petersburg, established in 2001, has now become one of the leading players in the local banking sector, with an extensive customer base, both corporate and private, and an inherent part of the banking community in the Northwest region.

Madina Butaeva graduated from Plekhanov Economic Academy in Moscow in 1997 with Cum Laude honours and majored in Finance and Investments. She received her MBA degree from South Bank University in London in 2001. Prior to Raiffeisenbank, Madina was employed by Aton Capital as an Equity Analyst. She joined Aton from Russian oil major, Sibneft, where she was heading an Investor Relations department. Madina also spent a considerable amount of time involved in various exploration projects while working at Schlumberger Oil Services from 1997 to 2000. She joined Raiffeisenbank as a Research Analyst in 2003 and became Head of Research in 2005. In this capacity, she has built up a team of local professionals whose mission is to seek out investment opportunities and provide Russian and international clients with top ideas and service.

Sebastian FitzLyon, founder of **S. Zinovieff & Co. Chartered Valuation Surveyors**, arrived in St Petersburg from Sydney (Australia) in 1992 to open an office and was the first local firm to provide valuation, architectural and real estate agency services under one roof. After two years the company was bought out by DTZ, a large chain of international real estate agents, which kept Sebastian as the branch manager. Since July 1997, Sebastian Fitzlyon has owned and run his own real estate consultancy in St Petersburg: S. Zinovieff & Co. Chartered Valuation Surveyors, registered locally as a foreign-owned company (see www.zinovieff.ru). The company's clients have included many of the leading names in international business, including Pricewaterhouse Coopers, Raiffeisenbank, RJR/Japan Tobacco, Rothmans/British American Tobacco, Samsung, Shell, Mitsubishi, KPMG, Ernst & Young and many others.

S. Zinovieff & Co. specializes in valuations, architectural/building surveying/project management work, and the leasing/sale of commercial and residential real estate as licensed agents. It also manages Sweden House, St Petersburg's most prestigious office and residential centre. Apart from the St Petersburg region, it also sometimes has valuation assignments elsewhere in the CIS. The firm was the first ever foreign-owned firm in the Russian Federation to receive the federal valuation licence, following the introduction of compulsory licensing in 2002. It is licensed to value/appraise all types of real estate, plant and machinery, businesses, etc. Sebastian FitzLyon was a member of the St Petersburg City government annual delegation to the international real estate exhibition, MIPIM, in Cannes, France, for two years running. Furthermore, as Honorary Consul, he represents Australia's interests in the Northwest region of the Russian Federation. He is a member of the Executive Committee of the St Petersburg International Business Association (SPIBA), and is a founding member of the Association. Sebastian Fitzlyon was born in London in 1948. His ancestors on his father's side were in the timber industry and government and military service in St Petersburg and they left in 1918. Their surname was Zinovieff before being changed to Fitzlyon in the 1930s. His ancestors on his mother's side were from Dorset in England. Sebastian is an Australian as well as a British citizen.

In the course of a relatively short period of time, **Web-invest Bank** has become a bright example of a leading investment bank, having established an independent finance group in order to promote the best investment business practices in the Russian market. According to the authoritative British magazine, *The Banker*, Web-invest Bank was ranked third amongst the fastest growing banks in Russia and eighth in the CIS. The Bank specializes in the underwriting of bond issues for Russian corporations and regions, and in corporate finance. In the period 2001–2005, the Bank participated in the origination and underwriting of debt issues for an aggregate amount in excess of 150 billion roubles (more than US$5 billion). The Bank is the arranger and underwriter of bonded debts of the following companies and regions: Russian Railways (RZD), Leningrad region, Nizhny Novgorod and Tver regions, Republic of Sakha (Yakutia), Khunty-Mansiysk Autonomous Region, UralSvyazInform, Northwest Telecom, Alrosa, Ilim Pulp Finance, LENSTRO Group, Severalmaz, VINAP-INVEST, Yakutskenergo, Central Telegraph and others. Web-invest Bank is the absolute leader on the secondary bond market, and it is ranked first by trading volume of corporate and regional bonds on the MICEX exchange. Its status as one of the biggest players in the Russian bond market enables the Bank to provide high-quality services for all categories of clients, ranging from governments and financial institutions to companies and private investors.

In April 2004, the merger of Web-invest Bank and LYNX Finance was announced, as a result, the range of the bank's services was fulfilled by corporate finance services, and the department of trade operation was also strengthened. In 2004, the bank's main projects in the sphere of corporate finance were for RAO UES, consulting in the project for the completion of Boguchanskaya HPP (hydro power plant); finance consulting for Energomash Group in the Uralelectrotyazhmash and Uralhydromash consolidation project. Also the Bank acted as financial advisor during the sale of brewing company Sobol Beer to a strategic investor and during Northwest Telecom's acquisition of telecom operators in Novgorod. The Bank is the heart of the Web-invest Group, which also includes the asset management company Creative Investment Technologies (CIT) and the brokerage company Web-invest.ru. CIT AM manages over 10,000 client accounts and it offers the widest range of mutual funds in Russia. The total assets under Web-invest Bank management now exceed over three billion rubles (over US$100 million). Web-invest.ru is the largest operator in the Russian exchange market and one of the largest brokerage companies.

Alla Petrova graduated from Leningrad State University, Department of Physics and holds a PhD. Her second education was at the school of finance management, specializing in the securities market. She has nearly 10 years' professional experience under her specialization (securities market).

Elena Vishnikova graduated from St Petersburg State University of Economics and Finance, specializing in finance and credit and evaluation of property. She has three years' professional experience under her specialization with the bank.

Acknowledgements

Mr Arkady Volsky, President, Russian Union of Industrialists and Entrepreneurs

The publishers (GMB Publishing Ltd and Kogan Page Ltd of the United Kingdom and Adaptec Company of Russia) would like to express their wholehearted appreciation to the Russian Union of Industrialists and Entrepreneurs and, in particular, the organization's President, Mr Arkady Volsky, for his support of our publishing projects relating to Russia's investment potential.

Introduction

Tom Stansmore, Head of St Petersburg Representation, Pepeliaev, Goltsblat & Partners, and Dr Marat Terterov, Senior Editor, GMB Publishing, London

Considering history

St Petersburg is one of those unique international destinations that truly captivates the imagination. Whilst a relatively young city by European standards, few cities have been witness to such tumultuous historical events as St Petersburg. The city was founded in 1703 on territory taken from Sweden and was intended to be not only the country's 'window to the West' but its capital as well, which was moved from Moscow. St Petersburg takes its name not from the man that founded it, Russian Tsar (emperor) Peter the Great, but from the Tsar's patron saint. Peter, revered as perhaps the greatest of all the Russian Tsars, modelled his new capital on the most important European – as opposed to Russian – cities and began a major campaign of reforms and innovations aimed at modernizing Russia and seeking to raise the country out of its state of eternal backwardness. St Petersburg was at the heart of Peter's reform project and, since that time, the city has been regarded as the focus of modernity and progress on the Russian-dominated Eurasian landmass. To the present day, with contemporary St Petersburg being such as important transportation hub for international commercial and civil application, the city has always served as one of Eurasian Russia's vital conduits to European civilization.

During the late 19th and early 20th centuries, the city's rapid economic growth and thriving cultural life empowered the Russian Empire with a sense of prestige and power, which allowed it to stand firmly amongst the great empires and nation states of

Europe. However, the city witnessed two revolutions during 1917 – one (February) bringing the end of Tsarist rule, whilst the other (October) heralded the commencement of the world's first socialist political regime successfully taking power in any country. The city has been renamed a number of times since its founding: during World War I the city of Peter was briefly renamed Petrograd. Following the death of Lenin in 1924, the city was again renamed to honour the Communist revolutionary, and finally, in a 1991 referendum, the residents of the city voted to restore the original name.

In 1934, with Stalin's regime consolidating power in Moscow and throughout the Soviet Union, the assassination of Leningrad (Communist) Party boss, Sergei Kirov, commenced one of the bloodiest purges in European history. The death toll during Stalin's purges of the 1930s was overshadowed, however, during the Great Patriotic War, in which Leningrad was a direct combatant from September 1941 to January 1944. Over a million Leningraders perished during these years, when German pincers held the city under an insurmountable blockade. Leningrad and its population were accorded the title of Hero City, due to its people's bravery and the inexorable hardship the city endured during the war years.

Political and economic reform resulted in the demise and eventual disbandment of the once mighty Soviet Union during the late 1980s and start of the 1990s. A nominally democratic revolution swept the region, and Leningrad, again about to become St Petersburg, returned to the forefront of the revolutionary events. Given the fact that the city was always such an important centre for cultural, political and intellectual life, many of the individuals and events that gave rise to the former Soviet Union's pro-democratic, liberal forces, concentrated themselves in St Petersburg in the late-Soviet period. Because of the city's close proximity to Europe and the Baltics (amongst the first regions of the USSR to witness wholesale pro-independence and pro-democracy demonstrations), it is hardly surprising that civil society forces in Leningrad were likewise rumbling with the call for greater liberalization of the political regime. As the Russian Federation and 14 other newly-sovereign state entities emerged out of the Soviet Union, it appeared that St Petersburg was, once again, ready to take its pivotal place as Russia's gateway to Europe and the Western world.

Developing business

From a business standpoint, one could not have been blamed for holding an optimistic outlook towards the development of private enterprise and foreign investment in St Petersburg at the start of the 1990s. The city was already the site of joint venture investments involving foreign capital during the late 1980s, and Russia's market reforms liberalizing the state-controlled Soviet economy were being driven by up-and-coming young, radical reformers including Anatoly Chubais, a St Petersburg native. The city had enormous economic potential, with its highly industrialized enterprise base, the significance of St Petersburg seaport as a world-class port for the development of regional and international trade, and Soviet Leningrad's role in developing an impressive scientific and technical capability. While seasoned foreign businessmen already realized that the Soviet Union was well endowed with a work-force comprised of qualitative and quantitative human capital, St Petersburg was arguably at the top of the Soviet educational pyramid and was widely regarded as Russia's intellectual and cultural capital.

The world famous Hermitage Museum, the opera performances of the Mariinsky and St Petersburg's numerous other grand theatres, the parks and fountains of Peterhoff, and the city's numerous other palaces and monuments all emerged out of St Petersburg's cultural and intellectual tradition. Needless to say, the city's potential to derive income from tourism (as a mystical name in history requiring minimal effort to persuade European consumers hungry for new destinations to visit) or attract investment into the renovation and restoration of its historical real estate also seemed boundless. Furthermore, the city's investment attractiveness was reinforced further by the extremely advantageous position of the city's political geography, connecting the Russian Northwest via Europe through the Baltics, hence allowing St Petersburg to become a natural transit bridge, located in the centre of an international transport corridor (St Petersburg is physically closer to Tallinn and Helsinki, than it is to Moscow).

However, despite the early promise, it is evident that neither St Petersburg nor Russia as a whole, experienced whole-hearted success in attracting high volumes of foreign capital or domestic private investment during the 1990s. Major factors inhibiting significant inflows of capital into St Petersburg's economy for the most part mirrored those for Russia (and the former USSR) as a whole. Among the obstacles cited by those contemplating doing business

in Russia was the lack of a clear rule of law and predictability in
the legal system; political and monetary instability; the state's lack
of ability (or willingness) to enforce and safeguard commercial contracts and private property; corruption; and a constantly changing
legal system. Moreover, the private investment that did come into
Russia during the 1990s was largely absorbed by Moscow, and the
once glorious capital of the former Russian empire was marginal-
ized to the periphery.

The city's economy accelerates

Like Russia as a whole, St Petersburg has not only been recovering
in economic terms during recent years, but the city is now in the
midst of a noticeable economic upturn. A number of sectors in particular have been proving themselves as a major source of economic
growth in the city during recent years. One example is the construction industry. The city is currently witnessing a building
boom, which is spurred by numerous development projects, including investments such as the *Baltic Pearl*, a US$1.25 billion Chinese
foreign investment in the city, which envisages the development of
a 180 hectare, multifunctional complex of housing, social, public
and business land plots. The real estate sector is likewise a major
economic driver for the city and, at the time of writing, the British
hospitality chain, Orient-Express Hotels, acquired a 93.5 per cent
stake in one of the city's architectural treasures, the Grand Hotel
Europe. Orient Express is reported to have paid over US$100 million
to acquire this historically significant property from its previous
owners (the government of St Petersburg) and has recently stated
its intention to invest some US$30 million further into renovating
the property within the next few years. The city's retail sector is
also experiencing rapid growth, with major European and US-style
hypermarket complexes, such as *Lenta,* opening at various locations throughout the city and effectively capturing the attention of
the city's consumer sector. A positive note about such investments
is that much of the capital originates from the Russian private sector, signifying Russia's willingness to invest in itself. Furthermore,
important spheres of economic activity such as food production,
brewing and beverages, tobacco, telecommunications and transport
infrastructure, which were all already a force in their own right
during the more troubled 1990s, are continuing to grow impres-
sively in St Petersburg at present.

The official position of the government of St Petersburg is to support the establishment and further development of these investments, and to attract additional investment into the city by working to create a more attractive business climate. Rivalries between the Moscow and St Petersburg political elite (which some analysts claimed worked to the detriment of the city's investment climate during the late 1990s and early 2000s), subsided during 2003, when the Moscow backed Valentina Matvienko became governor of the city. Governor Matvienko's administration has put the city's economy as one of its top policy priorities and has generally promoted a pro-business orientation. The new governor has elevated individuals from the private sector to the position of vice-governors (including the position of Vice- Governor for Investment), established the Committee for Investments and Strategic Projects, created two new state investment agencies, and pushed an initial draft of the St Petersburg Investment Code through the city parliament. All of these measures were designed to assist investors and provide assistance for investment projects where possible.

As already alluded to above, such measures have had a seemingly positive effect on the city's economy and on the level of foreign investment being attracted into the city. According to government figures, foreign investments coming into St Petersburg during 2004 outstripped those of 2003 by some 40 per cent, reaching around US$900 million. Overall investments flowing into the city during 2004 reached US$4 billion, an increase of some 22 per cent from 2003. While it is difficult to verify such figures independently, the city's investment ratings outlook is largely positive: Moody's (ratings agency) raised the city's long-term investment rating to Baa3, while Standard & Poor's, and Fitch, approved ratings of BB and BB+ respectively. Over one third of total investments coming into the city (36 per cent) is currently flowing into the building industry, with transport (19 per cent) and industrial manufacturing (15 per cent) also proving attractive sectors. Sources of foreign investments are highly diverse in origin, with major economic powers such as the United States (28 per cent) and the United Kingdom (11 per cent), EU states such as Holland (8.5 per cent), neighbouring Nordic countries such as Finland (10.5 per cent) and offshore-based Russian/ex-Soviet entrepreneurs (Cyprus – 14 per cent) proving themselves to be the major regions from where such investments into St Petersburg currently originate. Furthermore, St Petersburg's major trading partners are becoming increasingly more diverse in their origins, with businessmen from as far away as India and China seeking to make their fortunes in Russia's second largest city.

About this book

It is becoming evident from the expansion of investments into St Petersburg's economy, as briefly outlined above, that no matter how challenging an emerging market Russia is perceived to be within international business circles, investments coming into both St Petersburg and the Russian Federation as a whole are only likely to increase further in future years. Despite all the criticism that the Russian investment climate has taken in recent months as a result of the break-up of the oil giant Yukos Oil, foreign investments have not, on the whole, been deterred and Russia remains a source of major interest for both international and domestic private capital. From the early 1990s when private investment started entering Russia in noticeable volumes, Moscow has absorbed the overwhelming majority of such investments. Some sources have even suggesting that as much as nine out of every 10 dollars invested into Russia have remained in Moscow. However, many analysts suggest further that the Moscow area is fast approaching investment saturation and the next big investment targets in Russia will be in the major urban centres of its vast regions. St Petersburg is in a pivotal position to absorb substantial investment volumes during the next three to five years, given the city's excellent political geography, established industrial and technological base, its transport infrastructure and seaport, its dynamic human capital, its renowned name in international tourism and the pro-business stance of its government.

The central objective of this book, therefore, is to go beyond the purely macro level analysis of doing business with Russia – as we have traditionally done in our other publications in this series – and to present the reader with a deeper look at business development at the regional level. St Petersburg is one of Russia's most attractive and interesting regions from a cultural, historical and inevitably commercial perspective. This publication sets out to present the reader with an introductory, yet relatively comprehensive account of doing business in St Petersburg and is based on a collection of almost 40 specialized articles addressing different aspects of the city's commercial life.

Part One of the book covers the topics of government policy towards investments, overviews the development of foreign investments flowing into the city from the perspective of recent history as well as contemporary analysis, and provides an insight into the fascinating topic of Russian business culture. Part Two delves into the economy, banking, the securities market, currency regulation and reviews the labour and recruitment market in the city.

Part Three explores the city's more dynamic economic sectors, providing information that has rarely been available together in one comprehensive publication. These include the real estate market (to which we devote an entire sub-section), engineering, electrical energy, transport, retail, telecoms and the building industry. We also include a special section on the practical experiences of foreign investors through their joint ventures with domestic firms, and include several company profiles.

Part Four, the final main section of the book, provides the reader with a detailed account of the laws and regulations for investing in the city, which is invaluable information required by any commercial enterprise seriously contemplating the prospect of conducting business with this most important of Russian cities.

American
Chamber of
Commerce in
Russia

American Chamber of Commerce in Russia St Petersburg Chapter

Vision

The St Petersburg Chapter of the American Chamber of Commerce in Russia (AmCham) was established in 1997 to represent the interests of the international business community in St Petersburg and Northwest Russia. As the first regional Chapter of AmCham Russia, we have the resources and experience of the leading business advocacy group in the Russian Federation at our disposal. AmCham Russia's key role in the Russian–American Business Dialogue, started by Presidents Putin and Bush in 2001, is a testament to the success and influence of the organization.

Mission

The core mission of AmCham St Petersburg is to promote favourable conditions for investment and trade in Northwest Russia by endorsing solutions to trade and investment issues that protect and benefit our members' interests. In the last seven years, AmCham St Petersburg has become a key player in the local investment scene thanks, in large part, to the impressive work of our members. From a modest beginning of 11 member companies in 1997, we have grown to 108 today, encompassing practically all industry sectors. By 2004, the total amount of our members' investment into the economy of the Northwest Region of Russia had exceeded US$4 billion.

Strategy

In pursuit of our strategic goals, we maintain excellent working relationships with regional, municipal and district level government officials in Northwest Russia, as well as with representatives of the US government and other international organizations in the region. AmCham St Petersburg works closely with AmCham's head office in Moscow, especially on federal issues. Our wide-ranging advocacy and policy work ensures that our members' voices are heard by policymakers in Moscow and in Washington DC. The Chamber has solid relationships with key policymakers in all branches of the Russian government, including the State Duma, the Federation Council, and the Presidential administration.

Membership and services

AmCham St Petersburg's seven industry committees (Human Resources, Information Technology & Telecommunications, Investment & Legal, Public Relations, Safety & Security, Taxation, Tourism & Hospitality) form the backbone of our work. The committees serve as forums to address members' common interests and goals, to discuss ideas, exchange information, and develop policy positions for the Chamber. They also coordinate briefings, seminars and roundtables featuring top-notch industry experts and relevant government leaders.

Membership in AmCham St Petersburg also allows for many networking and marketing opportunities among the other members and beyond. Furthermore, AmCham strives to provide its members with a sense of community as well as the services and day-to-day support generally found in AmChams around the world.

Advocacy

We work to facilitate business and to reduce the bureaucratic burden on operations by presenting issues to government and business decision-makers:

- advocating members' interests to the government at all levels;

- representation of your views to the US Government through close working relationship with the US Consulate General in St Petersburg and the Russian-American Business Dialog (RABD);

- documenting the issues of critical importance to our member companies and sending these concerns to appropriate government officials;

- AmCham's ongoing dialog with the respective authorities at all levels;

Contacts & networking

- breakfast and luncheon meetings with prominent representatives of local and international political and business communities;
- government and business contact information for St Petersburg and the Leningrad Oblast;
- bi-monthly General Membership Meetings featuring prominent guest speakers and networking opportunities;
- social events for the membership, including Annual Meeting, Awards Ceremony and Gala Dinner, American Independence Day Celebration, Thanksgiving Party, December Holiday Party, etc.

Helpful information on running a business in Russia

- seven sector-based Committees meeting on a monthly basis;
- seminars and conferences on the most important developments in the business-related legislation featuring high-profile speakers and useful handout brochures;
- Issue Papers prepared by the Chapter;
- providing timely and accurate updates on the Russian market business trends and development policies.

Marketing

Exposure for member companies through:

- corporate news in the "Off-the-Wire" section of the AmCham News;
- description of and contact information in AmCham's exhaustive Annual Membership Directory;
- AmCham St Petersburg Annual Report with articles describing member companies' successes in the previous year;
- St Petersburg section of AmCham's Web site.

AmCham web site

- monthly calendar of events and updates on all AmCham activities;
- event registration and meeting minutes;
- AmCham News and Northwest Russia News on-line;
- business information;
- member companies' press releases.

Publications

- Membership Directory with alphabetical listings of all AmCham member companies in Russia;
- AmCham St Petersburg Annual Report;
- brochures with seminar presentation materials;
- industry white papers;
- Issue Papers prepared by AmCham St Petersburg.

Administrative assistance

Apart from the day-to-day support in regards to all the Chapter's events and activities, our staff also assists member companies' employees in issues related to US non-immigrant visas.

Contact us

Maria Chernobrovkina
Executive Director
St Petersburg Chapter of the American Chamber of Commerce in Russia
25 Nevsky Prospect, Suite 318-B
St Petersburg 191186
Tel.: +7 (812) 326 2590
Fax: +7 (812) 326 2591
Email: info@spb.amcham.ru
Web: http://www.amcham.ru/stpete

Part One

Market Background to Investing in St Petersburg

1.1

Local Government of St Petersburg

Maxim Kalinin, Partner, Baker & McKenzie, St Petersburg

General overview

St Petersburg is one of 89 subjects of the Russian Federation, and (along with Moscow) is classified as a city of federal significance, enjoying powers similar to those of Russia's other federal subdivisions. Like other subjects of the federation, St Petersburg enjoys local autonomy in a number of constitutionally delegated policy areas, including, but not limited to: adoption of a city charter and legislative acts; formation of legislative, executive, and judicial bodies; adoption of a budget; collection of taxes; adoption of state, economic, environmental, social, and cultural development programmes; and regulation of construction activities. The structure of the local government is regulated by the Charter of St Petersburg, approved by the city Legislative Assembly on 14 January 1998 (the Charter), and comprises a legislative body (the Assembly) and an executive body, headed by the governor of St Petersburg (the administration).

The Legislative Assembly

The Assembly is comprised of 50 deputies, elected for a four-year term. The main functions of the Assembly include:

- approval of the city budget and a report on its performance, as submitted by the governor;

- confirmation of candidates for certain government positions;

- approval of various socio-economic development plans and reports on their performance;

- introduction of local taxes (within the federal tax structure);

- establishment of policies and regulation of entrepreneurial activities.

These issues are regulated by laws and legislative acts adopted by the government of St Petersburg. In addition to legislative functions, the Assembly also carries out a number of supervisory roles, including:

- compliance with the Charter, laws and other legislative acts adopted by the Assembly;

- supervision of the budget, and the distribution of transfers, credits and subsidies from the federal budget;

- supervision of programmes related to socio-economic development.

The administration

As set out in the Charter, the administration consists of:

- the governor of St Petersburg (the governor), who serves as chair of the executive branch;

- the government of St Petersburg (the government);

- the branch and territorial sub-divisions of executive authority, (committees);

- administrations of city districts, and the gubernatorial administration.

The governor

The governor is the highest executive authority in the governmental structure. Competencies of the office include:

- representation and power of signature in relations with federal, regional, municipal and foreign authorities;

- appointment of directors of enterprises, establishments and organizations that are city property (in accordance with federal legislation);

- signing laws of the Assembly and government Acts;

- issuance of gubernatorial Acts.

It should be noted that the governor is not authorized to act on behalf of the City in legal and commercial relations with private companies, as these functions fall within the competency of various administrative committees.

The government

The activity of the government is regulated by Law No 642-87 'On the Government of St Petersburg', dated 30 October 2003. The government is headed by the governor and an adjunct deputy-governor, who serves as head of the gubernatorial administration. Six additional deputies are responsible for economic development, social policy, transport, construction, education and external affairs, respectively. The remainder of the government consists of the gubernatorial representative to the assembly, various committee and district administration heads, as well as the representative of a regional branch of the federal executive in St Petersburg. Currently this position is occupied by the head of the Federal Department of Internal Affairs (MVD) for St Petersburg and the Leningrad Oblast (region). In all there are 15 positions in the government.

Candidates for government positions are put before the Assembly upon recommendation of the governor. Once confirmed by the legislature, candidates are appointed to their position by the governor.

The competencies of the government include:

- consideration of, and amendments to, the draft budget, as well as a draft report on its performance;

- consideration of plans and programmes relating to socio-economic development;

- review of draft laws on the introduction or cancellation of regional taxes and tax incentives, or relating to any changes in financial obligations or expenses to be compensated from the budget;

- management and disposal of city property or federal property transferred to the city in accordance with federal law.

Additionally, upon request of the governor, the government may consider any other issue within the competency of the administration. All activities of the government are supported by the gubernatorial administration.

Branches of executive authority

According to Government Resolution No 8 'On the List of Executive Bodies of St Petersburg', dated 5 November 2003, there are over 60 branch and territorial divisions of the executive in operation. Some of the most important divisions are outlined below.

Property Management Committee

The Property Management Committee (the KUGI) is regulated by Government Resolution No 1589 'On the City Property Management Committee', dated 21 September 2004. Under this resolution the KUGI performs the following functions:

- record keeping and evaluation;

- management and disposal of city property, including lease, transfer in trust and transfer of property to third parties for reconstruction;

- acting as landlord in respect of leased city property, including leases of real estate and land plots;

- control over the use and preservation of city property, including the property of state enterprises;

- participating in commercial organizations on behalf of the city, within the scope allowed by law.

Construction Committee

The Construction Committee is regulated by Government Resolution No 650 'On the Construction Committee', dated 28 April 2004. Under this resolution the committee performs the following functions:

- management of documentation for capital construction, investment programmes and real estate projects;

- development of plans for industrial construction programmes and reconstruction of industrial and civil objects;

- acting on behalf of the city as a customer in relation to construction and reconstruction of industrial and civil objects;

- organization and execution of tenders for state construction orders;

- signing agreements for construction and reconstruction of industrial and civil properties financed from the city budget;

- enforcement of federal legislation and local laws in the sphere of capital construction and reconstruction.

Committee for Land Resources and Land Surveys
The Committee for Land Resources and Land Surveys (the KZRZ) is
regulated by Administrative Resolution No 2627-ra 'On Amending the
Resolutions of the Mayor of St Petersburg', dated 18 December 2002.
Under this resolution the committee performs the following functions:

- inventory of city land plots;

- legal description of land plots and maintenance of the city land
  cadastre;

- monitoring city land;

- recommendations on the determination of land payments.

Planning and Architectural Committee
The Planning and Architectural Committee (the KGA) is regulated by
Government Resolution No 1679 'On the City Planning and Architectural Committee', dated 19 October 2004. Under this resolution the
committee performs the following functions:

- organization and approval of urban development documentation;

- determining the strategy for city development and zoning;

- preparation of proposals on the selection of land plots for urban
  development;

- preparation and issue of architectural planning tasks and reference
  data for project design (in relation to urban development);

- preparation and issue to citizens and legal entities of permits for
  construction (or demolition), reconstruction, expansion of buildings
  and structures;

- customer functions in relation to urban development documentation.

Transport Committee
The Transport Committee is regulated by Government Resolution
No 226 'On the Transport Committee', dated 24 February 2004. Under
this resolution the committee performs the following functions:

- organization of public transportation services;

- enforcement of local legislation on automobile, railway and water
  transport;

- participation in project design for development of urban, suburban
  and international public transport;

- customer functions in contracts concluded for state purposes;

- determination of above-ground public transport routes;

- establishing favourable and safe conditions for public transport, including scheduling and rules governing the provision of services by transportation organizations;

- execution of tenders for providing transportation services;

- conclusion of agreements with transportation organizations;

- approval of compensation to transportation organizations relating to services with a regulated tariff, as well as compensation in regards to discounted fares for certain passengers;

- alteration of transport schedules on social routes;

- preservation of records on all above-ground public transport routes, and public dissemination of such information.

Finance Committee
The Finance Committee is regulated by Government Resolution No 721 'On the Finance Committee of St Petersburg', dated 5 May 2004. Under this resolution the committee performs (in relation to the city) the following functions:

- preparation and performance of the budget;

- control over the use of budget funds;

- management of the issuance and placement of securities;

- execution of financial obligations;

- management of the proper functioning of the securities market;

- provision of loans to third parties;

- conduct of financial reviews of investment projects.

Committee for Economic Development, Industrial Policy and Trade
The Committee for Economic Development, Industrial Policy and Trade is regulated by Government Resolution No 177 'On the Committee for Economic Development, Industrial Policy and Trade', dated 10 February 2004. Under this resolution the committee performs the following functions:

- organization of programmes for socio-economic and transport development;

- preparation of investment programmes;

- development and carrying through of target programmes according to financial, monetary, investment, innovation, and tariff guidelines.

Improvements and Roads Committee
The Improvements and Roads Committee is regulated by Government Resolution No 222 'On the City Improvements and Road Committee', dated 24 February 2004. Under this resolution the committee performs the following functions:

- management of proposals for capital repair of roads and transport infrastructure;

- road construction and maintenance;

- maintenance and development of parks;

- construction and maintenance of bridges;

- organization of specialized clean-up activities.

1.2

Economic Policies of the Government of St Petersburg and Emerging Market Opportunities

Igor Yegorov, BISNIS Representative in Northwest Russia

Introduction

When the new administration of St Petersburg came to office in the autumn of 2003, on the back of powerful support from the Kremlin, the new Governor, Ms Matvienko, pledged to prioritize development of the city economy and equal treatment of all businesses. Although the change of the city government in October 2003 was broadly expected to bring many benefits to the city, the real outcomes so far have been insignificant. It is not surprising that it has been hard to reconcile the multitude of pre-election promises with the hard realities of daily life. The idealistic rhetoric of a new city administration has inevitably led to initial policy declarations that proved difficult to implement in practice, given the existing problems of St Petersburg's economy. This is a clear indication that groundbreaking reforms require a change of mentality, not just a reshuffle of transient ruling groups. Nevertheless, some of the administrative measures the new administration is undertaking may lead to the emergence of new local markets in the near future. The following description of the plans and concrete measures of the new city government is based on the speeches of vice-governors before St Petersburg's Chapter of American Chamber of Commerce, interviews, press articles and other relevant information resources.

Policy priorities

After re-election for his second term in office, President Putin has set a doubling of Russia's GDP as a policy priority of his cabinet. In line with the President's directive, the new Governor of St Petersburg, Ms Matvienko, has vowed to double the budget of the city during her term in office (four years). This ambitious plan can only be realized if the economy of the city grows steadily during that period. In reality, the goal of doubling the income of the budget is being transformed into a policy of squeezing revenues from all possible sources (including private businesses and the federal budget) instead of giving real stimulus to private initiatives. Needless to say, the nominal growth figures used in the forecast are based on an assumption that there will be low inflation. The government will thus be able to report growth (as expressed in nominal gross regional product) even if real economic growth is jeopardized. Since official statistical reports are based on Soviet-style accounting principles, it is very difficult to get a clear picture of the real situation in the regional economy.

The new governor has brought to office new vice-governors from private businesses to take responsibility for the economic aspect of the city government's work: Mr Oseyevsky (who worked in the Industry and Construction Bank), Mr Blank (Industry and Construction Bank) and Mr Molchanov (previously a consultant for the Business Link company). The new vice-governors are described as 'effective' managers rather than politicians. The first phase of their activity involves making an inventory of current projects, searching for ways to maximize the financial revenues of the budget, reforming the purchasing system for the needs of the city, and promising to solve the numerous economic problems the city is facing. It is revealing that the new 'managers' have narrowed the spectrum of problems and decided to focus their efforts on just a few areas:

- real estate and development of the territory of the city;
- public utilities and residential maintenance services;
- development of transportation infrastructure and tourism;
- personnel training.

According to the vice-governor of St Petersburg, Mr Molchanov, the economic priorities of the new city government do not include proactive development of incentives for high-tech industries and R&D activities. The excuse for inaction is a lack of financial resources in the budget of St Petersburg. The new government seems to be expressly focused on utilities, real estate and territorial development, leaving aside many strategic matters. 'Common sense' is too often used as a substitute for a much-needed economic policy when solving particular problems related to business interests. Lack of understanding of fundamental economic principles on the part of the post-Soviet 'managers' leads to an inability to propose a working economic policy for the city. Financial instruments are prioritized because of their perceived omnipotence, while real measures that could give impetus to the development of manufacturing and service sectors are overlooked.

Real estate and development of the territory of the city

The city has experienced a tangle of problems linked to ineffective management of sites in the centre of the city (in the so-called industrial circle around the historical centre), decay of a large number of residential buildings (caused by inadequate maintenance), lack of sites for new construction, lack of infrastructure (roads, energy and water supply networks), and similar problems. To ensure long-term development of the city, a new Master Plan is urgently required, as the old plan is due to expire. The city government has promised to finance the preparation of a new Master Plan, which is set for release sometime in 2006. In the meantime, the government has proposed a set of measures to address the most pressing problems. Surprisingly, the problems of the remaining local industry do not seem to be addressed, although it is clear that without growth in the manufacturing sector it would be very difficult to achieve the target for GDP growth. The government is preoccupied with simple administrative measures and with distributing land sites for construction of leisure, trade and office real estate. It has decided to gradually minimize the role of the Investment and Tenders Commission of the administration (which was specially created by the former governor to evaluate real estate projects and make recommendations to the governor), and to allocate houses that need renovation and some construction sites to investors through a tender procedure. However, the government has retained the right to bypass the tender procedure and grant land plots to investors for residential construction and hotels.

The new government has revitalized plans to sell New Holland island (located in the historical centre of the city and currently occupied by the military), either to a number of private companies or to a single investor. Previous plans for the territory included the construction of a leisure and hotel complex on the island. It remains to be seen whether the new government can ensure that real investment projects are launched there, as numerous attempts by previous administrations have failed. Another big sale plan is to auction a huge territory near the former Warsaw railway station. Several companies are said to be willing to build hotels, trade complexes and office buildings there.

A large project in the centre of the city is the building of a trade and leisure complex near the Moscow railway station on the former RAO VSM construction site (RAO VSM was established to build a high-speed railway link between St Petersburg and Moscow, but went bankrupt after having ploughed millions of dollars into a huge pit near the old Moscow railway station, just beside Nevsky Prospect, the city's main avenue). A consortium of investors led by Vneshtorgbank has acquired the site for US$80 million and has already started to implement the project. The city has also strongly supported a project for the construction of a new building for the Mariinsky Theatre, which is expected to cost approximately US$200 million.

In addition, the city government plans to auction territories on the outskirts, which are currently lying idle. The construction companies that win the tenders will obtain rights to construct residential houses and other structures. The proceeds of the auctions will be earmarked for the construction of basic infrastructure. An important piece of news in the real estate sector of the regional economy was announced recently by vice-governor Mr Molchanov: the city government has agreed to sell a wide area bordering the Gulf of Finland in the southwest part of the city to a group of Chinese companies, in return for a memorandum of understanding promising to invest US$1 billion in the construction of a Chinese residential area there. In order to support the local building sector, the government also insists that local construction and industrial companies are involved in the project.

Overall, the city government aims to free up the 1,000 hectares of land currently being used by industrial enterprises in the centre of the city, by relocating these plants to the outskirts. It is said that the economic stimulus given by rising land prices will prompt the owners of these enterprises to sell the land to investors and move production to new industrial sites. In reality, this process is complicated by a variety of factors, most importantly the lack of developed industrial parks and infrastructure around the city. The government lacks the resources to invest sufficient funds in the construction of new infrastructure, but hopes to raise the necessary capital from private investors willing to acquire property in the city, through the imposition of a higher 'infrastructure fee' (which is charged per square metre of a land plot acquired by an investor – currently no less than US$80 per m^2 – and is transferred to a special infrastructure fund). Recent history has shown that the economic foundations of this plan are rather vague and it remains to be seen if it will lead to large-scale relocation projects.

Whatever procedure is in fact used to obtain land plots and construction approvals, US and other foreign companies can benefit from rising construction volumes. All sectors of the market are currently on the upswing, including hotel, retail, office and residential buildings, as well as industrial premises. Increasing competition is leading to interest in new construction technologies and building materials, as well as the emergence of new market sectors, such as individual housing. More people want to live in their own homes, and this segment of the market is likely to grow. Also important are energy saving technologies and materials that help to decrease energy consumption and reduce the cost of maintenance.

Development of transportation infrastructure and tourism

St Petersburg faces transportation problems that have been amplified by a long period during the 1990s of low spending on transportation infrastructure. As the city's residential areas expand, fast and reliable forms of transport are becoming a pressing need. A significant project under consideration by the government is to build an elevated high-speed tramway in the southern part of the city, which would deliver passengers from remote residential areas to an underground station. A Canadian firm, Bombardier, has proposed the project, whose cost is estimated at US$150 million. The government will decide on the deal later this year, after carrying out the necessary studies. Naturally, a requirement is that Bombardier involves as many local tool-building and construction companies in the project as possible. However, it is not clear why Bombardier would want to finance local production rather than employing its own plants.

One of the priorities of the new government is to ensure better international access to the city for foreign tourists and cargo flows. Construction of a ring road, expansion of port facilities and the building of a new high-speed rail link to Helsinki (Finland) are the key projects in this area. Construction of a new marine passenger terminal, which would enable large ocean cruise vessels and ferries from all around the world to call on the city, is also important. Seeking the right words to put the project into perspective, the Governor of St Petersburg, Ms Matvienko, explained that the new marine passenger terminal must become a 'project of the 22nd Century'. A new passenger terminal near Pribaltiyskaya hotel is planned for construction in St Petersburg by 2008, at an estimated cost of US$220 million. The navigating channel will be deepened from three to ten metres. A berth for ocean passenger liners and ferries about 1.3 km long, and a berth for smaller vessels that are about 200 metres long will also be built. The project will be financed through federal and regional budgets and by private investors. The payback period is estimated to be six to seven years. The new terminal will serve 1.2 million passengers a year.

Another important measure designed to boost the volume of investment in hotel infrastructure and improve the management of hotel complexes is the privatization of the city's stakes in 14 hotels, among which are the most profitable ones such as the Grand Europe and the Astoria. The idea that privatization in itself can solve the problems of economic efficiency demonstrates that Marxist postulates are still in the consciousness of many politicians, despite their formal recognition of market economy principles.

Public utilities and residential maintenance services

The topic of public utilities has become very sensitive in Russia, because the low tariffs on these services are often exploited by politicians for votes and popular recognition, at both federal and regional levels. Instead of thinking of how to improve the efficiency of capital investments in the sector, politicians are using it as a cash cow. Such policies are inevitably leading to underfunding and the subsequent decay in the sector. The St Petersburg government is trapped in a difficult situation, as it faces the need to reform the sector and raise tariffs, but simultaneously fears public discontent. Lack of decisive action now will lead to further deterioration of networks and facilities, and to an increasing number of accidents and breakdowns, which are especially damaging during the cold winter periods (the number of accidents increased 1.9 times during the 2003–04 heating season alone). The government therefore needs to introduce a plan that would facilitate investment in public utilities and simultaneously persuade the public that the proposed measures are effective and inevitable. The government tends to assume that the main cause of the many problems in this sector is its underfunding, which in turn is caused by a great number of concessions to various different groups of the population (and some categories of enterprises as well) inherited from the Soviet times and the perestroika period, and by low tariffs. In reality, the modification of financial flow patterns is a less important issue for reform than the urgent need to create a result-oriented structure in the sector and to implement efficiency-control mechanisms.

If the government's plans for annual economic growth of 6–7 per cent materialize, the city will very soon start to experience a lack of basic infrastructure and resources. For instance, consumption of gas will most likely increase from the current 8.6 billion cubic metres to 9.6 billion, and electricity from around 10.6 billion kWh to about 12.6 billion kWh. It will be necessary to build new power generation facilities and to lay new networks. According to estimates of the government of St Petersburg, for the period until 2010 the combined capital needs of public utilities companies in St Petersburg are well over 200 billion: Lenenergo would need 63 billion RUB (US$2.2 billion), Vodokanal 98 billion (US$3.4 billion), TEK St Petersburg 40 billion (US$1.4 billion), and Lengas 30 billion (US$1.1 billion). Mr Oseyevsky, vice-governor of St Petersburg, has claimed that during this period the city budget would be able to provide 60 billion RUB (approximately US$2 billion at the current exchange rate), while the rest is expected to come from private capital. However, it is unclear how the above 'capital investment' figures were obtained (ie what economic and technical characteristics of equipment and technology, required return on investment, etc the estimates were based on).

The fact that huge resources are required for the overhaul of public utilities companies is obviously an argument for attracting private capital as the primary way of financing the industry. The stable nature of revenues from public utilities and an opportunity to enter a large market have already attracted the attention of the affiliated structures of many Russian companies (including Interros, a financial-industrial group, RAO UES, an electrical monopoly and RAO Gasprom, a gas monopoly). As soon as the tariffs, rules and regulations are adjusted to fit the requirements of private capital, it is likely that the sector will experience an influx of investment. While the details of reform implementation are not yet clear, the guiding principles are formally very similar to those introduced in some Western countries. The ownership and management of networks will be separated (ownership of monopoly networks will be left with the city through wholly-owned companies, while operational management will be assigned to private companies for a set period of time). To promote competition, the generation market will be deregulated and investors will be allowed to build heat and power generation facilities, as well as to supply services to the public through the publicly owned networks.

One policy of the new St Petersburg government is to privatize municipal companies that are not important for the performance of the governmental functions. A list of state unitary enterprises for transformation into joint stock companies is being prepared (these are enterprises that were established by either the federal, regional or municipal authorities; ownership and control of such enterprises is subject to special rules contained in the Civil Code and relevant laws). At the first stage, ownership of all shares will remain with the city, and operational management will be transferred to private companies, but it is not unlikely that some companies would be privatized later. The reasoning behind transferring the management of state property to private companies is that private companies would be run operations more efficiently. As the current director of GUP

Vodokanal, Mr Karmazinov, phrased it, the 'unitary form of enterprise has exhausted its potentialities'. It remains an open question whether enterprises established for the public benefit can be privatized without sacrificing the ideals on which they were founded.

The real immediate outcome of all these factors will be rising tariffs for the population and industry, justified by the significant investment needs of the city's basic infrastructure. The current proposal of St Petersburg's government is to raise tariffs by 17–25 per cent in the summer of 2005, while providing a legal basis for further increases. If the scenario of transferring operational management of the utilities to private companies unfolds, the tariffs are set to grow (in the absence of proper cost management), as companies invest in reconstruction and new technologies. The concern of private investors is that a reasonable return on investment should be stipulated in law (these sectors are regulated by many federal and regional laws and regulations) to ensure that these costly long-term projects can attract financial resources. Ideally, the tariff setting procedure should be designed in such a way that an investment portion of a tariff, as well as a fixed minimum return on investment, would be protected (as opposed to the current situation where, in many cases, utilities companies have to justify the inclusion of incurred costs in the calculation of tariffs). Among the first candidates for reform are Lenenergo (electricity and heat supply), Vodokanal (water supply utility), Lengas (gas supply) and TEK St Petersburg (Fuel and Energy Complex of St Petersburg, a utility that operates a very significant proportion of boiler-houses and heat distribution networks in the city). The Bank of St Petersburg, together with GUP Vodokanal and several ex-owners of the Industrial and Construction Bank have announced the establishment of a separate company, which will apply for management of Vodokanal networks. On the heat supply front, Gasprom wants to utilize one of its local subsidiaries, Peterburgteploenergo, to apply for the right to manage the heat supply networks in the city. The heating market alone is currently estimated at 20 billion RUB (US$690 million) per annum.

The most pressing problems faced by utilities companies in St Petersburg include:

- Outdated equipment (power generation equipment, boiler-houses, water purification equipment, electrical substations, etc). For example, more than half the boiler-houses in St Petersburg are totally depreciated and need replacement.

- Low penetration of environmentally friendly technologies.

- Old pipe networks. The percentage of leakage of water/heat during transportation sometimes reaches 25–30 per cent.

- Lack of meters, resulting in uncontrolled usage of resources. Many residential buildings have no water, heat, electricity or gas meters, thus making it impossible to impose different charges to each apartment based on actual consumption, or to promote energy efficiency. For example, before 1996 the daily per capita consumption was 150 litres of water, whereas currently tariffs are set on the basis of an estimated 450 litres of daily consumption.

- Very low penetration of energy-saving technologies. Some estimates show that the consumption of energy could be reduced by 30–40 per cent just through a broad application of energy-saving measures.

When regulatory problems are resolved and the redistribution of ownership of public utility companies is accomplished, the issue of efficiency is likely to emerge as the most important factor of profitability (assuming that the law would allow private management companies to benefit from energy efficiency improvements). At the same time, rising utility tariffs will prompt the population and businesses to invest in various energy/water-saving technologies. This may open new market opportunities to US and other foreign companies in the area of new construction materials and techniques (especially for underground communications), energy efficiency equipment and services, heating and power producing installations, metering equipment and the like.

Personnel training and financial incentives

The government of the city is aware that one of the problems facing local industry is the shortage of qualified workers in many sectors. This impedes the development of new technology and products, burdens local companies with additional costs (to train and retain staff) and hampers economic growth. The city government estimates that the economy of St Petersburg currently has a shortfall of 60,000–90,000 qualified workers and technicians. The spectrum of measures to be introduced in this area is unimpressive; the city claims that its budget cannot accommodate increased spending on professional schools. According to the chairman of the Committee for Economic Development, Industrial Policy and Trade, Mr Blank, there will be improvements in the managements of funds from the federal budget (US$50 million annually), although it is unclear how that will be achieved, and companies will be urged to collaborate with technical schools and to financially support the educational process.

The idea of public–private partnerships (PPPs) is being actively promoted by the new city government as a model that can help solve the problem of lack of investment resources (the application of the PPP concept is reminiscent of the idea of off-shore companies, which was widely promoted in Russia several years ago as the best method of 'optimization of financial flows and tax obligations'). PPPs, which will be discussed in more detail in Chapter 1.3, will be created with private companies willing to collaborate with the city on the implementation of large-scale projects. The city also plans to assign curators within the administrations of the most important private undertakings. The government is also contemplating introducing regional tax privileges for investors (relating to parts of the regional profit and property taxes), and promising to stabilize the tax burden for the forthcoming four years. If the legislative assembly of the city adopts the proposals, the profit tax for investors will be decreased by four per cent.

1.3

St Petersburg Government Strategy for Business Development and Attracting Foreign Investment

Pavel Brusser, St Petersburg City Committee for Investments and Strategic Projects, and Victoria Kovaleva, Hansa Leasing

Government–investor relations in the cultural and intellectual capital of Russia

St Petersburg is considered Russia's cultural and intellectual capital – a city of high scientific as well as industrial potential. The key factor for further development of these features is investment. Direct investment is probably the most effective mechanism for realizing the inner potential of the city. However, capital flows tend to follow their own principles, moving in the direction of a prompt, reliable and optimum return.

The financial crisis of August 1998, continued depreciation of the national currency as well as high global prices for Russian energy exports have combined to create a unique macro-economic situation for Russia as a whole and St Petersburg in particular. A low and basically stable exchange value for the Russian rouble and a considerable foreign trade surplus have stimulated home production and import substitution. Russia has benefited from these developments and has now reached a position where it can sustain its current levels of economic growth. As one of the regions with the highest investment potential, St Petersburg has thus obtained an advantageous position in the investment market.

However, it is evident that awareness of the positive statistical outlook in the investment climate of a particular region is not in itself sufficient to secure investments to that region. Before an investment is made, one has to take account of the specific terms and conditions that have been established by the authorities in a particular region or city. From this perspective, the government of St Petersburg has done away with the archaic bureaucracy of the Soviet period. The city's system of government, at present, basically consists of two bodies, and this has simplified the process of government–investor relations in the city. The government bodies are the Administration (executive body) and the Legislative Assembly (legislative body), and both have their own instruments for influencing the city's investment climate. The Assembly is responsible for creating a suitable legislative framework to support investment activities, while issues relevant to policy formation, policy execution and project tracing are determined by the Administration.

The Committee for Investment and Strategic Projects

The establishment of a new government committee, the Committee for Investment and Strategic Projects (henceforth 'the Committee'), is one of the recent measures taken by the Administration and the Governor of St Petersburg, Valentina Matvienko. The Committee was established in 2003 and is responsible for the implementation of public investment policy and the coordination of major investment projects in St Petersburg. Its main tasks are as follows:

- to formulate and implement public investment policy in St Petersburg;

- to develop strategic planning of investment projects;

- to work out measures to support implementation of various investment projects;

- to coordinate the activities of governmental executive bodies of St Petersburg over investment issues.

The Committee has laid down the following principles of investment policy in St Petersburg:

- mutual unselfishness and honesty;

- equilibrium of private and public interests;

- open access to information needed for investment activity;

- a clear and coherent investment policy;

- equal rights of all investors and commonality of all public procedures;

- objectivity in decision making;

- consistency of decisions;

- mutual responsibility of St Petersburg and investors.

Facilitating investments

The city's great willingness to become involved in investment processes is emphasized by the well-known slogans 'St Petersburg – an open city' and 'St Petersburg – a city of European standards'. In 2004 the government of St Petersburg took the following steps to attract investors:

- Changes to the Law of St Petersburg 'On tax remissions' was adopted. The changes introduce profit tax and property tax allowances for organizations.

- The City Agency for Industrial Investment was established. Its role is to stimulate the development of non-residential areas and of engineering infrastructure, and to monitor investment projects within the industrial sector.

- The Law of St Petersburg 'On provision of real estate objects in property of St Petersburg' was introduced. The law simplifies the procedures of real-estate provision.

- The St Petersburg Administration passed a regulation 'On strategic investment projects in St Petersburg', which ensures a better investment climate and increases the efficiency of investment processes. From now, on the Administration will be authorized to provide information and administrative and legal support to investors and independent entrepreneurs.

- The procedure of building-lot assignation was changed. 'Short packet' tenancies will from now on be put up for auction. This implies reduced documentation requirements, which are to be specified for each particular case.

- Open auctions were introduced in 2004 as a means of allocating housing stock, non-residential areas, buildings in disrepair with surrounding grounds, and building lots assigned for the construction of shopping malls, supermarkets, business centres and hotels. The lots vary in their location and area. Open auctions are held by the Property Fond, one of the sub-units of the city Administration (www.property-fond.ru). The Fond had been specially created to conduct municipal land transactions. Transactions are VAT free, which brings additional tax benefits to investors. A total of 24 building lots with an overall value of US$14 million were sold in 2004, and sales are expected to rise to US$44 million in 2005. Open auctions comprise the following stages: filling out a participant application form, making necessary deposits, bidding and signing a contract.

- The Administration approved a list of building lots for con-struction of hotels in different parts of St Petersburg (www.hotelinvest.ru).

We should also highlight the fact that, during 2004 and the first quarter of 2005, the Fond sold more than 55 lots, and conducted buyouts of 11 hotels in St Petersburg. Starting from 2005, the Fond is to initiate the auction sale of privately owned property.

Investing in urban infrastructure

The government of St Petersburg pays close attention to city planning. Among the most significant projects are those aimed at developing the transport infrastructure of the city: ring-road construction, reconstruction of airport complexes, road-building at the West High Speed Diameter, construction of a new ferry terminal and an elevated express route.

Other projects initiated by the city's Administration provide for further development of the urban territories. Reconstruction of the island area known as New Holland is one of these projects. The Administration of St Petersburg has already announced a competition for investors willing to develop these territories. The investment contract is to be signed in 2005.

Foreign investments in St Petersburg

A brief review of investment figures clearly demonstrates the increased interest being shown by foreign investors in St Petersburg.

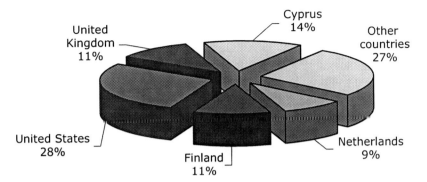

Source: Government of St Petersburg.

Figure 1.3.1 Foreign investments in St Petersburg for 2004 (total foreign investments of US$985.1 million in 2004, a 41.6 per cent increase over 2003)

In 2004, the total volume of foreign investment inflow into St Petersburg came to US$985.1 million, which was 41.6 per cent more than in 2003. The leading source countries of foreign investment into the city were the United States (28 per cent of total foreign investment in 2004), Cyprus (14 per cent), the United Kingdom (11 per cent), Finland (11 per cent) and the Netherlands (9 per cent) (see Figure 1.3.1). Foreign direct investment (FDI) comprised 12 per cent of the total investment volume flowing into the city; portfolio investment comprised close to 5 per cent, with the rest of the investment stock coming from other forms of investment activity. The total volume of investment into St Petersburg's economy increased by US$4 billion in 2004, 22 per cent more than in 2003.

Total investments flowing into St Petersburg's economy during 2004 were distributed amongst the following sectors (see also Figure 1.3.2):

- construction – 36 per cent;

- transportation – 19 per cent;

- industrial sector – 15 per cent;

- housing and communal services – 10 per cent;

- communication – 5 per cent;

- education and science – 2 per cent;

- trade and public catering –2 per cent;

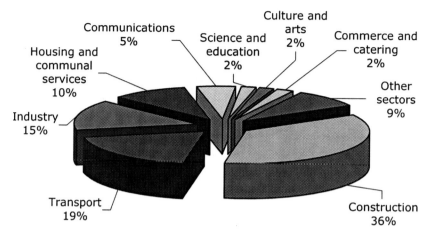

Source: Government of St Petersburg.

Figure 1.3.2 Total investments in St Petersburg for 2004 (total investments of $US4 billion, a 22 per cent increase over 2003)

- culture and art – 2 per cent;
- other sectors – 9 per cent.

Investment ratings

According to leading international rating agencies, the economy of St Petersburg is developing at a steady pace. Higher credit ratings, Stable (BB+) and Positive (Baa3) were attributed to the city by the Standard & Poor's agency and Moody's investors service respectively in 2004.

St Petersburg as seen by rating agencies

- Standard & Poor's

    - Long-term credit rating BB+
    - Stable forecast

- Moody's Investors Service

    - Long-term credit rating Baa3

- Positive forecast

- AAA (Rus)

- Fitch Ratings

    - Long-term credit rating BB+

    - Positive forecast

    - AA (Rus)

Newly commenced investment projects

The following large-scale investment projects were started in 2004 in St Petersburg's industrial sector:

- construction of the telecoms equipment plant, Elcoteck – US$100 million (in value);

- construction of the Russian Standard vodka distillery – US$25 million;

- construction of a production and storage complex for the Pepsi Bottling Group – US$20 million;

- development of the Petersburg Products International production complex – US$20 million.

All of the above projects are to be completed in 2005. The well-known European companies Electrolux and Bosch-Siemens have also signed agreements to build plants in St Petersburg. A number of Japanese companies, including Sumitomo Corporation, Marubeni and Hitachi, are showing strong interest in investing in the region. Furthermore, the Shanghai Foreign Investment Company intends to invest more than a billion dollars in a project aimed at developing the southwestern part of the city (a project that has been dubbed the 'Baltic Pearl').

Public–private partnerships

Public–private partnerships (PPPs) are among the keys to strategic investment, and are becoming more and more popular throughout the world today. PPPs provide an effective mechanism for attracting investment to the city and are actively supported by the government of St Petersburg. This form of cooperation between the state and private agents was previously impossible, when the economy of the USSR was tied to the model of socialist rather than private ownership.

The first examples of PPPs emerged with the processes of property differentiation and the fast development of the private sector. The model was first applied in St Petersburg in the marine terminal construction project eight years ago. The completion of a southwest treatment plant construction project has also been achieved by a partnership of the city Administration, State Unitary Enterprise Vodokanal, the Nordic Environmental Finance Corporation (NEFCO) and the NCC, SKANSKA and YIT companies. This 174.7 million euro project was a PPP project designed to achieve environmental protection and investment in municipal infrastructure.

The willingness of both the city and investor to be engaged in an investment project is determined by various benefits and favourable terms that the parties can offer each other. The PPP pattern usually implies the mutual contributions outlined in Table 1.3.1.

Table 1.3.1 Contributions by the parties to a PPP

Investor's contributions	City contributions
Knowledge, experience, innovation	Property
Effective management methods	Tax benefits and other favourable terms
Financial resources	
Efficient decision making	Financial support in some cases
Carrying out multinational investment projects contributes to city development by:	Redistribution of city resources results in:
– introducing new and more effective operation methods	– widespread support for social programmes of education, public health and culture
– technological and technical improvement	– improvement of human environment and economic conditions
– forming commercial bonds between suppliers and contractors	Hence an indirect effect on facilitating investment
– building business with foreign capital	
– stimulating demand for qualified labour	
– creating new jobs	

Investor's contributions	*City contributions*
Investor's interest in PPP depends on:	*City's interest in PPP depends on:*
– favourable conditions for carrying on business such as guarantees from the state, opportunities for long-term project development and flexibility in contract terms in case of unexpected negative exposure	– opportunities for attracting capital funds from the private sector
– competitive investment revenue in exchange for expertise and contract financing	– opportunity for final enjoyment of property with partial transfer of financial risks to private sector
– availability of a legal basis for contract regulations (SPC, concession contract, credit) and administration of guarantees	– opportunity to use management expertise of the private sector in public projects
– political climate and willingness of the state to support private sector and measures for a better investment climate	– readiness and capability of the state to bear responsibility for control and regulation with respect to public opinion

The Committee for Investment and Strategic Projects is currently working on a list of conditions that should be met by an investor in order to be acknowledged as a strategic investor or a strategic investment project. Some basic requirements here would be GDP growth after project completion, an increase in employment rates and the introduction of new technologies. In addition, the minimum cost of a strategic investment project is set at US$100 million.

It is reasonable to note that the progress of strategic investment depends, in many respects, on the PPP schemes offered by the Administration of St Petersburg.

The basic forms of PPPs relevant for Russia and St Petersburg are:

- contractor's agreement;

- technical assistance agreement;

- administration agreement;

- leasing;

- investment contract;

- concessions (not fully relevant yet, Russian Federal Law is being corrected);

- agreement on the sharing of profits;

- joint venture.

Some of the forms of PPPs listed above could be presented as separate alternative elements, as shown in Table 1.3.2.

Table 1.3.2 Elements of PPP agreements

Contractor's agreement	— operation
	— execution
	— designing-construction
Leasing	— leasing-buying
	— leasing-developing-operation
Joint venture	— co-ownership
Concession	— concession on operation
Privatization	— partial privatization
	— complete privatization
	— prompt privatization

There are various kinds of PPPs, and the most common include:

- *BOO (Build, Own, and Operate)*. A private company finances, builds, owns and operates the unit of infrastructure in question for an unlimited period of time.

- *BOOT (Build, Own, Operate, Transfer)*. The model proposes the same initial terms as the BOO model, with the stipulation that ownership of the infrastructure unit will be transferred to the city in 20–30 years. An inverse alternative, where the state finances and builds a unit on condition that ownership is subsequently transferred to a private actor, is also possible.

- *BOT (Build, Operate, Transfer)*. The private sector finances, builds and operates the unit during a period needed to finalize the project (for example, 30 years). At the expiration of the prescribed period, ownership rights are transferred to the city. One may also apply the models of ROT (Reconstruct, Operate, Transfer) and PBO (Plan, Build, Operate) that correspondingly imply reconstruction and planning.

- *BTO (Build, Transfer, Operate)*. A private company finances and builds the infrastructure unit and transfers ownership to the city once construction is completed. The unit may be transferred to a different private agent for contract operation.

- *Prompt privatization*. The ownership of the unit is to be transferred to a private investor who finances, plans and carries out a project of unit reconstruction or unit development. The unit may well be operated by the investor for a limited period and then passed over to the state. The operation period may be fixed, or determined by a certain level of revenue.

- *LDO (Lease, Develop, Operate)*. A private agent takes an infrastructure unit on lease, finances and develops (or reconstructs) the unit, operates the unit for some limited period and later on transfers ownership back to the city.

- *Lease and sell*. A private investor finances, plans and builds a unit and then leases it to the state for a fixed period of time. As owner of the unit, the investor receives rental revenue. At the expiration of the fixed period of ownership, rights are transferred to the state.

- *Unit extension*. A private agent finances, plans and builds on to an existing infrastructure unit. The investor's operation of the unit is to be followed by ownership transfer to the state.

- *Turn-key*. The project is financed by the state and carried out by a private investor. The state determines the requirements for using this particular PPP model.

- *Design and build*. This model is designed for road infrastructure projects. Planning and construction works are carried out by a private investor in accordance with the standards and requirements of the city. After project completion, the state owns and operates the unit.

- *Leasing agreement*. The state finances, builds and owns an infrastructure unit and leases it to a private agent. The latter is responsible for operating, maintaining and managing the unit, including collecting revenue, for some fixed period of time. The state retains ownership of the unit, however, together with the responsibility for attracting investment, debt control, setting tariffs and regulating compensation of costs.

- *Contract operation*. Contracts to operate a unit offer additional opportunities to private investors. This type of contract permits a private agent to administer the state enterprise while the state neither attracts the private capital assets nor assumes the economic risks connected to revenue collection. Contract payment may be fixed or tied to productivity and revenue rates. An average contract period is three to five years.

- *Concession.* Concession investment is a form of PPP that uses various units of state or municipal property, such as enterprises, ground areas, engineering or transportation units and other public establishments, as concession objects. Concession investment results in a more effective asset distribution for both investor and the city. The term 'concession' has not yet been adopted by the Russian legal system: the law to regulate the concession mechanism is currently being drafted by both federal and local governments, namely the State Duma and St Petersburg Legislative Assembly. Until a new legislative basis is created, lawyers working with concession investment have successfully used the Civil Code and other legislation as legal support for PPP projects.

- *Contractor's agreement.* This type of agreement implies a transfer of authority to operate and maintain the unit to the private sector for a period. The municipality assigns key parameters of efficiency, evaluates contractors, controls their activities and pays at an agreed rate for services rendered. The government is also responsible for financing investments needed to develop the infrastructure. The average contract period is one to two years.

The fundamental step in any project is the elaboration of a finance plan, which takes into account the goals and the limiting factors of all project participants, and indicates possible sources for project financing such as financial markets and financial institutions.

Public investment is crucial to project realization. The degree of state participation determines the strategies and plans for attracting private capital. That is why defining and prioritizing targets in government financing is a matter of primary importance to any investment project. The goals of public financing may include:

- reducing the demand for capital and operation transfers;

- reducing the final cost of the project;

- attracting the private sector (sharing risks);

- reducing requirements on guarantees for project completion and expected revenue;

- restricting future tariffs and supporting tariff subsidies.

Probably the most effective way of financing a PPP investment project is to create a special purpose company (SPC), which is based on the principle of financing limited project shares. The investors' obligations in this case are limited to their initial capital investments and reserve capital designed to cover possible costs and excessive expenses. If the project fails due to unforeseen circumstances, investors are not required to support it beyond their initial obligations. This aspect provides for effective investment of private capital. Under the SPC scheme, financial institutions and other lenders correlate the security of their capital investment to the size of the anticipated revenue from the project. A developed contract structure that distributes the risk among reliable and experienced investors is needed to provide a stable inflow of financial assets. Attracting private capital on such a large scale requires high-level support and participation from the city authorities, especially when resources are scarce.

Financial cost optimization should be set as a main goal in elaborating financial strategies. Optimization implies that a debt can be settled before the due date, which, in turn, means reasonable interest on debt and effective property funding.

Below are potential sources of funding in the private sector that can be viewed as candidates to secure project property and debts:

- private investors of the project;

- investment and venture capital funds;[1]

- multilateral agencies;

- export credit agencies;

- Russian and international commercial banks;

- leasing companies.

Each funding source has its own distinct cost of capital, conditions and benefits. The main criteria in selecting a funding source are:

- optimization of risk distribution (in order to minimize risks and the total cost of the project);

- maximization of the borrowing period (longer borrowing periods provide additional benefits in the case of large-scale infrastructure projects; the length of the borrowing period may also affect the optimum duration of 'the operational period of concession');

- maximum increase of indebtedness at a lower rate in relation to the size of assets.

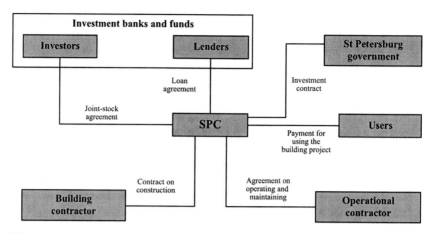

Figure 1.3.3 The structure of relationships among the participants in a PPP.

The development of an optimal financing strategy demands careful structuring of relationships among the participants (a contract structure), as well as the involvement of financial specialists, legal consultants and other professionals.

It is necessary to consider all existing ways of financing an SPC (including the issue of loan securities) and to accept the one that entails the minimum funding costs. The funding period should also be taken into account.

The contribution of St Petersburg to the authorized fund of an SPC may be made not only in the form of money but also as real estate, equipment and other assets. An SPC is usually created as an open joint stock company, although other forms of ownership are also possible under the agreement of the parties.

The major motivating force for such a PPP scheme for the potential investor and for St Petersburg is the desire of both parties to have low costs that will be quickly paid back by the project. This is a very important aspect for the city, as it aims to get a project finished as quickly as possible, and it is crucial for the investors to recoup their investment. Thus the advantage of a PPP scheme lies in linking the diverse interests of the city and the investor.

Figure 1.3.3 helps to demonstrate the structure of relationships among the participants in a large-scale infrastructure project. This example in fact shows a tripartite structure, with participation by the city authorities, the investors and the SPC.

Depending on the structure proposed, the St Petersburg government may consider an additional implicit set of guarantees in the form of a 'target programme' under a law approved by the city's Legislative Assembly. Under this programme, if (and only if) the SPC is unable to cover interest payments and due repayments of capital, the city treasury is authorized to advance the money. This scheme has advantages for both the investors and the city. The investors are protected against material losses (having the right to manage the SPC on profitable terms until the debt is paid). For its part, the city avoids having to pay for the entire project at the start, and is free of the heavy burden such a cost would impose on its budget. All the costs are borne by the SPC, which in turn recoups its costs through charges for services (for example, water tariffs).

Some infrastructure projects that exceed US$500 million would be almost impossible to carry through, because they would push up the liability index of the city's budget. In such cases, the target programme may be considered as one of the possible options for the St Petersburg government, enabling it to offer additional guarantees to the investor in certain cases.

The question of the provision of guarantees needs to be considered for each different case. Under a BOOT (Build, Own, Operate, Transfer) scheme, the SPC accepts the responsibility for organizing the whole system, and gains the right to own the unit for a fixed period of time after it is constructed. In this case, an agreement indicating the basic rights and duties of the parties needs to be concluded with the government of St Petersburg.

In some cases, such as water supplies, the city must retain control of infrastructure of crucial strategic importance, and so can never transfer property rights to any other owner. Under a modified BTO (Build, Transfer, Operate) scheme, the city owns the properties but the SPC has contractual rights to operate and maintain the unit (or to delegate these activities to an operating company or companies) and recoup its investment by charges for these services.

These arrangements are not BTO schemes in the general sense of the term. They are usually related to reconstruction projects rather than new buildings. Thus, when the structure or utility is reconstructed, it is 'transferred' to the city. Since the structure or utility is modified during the stages between building and transfer, it can in some sense be thought of as a BTO.

To avoid misunderstanding of certain complex aspects of Russian law on property rights, it is important to stress that in such an arrangement, the owner is always the city. Take for example the case of a 'unitary enterprise' (UE – an enterprise set up by a municipal body). In St Petersburg, the UE, Vodokanal, is the operator of the city's water supply infrastructure, but not its owner. Ownership of the infrastructure remains with the city.

The SPC has a central role, dealing with building and operating contractors, users, lenders and the state. It will contract with the building contractor to design and construct the unit, and conclude an agreement with the operating company (or companies) to operate and maintain it under SPC ownership. Where there is insufficient finance, the SPC borrows from the group of lenders, agreeing appropriate terms and conditions with them. The SPC is entitled to offer the unit (or its services or products) to potential users and to collect payment for these services. It will also have a right to be engaged in related commercial activities to generate additional profit. In addition, it may receive fixed annual premiums for rendering services in accordance with certain criteria.

The efficiency of project realization depends on the level of risk that investments, loans and the SPC's property is exposed to. The level of risk involved will affect the availability, cost and conditions of direct capital investment.

The potential groups of risks related to the realization of a strategic investment project are:

- the risk of not completing the project due to time or money constraints;

- risks connected to revenue collection;

- operational and repair risks;

- pre-schedule termination of the concession;

- funding risks;

- exchange rate risks;

- political risks;

- legal risks;

- *force majeure.*

Table 1.3.3. shows the possible distribution of risks during the various phases of a project. MR indicates that most of the risks are present during that phase; SR indicates that some risks are present; RR that only residual risks are present; I that risks are covered by insurance; and H that risks are hedged.

Table 1.3.3 The distribution of risk

Project Risks during various project phases	*Risks incurred by*			
	St Petersburg	SPC	Contractor	Third party
Risks during the design period				
Phase of proposals and evaluations		MR		
Phase of negotiations		MR		
Phase of termination of financing	MR			
Risks during the construction period				
Risks connected to real estate	MR			
Risks during confirmation phase	MR			
Risks connected to project completion				
Risks connected to technical parameters and matching		RR	MR	
Risks of delay		RR	MR	
Risks of overestimation		RR	MR	
Financial risks (inflation, interest on loans, exchange rate)	SR	SR		H
Risks of *force majeure*	SR	SR		I
Losses or damage		SR		I
Risks connected to responsibility of the parties		SR		I
Risks during the exploitation period				
Technical risks (availability, reliability, safety)			MR	
Risks of demand	MR	RR		
Risks of supply	SR		MR	
Risks of *force majeure*	SR	SR		I
Risks of exceeding the estimate		RR	MR	
Financial risks	SR	SR		H
Losses or damage of equipment		MR		I
Risks under obligations incurred		MR		I

Preliminary analysis leads to the conclusion that, assuming that risk is managed efficiently, PPP can be viewed as an adequate mechanism for realizing large-scale investment projects. A sound financial model indicating estimated costs and revenues would be essential to define the project requirements and the requirements for optimization of its financial structure. Defining the optimum length of the concession period is another important step in project development.

The PPP approach discussed above has already been successfully approved in St Petersburg and appears to be a Pareto-efficient solution. The government of St Petersburg is currently open to discussion regarding any investment offers and other proposals, including those related to the PPP scheme.

Note

1. Funds can also be raised by the issue of bonds or an additional issue of shares in the future company (SPC). In the case of a guarantee provided by the city, the loan bonds for an SPC can be issued for a longer period and at a lower price.

1.4

Foreign Investors and Joint Ventures in St Petersburg

A look into the past and a review of the present

Sergei V. Ochkivsky, Director of Development, Association of Joint Ventures of St Petersburg

St Petersburg in Russian history

The role of St Petersburg in Russian history has recently become a matter of public debate. The generally recognized rationale for building the new Russian capital in the early 1700s is being questioned by some scholars, who argue that many other Russian cities were eligible to serve as a Baltic Sea harbour, ship-building hub, administrative capital, naval base, and so on. The prevailing theory these days is that the new capital was built to fulfil a special mission, namely, to break Russia's isolation and bring it closer to Europe, transcending Russia's conservative, patriarchal lifestyle and tradition. The nation needed a new elite, a team of highly educated, dynamic people, open to new ideas. The new capital was built specifically to nurture a new generation of Russia's establishment. No other city would have been able to handle this task, which was critical to the success of Peter the Great's nascent reform. For the reform to advance, Russia needed a brand new capital with cohorts of new, reform-minded people. This was probably the greatest, most audacious reform initiative in human history, in terms of scale and historic timeline.

From then on, St Petersburg fulfilled its basic mission successfully for over 200 years, avidly absorbing the latest scientific thought and wooing the best exponents of foreign culture, science, art and architecture. The names of many European artistic and scientific luminaries are forever embedded in place names and whole neighbourhoods in St Petersburg's historical downtown. Over decades, the city evolved neighbourhoods heavy with the cultural heritage of many European nations, which is felt very strongly even to this day. In this cultural crucible, sampling the best of all national cultures, many generations of new Russian statesmen were forged. St Petersburg's educational institutions, such as the Page Corps, Tsarskoe Selo Lyceum and Smolny Institute produced all Russia's major historical figures in the 18th and 19th centuries.

Imported innovations were transformed to respond to Russia's needs, and then piloted successfully all across the Empire, but over time St Petersburg also emerged as the medium for a reverse process, as other countries began absorbing the best of Russia's scientific thought, culture, literature, art and, ultimately, Russian financial capital. The process became reciprocal and mutually rewarding. Foreign capital and entrepreneurs flocked to Russia, while Russian merchants and industrialists explored overseas markets.

Foreign investments during the Soviet period and the onset of Gorbachevian economic liberalization

The initial decade after the Soviets took over the country that subsequently became the Soviet Union, did not disrupt foreign capital participation in making Russia an industrialized economy. Foreign corporations effectively contributed to the groundwork for several industries that were to thrive in the Soviet Union: car manufacture, tractor building, aerospace, energy and a few others.

In many cases, the Soviet government simply purchased advanced technology and manufacturing equipment from foreign vendors for its major industrial projects. Later on, the participation of foreign capital and entrepreneurs in Russia's economy ground to a halt and, for many decades, would be limited to international trade. New companies established in partnership with foreign investors would not appear in Russia/the Soviet Union until the late 1980s.

Credit for liberalizing Russia's economy must go to the last Soviet leader, Mikhail Gorbachev, although his first mention of the term 'joint enterprise' was nothing more than a slip of the tongue. During his official visit to India, Gorbachev, the first Soviet leader who preferred to improvise rather than deliver a prepared speech as per protocol, mentioned 'joint enterprise' when talking to a business gathering. What he really meant was conventional international cooperation and trade, but members of the business community took the phrase at its face value. To the rest of the world, 'joint enterprise' has always meant businesses founded with a mixture of domestic and foreign capital.

Gorbachev found he had no choice but to live up to his own misuse of the term. In 1987, when Rajiv Gandhi paid a reciprocal visit to Moscow, the first Soviet-Indian joint venture – the Delhi Restaurant – was already there. In Leningrad, the first joint venture, established in 1988, was LenWest, a shoe-manufacturer established in partnership with Germany's Salamander. In the Soviet Union, which had never previously seen this type of business format, LenWest became the fourth private business to be recorded in the public companies register.

After a more than 50-year lull, foreign capital returned to help Russia reinvent itself as a market economy. One had to be brave to start a business in Russia at that time. While they certainly came to make a profit, foreign entrepreneurs faced tremendous risks: nobody could tell how things would go in the future.

By then the business landscape had changed beyond recognition in the Soviet Union. Following the enactment, in 1988, of the Cooperative Enterprise Act, the floodgate was opened for the advent of a new class, that of Russian entrepreneurs. Two years later, private business was already diversified and thriving in the consumer industry, retail, food and beverage, agriculture and service sectors. Early Soviet entrepreneurs shaped the market, which now offered attractive business opportunities for small and medium-sized foreign investors as well as major ones. Joint ventures, established with domestic and foreign capital, were on their way.

The advent of joint ventures gave a new impetus to foreign investment in Russia. From now on, international entrepreneurs could deal with emerging Russian private businesses rather than government-run colossi. But the development had a downside to it. On the positive side, projects could benefit from the dynamics of the Russian partners' private initiative. What was negative was that the majority of the up-and-coming Russian entrepreneurs were unfamiliar with business ethics. As a result, many foreign investors would subsequently suffer heavy losses when their Russian partners defaulted, or even fall victim to brazen fraud schemes perpetrated by the less scrupulous exponents of Russian business.

However, joint ventures were at least no longer viewed as an unwelcome alien intrusion into Russia's and St Petersburg's economy.

Joint ventures in St Petersburg during the disorder of the early 1990s

Political and economic turmoil followed in the wake of the Soviet Union's collapse in late 1991. Once again, the nation subjected itself to suffering by choosing a revolutionary rather than evolutionary course of progress. The fallacy of this choice soon became obvious in light of what happened next across the former Soviet Union, and when contrasted to China's economic miracle. The next four or five years saw an unprecedented economic collapse across the former Union; indeed, the economy suffered a blow exceeding the impact of the 1941–45 Russian involvement in the Second World War. The gross domestic product dropped 50 per cent; an enormous number of manufacturing enterprises went out of business. All this looked very sad in comparison to China's economy, which has shown a steady annual growth rate of 9–10 per cent over the past 25 years, and has seen a six-fold GDP increase. Russia's performance has been strikingly different, testifying to Russia's error in choosing radical liberal reform that has resulted in economic degradation.

In order to fully comprehend what went on, socially and economically, in Russia during the 1990s, it should be noted that the ill-conceived, sweeping privatization of government property caused a nationwide gangland war. Racketeers sprang up soon after the first cooperatives were formed, but early racketeering was mere child's play compared with what followed. In the 1990s, all-out battles were fought over enormous chunks of government property, in which the casualty count far exceeded the Soviet losses in the 10-year Afghan war.

Regardless of this, many international entrepreneurs stuck to the Russian market. In the investment community, some investors tend to be more aggressive than others, and show great appetite for risk when given the promise of more investment opportunities and higher returns. Around this time, restrictions were lifted, and businesses that were 100 per cent foreign-owned were allowed to operate. This was made possible by the 1991 Law on Foreign Investment in Russia, which provided guarantees of investment security for foreign investors.

Taking high risks paid off and, over the years, entire Russian industries found themselves dominated by foreign players, including the tobacco and food industries, construction supplies, telecommunications, chain superstores, the automotive industry and some others.

In the 1990s, Leningrad, having restored its historical name of St Petersburg, emerged alongside Moscow as an increasingly appealing destination for international entrepreneurs and investment dollars. To an extent, St Petersburg's investor appeal is explained by its advantages over other regions, such as:

- a convenient geographic location;

- a high level of industrialization;

- a solid transport infrastructure;

- a sufficient pool of qualified labour.

However, this is not all there was to it. The Soviet Union's first non-governmental association for foreign-owned businesses, the Leningrad (since 1991, St Petersburg) Joint Venture Association (JVA), was founded as early as 1990. Looking back, we can say that the JVA was one of Russia's first civil society institutions, formed when joint venture CEOs realized the need to consolidate their efforts as a lobby for the emerging joint venture sector. Entrepreneurs also needed a 'club,' or some place where they could meet and share their experiences and new ideas. The JVA was a body with the mission to represent the interests of international business in Russia.

An early role for Vladimir Putin

St Petersburg's investor appeal was also enhanced by the fact that the municipal government went out of its way to welcome foreign investors to the city. At the time, the City Hall officer in charge of foreign economic policy was deputy mayor of St Petersburg, Vladimir Putin, who headed the Committee for External Relations. While the federal government was in chaos and St Petersburg lacked any cohesive economic policy for domestic enterprise, the arrival and domiciling of foreign businesses in St Petersburg was encouraged in every way.

In 1993, it was St Petersburg, not Moscow, that hosted the national Joint Enterprise Forum to consolidate Russia's emerging joint venture sector. The forum addressed some of the more 'painful' issues plaguing foreign investors in Russia. While it would be wrong to say that all the recommendations issued at the forum were subsequently heeded by federal or regional authorities, some vital decisions were nonetheless made, and some legislative initiatives did go through.

It was on the initiative of the St Petersburg Joint Venture Association that Vladimir Putin was appointed head of the Cross-Agency Commission on Foreign-Owned Businesses, established under City Hall. Thanks to its focused policy, this body more than once diffused highly complex crises arising in the course of the business of foreign-owned companies in the city.

From Sobchak to Yakovlev: State efforts to improve the business climate

When Anatoly Sobchak was replaced by Vladimir Yakovlev as governor of St Petersburg in 1996, the Cross-Agency Commission was disbanded. Its successor, the Council on Attracting Foreign Investment, was established under the governor's auspices in 1997, but, unfortunately, this body was never to mature into an efficient tool for addressing the immediate challenges faced by foreign businesses in St Petersburg. Nor did the Council succeed in its stated mission of attracting foreign investment to the city.

However, some favourable changes did occur on the investment front. St Petersburg joined Moscow to become Russia's trailblazer in attracting investment dollars by issuing municipal securities. Some City Hall bodies succeeded in attracting substantial international borrowings, for example:

- A loan was raised for construction companies to renovate St Petersburg's historical Old Town.

- St Petersburg Vodokanal, the company providing water supply and sanitation and pipe and sewer maintenance services in the city, took out a loan to upgrade infrastructure and introduce new technology.

- More focused lending opportunities became available, such as loans for St Petersburg's small and medium-sized businesses.

The loans were issued by the European Bank for Reconstruction and Development (EBRD) and the World Bank. It should be noted that all these projects had been launched under the previous St Petersburg government, and were only formally and chronologically completed under its successor.

Investment in downtown reconstruction necessitated a Strategic Plan for St Petersburg, which was developed by the Leontief Centre and enacted in 1997. The Strategic Plan, setting forth the basic concepts and vision for the city, gave businesses, prospective investors, authorities and citizens a system of benchmarks to guide them. St Petersburg's pioneering experience in strategic planning was subsequently not only borrowed as a model by other major cities and regions in Russia, including Novosibirsk, Karelia, Saratov, Omsk, Surgut and others, but also used by Vilnius, Riga and Tallinn, the capitals of the former Soviet Union's Baltic republics.

The development and enactment of St Petersburg's Strategic Plan went ahead with no thanks to the then governor, Vladimir Yakovlev. Such a plan was required by the World Bank as a precondition for disbursing its downtown reconstruction loan to St Petersburg. In fact, once the loan came, the Plan was relegated to a back shelf. The development guidelines mapped out in the Plan never received financial support from the city coffers.

In 1998, the St Petersburg JVA, in partnership with a number of other business associations, succeeded in pushing through three new bills, offering better incentives for investors. These concerned:

- government support for investment in St Petersburg;

- tax incentives;

- investing in real estate in St Petersburg.

Paradoxically as it may seem, the city owes these crucial investment laws to the then-ongoing political standoff between Legislative Assembly lawmakers and Governor Yakovlev. Another consequence of that standoff was that City Hall never honoured the 1998 bill, Annual Address of the Governor of St Petersburg. Passed in 1998, this ordinance combined the ideas of the Strategic Plan with the 'open policy' concept, binding the city's executive and legislative authorities to work together to develop, annually adjust and enact a policy document outlining the city's values and priorities for a medium-term period of three to five years. The governor completely ignored this law. In the years that followed, he would never deliver a single policy address to the lawmakers.

It was thanks to St Petersburg lawmakers that, at that particular juncture, the city boasted the best legal framework for investment among all Russian regions; and it was only logical that more foreign investment dollars flowed into the city year on year, placing St Petersburg among Russia's top three favourite investment destinations.

The 1998 financial crash and the resilience of foreign investors

The 1998 currency crisis showed the error of Russia's economic ways. As the rouble crumbled, the economy was hit by three divergent trends:

- Companies geared towards the domestic market were ruined, and many went out of business.

- The goods and services prices of Russian exporters, including manufacturers, became more competitive internationally.

- When banks collapsed en masse, their clients, including successful businesses, suffered heavy and sometimes irreparable losses; paying through banks became problematic; many lawsuits were brought on grounds of *force majeure*.

Businesses with foreign investors proved more resilient than their Russian counterparts. The few losses they did incur had to do with their Russian partners defaulting or going out of business. The economic consequences that followed in the wake of the crisis played into the hands of foreign manufacturers doing business in Russia. As the rouble lost ground against the hard currencies, they were able to cut production costs and make more profit.

Overall, however, St Petersburg's manufacturing industries were hit much harder than their counterparts elsewhere in Russia, and here is why:

- St Petersburg is home to more defence industries, which were the ones most affected by the destructive processes unleashed by the 'liberal fundamentalists' in the government.

- The Sobchak administration had largely neglected the manufacturing sector.

These factors were chiefly to blame for the fact that the city's industrial output plummeted by 70 per cent, compared with the national average of around 50 per cent, although St Petersburg's banking sector emerged less scathed from the crisis. Not a single bank headquartered in St Petersburg went out of business. In fact, the St Petersburg branches of major Moscow-based/national banks stayed afloat when their parent banks defaulted. Some examples were Baltuneximbank (now Baltinvestbank) and Menatep St Petersburg. This augured well for the city's enterprise climate, which did not deteriorate as much as it did almost everywhere else in Russia.

Lower political risk, a relatively favourable legal framework, solid financial services, upbeat business activity and a municipal budget surplus were some of the factors that continued to bring international investors to St Petersburg. The bulk of investment dollars – around 75 per cent – flowed into the manufacturing industries, mainly food production and telecommunications, as well as retail and food and beverage services. Foreign investment peaked in St Petersburg at an annual total of nearly US$1.5 billion in 2000, up ten times from 1995.

Towards a new equilibrium under Putin

In 2000, Vladimir Putin was elected president of Russia. Most analysts attributed his lightning ascent to a combination of random circumstances. In fact, there were perfectly logical reasons why this particular person came into office at this particular point in time, but to explore these calls for a brief recapitulation of history. Under the Soviets, Leningrad had continued the mission envisioned by its founder, Peter I, as the forge of Russia's political, academic, economic and cultural elites, helping to absorb the best international ideas and practices and to transplant them to Russian soil. In light of this mission, the St Petersburg elite had always stood apart from other regional elites, which took over and ran the country from Moscow after the 1917 Bolshevik Revolution. In its early Soviet years, Leningrad was the de facto capital of all northwestern Russia, and the city's leaders were strong and even defiant of Moscow. Sergei Kirov, who headed the Leningrad communist party establishment at the time, enjoyed broader support among rank-and-file communists than Stalin. A major communist party congress was coming up, and more deputies were willing to vote for Kirov than for Stalin as their leader. The Leningrad party bosses were a real challenge and threat to Moscow. After Kirov was assassinated under mysterious circumstances, the entire Leningrad elite was annihilated by Stalin's secret police (NKVD) on trumped-up charges in the infamous 'Leningrad Case'.

Another 'Leningrad Case' was opened in the early 1950s, when Leningrad's leaders once again strengthened their clout, exerting major influence on Soviet policy-making via their representatives in the central government. With their business acumen and broad-based support among common party members, Leningrad's leaders aspired towards key government positions in Moscow, and this could not fail to alarm the senile dictator and his cronies, who were waiting expectantly for Stalin to depart and let them take over. In both 'Leningrad Cases', not only the top officials but also regular communists, scholars and artists were persecuted and killed.

In 1985, the Leningrad party head, G. Romanov, challenged Gorbachev for the party leadership. The former capital of imperial Russia, Leningrad and then St Petersburg has repeatedly, cyclically, pressed its claims to run the country. This is the objective, if somewhat mystical, reality of Russia's 'two capitals'. What we observe now is that many of Russia's top decision makers hail from St Petersburg, such as A. Chubais, A. Kudrin, H. Gref, along with less public, but also influential political figures like the president's envoys plenipotentiary I. Klebanov and G. Poltavchenko, government ministers A. Reiman, A. Fursenko, V. Yakovlev, S. Ivanov and V. Cherkesov, presidential chiefs of staff D. Medvedev, V. Ivanov and I. Sechin, and presidential office manager V. Kozhin. These have all remained in the government for a long time, and their political longevity proves that St Petersburg can, indeed, claim to be a crucible of successful statesmen and administrators. The dominant stature of St Petersburg politicians as strategic decision makers for the whole country appears to be a long-term trend.

By the year 2000, Russia had reached a new socio-economic equilibrium with an upturn in industrial production. In most Russian regions, top decision makers realized perfectly well how much foreign investment meant to their respective economies. Competition for investment flows increased rapidly among the regions. Whereas in 1993 only three of Russia's regions were interested in attracting foreign capital and had some sort of legal framework to show for it, by 1998 79 regions had investment ordinances in place, and 70 of them were offering attractive tax incentives to investors. Many governors went beyond updating the laws, and set the wheels in motion for a cohesive policy to encourage foreign investors. Regional executive authorities developed new government bodies focused exclusively on investment. As a result, St Petersburg was no longer a uniquely attractive destination for foreign capital. Other regions offered even better alternatives.

Federal vs regional political rivalries: negating the business climate

At that point, many top decision makers in St Petersburg were under the impression that the city was so unique and appealing to investors that investment dollars would simply keep flowing in. To make matters worse, Governor Yakovlev was busy fighting the federal authorities and changing the laws to allow himself to run for a third term to perform his daily duties. For the sake of fairness, a few attempts were made to institutionalize the city's investment policy in 2000 and 2001. The drafting of the following ordinances was initiated: Guidelines of a Municipal Investment Programme for St Petersburg, and a Strategic Investment Policy for Better Socio-Economic Development. But neither of these ordinances was developed to the point of becoming usable as a working investment policy tool.

Meanwhile, a succession of new federal laws slashed regional governments' discretion in granting investment incentives and curtailed the remit of regional investment laws. In 2000, the Expert RA rating agency moved St Petersburg way down the list, rating it 22nd most attractive investment destination in terms of legal framework. But the city's executive authorities learned nothing, and their policy on prospective investors remained the same. At that juncture, the City Hall bodies overseeing investment did not coordinate their work efficiently with investors.

As a result of all this, not only did St Petersburg stop being a prime investment magnet but the influx of investment money into the city began to decline year by year. Three major factors contributed to the decline:

- Fewer investors were willing to come to St Petersburg, where political risks were high; by then, St Petersburg had also earned notoriety as the 'crime capital' of Russia.

- Many other Russian regions offered equally or more attractive investment opportunities.

- Foreign-owned companies operating in St Petersburg, having saturated the markets of the city and neighbouring regions with their products and services and having no more room to increase sales, naturally sought to expand farther afield, investing in their new target regions.

Interestingly, the branding of St Petersburg as 'the Crime Capital of Russia,' designed by Kremlin spin doctors in an attempt to defeat Governor Yakovlev in the 2000 gubernatorial elections, did not work: Yakovlev won by a landslide in the first round, having garnered 70 per cent of the votes. But this negative image took root in the media, particularly outside Russia. The Western public and media are generally prone to greatly exaggerate the rate of crime in Russia and St Petersburg. Not that crime is not a problem, but harassment of businesses by organized crime groups is a thing of the past, even for Russian small businesses. Economically motivated assassinations do occur, but, like in the West, they belong in the realm of illegal business such as drug trafficking, prostitution or trafficking in guns.

Relieving the tensions: the role of St Petersburg's new government

When Valentina Matvienko was elected Governor of St Petersburg in 2003, tensions about high political risks were relieved and, in 2004, the downward trend in investment reversed towards modest growth. While the government had no statistics to support its claims of a 40 per cent increase in foreign investment, some growth did occur, and it would be unprofessional to give any other reasons for it than lower political risk expectations: the new St Petersburg administration had only recently stepped in. Meanwhile, some positive trends have emerged that promise to enhance the city's investment appeal in the long run. The St Petersburg government now has a post of Vice-Governor for Investment. A new Committee for Investment and Strategic Projects has been established. Two investment agencies have been formed, one reporting to the above-named Committee, the other operating under the Committee for Economic Development, Industrial Policy and Trade. The mission of these agencies is to assist investors and provide support for investment projects.

The first draft of the St Petersburg Investment Code was given a reading in parliament in the autumn of 2004. Drafted on the initiative of the St Petersburg JVA with contributions from its consultants, the draft bill is centred around the guidelines set forth within the St Petersburg Investment Policy Concept, drafted by the JVA in 2003. Once the Investment Code is passed by the Legislative Assembly, St Petersburg will again be one of Russia's vanguard regions, with one of the most investment-friendly legal frameworks in the country.

Foreign business and joint ventures in St Petersburg's economy

St Petersburg's foreign-owned business sector is not yet 20 years old. According to Internal Revenue files, upwards of 3,000 businesses have been established with foreign investment in the city, 676 of them major or medium-sized companies. The rest are regional and representative offices and small businesses. Table 1.4.1 shows the basic figures for St Petersburg's large and medium-sized businesses.

Table 1.4.1 St Petersburg-based large and medium-sized businesses with foreign capital, by industry: key performance indicators for January – December 2004

	No of entities	Output of goods and services	
		million RUB	% of total
Total	676	209,137	100
including:			
Manufacturing	195	143,362	68.6
Transportation	69	9,973	4.8
Telecommunications	24	28,935	13.8
Construction	21	4,012	1.9

	No of entities	Output of goods and services	
		million RUB	% of total
Retail and food and beverage	171	11,467	5.5
General services required for successful market operation	35	1,338	0.6
Housing and utilities	9	2,274	1.1
Culture and arts	19	3,352	1.6
Science and scientific services	26	1,176	0.6
Other business	107	3,248	1.5

Express poll data

	Average employee headcount		Average monthly wage per employee		
	People	% compared with previous year	Roubles	% compared with Previous year	General average wage
Total	130,505	97.2	14,282	123.7	100
Including:					
Manufacturing	77,311	93.5	13,806	125.1	96.7
Transportation	11,275	103.0	14,958	119.1	104.7
Telecommunications	10,803	94.6	19,195	126.0	134.4
Construction	2,506	108.7	9,755	87.2	68.3
Retail and food and beverage	11,753	105.7	10,978	132.9	76.9
General services required for successful market operation	1,374	89.5	17,630	118.4	123.4
Housing and utilities	1,732	101.9	17,393	108.1	121.8
Culture and arts	4,206	102.6	9,171	119.3	64.2
Science and scientific services	2,459	115.1	18,383	1.6	128.7
Other business	7,086	113.2	18,184	110.5	127.3

Source: Petrostat.

Joint ventures produce some 40 per cent of goods and services in St Petersburg. While no specific figures are available for small businesses, or regional and representative offices, these are estimated to produce another 7–9 per cent. Therefore, foreign-owned businesses (about 1,000 of which are 100 per cent foreign-owned) contribute approximately 50 per cent of the city's gross regional product (GRP). Of the city's top 10 taxpayers, six are partially or fully foreign-owned companies.

St Petersburg is proud to be home to the leading multinational corporations such as Otis, Radisson SAS, Bosch Siemens, Alcatel, Elcotec, Gillette, Electrolux, Knauf, Heineken, Nestlé, Philip Morris, British American Tobacco, JTI, Scania, PricewaterhouseCoopers, Wrigley, Kraft Foods, Soufflé Group, Raiffeisenbank, Dresdner Bank, Deutsche Bank, Credit Lyonnais, Baker & McKenzie, TNT Express, Wurt, Kelly Services, Mantsinen, Ives Roche. The three countries with the most number of businesses in St Petersburg are:

1. Finland with 547;

2. the United States with 408;

3. Germany with 393.

The leading investors in St Petersburg are the United States, Germany, the Netherlands, Cyprus, the United Kingdom and Switzerland, with others accounting for less than seven per cent of investment inflow. Notably, Swiss and Cypriot investments mostly represent returning Russian capital. Investments from Cyprus have shown more than 50 per cent annual growth for two years running.

Meanwhile, many great investment opportunities remain untapped by foreign investors:

- a hotel sector with so few 2 and 3-star hotels that they only provide 10 per cent of what should be expected from a prime international travel destination like St Petersburg;

- high-tech manufacturing in all industries;

- components for the automotive industry and other high-tech industries;

- venture investment in innovative projects;

- education services;

- housing and utilities.

According to the records of the Ministry of Economic Development, Industry and Trade, 70 per cent of foreign-owned businesses routinely earn upwards of 20 per cent in profits; 16 per cent of them operate at profit margins exceeding 50 per cent, and 24 per cent make over 30 per cent.

In polls of investors over the past two years, 80 per cent described their business in Russia as 'successful', 17 per cent said they were doing 'OK', and only 3 per cent thought they were not making it.

The majority of investors have radically rethought their values and priorities in the past four years:

- 71 per cent of foreign-owned companies consider corruption the main obstacle to business;

- 66 per cent said they were the most unhappy about 'administrative barriers';

- 56 per cent said their bane was 'selective interpretation and enforcement of laws';

- 51 per cent named 'unclear and mutually contradictory laws';

- 29 per cent cited conflict of interests between the state and private business.

Four years earlier, the most frequently named grievances were threats to security/safety and different laws in different regions. High taxes have completely vanished from the top 10 obstacles to business.

Investing in St Petersburg: ratings and outlook

For many years now, the Expert RA rating agency has placed St Petersburg second only to Moscow in terms of investment opportunity. In passing its judgement, Expert RA looks at macroeconomics, including industrialization levels, consumer demand, labour pool, financial institutions, infrastructure, natural resources and the 'institutional factor'. St Petersburg is third in Russia (Moscow not being in the top 10) in investment risk level, calculated as an integral total of seven types of risk: legislative, political, economic, financial, social, criminal and environmental.

In 2003 and 2004, St Petersburg joined Moscow, Moscow Region, Sverdlovsk Region and Khanty-Mansi Autonomous Region in the group of regions with 'high potential and moderate risk', with reference to investment climate. However, not a single region in Russia met the high criteria that would make it a region with 'maximum potential and minimal risk'.

St Petersburg's highest risks – political and legislative – are reducing, while Moscow has, to all intents and purposes, exhausted its resources for keeping its investment potential high. As new port facilities are built and opened in the Leningrad Region, St Petersburg's clout as a major hub of logistics, transportation and cargo handling is set to increase dramatically. The bottom line is that St Petersburg stands a very good chance of emerging as Russia's new investment capital within the next two to three years.

1.5

Understanding Russia's Business Environment with a View to Investing in St Petersburg

Sebastian Zinovieff FitzLyon FRICS, Australian Honorary Consul, Northwest Russian Consular District

Introduction

My observations and credentials are derived from my 12 years' work as a real estate appraiser in St Petersburg – after a lifetime working in the West – and my background as the Russian-speaking grandson of a businessman and politician from this city from before the 1917 Revolution. I was born and educated outside the Soviet Union. My position as Australia's representative in the northwestern part of Russia has given me added insight into why foreign investor penetration succeeds in some cases and fails in others, and grants me ready access to the provincial corridors of power.

As a Western consultant to Western organizations and sometimes Russian ones, I am often called upon to revitalize negotiations between foreign would-be investors and their Russian would-be partners, and sometimes to help them to divorce. This is my bread and butter and it has given me a grandstand view of the opportunities and pitfalls. In addition, working in a region bordering the West – next to Finland and Estonia – one can make comparisons more readily with the West than if one were based in Moscow. Also one often tends to be involved with enterprises active in cross-border commerce and cooperation, and consequently the reasons for success and failure become clear.

Who's who in business

It is as well to know whom you are dealing with in the new Russia, and an understanding of the pedigree of businesspeople is the key to deciding how to deal with them – or whether to deal with them at all. Knowing something about people's backgrounds in Russia will help to predict their behaviour and will assist you in your own approach towards them.

But I would advise against coming to Russia 'to do' or to start up business activities without local consultants – legal, tax, real estate – even if one is fluent in Russian. One needs local contacts who know a lot about the business climate and whom to avoid.

Contrary to common Western assumptions, business began to evolve in Russia and the region well before 'speculation' (or the carrying-on of commercial activity) ceased to be a crime punishable by a term in a labour camp. Distinct business castes began to form, and entered the scene when the Soviet Union collapsed at the end of 1991.

Heirs to the black economy

The 18 long years of stagnation under Leonid Brezhnev saw the evolution of a massive underground economy running in parallel with the state economic system and all its panoply of five-year plans and propaganda support. Simple economic pressure, together with the possibilities of making money out of an illegal state-wide distribution system for food and other essential commodities that ran in parallel with the official state system, created a hidden entrepreneurial layer of Soviet society. The state system was bound to fail owing to the lack of incentives, inefficient bureaucracy and reduced repressive force. Stalin and his milder version, Krushchev, had gone, and with them the initial Marxist purity; cynicism took root and the climate for an underground alternative capitalist economy was founded.

Actually the southern Soviet nationalities never took their communism too seriously, and their commercial trader instincts easily dovetailed into the black economy.

The businesses and businessmen created in this era had a flying start to legal capitalism with Perestroika. These were the first commercial enterprises to trade openly. This caste are the heirs to the black economy.

Closely allied to the heirs of the black economy are some of the former managers of state enterprises. For the black economy to work, the official economy had to leak, and before Perestroika a core of corrupt state managers worked with the underground distribution networks, supplying them with agricultural produce and raw materials through the back door. Eventually they, too, became private business people in their own right, legitimizing themselves in the post-Perestroika privatization era.

Thus unofficial business before Perestroika incubated a culture of corruption working through patronage and theft. Lack of money in circulation led to barter. Vicious reprisals were meted out for failure to meet obligations. In short, all the ingredients were present for widespread tax evasion and organized crime to flourish after Perestroika. Despite this, the trust necessary for the system to work in the absence of legally enforceable contracts has continued into modern business life, and the trustworthy element of this caste of business society greatly outweighs the criminal one. The problem is, how does one find out who falls into which camp? Many a joint venture with foreigners has foundered due to the foreign partner being abused by the worst representatives of this caste. And some newcomers to business in Russia unwittingly fall in with the criminal element, which I stress is in the minority.

Good or bad, one thing I can say with emphasis is that they are all extremely street-wise.

Voucher millionaires

The wealth acquired by people connected with pre-Perestroika business was used to buy up individuals' privatization vouchers in the early 1990s when state assets were divided up and one voucher assigned to each resident of the Russian Federation. Some of the earliest oligarchs built up their wealth by voucher accumulation. Ruthless, these people are not joint venture material.

Privatization tsars (and failures)

Those managers of large state enterprises who were lucky enough to be in the right place at the right time (1992–94) when mass privatization took place picked up the lion's share of the enterprises and the real estate that went with them. However, most of these people reached their positions of authority by climbing up the higher echelons of the Party, not by dint of any commercial acumen or characteristics – officially, there was no commerce. So when they became enterprise owners, many of them could not cope with the competition and the need to apply efficient work practices, or just to work hard. Thus a significant proportion of these former state businesses never became profitable, and eventually their new owners were forced to sell out to cleverer people who knew how to turn the business round, or to asset strippers. However, the successful ones, who also had the good fortune to inherit essential or monopoly enterprises, form a powerful lobby group in politics and have close ties to government. They are often motivated by power as much as by profit, and are not interested in sharing either with outside partners.

The security people

The best organized caste of business people is derived from the security forces (ex-KGB). Before Perestroika, the security system scooped up those of the Soviet Union's finest university graduates who had the right background and patriotic instincts, and employed them in this apparatus, which was vast enough to make up an identifiable layer of society. As well-educated people, with a network of support that transcended the collapse of the Old Order, they had major advantages over their cousins in less influential organizations.

After Perestroika, state security became more or less moribund. There was no totalitarianism to preserve anymore, and many of its members lost their jobs or left due to low pay and high inflation. They redeployed themselves into business if they were bright, found jobs with foreign companies, or just lay low till better times. The business elements were quick to snap up opportunities. They rely on their 'old boy' network – the best in Russia – for contacts and mutual assistance; they are extremely well organized, disciplined and mostly reliable, but lack the cunning of the heirs to the black economy. When you talk with them, you rapidly get a sense of their deep disdain for the 'heirs to the black economy'. It is generally possible to do business with them.

The ones who lay low or stayed behind in the 'organs' made their comeback under Putin, who is using them now for his reorganization of the country. Of course, the business element is well serviced by their former colleagues back in power. This is useful to know.

For business discipline, a Komsomol (Communist youth league) background is also good, and it did teach its members loyalty and organization.

They all make, by and large, conscientious and efficient managers.

The new boys and girls

The last caste is the new start-up business category. Mostly young but with some in early middle age and from the military, these people are the future of Russia. They are extremely able, and probably the majority wish to succeed by virtue of hard work and good planning, without resorting to bribery. Bereft of old Party contacts and not inheritors of state assets – or of parental wealth, for that matter – they are largely honest, and many have made a careful study of Western practices. Still unable to have access to bank finance – because of high interest rates and impossible loan criteria – they start their businesses from very humble beginnings and build them up through sheer effort.

If there is a difference between them and young business people in the West, it is that the Russians are learning the hard way and are much better at coping with obstacles.

However one should not generalize too much about this caste, and one should take great care when dealing with 'new' unproven entrepreneurs and potential partners. I suggest a gradual build-up of commercial relations until absolute mutual trust is reached. The Japanese approach to dealing with foreigners – extreme caution and a trial period of low-key business – is what is needed.

Business life

Employment practices

Discipline in the workplace varies from virtually nil in some former state enterprises to very tight rules and sanctions and a high standard of behaviour in other businesses. Alcoholism is a declining problem, but it still exists and some manufacturing enterprises even carry out random tests for alcohol levels at the gate, dismissing transgressors.

The concept of seeking promotion, and particularly added responsibility, is still largely absent in a high proportion of the Russian workforce. So is initiative. This is because tall poppies were ruthlessly cut down in Stalin's Russia and there were no advantages in being promoted (greater responsibility brought little or no added pay). Initiative was almost regarded as an aberration. People kept their heads down. This is so much stamped into the national psyche as a result of the Purges and later repression that only the teenage generation born in Gorbachev's time displays signs of initiative in the workplace. The creation of cadres who actually want responsibility is one of business's greatest problems.

The idea that Russians inherently reject responsibility, or are bereft of initiative because of ethnic Slavic traits, is incorrect. In other former Soviet states such as Estonia where the native population is non-Slav, exactly the same Soviet-inherited passivity is found today in the older generation.

Successful enterprises are usually ruled with a fairly iron hand; democracy in the workplace is seen as weakness. However, respect for the individual and for his/her skills and contribution is enormously appreciated; it is a managerial trait that seems to have been largely absent in Soviet times.

It is common to entertain one's staff quite lavishly on occasions such as Women's Day (8th March) and the New Year, and increasingly to arrange restaurant outings and trips to spas and weekend retreats. I think I can explain this as a mixture of natural Russian generosity and hospitality, and the feeling of togetherness that Russians always feel comfortable with. Russian employers, although often fairly tyrannical and quite mean with wages, are generous in a paternalistic sort of way when it comes to collective activities.

Generosity also expresses itself in the extraordinary amount of money employees will spend on gifts and imported flowers to each other on birthdays. Birthdays, by the way, are extremely important in Russian culture. Unless you lay down the rules when you open your business, you will find that there is little work done on somebody's birthday as a party will be organized in the workplace well before closing time. Businesses pay Byzantine homage to female tax and other inspectors with birthday bouquets. Productivity on the eve of national holidays is usually low; the common expectation in many enterprises is that everybody will be released to go home at lunchtime.

After a dozen years living and working in Russia, there are one or two features of business life that I still find too absurd to accept, but at the same time I know they must be accepted. Foremost is the acceptance of bureaucratic requirements bordering on the insane.

I now realize that a good proportion of the people one sees during normal working hours going about town, and riding on public transport, are carrying out the most ridiculous bureaucratic tasks, which because of their sheer scale almost dwarf productive administrative work in the country. Government departments such as tax offices require original documents to be delivered to their offices confirming the most routine, petty of events in the financial life of enterprises as and when those events occur.

It is not enough to post documents to the administration: use of the postal service is their prerogative, not yours. So at any one time of the day, one or two of your employees will be crossing town to deliver a letter or a form to a government department and getting written confirmation that it has been delivered.

This absurdity reached its zenith for me when recently I had to wait in line at a notary's office for almost an hour so that I could arrange to notarize a power of attorney to my driver, authorizing him to wait in a longer line to receive from a local government department a photocopy of a simple floor plan of the premises above my office, so that I could pass this document to another local government office who would be considering my application to construct a new front entrance. In any other society, I would have asked my upstairs neighbour for the plan, or written to the government department with a similar request, or expected one government department to go direct to the other. But no, two busy people had to waste hours to get this trifling piece of paper.

This was an example of local government being hamstrung by federal government rules and legislation, as normally one gets quite helpful service from municipal government departments, who try hard on behalf of the citizenry.

Driving a motor vehicle in Russia is most instructive when it comes to explaining the Russian business psyche, and also the mentality of bureaucrats. Up until about six years ago, there were few cars on the roads and now, with the huge number of new inexperienced drivers and virtually no police control of behaviour behind the wheel, driving standards are appalling. The most tiresome aspect is the way cars will race to fill up the slightest gap in front of another car in any lane, and switch from lane to lane taking any opportunity to move ahead of the pack, ultimately saving only seconds in their journey.

This characterizes the approach to some fields of business, where entrepreneurs are so impatient for returns that they will chop and change their approach and their partners and suppliers at the drop of a hat when they see a gap they can fill. As for the traffic police, they seem oblivious of the mayhem and breaking of traffic rules around them. They are little more than document checkers who constantly stop cars and go to inordinate lengths to check every one of the many documents that driving a company motor vehicle in Russia entails. This is a classic example of how form overrules substance in Russia.

Tangling with the bureaucracy

Bureaucratic red tape is the greatest hindrance to business development in Russia, and ultimately to the development of the country. There is little concept of a public service serving the public: you could easily imagine the principle is the reverse, that the general public exist for the benefit of the public servants. If you want to look for logic in the actions and decisions of federal bodies, stop now: you won't find it.

The foreigner will have a first taste of intractable bureaucracy when attempting to obtain a visa for employment purposes and a work permit. Firms employing foreigners will have a staff member whose principal job is to obtain these documents – sometimes even if there is only one foreign employee. The situation is actually getting even worse, particularly as far as work permits are concerned.

There are at last signs that the younger generation do not take for granted the unhelpfulness of some public servants and the absurdity of the red tape. Many are becoming more demanding and critical of government – which no longer frightens them – and within the next 10 years or so I think that these young people will increasingly influence political life, demanding real service and value for money.

The trouble is that Soviet society was largely built on control and lack of trust. The government's basic premise was that people are dishonest and can be expected to cheat the system if they can. Western society is largely built on the opposite assumption, that people should be trusted until they are foolish enough to get caught cheating the system – which everybody has the opportunity to do – and that this will usually be their last easy opportunity to do so.

The huge effort put into controlling the public by making people fill out forms and deposit them with various overlapping controlling departments, and notarizing powers of attorney for the most minor of actions, is a real drain on productive activity time which is impossible to overstate.

Of course, it has to be said that in becoming a capitalist society once again, Russia did not abandon its anti-capitalist legal base. Rather it tended in the 1990s to add new layers of amending legislation on top of the inherited Soviet legislation, to try to turn it into capitalist-friendly law. This renders some of the legislation more opaque and contrasts with other former communist countries which have sensibly abandoned communist law altogether in favour of modern legislation.

Crime

Crime is no more endemic in Russian society than in many Western countries; it is just that the Soviet Union endlessly informed the world that there wasn't any to speak of, and the discovery that Russia is no different to anywhere else is a shock that the Russian and Western media have not got over yet.

The 'Mafia' is an interesting sociological topic in its own right and it is as well to try to explain its composition, its transmogrification and its effect on business life. As a sub-culture in Russia, it largely owes its origins to the black economy and the underground business groupings driving it. These groupings have consolidated somewhat, and as legalization of business eroded their traditional opportunities, they branched out into extortion, protection rackets and privatization scandals in the early 1990s.

Several such publicly identifiable groupings evolved in St Petersburg, and over the next six years or so they largely eliminated each other or were themselves eliminated by the police in a gory war of attrition. Mafia members either died in the cross-fire, were imprisoned for long terms, or quietly became more or less respectable employees and business people. It seems some organizations remained intact and moved into highly profitable spheres of legitimate business.

A security industry staffed by former state security personnel has developed and, together with the forces of law and order, largely keeps the situation under control for law-abiding tax-paying firms. The picture in regards to cash businesses is bleaker, however.

Various business spheres in Russia are more criminalized than others. The Mafia as such has changed from being a purely geographically delineated phenomenon into primarily an industry-delineated one, albeit operating on a regional basis. In March 2005 this was underlined when the Interior Minister stated that 500 major Russian firms are infiltrated by criminals, including many in the natural resources, primary industry, and vehicle distribution sectors.

Working in St Petersburg

As one of Russia's only two really major cities, St Petersburg does have a foreign business community, albeit quite small. The St Petersburg International Business Association is the oldest established forum for foreigners to meet and discuss common problems socially, and for business bonding at seminars (www.spiba.spb.ru). However St Petersburg is very different from Moscow as a place to live and do business: its local authorities are much more transparent (especially in the surrounding Leningrad Region, which is consistently rated as one of Russia's friendliest investment destinations), and there is far less corruption.

The city government recognizes its bureaucracy is inflexible and cumbersome and is making real efforts to change for the good.

The underlying foundation of the St Petersburg workforce is an excellent primary, secondary and higher education system, by anyone's standards. It is adapting itself extremely well to massive continuing change and constant experimentation with the economy by the Federal government. This is the most underestimated and potent element in the entrepreneurial environment today and for the foreseeable future.

Some concluding remarks

Why, given the negative features of doing business in Russia, should anyone consider doing it?

The answer lies in the fact that Russia, as the world's largest oil producer and holder of the largest reserves of natural resources, with a population which is undersupplied with basic and luxury commodities and much else, has enormous potential to become very wealthy. Indeed an increasingly wealthy middle class is growing rapidly. Anyone involved in that enrichment process has the potential to benefit quite dramatically. The difficulties are not unique to foreigners, and the playing field is becoming more level now for foreigners and Russians alike.

The efforts of the Federal Government to make standards in Russia acceptable to the WTO are beginning to have a noticeable effect. People at every level (except corrupt officials) understand they will benefit from structural change and that all businesspeople – foreigners and locals alike – are victims of problems inherited from an anti-capitalist regime; people are united in supporting change.

My own forecasts made two, five and even 10 years ago for the economy, based on various political scenarios, have been surprisingly accurate; currently, the political climate may not appeal to Western observers but it is largely positive for business. The business climate is becoming more acceptable, as in the case of the tax regime. I still forecast good progress for the next 10 years, provided there is no unexpected cataclysmic political upheaval.

A 'can do' attitude, sadly lacking in many parts of 'old Europe' nowadays, is creeping into and pervading business life in Russia, certainly in St Petersburg.

Bureaucracy is the main drawback, along with the things which stem from it such as corruption. There are other hindrances: for example, some prejudice against foreigners is certainly still there on an official basis; there are tiresome visa and employment bureaucratic hurdles; and vehicle registration is still limited by the period of visa registration.

As for St Petersburg, its locals are relatively open to foreign attitudes, being on Western Europe's doorstep.

I have left one of the most important pieces of advice to the end: the need to employ a local manager before embarking on business operations that you hope to establish on a long-term basis. The selection of that person is extremely important and will make or break your business.

Part Two
Business Development

2.1

An Economic and Political Outlook for Russia

Madina Butaeva, Head of Research, Raiffeisenbank Austria

To be sure, 2004 could be described as a year of both big hopes and big disappointments. Hopes last March that President Putin would use the political momentum gained from his earlier-than-expected Cabinet reshuffle and decisive electoral victory to spearhead a decidedly liberal economic and political agenda proved to be overly optimistic. Together with the rollback of gubernatorial elections, the Yukos endgame erased any doubts that may have lingered about the lengths to which the Kremlin would go to consolidate its grip over the country's political institutions and strategic economic assets. As economic policy took a backseat to political power plays, in-fighting nearly paralyzed the government, causing some major structural reform initiatives to stall. Despite the letdowns, however, there are grounds for optimism, as well as a need for healthy caution.

The economy

Policy implementation is a key factor here. From a purely static viewpoint, Russia's economic situation looks superb, with strong trade and budget surpluses, low debt and high economic growth rates. However, from a dynamic perspective, the economic situation is clearly deteriorating, as evidenced by lower investment, looser fiscal policy and higher inflation. The growth rate is expected to slow further until key structural reforms (such as judicial, administrative, utilities and banking reforms) are realized. GDP growth of 5.5 per cent is expected in 2005, versus 6.8 per cent in 2004, which is notably less than the 7.3 per cent annual average required to double GDP within ten years. Despite widely touted efforts to diversify the economy, energy will remain an engine of key growth.

The strength of commodity markets means that Russia, the world's principal resource exporter, is enjoying ideal conditions for loose monetary and tight fiscal policies. Despite this, significant fiscal loosening (to the tune of 2 per cent of GDP) is the likely scenario for 2005. So far, the Russian authorities have been extremely impressive in their fiscal strictness. However, as the state's balance sheet becomes evidently strong on the back of petrodollars galore, the hawkish line is proving increasingly hard to hold. Increased expenditures in response to protests over the monetization of benefits, together with the big cuts in VAT (down to a unified 13 per cent rate) advocated by Prime Minister Fradkov, are part of the larger ideological aim to meet Putin's target of doubling GDP. However, the quality and sustainability of this growth is more important than just hitting that target, as more loosening would inevitably increase Russia's vulnerability to negative oil price shocks. At the same time, trying to improve the investment climate through the strengthening of institutions and a better-incentivized tax system would spur more private investment and help sustain economic growth in the long term.

The temptation for the government to shore up spending (ie from the Stabilization Fund) creates another economic concern: rising prices. The Central Bank of Russia has, since 2000, been remarkably successful at managing to keep inflation low while limiting appreciation of the nominal exchange rate. However, money supply expansion, which reached 36 per cent in 2004, appears to be finally taking its toll on producer prices, which rose by 29 per cent in that year. Restoring control over the fiscal situation, and in particular the Stabilization Fund, is especially important.

Politics and economic reform: overcoming old ways of thinking

The Kremlin has been pursuing two agendas – political centralization and economic modernization – in the belief that the former (which includes shoring up the state's position in the energy sector) is an important prerequisite for the latter. The political part of the equation was certainly dominant throughout 2004.

As 2005 progresses, we believe that the president's economic goals could well return to the forefront. There are still a full two years or so before election-year passions begin to resurge. Putin's popularity, albeit dented by the backlash against the unpopular move to monetize social benefits in early 2005, is still high enough to allow him room to

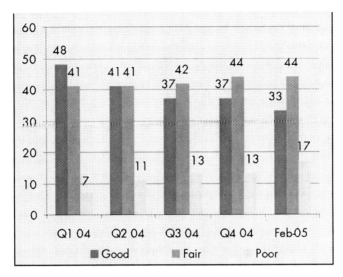

Figure 2.1.1 Opinion polls about president's performance (%)

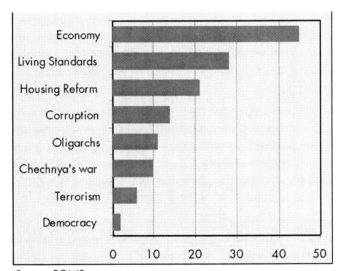

Source: ROMIR

Figure 2.1.2 Public perception of most important problems (%, as of January 2005)

manoeuvre and get back on track with his reform programme (see Figure 1). Doing so would help him to build a positive domestic policy legacy, allowing him more leeway to get his successor elected in 2008. Recent polls show that the development of the economy tops the list of concerns among Russian citizens (see Figure 2.1.2).

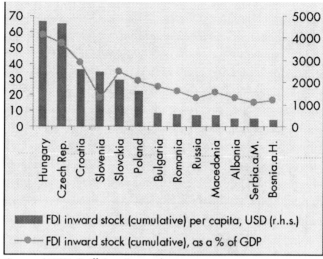

Source: WiiW; Raiffeisen Research

Figure 2.1.3 Foreign direct investment in Russia and CEE

Structural factors will play an important role in the medium-term scenario, in particular the role of foreign direct investment (FDI). Healthy FDI could be an important disciplining factor to help keep the state at arm's length from the economy. Given its vast mineral endowments and skilled labour potential, Russia still attracts too little investment compared to its CEE and CIS neighbours (see Figure 2.1.3).

The fact that FDI outflows are much higher reflects in part the uncertainty in the business environment at home (eg the capital flight caused by oligarchs taking their capital out of Russia and investing in safer markets elsewhere), as well as an increasingly nationalistic tinge to investment policy disseminating from the Kremlin. Clearly, companies with non-Russian majority shareholders are being squeezed out of the competition for choice mineral deposits.

In this respect, Russia's accession to the WTO, which optimists hope could take place towards the end of 2005, would be an important milestone on the road to establishing transparent and fair rules for foreign participation in the economy.

By fostering foreign investment in domestic industries and the transfer of know-how, WTO accession could also help to diversify the Russian economy, reducing the sensitivity of the state budget to commodity prices. Indeed, as a percentage of GDP (see Figure 2.1.4), the relative significance of Russia's largest industrial enterprises (with the top 20 mainly consisting of oil and metal giants) in the economy is gradually declining, which could be a healthy indication of diversification

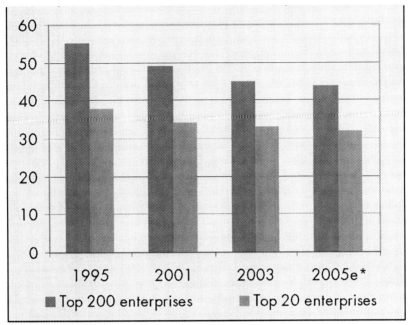

Source: Expert RA, Raiffeisen Research

Figure 2.1.4 Russia largest enterprises as a % of GDP (ranked by sales volume)

and the growth of small and medium-sized enterprises in the manufacturing and high-technology sectors.

2.2

The Banking Sector in St Petersburg

Elena Vishnyakova and Alla Petrova,
Web-invest Bank Plc

Introduction

The beginning of the 1990s saw the emergence of the banking system and the transformation of the market in St Petersburg's economy. Even in the 1980s, however, when reforms had not yet been initiated, St Petersburg was a leader in developing banking in Russia. At that time, three retail banks were created as an experiment. Two of these were closely related to governmental industrial enterprises that had been freed of state control: Tehnohimbank was set up to service companies in the chemical sector, while Energomashbank focused on the power machine building industry.

The busiest period in banking development was the last decade of the 20th century. The crisis of 1998 wiped out ineffective organizations and allowed new names to appear in the banking arena, as well as strengthening previous leaders in the sector. Alongside newly created independent banks, subsidiaries of banks headquartered in other cities sprang up in St Petersburg, where there are now branches of more than 70 banks from all over Russia.

As of 1 February 2005, 1,296 credit organizations were registered in the territory of the Russian Federation, of which 668 companies (51.5 per cent) are registered in Moscow Region.

In terms of the number of banks registered in one city, the leader is Moscow with 653, followed by St Petersburg with 44. Most of the Moscow-based banks have subsidiaries and representative offices in St Petersburg. The Northwest Federal Region is in fourth place after the Moscow, Privolzhsky and Southern Federal Regions. Its banking sector includes 87 banks and 367 branches of credit organizations.

The events of 2004 once again proved that banks of the Moscow region are less stable and less able to cope with external changes. The high level of market saturation in Moscow, tough competition and weaknesses in financial planning cause risks throughout the system. However unusual it may seem, regional banks, whose business models are based around client asset management as well as provision of credit facilities to other sectors and private individuals, proved to be more stable during the 'crisis of confidence' in the summer of 2004. Although the St Petersburg banking sector is far from insulated from events outside the city, by having around 80 branches of banks based in other cities, the consequences of the summer liquidity crisis were less damaging for the city's banking sector.

The main financial resources are concentrated in Moscow, while industrial production is mainly based in other regions. This causes real difficulties for regional banks when servicing industrial enterprises. Expansion into the Moscow market by regional banks is perceived as a means of gaining access to speculative instruments and the credit market, not as a challenge to local participants. Conversely, Moscow banks undertake moves into regions as a way of expanding their client bases.

Capital

In contrast to the overall Russian trend, St Petersburg's banks demonstrate a higher growth rate of capital than of assets. Net profit represents the main source of capitalization of banks in St Petersburg. Web-invest Bank Plc has the fastest capital growth rate among St Petersburg's financial companies. It moved from the bottom of rating charts to the Russian top 10 after capitalizing its retained earning.

Table 2.2.1 The top five St Petersburg banks by size of authorized capital as at 1 January 2005

Ranking	Bank	Authorized capital (million $)
1	Web-invest Bank	73.7
2	Menatep St Petersburg	51.7
3	Industry and Construction Bank	39.4
4	Dresdner Bank	25.2
5	Kalion Rusbank	16.3

Table 2.2.2 The top 10 St Petersburg banks by equity as at
1 January 2005

Ranking	Bank	Equity capital (million $)
1	Industry and Construction Bank	310.80
2	Menatep St Petersburg	126.58
3	Web-invest Bank	89.25
4	Dresdner Bank	82.86
5	Baltic Bank	78.58
6	International Bank St Petersburg	71.11
7	Kalion Rusbank	62.42
8	Bank St Petersburg	60.52
9	Tavricheskiy	43.09
10	Russia	42.66

The 2004 results show the combined assets of regional banks as slightly over a trillion RUB (around US$36 billion), which is only half the assets of the state-monopoly Sberbank. Clearly, the regional banking system is much smaller than the large banking business.

Only 4.18 per cent of the total assets of the Russian banking industry and 27.87 per cent of regional banks' assets are located in the northwestern region. For comparison, bank assets in the Moscow region amount to 83.78 per cent of total assets in the country. Most of the financial capital of the northwestern region is concentrated in St Petersburg.

Table 2.2.3 The top 10 St Petersburg banks by assets (excluding branch offices of out-of-town banks) as at 1 January 2005

Ranking	Bank	Assets (million $)
1	Industry and Construction Bank	6,517
2	Menatep St Petersburg	1,525
3	Baltic Bank	845
4	Bank St Petersburg	701
5	Web-invest Bank	593
6	International Bank St Petersburg	592
7	Russia	446

Ranking	Bank	Assets (million $)
8	MDM-Bank St Petersburg	427
9	Dresdner Bank	415
10	Tavricheskiy	262

The Industry and Construction Bank (ICB) is the largest regional Russian bank by assets. The only bank that experienced a squeeze in assets last year was Menatep St Petersburg, which suffered a fall of 21.34 per cent because of the Yukos case; however the bank is still the second largest by assets among its St Petersburg based rivals.

Table 2.2.4 The top 10 St Petersburg banks by size of assets as at 1 January 2005

Ranking	Bank	Liquid assets (million $)	% change from previous year
1	Menatep St Petersburg	332.62	-22.14
2	Industry and Construction Bank	221.94	-51.17
3	Baltic Bank	72.51	-42.26
4	Tavricheskiy	61.49	70.11
5	Bank St Petersburg	50.91	-35.26
6	MDM-Bank St Petersburg	47.45	-12.18
7	Russia	45.31	56.78
8	Web-invest Bank	45.15	33.73
9	St Petersburg Social Commercial Bank	41.54	63.78
10	Kalion Rusbank	26.43	45.91

In the context of the banking sector's development strategy, serious work has to be done in order to increase the capitalization of banks, both in terms of initial public offerings (IPOs) and higher profitability. The task of capitalization increase has become a priority for those Russian banks whose asset growth rate is higher than their equity capital growth rate. In that sense, one can say that the St Petersburg banks have a healthy capital position, which provides a reliable foundation for future development.

Table 2.2.5 The top 10 most profitable St Petersburg banks as at 1 January 2005

Ranking	Bank	Profit (million $)
1	Industry and Construction Bank	113.65
2	Web-invest Bank	17.39
3	Bank St Petersburg	11.63
4	MDM-Bank St Petersburg	10.78
5	Baltic Bank	9.18
6	Russia	9.18
7	International Bank St Petersburg	7.16
8	Dresdner Bank	7.05
9	Menatep St Petersburg	6.34
10	Tavricheskiy	5.51

The St Petersburg banking sector and international capital markets

The St Petersburg banking sector is one of the most developed in Russia, but its role in developing the regional economy is not substantial. There are many large-scale projects in the region that could benefit from an investment process, but few banks have disposable funds to finance them. That is why they are entering international markets for capital.

Western banks, on the other hand, take part in organizing syndicated loans for banks in St Petersburg. In October 2003 a consortium of European banks, led by Raiffeisen and RZB, offered a syndicated loan of US$25 million to the ICB, and in February 2005 the ICB agreed on a 12-month loan with a syndicate of 20 banks. The leading underwriters of the 2005 loan were the Bank of Tokyo-Mitsubishi Ltd, Commerzbank, Aktiengesellschaft and Standard Bank London Ltd. As a result of excess investor interest, the amount loaned increased to US$90 million from the initially agreed US$50 million. The purpose of the loan was to enable the ICB to finance client projects in various industries, and one condition of the agreement was a possible extension of the loan for another 12 months. The coupon rate was set at LIBOR +2.95 per cent. Since coupon rates in Russia rarely go below 10 per cent per annum, the difference in rates allows banks to receive additional income from international fund raising.

Foreign companies have had a positive influence as they enter the sector and offer quality banking products to a wide range of businesses and individuals at reasonable prices.

Lending

Regional banks are increasing their volumes of lending to both businesses and households faster than banks in Moscow. In 2004, a business lending growth of 52 per cent (418 billion RUB, US$14.5 billion) was achieved in St Petersburg, compared with 46 per cent in Moscow. Household lending grew 119 per cent.

The credit portfolios of all Russian banks by the end of 2004 amounted to 3.3 trillion RUB (more than US$117 billion). The proportion of loans to net assets of Russian banks increased by 10 per cent to 53 per cent last year. Expert opinion is that the maximum possible share is 80 per cent, so the growth potential remains significant. St Petersburg banks have that potential. However, none of them is rated among the top 10 Russian banks in terms of the volume of lending. The ICB ranks only 11th in the list of the largest Russian lenders.

Although the proportion of debt in the resource base of enterprises in the Northwestern Federal Region varies from sector to sector, an overall trend is evident, with the major part of capital being borrowed. The role of banks as financial intermediaries in reallocating resources among economic agents of St Petersburg should therefore not be underestimated. However, banks in St Petersburg do not yet have 'long-term', sufficiently 'cheap' resources at their disposal to finance long-term investment projects, although most enterprises require loans with maturities of over three years.

The high risk associated with provision of credit by St Petersburg banks can be explained by the following factors:

- insufficiently wide diversification of the banks' resource bases;

- liquidity management problems: unbalanced structures of assets and liabilities of banks by durations;[1]

- absence of accurate mechanism for interaction between real and banking sectors: lack of business transparency (unwillingness of companies to disclose information to banks), absence of default statistics (credit agency);

- ineffective risk and internal control systems in banks.

All these factors result in a high level of interest rates on credit. Interest rates charged to small and medium-sized enterprises (SMEs) total

22 per cent per annum, which is more than 50 per cent higher than the average rate charged to non-financial organizations in all of Russia (11.9 per cent).

Table 2.2.6 Comparison of car-purchase loan rates of Northwest Federal District banks (including branch offices of out-of-town banks)

Bank	Range of interest rates for credits in foreign currency (% per annum)	Credit period(days)	
		From	To
Raiffeseinbank	9.0–12.0	365	1,095
MMB	9.5–11.0	365	1,095
Baltic Bank	9.9–14.0	365	1,095
MDM-Bank St Petersburg	9.0–11.5	730	1,095
Sberbank NWFD	9.0–11.5	365	1,825
Industry and Construction Bank	12	180	1,825

Table 2.2.7 Comparison table of consumer credit rates of Northwest Federal District banks to households (including branch offices of out-of-town banks)

Bank	Range of interest rates (depending on credit programme) (%)*
Sberbank NWFD	11.5–20.0
Home Credit and Finance Bank	12.0–28.0
Russian Standart	29.0

* average credit period is 12–24 months

The proportion of bank loans on the balance sheets of enterprises in the northwestern region is low (4.6 per cent), and these funds are mainly short-term debts used for extension of turnover resources. The main source of funds is the accumulation of creditor liability to suppliers. Resources for developing enterprises come from bond underwriting on the Russian market, which is implemented by large organizations that disclose their shareholder structures and regularly issue financial reports.

Table 2.2.8 The top five St Petersburg banks by volume of loans granted as at 1 January 2005

Ranking	Bank	Volume of loans granted (million $)	Change over one year (%)
1	Industry and Construction Bank	1,388.92	41.42
2	Baltic Bank	400.04	88.61
3	Bank St Petersburg	361.71	89.49
4	Kalion Rusbank	270.70	34.16
5	Menatep St Petersburg	236.33	-35.19

The most vital niche for regional banks is management of the assets of small and medium-sized enterprises. The fact that small regional banks specialize in loan provision to SMEs is a natural process of the 'division of labour' between large, medium and small-scale financial institutions. The need for a prompt diversification into a small-business niche by regional banks is reinforced by the recent increase in competition from large and international financial companies that are entering this market. These include financial institutions working alongside international donor-organizations such as European Bank for Reconstruction and Development (EBRD), the International Finance Corporation (IFC) and others, which have announced plans to start small-business financing programmes. It should be observed that companies working within the boundaries of such special schemes (the EBRD programme for example) and working with small enterprises set their interest rates in the range of 12–15.5 per cent per annum.

In 2004 the Bank for Foreign Trade (Vneshtorgbank) allocated US$1 billion for purposes of small-business financing in 12 cities, and the plan for 2005 is to add 10 more. Small regional banks will soon face tough competition, and need to extend their client lists now.

The large banking businesses have certain advantages. However, most of the largest Russian banks are affiliated with industrial financial groups, and are therefore exposed to risks associated with the financial performance of the conglomerates they belong to. As a result, most banks do not take a long-term view in their debtor selection process. When providing credit, banks base their decisions on the financial results, debt provisions and credit history of companies. Companies with satisfactory indicators can choose the bank that will offer the best credit terms. This approach offers very little prospect of developing a credit system for small businesses.

Fund raising

In 2004 the volume of deposits increased by 915 billion RUB (US$31.76 billion) to 3.8 trillion RUB (about US$320 billion). The proportion of deposits in the value of total assets rose by 3 per cent to 61 per cent. The growth rate of deposits is significantly lower than the growth rate of banks' credit portfolios (32 per cent against 52 per cent). In 2005, the volume of funds held in accounts has been rising, mainly thanks to business deposits. Meanwhile, householders have shown less interest in keeping money on deposit; this is due to the development of customer loan provision in Russia, so that people do not have to save up in order to make major purchases. The 2004 summer crisis of trust in banking has also played its role.

Overall, business and household deposits in banks of the north-western region increased 1.24 times in 2004, to 212.4 billion RUB (US$7.37 billion). It should be noted that 73 per cent of all households' deposits are rouble-denominated funds, which provide higher rates of return than dollar deposits, which in turn are losing value as the US dollar weakens on international markets.

Table 2.2.9 St Petersburg banks by volume of household deposits (including branch offices of out-of-town banks) as at 1 January 2005

Rate	Bank	Outstanding funds on individual accounts (million $)
1	Northwest Bank of Sberbank RF	3,300
2	Industry and Construction Bank	573
3	Baltic Bank	289
4	Menatep St Petersburg	183
5	MDM-Bank St Petersburg	158
6	Bank St Petersburg	135
7	Alfa-Bank (Branch Office)	65
8	Uralsib (Branch Office)	55

Due to a deficit of funds, banks issue their own securities: notes, bonds and shares. Note issues are the largest by volume because of simplicity of the issue procedure. The market for bonds is seriously fragmented, and only large banks have the opportunity to obtain cheap funds on the market for securities.

Business diversification

Regional banks in Russia are not just credit- and payment-processing institutions. Quite often they also provide consulting services. The range of services offered by credit organizations in St Petersburg is considerable. Apart from payment processing, credit provision and consulting, they implement operations with bills of exchange, export–import transactions (guarantees, letters of credit), factoring, management of temporarily free accounts, encashment. Banks assist in financial and tax planning, and help in the formation and expansion of the market for small enterprises, demonstrating that small and medium-sized banks are working in partnership with the small business sector, providing a diversified range of services.

Apart from business loans, there are alternative ways for enterprises in St Petersburg to raise funds for investment activity. The most popular are bond issues and, less frequently, initial public offerings (IPOs).

Bond issues enable companies to raise funds for longer periods, and unlike IPOs do not cause changes in shareholder structure. However the procedure of bond underwriting requires substantial time spent on registration and compliance as well as significant transaction costs.

For some banks in St Petersburg, bond underwriting has become one of their main activities. According to an independent bond underwriting rating published by Cbonds.ru, the Industry and Construction Bank (Promstroibank) and Web-invest Bank are ranked fifth and sixth respectively, with only large investment houses (such as Renaissance Capital and the Bank for Foreign Trade (Vneshtorgbank) ahead of them. The ICB is a commercial bank that also offers fund raising for businesses together with retail banking services. In contrast, investment business is a core activity for Web-invest Bank, which is the heart of a diversified financial group. Its independent investment bank specializes in bond underwriting, corporate finance, mergers and acquisitions, asset management and brokerage services. Between 2001 and 2005, Web-invest Bank took part in over 90 fund raising deals for the largest Russian corporations and municipal agencies.

Forecast

The distrust of the banking system that was prevalent after the crisis of 1998 has caused a deficit of resources. The leader in gaining and serving private customers in the northwestern region has been the northwestern branch of Sberbank.

In 2005 the growth in demand for consumer credit will continue, and will consequently fuel a growth in consumption by the private sector. On the one hand, this will contribute to the prosperity of the population and an increase in production. On the other hand, it may reduce savings (including deposits) and increase inflation, which is currently estimated at a level of 8.5 per cent. In an unstable macro-economic environment, households prefer to purchase goods on credit and not to leave spare cash in deposit accounts, mainly because the rates for rouble-denominated deposits do not cover the rate of inflation. Banks in St Petersburg region will continue to focus on expanding their retail business.

With significant differences between internal and international rates for capital, as well as a weakening dollar in relation to the rouble, foreign-currency-denominated investments in the Russian banking sector remain attractive for foreign investors despite the continuing associated risks. Thus, volumes of foreign liabilities of banks in Russia will rise, and at the same time St Petersburg banks will actively participate in raising international capital.

Among the major negative factors that affect the competitive development of the banking sector in St Petersburg are the presence of state monopolies (Sberbank, Vneshtorgbank, and Vnesheconombank) and the high concentration of assets, with 80 per cent in the hands of 13 banks based in the St Petersburg region.

Difficulties associated with de-monopolization imply that the competitive model of the banking sector in St Petersburg will be dominated by governmental and foreign capital in the proximate future. Acquisitions by larger Moscow and foreign banks to increase their opportunities to enter the market are also feasible. The fist deal of this type was initiated in 2004. Vneshtorgbank gained ownership of 25 per cent+1 stake in Promstroibank. According to a spokesperson for Vneshtorgbank, this deal is a completion of the first stage of the agreement between Vneshtorgbank and Promstroibank shareholders, outlined in the memorandum signed in September 2004. Vneshtorgbank and shareholders of Promstroibank are willing to create favourable conditions to implement the second stage of the deal in the near future, which will result in Vneshtorgbank gaining a 75 per cent stake in Promstroibank. This acquisition will allow both parties to strengthen their competitive positions in business and household financing in the Northwestern Federal Region, will facilitate development of the Vneshtorgbank Group and implement the strategic task of transforming Vneshtorgbank into a generic financial network with European status.

Note

1. The problem of liabilities of banks by duration relates to the fact that the structure of bank assets and liabilities is not balanced in terms of their time period(eg long-term assets are financed by short-term liabilities), which causes a problem for liquidity management.

2.3

The Stock and Fixed-income Market in St Petersburg

Alla Petrova, Head of Equities Research Department, Web-invest Bank Plc

Although the territory and population of St Petersburg and the Northwest Federal Region of Russia are larger than many European countries, the city does not have (and actually cannot have during a period of globalization) its own stock market, separated from the other world markets. St Petersburg's stock market is naturally integrated into the Russian stock market system by means of modern communication facilities.

Commercial and investment banks, investment companies, management companies of mutual funds and non-governmental pension funds are among the professional participants in St Petersburg's stock market, which offers access to almost all the trading floors of Russia and the world. There are also closed-end (private) investment funds operating as hedge funds, which are usually based on the available capital of a group of well-to-do citizens. The assets of these funds are usually managed by professional market participants.

There are also many private investors among the market participants, who first appeared in the 1990s, when the process of privatizing state property started. It is worth noting that the number of private investors who act independently on the stock market and get access to the trading terminals through brokerage houses has substantially increased recently. Now private investors of the Northwest Federal Region have opportunities to obtain brokerage and depositary services not only through St Petersburg companies, but also through large Moscow investment companies using modern communication facilities.

The stock exchanges of St Petersburg

There are several stock exchanges in St Petersburg, functioning in accordance with Russian Security legislation.

The St Petersburg Currency Exchange (SPCEX) closed joint-stock company

The SPCEX was founded in 1992. The exchange is licensed to carry out professional activities organizing trade in all sectors of the Russian financial market: to organize operations in buying and selling foreign currency for RUB and to carry out settlements on transactions; to trade on the securities market; to perform clearing activities; and to organize exchange trades in commodities (standard contracts, power, ferrous metals, etc). Its core areas of activity are trades in currency, St Petersburg's bonds, corporate bonds, shares and futures contracts. The Web site of the SPCEX is http://www.spcex.ru.

'St Petersburg Stock Exchange' non-commercial partnership

The St Petersburg Stock Exchange was founded in 1997. It is licensed to carry out activities as a stock exchange, to carry out clearing activities and to organize exchange trades in futures contracts.

In October 2002 the St Petersburg Stock Exchange and the Moscow-based Russian Stock Exchange (RTS) organized the Stock Market on the basis of a guaranteed trading system (GTS) and united Gazprom shares' market. The Stock Market functions as a floor for anonymous trading in common and preferred shares of Russian companies with preliminary deposition of assets.[1] The accounting currency is the Russian rouble. Thus, the St Petersburg Stock Exchange is the only government-authorized trading floor in Russia where Gazprom shares are traded. In 2004 the total trading volume of transactions in Gazprom shares exceeded US$24 billion. Distant access enables participants from different regions of Russia to join the trading on the St Petersburg stock exchange. At present the Exchange's members comprise 258 banks and companies.

The shares that are included in the Guaranteed Trading System of the RTS Stock Exchange can be traded on the St Petersburg Stock Exchange. So the list of shares traded on the St Petersburg Stock Exchange consists of 374 stocks of 238 issuers, including Gazprom.

The Stock Exchange's Web site can be accessed on http://www.spbex.ru/TFB/index.htm.

The closed joint-stock company 'St Petersburg Exchange'

The St Petersburg Exchange is a supplier and technical support provider for the FORTS (Futures and Options on the RTS) trading system. Since it began in 2004, the total trading volume on the FORTS amounted to US$11.7 billion, comprising 1.5 million deals with 42 million contracts. Futures contracts on the shares of RAO UES of Russia, Gazprom, Lukoil and Surgutneftegaz are the most liquid. In 2005 it is expected to create an oil products market and to extend futures contracts market.

The Web site can be accessed at http://www.spbex.ru/TFB/index.htm,

The closed joint-stock company 'St Petersburg Futures Exchange'

This is gradually losing its position on the futures market due to take up of futures trading on the other St Petersburg's exchanges. Details can be found at http://www.spbfe.futures.ru/intro/common/index.shtml.

Investment companies of St Petersburg

Investment and brokerage companies located in St Petersburg can provide brokerage and depositary services for residents of the North-west Federal Region and for any potential client regardless of the client's location.

Pioneering investment and brokerage companies were set up in St Petersburg in the early 1990s, when the privatization of the state property began, and these companies participated in every event on the emerging Russian financial market. Brokers and their clients executed almost all operations, from resale of the notes of 'Ponzi schemes' (financial pyramids) to trading operations on paper vouchers and savings bonds issued by the Ministry of Finance, along with dealing in currency and shares of St Petersburg's and other regions' companies offered on the market.

During the 1998 crisis, the number of investment companies represented on the stock market decreased substantially. Some went out of business, some changed their profile. A few remained on the capital market and now continue their operations, expanding their services and increasing the volume of transactions by attracting new clients and using new technologies of exchange trading. Thus the age of the oldest St Petersburg investment companies is approximately

10–15 years. Since the 1998 crisis, new companies have also entered the market for investment and brokerage services.

Table 2.3.1 The most popular St Petersburg companies: professional stock market participants

Name	Assets ($ million)	Equity ($ million)	Total transaction volume in Q3, 2004, ($ million)
OJSC 'IC AVK'	11.65	3.31	763.90
OJSC 'Baltic Finance Agency'	66.91	2.36	266.69
Brokerage company 'Hedge Fund' Ltd	3.44	N/A	54.96
'Web-invest.ru' Ltd	105.85	9.76	10,263.47
OJSC IC 'Lenmontagstroy'	1.28	0.78	168.12
OJSC BF 'Lenstroimaterials'	10.59	1.54	60.32
OJSC IC 'Neva-Invest'	5.44	2.89	54.04
OJSC IC 'Eltra'	5.87	1.38	200.17
OJSC IC 'Energocapital'	6.59	1.38	324.86

Source: National Association of the Stock Market Participants, figures for the end of third quarter of 2004.

Participation of brokerage companies in the process of mergers and acquisitions

The expansion of the customers' service area gives St Petersburg's investment companies an opportunity to take an active part in the process of market redistribution of properties from ineffective owners to effective ones. There are still a lot of small-cap companies on the Russian stock market, the shares of which are non-liquid on the market and can only be traded in the negotiated deals mode, either on the RTS stock exchange (the RTS Board, where participants declare their bid and request share prices that are merely indicative and do not guarantee deals to be done at these prices) or on the over-the-counter market. Thus, private investors who received such shares during the privatization process and would now like to sell them may offer these stocks to strategic investors through investment companies located in St Petersburg. Modern communication facilities allow shareholders and brokers to cut down transaction costs. Brokerage companies such as Web-invest.ru (which is in the top 10 by the volume of transaction on the over-the-counter market), Energocapital, Eltra and Lenmontagzstroi are the key players among St Petersburg's companies in the over-the-counter market.

After the 1998 crisis, brokerage companies helped investors to accumulate large blocks of shares in those companies that are now key players in their market segments. Among the most important M&A deals, arranged by St Petersburg's brokerage companies, are the following:

- the foundation of Brewery Holding 'Baltika' (PKBA.RTS), including all its breweries located throughout Russia;

- the creation of the Russian holding company Power Machines (SILM.RTS), whose core production assets are Leningradsky Metal Plant (LMZ), Electrosila and Turbine Blades' Plant (ZTL), situated in St Petersburg;

- the foundation of OMZ (Uralmash-Izora Group) (OMZZ.RTS), which consists of the Igzorsky plant, located in the St Petersburg region, and St Petersburg Scientific Centre 'Mechanobr'.

New types of investors and new opportunities for investment

In the past only 'hot money' turned over on the Russian stock market. It came either from foreign hedge funds or from Russian short-term speculators. High volatility enabled speculators to make money from market fluctuations. But if any large (according to the Russian scale) funds left the market, such considerable sales led to a downside market correction and following side trend that would last for the next six months or even longer.

Since the 1998 crisis, the stock market has seen the beginning of capital concentration by investors buying large blocks of shares, and its dynamics have changed substantially. Investors who intended to take over some company's business and develop it did not sell their stocks when the market went down, but took advantage of the lower prices to increase their holdings.

Since 2000 investors have been showing increasing interest in second-tier shares. During the process of buying out, strategic investors consolidated large blocks of shares in petrochemical, metallurgical, machine-building production, tyre and bus plants, breweries and chemical fertilizer companies.

When the process of asset consolidation started to calm down, a new type of investor appeared on the market and kept the market from falling below its minimum values. Even in 2004, when the oil company

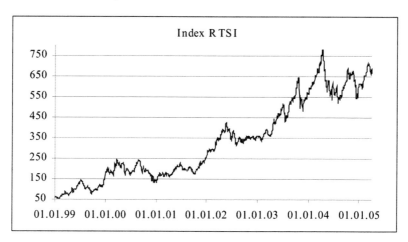

Figure 2.3.1 The RTSI index

Yukos was actually thrown out of the market, the stock market did not fall below its minimum value. Yukos' capitalization amounted to US$41.6 billion at its all-time-high, and accounted for almost 19 per cent of the total market capitalization on the RTS classical market.

Among the 'new investors' were mutual funds and private pension funds (PPFs), which placed available assets of future pensioners on the stock market. Corporate PPFs are usually the largest in this sector, while individual PPFs are not really popular in either Moscow or St Petersburg. At the same time, however, mutual funds, which invest the money of private investors, became really popular among the general population. Open-end and interval mutual funds turned out to be attractive for investors who had a certain amount of spare money.

Private asset management (AM) companies were founded to manage assets of mutual funds and PPFs, and St Petersburg shared in this development. Commercial banks and investment companies established AM companies, which had to manage mutual funds' assets according to requirements of the Russian security law. The years 2003 and 2004 appeared to be the most profitable for the mutual funds in terms of the volume of attracted private capital.

According to data from Investfunds.ru, at the end of the first quarter of 2005, the top 10 mutual funds (most of which are located in Moscow) accounted for about 70 per cent of the total asset management market by net asset value (NAV) of open mutual funds. Troika Dialog holds the leading position in this segment; its NAV of open mutual funds amounts to 3.9 billion RUB (US$136 million) and its market share is 22.93 per cent.

The AM company CIT (Creative Investment Technologies) is the leading company among St Petersburg's mutual funds and ranked fourth among all Russian AM companies, with NAV at the value of 1,079.89 million RUB (US$37.68 million). The AM company AVK 'Palace Square' (480.5 million RUB or US$17.3 million) and AM company of the Industry and Construction Bank (425.18 million RUB or US$15.3 million) follow CIT in the St Petersburg region and are ranked seventh and eighth among all Russian asset management companies.

Obviously 'new investors', represented by private pension funds and mutual funds, required an adequate volume of investment instruments to work with on the market. For the most part, demand for new assets was satisfied by the growing volume of the corporate and municipal bond markets. In 2004 the total trading volume on fixed-income instruments increased to 1.325 billion RUB (US$47 billion). The net placement/redemption balance on the corporate bonds market over 2004 amounted to 108.3 billion RUB (US$3.76 billion).

Table 2.3.2 Change in Russia's corporate and regional bonds (US$ billion)

Ratio	2003	2004	% change
Volume of regional debt market	2.7	4.42	64
Trading volume on regional debt market	8.1	19.5	141
Volume of corporate bond market	5.2	8.93	72
Trading volume on corporate bond market	16.03	27.4	71
Volume of 'blue chip' bond market	0.52	1.94	273

The placement volumes of St Petersburg's governmental registered bonds (GRB) are not as large as those of Moscow's or of corporate bonds. But St Petersburg was the first region to issue bonds, doing so in 1996. Since the 1998 crisis (when St Petersburg was the only region in Russia that did not default on its payments) the Finance Committee of St Petersburg's government has decided to gradually increase the duration of internal debt. As of 1 March 2005, the total volume of St Petersburg's liabilities in municipal bonds amounted to 9.74 billion RUB (US$0.35 billion). These liabilities account for 87.3 per cent of St Petersburg's total debt. According to IC AVK, as of 28 March 2005, the duration of St Petersburg's debt had increased to 1,088 days, and the market price of St Petersburg's debt portfolio amounted to 10.76 billion RUB (US$0.39 billion). The yield of the longest governmental registered bonds varies from 8.5 per cent to 9 per cent per annum. St Petersburg's bonds, together with the other regional bonds, are traded on the SPCEX. The Moscow Interbank Currency Exchange (MICEX) is Russia's main exchange with the largest trading volume, and has several sections, including ones for trade in regional and corporate bonds. But St Petersburg's bonds are listed only on the SPCEX, which limits the number of investors who might be interested in such instruments. The insignificant trading volumes of the St Petersburg debt market also limit the number of investors trading on the SPCEX.

St Petersburg's private companies on the stock market

During the period of privatization, shares of most of St Petersburg's privatized companies were presented on the formal stock market that came into being at that time. The over-the-counter market was also quite popular.

Among the shares traded on the formal stock market were those of St Petersburg's telephone system and International Telephone Net, Izorski plants and Leningradsky Metal plant, Electrosila plant and Turbine Blades' plant, Kirovsky, Proletarsky and Nevsky plants, Svetlana union and Leningradsky optical mechanical union (LOMO), Krasnyi Vuborgzez plant, and Northwest Shipping Company, Lenenergo and Plastpolimer. The list is necessarily incomplete, as it is too long to be covered in a short research chapter. St Petersburg is a city where enterprises from nearly all industry sectors are represented, from steel-casting to precision optics and modern electronics. According to the information disclosure system for the Russian companies, over 1,200 public companies are registered in St Petersburg. However, from the time the privatization process started until now, many public companies have ceased to offer their shares on the open market, because their free-float[2] ratio (1–5 per cent of authorized capital stock) and the number of shareholders (as a rule, affiliated persons) are too low.

There are few truly public companies in St Petersburg. Their shares are presented on the formal and over-the-counter markets and have quite high free-float ratios, and are already listed on several trading floors. Northwest Telecom has American Depositary Receipts (ADR), which are traded on foreign exchanges.

Enterprises whose shares are traded on the formal market publish their financial statements regularly and disclose their shareholder structures, important changes and any other relevant information. Official sources of such information are large information agencies, such as Interfax. The activities of public companies activities are regulated by the Law on Public Societies and by the Security Market Law.

Table 2.2.3 Shares of St Petersburg-based issuers traded on RTS

Company	Ticker, RTS classical market	Free float (%)	Market cap, ($ million, on 31 March 2005)	Industry
OJSC Lenenergo	LSNG, LSNGP	20.30	451.96	Electric power production and sale
OJSC North-West Telecom	SPTL, SPTLP	35.50	529.07	Fixed line services in the North-West Federal Region
OJSC Power machines	SILM	17	357.91	Power machine-building
OJSC Kirovsky plant	KIRZ	29.06	61.66	Power machine-building
OJSC Farmakom	FARM	13.68	n/a	Pharmaceuticals
OJSC Brewery Holding Baltika	PKBA, PKBAP	24.85	2 272.92	Brewery
OJSC Russkiye samosvety	RSAM	21.31	2.50	Gem production
OJSC North-West Shipping Company	SZRP	12	1.92	Water transport
OJSC Machine-building plant Arsenal	arse	17.12	0.72	Machine-building
OJSC Baltic plant	balz	17.18	55.55	Metallurgical machine-building
OJSC Bread house	hleb	11.00	2.12	Food industry
OJSC Sovetsky Hotel	gsov	14.20	0.11	Housing services
OJSC Lenexpo	lnep	54.70	n/a	Exhibition centre
OJSC Lentelefonstroi	ltst	79.90	n/a	Building and construction
OJSC Holding company Petrobread	pehl	18.90	0.02	Food industry
OJSC Pirometre	piro	16.00	19.66	Aircraft industry

Company	Ticker, RTS classical market	Free float (%)	Market cap, ($ million, on 31 March 2005)	Industry
OJSC Combine named after Stepan Razin	praz	28.18	0.26	Chemical industry
OJSC Red October	spkr, spkr	66.90	5.96	Aircraft industry
OJSC Svetlana	svna	46.50	6.20	Electronic production
OJSC Techpribor	thpr,thprp	39.00	2.15	Aircraft instrument making

Note: Official capitalization figures shown in the table above (especially for companies whose shares are listed on the RTS Board) are calculated according to bid quotes in the absence of real deals. Sometimes low-liquid equities' quote spread amounts to 100 per cent and above, which is why official capitalization of low-liquid companies turns out to be much lower than the real company's value when demand for its assets exists on the market.

Unfortunately, St Petersburg companies still do not see the stock market as a good opportunity to attract capital to finance restructuring and production expansion projects. Most companies prefer to attract financial resources through the corporate bond market or bank loans, creating and supporting their credit history.

At present there are a lot of new St Petersburg companies in the sector of enterprises that produce goods with high added value. However, they still remain non-public and do not issue financial statements or disclose their ownership structures. Until interest rates on the corporate rouble fixed-income market are acceptable to such companies, we are unlikely to see their public placements on the Russian and foreign stock markets. But as the inflation rate and interest rate on the capital market for public companies go down, borrowings on bond markets will rise in price for non-public companies (relative to the level of inflation). Thus, it is not improbable that a boom of companies' initial public offerings (IPOs) will start as early as 2006–07. At present, companies are conducting asset consolidation and restructuring of their businesses, which quite often belong to different sectors of the economy. Moreover, companies are switching to international accounting standards and considering the possibilities of future IPOs.

Notes

1. 'Preliminary deposition of assets' refers to traded stocks deposited at a special trading account in advance in order to make a deal at

a particular moment without delay on delivery. The same rule applies to monetary assets in a deal.

2. Free float: the total number of shares publicly owned and available for trading.

2.4

Currency Regulation

Stanislav Denisenko, Head of KPMG
St Petersburg Legal Group

The previous currency regulation regime

The currency regulation regime in effect from the end of 1992 to the middle of 2004 was based on Law of the Russian Federation No 3615-1 of 9 October 1992 On Currency Regulation and Currency Control (referred to here as 'the Previous Law'). For a long time it was one of the major constraints affecting foreign investment in Russia; its main principle was that 'whatever is not permitted is forbidden'.

Under the Previous Law all operations with foreign currency and foreign securities were classified into:

- current currency operations;

- currency operations related to capital movement.

Although 'current currency operations' were performed without restrictions, they were limited to those directly stipulated by the Previous Law. All other currency operations were considered to be 'currency operations related to capital movement' and were subject to strict control by the currency control authorities. For most of those currency operations it was necessary to obtain individual special permits issued by the Central Bank of Russia. This involved a bureaucratic and time-consuming procedure, entailing the preparation of a considerable number of documents and going through a number of stages that could take several months. This slowed down cross-border transactions and was one of the stumbling blocks for planning investments into Russia.

This currency regulation regime was a cause of concern for the business community, which lobbied for an extension of the list of current currency operations and for faster and simpler procedures to obtain the relevant permits.

The new Currency Law

The recommendations of the business community did not go unheeded. The need to liberalize the currency regulation regime and significantly reduce state control over currency operations was recognized, and on 10 December 2003 Federal Law No 173-FZ On Currency Regulation and Currency Control ('the new Currency Law') was signed by President Putin. Most of its provisions came into force on 18 June 2004.

The new Currency Law is based on the principle that 'whatever is not forbidden is permitted'. The law no longer formally stipulates that currency operations are classified into the two types defined under the Previous Law. It does not mention current currency operations but instead sets out an exhaustive list of currency operations that may be subject to certain restrictions (see the 'Restrictions on currency operations' section of this chapter), while all other operations may be effected without restriction. Currency operations between Russian residents and non-residents (including foreign individuals, foreign companies and their branches and representative offices in Russia) are regulated by the government and the Central Bank of Russia in accordance with the new Currency Law. The Russian government regulates currency operations in connection with foreign trade, while the Central Bank of Russia regulates currency operations related to banking, finance and the capital markets.

The Russian government and the Central Bank of Russia are also empowered with currency control functions. In addition, the Federal Service for Financial and Budgetary Supervision and the Federal Tax Service control and supervise currency operations. Authorized banks, professional holders of registers of securities and the Russian customs authorities, as currency control agents, are required to monitor the performance of currency operations and notify the currency control authorities of any violations so that the corresponding liability can be imposed.

Restrictions on currency operations

With the abolition of the Previous Law, the new Currency Law has significantly changed the currency regulation regime. The currency regulation authorities can no longer demand individual permits for the performance of currency operations. Instead of regulation by means of individual permits, the new Currency Law stipulates that the government and the Central Bank of Russia may impose administrative and economic restrictions (described more fully below) with respect to certain types of currency operations.

The Russian government and the Central Bank of Russia decide whether to introduce such restrictions on the basis of economic factors in Russia. Where no such measures have been introduced, currency operations can be conducted without restriction.

The list of restrictions that may be currently introduced by the government and the Central Bank of Russia is as follows: 1) use of special accounts; 2) the requirement to place a reserve amount on deposit ('reservation'); 3) advance registration. The new Currency Law also introduces: 4) restrictions on the selection of the currency for settlements when performing certain currency operations.

Use of special accounts

The requirement to use special accounts is a restriction that may be introduced by the Russian government or the Central Bank of Russia. It is a formal requirement established mainly for the purpose of administrative recording and monitoring of currency operations. This implies that certain currency operations may not be performed through ordinary accounts and that Russian residents or non-residents must open special accounts to perform such operations. These might include a special bank account opened with an authorized bank for currency operations with foreign currency, or a special section of a personal account opened by the holders of registers of securities for currency operations with securities. In practice, opening such special accounts is not particularly difficult.

The requirement to use special accounts may only be imposed with regard to a limited number of currency operations expressly listed in the new Currency Law, such as the provision of bank and other loans, the acquisition of foreign and Russian securities and certain other currency operations.

The Central Bank of Russia has already introduced the majority of special accounts stipulated by the new Currency Law. For example, when the other party to a transaction is a Russian resident, a non-resident must open special Russian rouble (RUB) bank accounts when buying or selling shares in Russian joint stock companies, investment securities in Russian unit investment funds, or bonds and promissory notes issued by Russian residents, and when obtaining and providing bank and other loans in RUB. In all these cases, the corresponding settlements must be performed through special RUB bank accounts opened by non-residents at authorized banks that are distinct from their ordinary bank accounts.

Reservation

Reservation of funds implies that for some currency operations, the list of which is strictly limited, RUB funds must be transferred by Russian residents or non-residents to a deposit account at an authorized bank in an amount and for a period determined by the government or the Central Bank within the limits established by the new Currency Law. No interest is accrued on the funds deposited.

As a general rule, currency operations may be performed as soon as the funds have been deposited. However, some operations (for example, those with foreign securities issued abroad) may only be performed once the reservation period has expired.

Such economic restrictions result in funds being withdrawn from business turnover and frozen for a certain period of time. For example, the Central Bank of Russia may require that an amount not exceeding 20 per cent of the currency operation amount be deposited for a period of up to a year. This may be stipulated for operations where there is an inflow of capital, such as the provision of loans by non-residents to Russian residents or the acquisition by non-residents of title to Russian securities from Russian residents.

A requirement to deposit an amount not exceeding 100 per cent of the currency operation amount for a period of up to 60 days may be imposed by the Central Bank in the case of operations that involve an outflow of capital, such as the provision of loans by Russian residents to non-residents, the acquisition of foreign securities by Russian residents or the discharge of liabilities with regard to Russian securities by Russian residents (eg payment of dividends by Russian joint stock companies).

The Russian government may establish a requirement that funds be deposited for up to two years for some currency operations related to foreign trade.

The percentages and periods for reservation indicated above are the maximum that may be required by the government or Central Bank under the new Currency Law, and in practice they impose less stringent requirements. For example, where non-residents make RUB loans to residents and acquire Russian promissory notes and bonds (except in the case of bonds issued by the Russian Federation), the Central Bank has introduced a requirement for non-residents to deposit 2 per cent of the transaction amount for a period of 365 days. The Russian government has not yet introduced any reservation requirements.

Advance registration in connection with performing currency operations

The new Currency Law also stipulates that requirements may be established for both Russian residents and non-residents to register in advance currency operations such as the import or export of RUB or Russian securities in documentary form

The law includes general instructions with regard to advance registration and establishes a full list of documents to be submitted for the process, documents that are relatively easy to compile. The law indicates that an application for advance registration should be considered within 10 days, and either a registration certificate should be issued or, if advance registration is refused, the grounds for refusal should be stated. The possible reasons for refusal are explicitly stipulated in the new Currency Law, which does not allow refusals merely because the currency operation is considered inexpedient.

The specific procedure for performing advance registration is to be established by the Russian government. As it has not yet been approved, the import and export of RUBs and Russian securities in documentary form at present take place without advance registration. However, customs regulation requirements should be taken into consideration when performing such operations.

Restrictions imposed on the choice of currency for settlements

In certain instances, the new Currency Law also prescribes the currency to be used for settlements in currency operations. For example, it stipulates that settlements between Russian residents and non-residents related to operations with Russian securities are to be made in RUBs.

In addition, although settlements between Russian residents and non-residents related to operations with foreign securities may currently be performed both in foreign currencies and in RUB, the Central Bank of Russia may prohibit the use of any particular currency for such settlements.

Currency operations of non-residents

Currency operations between non-residents

There are no restrictions on transfers of foreign currency by non-residents to other non-residents from bank accounts outside the

Russian Federation to bank accounts held with authorized banks inside the Russian Federation, and vice versa. However, currency operations between non-residents in the Russian Federation in RUB must be performed via bank accounts opened at authorized banks.

Transfers of currency into and out of Russia

There are also no restrictions on non-residents transferring foreign currency from their bank accounts held with banks outside the Russian Federation to their bank accounts held with authorized banks in the Russian Federation, or vice versa. Accordingly, foreign currency may be transferred from the head office of a foreign company to its Russian representative office or branch, and vice versa, without any restrictions.

Administrative responsibility for violation of currency legislation

Administrative responsibility for violation of currency legislation is currently regulated by the Code on Administrative Violations.

Administrative penalties for violation of currency legislation are still very high, usually between 75 per cent and 100 per cent of the amount of the currency operation. To avoid such heavy penalties, anyone responsible for currency operations should take great care to observe the provisions of currency legislation.

In practice, where currency legislation can be interpreted ambiguously or clarification is needed from the currency regulation authorities about the official position, it is possible to approach the Central Bank of Russia with a request for clarification of a particular currency rule. In St Petersburg, such requests may be addressed to the Main Department of the Central Bank of Russia, which usually replies and provides the relevant official clarification within a month.

Conclusion

New currency legislation was recently brought in, designed to liberalize the Russian currency regulation regime considerably. This liberalization is evident in many significant aspects; for example, the requirement to obtain special permits for the performance of currency operations has been abolished and currency transactions are now performed without restriction unless directly stipulated by the new Currency Law. Nevertheless, new economic restrictions have been introduced which apply to both Russian residents and non-residents and are perceived by the business community as onerous.

The good news is that the new Currency Law stipulates that the special account and reservation restrictions, as well as restrictions on the choice of currency for settlements, are of a temporary nature. Unless new laws change this in the meantime, these restrictions will cease to apply as of 1 January 2007.

2.5

Brownfield Investments

Vitaly Mozharowski, Partner, Pepeliaev,
Goltsblat and Partners

Brownfield investments

The term 'brownfield investment' is widely used to describe investment
in land that has previously been used for industrial purposes. Such an
area is called a 'brownfield site', and actually consists of two separate
items: the buildings located on the land and the land itself. Investors
evaluating the prospects of a brownfield investment thus need to exam-
ine the legal status of the land plot and the buildings separately. This
is one of the main differences between brownfield and 'greenfield
projects', a 'greenfield site' being one with no buildings located on it.
The independence of buildings from land plots is at odds with one of
the fundamental principles of the Russian Land Code, which states
that land is inalienable from the buildings located on it. However, in
many cases, mostly involving state-owned land, a contradictory situation arises, in which a land plot belongs to one person, generally the
state, whereas the buildings on it, a factory for instance, belong to a
private owner.

In practice, this gives rise to three possible ownership scenarios for
brownfield sites. The first and most common is that the land belongs
to a public owner and the buildings to a private owner. The second scenario is that both land and buildings belong to a public owner, which
is less common. The third scenario is that both land and buildings
belong to a private owner. This scenario, needless to say, is preferable
for investors, as it means that both the land and buildings can be
acquired through private sale. Unfortunately, this is seldom the case.

The implementation of a brownfield investment is a long and complicated process. As a rule, it can be broken down into four main stages.
First, a potential site must be selected. Then due diligence must be
performed in order to reveal all the legal risks associated with the
transaction and to confirm the legality of the existing title to the land.
The third stage is the actual acquisition, which is followed by the final

stage: the redevelopment of the site to meet the specific needs of the investor. From a legal perspective, the second and third stages are the most critical for the success of the investment, and they will therefore be examined in greater detail below. It is also possible to acquire a land plot and buildings located on it by acquiring an ownership interest in the company that owns the buildings. However, this strategy is outside the scope of this chapter.

Due diligence

The dual nature of a brownfield site means that due diligence must be performed on both the buildings and the land plot on which they are located. In addition to this, a range of corporate issues must be dealt with, such as legal capacity, powers of directors, preliminary board or shareholder approval, and compliance with anti-monopoly laws. In the course of the due diligence, the legality of the seller's title to each real estate item must also be thoroughly checked. The validity of the title depends, in turn, on the validity of the transactions under which the title was acquired.

Under current Russian law, titles to buildings and land plots must be registered with the Realty Registry, and come into effect only on the date of registration. In certain cases, however, the absence of an entry in the Realty Registry does not mean that a person or company does not have a right to the land. Real estate rights that were acquired prior to 1998 fall into this category, as they were acquired before the state registration system was established. Such rights must be confirmed by documents stating the grounds on which the rights were acquired, such as contracts, court decisions and governmental acts. In addition to checking the Realty Registry, it is necessary to verify the status of the real estate with the Land Cadastre Chambers and Technical Inventory Bureaux. The Land Cadastre deals with land parcels, whereas the Technical Inventory Bureaux keep records of technical information on buildings.

As for the buildings themselves, the scope of the due diligence may differ, depending on whether the seller acquired the title to these buildings through outright purchase, privatization or construction. For example when the buildings being acquired were constructed by the seller, examination generally focuses on whether the seller received the land plot for construction by legal means, as well as on the legality of the construction permits, the function of the building and its commissioning.

Acquisition of a brownfield site

As noted above, there are three possible scenarios for the ownership of a brownfield site. The first ownership scenario, where the land belongs to a public owner while the buildings are privately owned, is the most widespread. In Russia, land legislation is an area of joint competence of the Russian Federation and its constituent entities, and public ownership may imply that land plots are owned by the Russian Federation, regions or municipalities. State lands, ownership of which has not been specified, are normally managed by local governments. However, regional legislation on such issues varies from place to place. In the Leningrad Region, for example, municipalities are authorized to dispose of state lands with an area not exceeding 3.0 ha. In some other regions, the powers of municipalities to dispose of state lands have not been regulated at all. In such cases the owner of the buildings generally holds the land parcel on the basis of either a perpetual use title or lease right.

The owner of buildings located on a site that is owned by a third party has the right to dispose of the buildings (for instance, sell them) at his or her own discretion; that is, without the consent of the owner of the land. However, such a sale also implies a certain degree of entitlement to the land on which the buildings are located. A private owner or buyer of buildings located on state-owned land has an exclusive right, by virtue of law, to acquire ownership of the land, subject to certain restrictions. The owner also has the right to obtain a lease for the whole plot (or part of it) at his or her discretion.

When a land plot is purchased from a public owner by the private owner of the buildings located on this land, payment is always made at a fixed price, which is calculated on the basis of the land tax rates. In the Leningrad Region, for example, the fixed price is equal to 10 times the land tax rate, while in St Petersburg it is set at nine times the land tax rate. The price calculated in this way is considerably lower than the market price of the site concerned. Where land is leased, the rent is fixed according to rules set down in regional or municipal laws. It is clear that a tenant who leases a site will not have the same freedom and legal protection as one who owns it. Therefore, from a legal perspective it is preferable to buy the land. The legal right for the owner to buy the land on which its buildings are located also means that this can be done prior to selling the brownfield site to an investor. In other words, the owner of the buildings may buy out the land plot from the state or municipality and, having become the owner of both the buildings and the land, sell them both to an investor. This will result in the third, and most preferable, of the three ownership scenarios.

Thus, to summarise, if the site on which the seller's buildings are located is held in public ownership, investors can acquire the land title in three ways. First, they could buy the buildings from the private owner and obtain a lease of the publicly owned land on which these buildings are located. Second, they could buy the buildings from the private owner and later buy the land from the public owner. Third, the private seller of the buildings could buy the site from the public owner, and then sell the buildings and the land to the investor.

The second of the scenarios mentioned earlier is when both the land and the buildings on it belong to a public owner. A brownfield site (buildings and land) owned by the state or a municipality can be acquired through one of about 10 legal ways in compliance with the procedures established in the Federal Law on Privatization. The most common options are the privatization of either the assets (the buildings and land) or the shares (securities) in a joint-stock company. As a general rule, a public tender is required in these circumstances. As mentioned previously, the third scenario, where both land and buildings are privately owned, is ideal for investors, but the least common of the three. The fundamental advantage of this scenario is that the investor acquires title to both the buildings and the land plot simultaneously, unlike in the other scenarios illustrated above. The price in this case can be negotiated with the owner.

Brownfield and greenfield investments involve different legal procedures. Consequently they entail different kinds of issues for the potential investor. The main differences lie in such issues as land category, public utilities, land pricing and environmental planning. In most greenfield projects, the allocation of a land plot involves a change in the land category. Most often, agricultural land is to be converted into industrial or residential land in order to allow for construction. The land conversion procedure is time consuming and costly, normally taking from eight to 11 months. When the land category has been converted, compensation for crop losses must be paid to the municipal budget (the amount is not negotiable and depends on the quality of the soil). Private landholders or users also must be compensated for any losses, and in these cases the amount is negotiable. Brownfield sites, on the other hand, do not generally belong to the category of agricultural lands and thus do not require conversion.

When a greenfield site is acquired, an investor has to construct industrial buildings and ensure provision of public utilities like electricity, water, wastewater treatment, access roads and so forth. A brownfield site generally has industrial buildings and all the necessary infrastructure in place, although these facilities may need upgrading and renovating. Both brownfield and greenfield investment options usually require land cadastral works, and the newly created land plots must be registered with the Realty Registry.

In implementing a greenfield project, where the land is in public ownership the investor will need to do due diligence only on the land plot, while in a brownfield project due diligence should be performed on both the land plot and the buildings on it, as well as on the various corporate matters listed above.

On a brownfield site, when the owner of a building does not own the site on which it stands, he or she has the option to buy the land at a fixed price, which is in most cases significantly lower than the market rate. A greenfield site, on the other hand, may be purchased from the state or municipality prior to construction at a public tender, and only at the market price. However, this can usually be avoided if an investor first leases the greenfield site, through the so-called preliminary facilities location approval procedure, and begins building on it. After the facilities have been commissioned, put into operation and registered in the Realty Registry, the investor is entitled (but not obliged) to purchase the leased site at a fixed price without a tender, as it is now considered a brownfield site.

When assessing the investment appeal of a particular brownfield site, it is also necessary to take into account certain environmental aspects of the site. For instance, in order to determine the quality of the air and subsoil water, or the level of soil pollution, it is generally necessary for air, water and soil samples to be taken by specialized organizations for laboratory testing. In addition, it should be kept in mind that industrial facilities must be separated from residential and recreation areas by buffer zones. For instance, the size of a buffer zone for glass manufacturing facilities may vary from 300 to 1,000 metres, depending on a range of factors.

As is clear from the above, an investor considering the acquisition of a brownfield site must consider a wide variety of issues. The most crucial is undoubtedly the question of land title, of whether the land plot and buildings are in state or private ownership. Depending on the title to the land and buildings, the legal steps to be taken by the investor vary considerably. As concerns due diligence, the most important elements are the legitimacy of the title to the land and the lawfulness of the construction performed on it, as well as the need to make thorough and comprehensive checks in all the relevant state registry bodies. Despite the complexities of brownfield investment in Russia, however, foreign investors can acquire suitable sites for their operations, as has been demonstrated in a number of successful acquisitions in recent years. Perhaps the key factor in the success of this process is having reliable and professional legal support in Russia at all stages of the transaction.

2.6

St Petersburg's Labour Market

Igor Yegorov, BISNIS Representative for Northwest Russia

Introduction

Labour is one of the key production factors, as access to professional and motivated employees is a decisive factor in competitive markets. Due to a prolonged stagnation of professional education and economic weakness, Russia is starting to experience a deficit of professionals in many fields. St Petersburg is not exempt from this problem. This chapter aims to describe the current status of the labour market in the area. As is true for almost every other sector of the Russian economy, it is not easy to get reliable, detailed information about the labour market. This chapter is therefore based on information from the St Petersburg State Statistical Committee, St Petersburg Department of the Federal Employment Agency, recruitment agencies, and, in some cases, on expert estimates and articles in the local press.

Demand for qualified specialists and workers is steadily increasing as the Russian economy gathers steam, but many companies have problems in finding staff and meeting rising employment costs. The gap in the labour market is caused by a structural mismatch between supply of and demand for labour. The educational gap in the last ten years has led to a deficit of skilled workers and professionals in a number of specialties, especially in technically oriented spheres. St Petersburg is the major centre for training and education in northwest Russia and plays a significant role in the training of specialists for northwest Russia's industries. But the system of professional education does not deliver the needed quantity and quality of specialists due to a number of inherent problems, most notably its isolation from industry and practical research, low-paid teachers and corruption. In addition, there is no link between training programmes and strategic planning in the country or in the city (as there is no such planning). No one knows which industrial sectors will develop or which specialists will be in demand in several years.

The quality and motivation of employees are increasingly perceived as crucial factors for ensuring stable business development. In contrast to earlier years, when family members and acquaintances were often hired to fill important positions, Russian companies are now paying close attention to candidates' experience and achievements. Hiring is now done through recruitment agencies, newspaper announcements, web sites, referrals, municipal employment centres and advertisements of vacancies. Since the supply of good staff is limited, retaining policies are required to ensure that employees stay with a company and work efficiently. These may include improving working conditions and environment, higher safety standards than are legally required, bonus schemes, healthcare insurance, access to sport and recreation facilities, flexible hours, periodical rotation and additional training.

Business in Russia: professionals becoming the key resource?

The improvements in the capacity utilization of those sectors of the Russian economy that remain economically viable (accompanied by minimal investment), which have been described as a re-emergence of economic growth, have put a heavy strain on all major production assets such as infrastructure, technology, capital, and especially labour resources. Among the chief obstacles that prevent companies from increasing production (apart from the unavailability of long-term capital at affordable rates) are a deficit of skilled labour and rising employment costs. Even most official statistics (which are unreliable when it comes to real pay levels) demonstrate that nominal labour costs increased 25–30 per cent in northwest Russia in 2003 alone, while nominal industrial production grew to around 110 per cent. Although one can dispute the underlying methodology of the statistics, it is highly likely that the general inflation of labour costs in Russia, and in northwest Russia in particular, has been higher than productivity growth.

When comparing the government's initial economic reform goals with tangible achievements, the positive statistics produced can be misleading; they do not reflect the ineffectiveness of the government's economic reform efforts. Russian businesses have suffered from a lack of ideas and of strategic concepts for development. This problem stems from a failure to think creatively about the future of society, or to evolve an economic strategy for the country as a whole. Simple extrapolation of the Soviet economy's imbalances, accompanied by the collapse of the military-industrial sector, which had demonstrated the potential to become the main producer of high-tech products (if properly reformed), has given a predominant economic role to companies producing basic commodities such as oil, gas, metals, timber, electricity and chemical products. Since the potential created during Soviet times has already been exhausted, the growth of these industries has reached a point where major, long-term investments are required to sustain and increase production volumes and efficiency. Future business planning is inhibited by the lack of long-term resources available to implement fundamental investment projects that will lay the grounds for the ongoing economic development of any business in the country.

The need for new ideas and creative thinking is obvious. However, the investment plans of most of Russia's largest companies rarely venture beyond such sectors as extraction and processing of raw material, telecommunications, food processing, services, pipelines, real estate, and most recently, water, electricity and sewage networks. Lack of vision or a sense of reality is obvious at both state and company level. Sadly, the ultimate goal of many business owners is money (in the form of US dollars) and not profitability as a means of improving efficiency.

Although Russia is still (and has always been) a country of many unexploited opportunities, the private initiative of small and medium businesses is undermined by the lack of realistic and forward-looking economic strategies or of concrete, broadly accepted economic policies (by some estimates, 26 individuals control 34 per cent of Russia's GDP). The re-emergence of vertically integrated business structures reminiscent of the Soviet system explicitly demonstrate the lack of transparency and trust in Russia's post-Soviet business circles. The need for able, qualified people is at the core of the problem. The development of the country as a whole and its businesses in particular is stalled by the lack of well-educated, responsible and thinking professionals, who would be able to identify and capitalize on new opportunities and counter new threats. Moreover, the government does not send clear signals about where the country is heading in terms of real policy priorities and reform plans. Post-Soviet basic social science has not been able to produce a new ideology, and since the fall of Soviet ideologies and illusions the government has not adopted any clear concept of the country's future. Analysts in financial planning departments have no basic policy priorities on which to build their business planning models. This causes inherent instability in any Russian business, and difficulties with long-term investments in new product and technology development, equipment modernization and so on.

Demand for labour

Market developments taking place in the past few years in St Petersburg prove the larger picture of scarcity of qualified labour. Demand for qualified personnel has been gradually increasing since 2000. The market has now reached a point where it is driven by supply, with a pool of professionals no longer large enough to satisfy the demand for qualified professionals in some specialties. Companies have come to realize that the availability of labour has become one of the chief threats to their survival. In a recent interview the Director of the St Petersburg Department of the Federal Employment Agency, Mr Dimity Cherneyko, emphasized that the gap between supply and demand on the labour market is becoming a problem. The time it takes to find a job has increased simultaneously with the number of vacancies filed by employers, indicating the discrepancy between supply and demand. In other words, people are not qualified for the specialties in demand, or employers are not willing to offer reasonable salaries and working conditions. St Petersburg's economy experiences structural unemployment, when a significant portion of the available labour force can't be hired because there is a mismatch between available and required qualifications.

Demand is growing first and foremost for qualified labour. As of May 2004, the total number of vacancies available through the Federal Employment Agency in St Petersburg was 68,000, and 3,482 organizations and enterprises gave notice that they needed employees in May alone for as many as 13,527 vacancies. The largest number of vacancies has come from industrial enterprises, which need such highly skilled workers as metalworkers, electricians, welders, turners, carpenters, bricklayers and milling-machine operators. On the non-industrial front, sales agents, nurses, accountants, engineers, IT specialists, project managers and financial specialists are in demand. According to information from recruitment agencies, the largest demand from their clients is for such specialties as sales, finance, IT specialists, personnel managers and administrators. A recent trend is an increasing demand for technically skilled professionals, such as plant managers, construction engineers, production engineers, maintenance personnel and so forth (that is, specialists in various technologies, who manage the production process and are a key element in ensuring the quality of end products).

Official statistics for the first quarter of 2004 indicate that salaries per month (benefits and bonuses not included) in various sectors of the economy of St Petersburg were as shown in Tables 2.6.1 and 2.6.2. Actual salaries can be much higher than the official statistics suggest; many firms officially report that they pay much less than they in fact

Table 2.6.1 Salaries per month (benefits and bonuses not included) in various sectors of St Petersburg's economy in the first quarter of 2004

Sector	Salary (RUB)	Salary (US$)
Industry	8,204	283
Transport	9,456	326
Railway	10,223	352
Pipeline	21,617	745
Sea	15,798	544
Air	14,984	517
Communication	12,684	437
Construction	7,130	246
Trade and catering	3,306	114
Data processing services	7,451	257
Housing services	7,942	274
Medicine	6,580	227
Education	5,720	197
Science	8,086	279
Culture and art	5,711	197
Finance	19,093	658
Management	10,187	351

Source: St Petersburg Statistical Committee

Table 2.6.2 Average salaries per month in various industry sectors in the first quarter of 2004

Industry	Salary (RUB)	Salary (US$)
Power generation	12,120	418
Fuel	14,974	516
Ferrous metallurgy	9,481	327
Chemical and petrochemical	5,201	179
Machine-tool making and metalworking	8,234	284
Forestry and wood processing	4,515	156
Building materials manufacturing	8,502	293
Light industry	4,427	153

Industry	Salary (RUB)	Salary (US$)
Food processing industry	10,587	365
Microbiology	7,097	245
Medical	5,415	187
Printing	6,529	225

Source: St Petersburg Statistical Committee

do, and a large number pay unreported cash sums to their staff. Of course, such payments are particularly widespread in such sectors as construction, public catering and medical services, which collect cash directly from consumers and thus have better opportunities to run various schemes. Such heavily regulated and controlled industries as banking and finance, on the other hand, have fewer chances of avoiding payroll taxes, and so usually pay salaries that are officially reported in full. This is reflected in officially registered figures for the financial sector, which pays US$658 per month, substantially higher than reported in most other sectors. Higher-than-average wages are also registered in profitable consumer-oriented industries such as food-processing (US$365), or export-oriented pipeline transport (US$745). It should be noted that industrial enterprises and educational institutions usually pay the whole salary officially (there is widespread corruption in those sectors due to low wages). Official statistics are thus reliable for some sectors, whereas for others this is not the case. The gap in incomes between managers and medium-level staff and workers is tremendous, reaching 10:1 or 20:1. This undermines work morale and work ethics, as well as inflow of skilled labour into business.

According to Ms Maria Margulis of Ancor recruitment agency (www.ancor.spb.ru), the real pay levels (monthly salary in US dollars) for such professionals as IT specialists, engineers, lawyers, managers, construction managers, sales personnel are those shown in Table 2.6.3.

Table 2.6.3 Ancor figures for real salary levels (US$)

Job	Salary		
	Minimum	Average	Maximum
Software developer	400	971	2,207
Project manager	800	1,722	5,287
Production manager	760	2,442	4,992
Chief engineer	379	1,351	4,018
Chief accountant	516	1,877	4,153

Job	Salary		
	Minimum	Average	Maximum
Regional sales manager	2,926	3,371	4,215
Financial analyst	296	1,012	1,967
Lawyer	902	3,302	11,911

This information is based on results of a special survey of the labour market in St Petersburg, and has been provided by Ancor. Companies interested in obtaining more information about pay levels in St Petersburg should contact Ancor directly: tel./fax +7-812-329-5770.

Supply of labour

The supply side is largely beyond the control of private business. The demographic situation in St Petersburg is not improving, and even if it did, that would not have any immediate positive effect on the labour force. Indeed, the problem would be worsened by a growing number of women going on maternity leave. The average age of the labour force is increasing, while the city's population is decreasing and its health worsening. In 2003, the labour pool in St Petersburg was estimated at 2.48 million economically active individuals (people residing in St Petersburg who are of working age and are not disabled), falling significantly from 2.64 million in 1992. Among them, the officially employed made up 2.38 million, while 102,000 were unemployed. The unemployment rate was 4.1 per cent, but various estimates put it at more like 10–20 per cent in reality, because a lot of people are involved in the 'shuttle trade' (going abroad to buy things and bring them back for re-sale) and similar activities to earn their leaving. This has proven to be an ineffective use of scarce labour resources.

It is known that training any qualified specialist (engineer, economist, etc) takes 10–15 years on average. The supply gap experienced today is caused by a severe interruption of the normal educational process in the reform period. Times were especially harsh between 1991 and 2001, which amounts to the ten years required to train a skilled professional. Many specialists had to quit their jobs in the 1990s and take paid work in such sectors as trade and services. Many of them were well-qualified engineers, teachers and scientists in their 40s. The resulting loss of continuity has led to a situation where experienced workers and specialists left work without having successors to replace them.

Professional education in Russia is basically carried out in specialized educational institutions, and in the higher educational institutions: universities, academies, institutes and the like. Specialized educational institutions usually train specialists and workers in narrow fields, whereas universities and academies strive to educate students in a broader but less practically oriented range of disciplines. St Petersburg is the educational centre of northwest Russia. However, the educational system is plagued by its isolation from real needs and problems of the economy. Many teachers have little practical experience or knowledge of modern requirements and trends within the industries they are preparing students for. The shortage of well-paid professors and the isolation of most educational institutions from practical research has led to a gradual devaluation of the perceived importance of academic degrees and academic knowledge in Russia. Low official salaries in educational institutions pave the way for corruption, thus preventing clever but less wealthy entrants from getting into a university. There are currently 76 special educational institutions (with 75,000 students) in St Petersburg, and 47 higher educational institutions with 319,000 students (counting only state-financed ones, which are currently a majority).

Table 2.6.4 Number of graduates classified by sector specialization, 2002/2003

	Medium-special educational institutions	Higher educational institutions
Industry and construction	40,700	153,200
Agriculture	n/a	9,800
Transport and communications	9,000	40,400
Economy and law	7,800	33,800
Medical and sports	8,100	14,400
Education	7,900	62,100
Cinematography and culture	1,500	5,200

Source: St Petersburg Statistical Committee

Table 2.6.5 Number of graduates by specialty groups in medium-special educational institutions, 2002

Specialty group	Number of graduates
Law, social work and publishing	2,617
Education	2,134
Medical	2,608
Economics and management	5,250

Specialty group	Number of graduates
Energy	260
Metallurgy	84
Machine-tool making	523
Technological equipment, machines and transportation equipment	670
Electro technology	313
Instrument-making	167
Microelectronics, radio technology and telecommunications	593
Automatic machinery and management	336
Informatics and computer engineering	1,073
Construction and architecture	722
Operation of transport	795
Food product technology	473

Source: St Petersburg Statistical Committee

Table 2.6.6 Number of graduates by specialty groups, and by courses in higher educational institutions, 2002

Courses	Number of graduates
Natural sciences and mathematics	1,015
Humanitarian and socio-economic sciences	1,804
Education	1,268
Technical sciences	2,185
Specialty groups	
Natural sciences	1,163
Humanitarian and social	6,938
Educational	1,581
Medical	1,680
Culture and art	1,746
Economics and management	11,929
Interdisciplinary and technical science	1,243
Geology and prospecting	105
Extraction of natural resources	278

Courses	Number of graduates
Energy and power machine building	484
Metallurgy	120
Machine-tool making and material handling	683
Technological machines and equipment	820
Electro-technology	503
Instrument-making	565
Electronics, radio technology and communication	1,548
Automatic machinery and management	1,132
Informatics and computer engineering	1,131
Operation of transport	1,590
Chemical technology	520
Forestry and wood processing	746
Technology of food products	246
Construction and architecture	1,154
Agriculture and fish industry	864
Ecology	186

Source: St Petersburg Statistical Committee

Only 6 per cent of graduates do not find work, while approximately 23 per cent continue education to the next level (although in reality this often means working and studying simultaneously). Educational institutions produce graduates who often do not possess the required skills and qualifications to work in a modern enterprise. Moreover, 60 per cent of graduates do not find work within their specialty; the starting wages in small and medium-sized companies are US$400–600, but industrial enterprises are seldom prepared to pay more than US$200 per month to an inexperienced person.

Prevailing hiring and retaining methods

Companies use a variety of methods to recruit new staff. They search for qualified staff mainly through personal contacts and referrals, but also increasingly through recruitment and headhunting firms. Today outsourcing of recruitment has become popular not only among subsidiaries of foreign companies, but also among Russian firms. The choice of method depends on the types of positions to be filled, pay levels and other factors. Well-paid positions are usually filled with the help of recruitment agencies or through referrals, but also through newspaper announcements (The *St Petersburg Times* and *Delovoy Peterburg* being the best-known in this sphere) and sometimes through web sites. The hiring of qualified personnel too often entails enticing people from competing firms. People are pressurized to work as much as possible without regard for their personal time or their families. Candidates are required to have extensive experience and proven track records, but little or no additional training is provided once a person is hired and has started to work for a company. Such short-sighted policies lead to low employee loyalty and high staff turnover. Lower-paid vacancies are usually announced through municipal employment centres or through newspaper announcements in free newspapers (handed out in the underground and other places). A popular method is the organization of shows of vacancies, which is usually done in partnership with municipal hiring centres and recruitment firms.

Industrial enterprises have found that it is very difficult to fill multiple vacancies, because there is limited supply of qualified workers. The situation is complicated by the fact that there is a certification requirement for many specialized occupations. Without a certificate, an individual cannot be hired for such positions. The retraining system for workers and engineers that was maintained by the former Soviet ministries has collapsed. Since professional education institutions have ceased to train workers in many fields, and in addition, since those who are trained often do not master the practical skills required, manufacturers have faced an urgent need to counter the problem.

According to local business newspaper *Delovoy Peterburg*, some enterprises have received licences to train workers. For example, Sevkabel Holding trains in 38 worker specialties, Kirovskiy Zavod in 58 and Elektrosila in eight. Ford Motors Vsevolozhsk has opened its own worker-training centre. According to reports, local employers plan to spend up to 2.5 per cent of their total 2004 payroll on various personnel training programmes. Regrettably, most enterprises still don't have their own retraining programmes. Another important measure for many companies is to establish long-term ties with educational institutions, which prepare specialists in their fields. Some companies have started direct collaboration with educational institutions to finance various courses, supply training equipment and materials, invite students to practise at their facilities and other forms of assistance. Inviting interns from the latest courses for a part-time job is becoming a widespread practice, as a significant proportion (up to 50 per cent) of interns stay with a company after graduation. It is also a good method of training specialists and choosing the most promising students.

To prevent high turnover of acquired employees, a growing number of companies are thinking of ways to retain personnel. Otherwise the long-term stability and prospects of the company can be jeopardized, especially if a group of talented employees leaves in the middle of an important project or amidst increasing market pressures. For younger and well-educated people (in the age range of 25–40), it is usually not a big problem to find work. Such people tend to be ambitious, progressively minded and with high expectations. Polls show that for this group, working environments, benefits and promotion prospects are no less important than salary levels. For many Russian companies, attracting and retaining qualified personnel is an increasing problem, which is caused not only by the relative scarcity of labour but by weak management culture.

As one manager put it, the problem of an average Russian business lies in the juncture of ownership structure and level of corporate management, company management and personnel quality.

- Ownership structure and corporate management:

  - ownership structures are unstable and procedures of investment decision-making are not settled or formalized;

  - shareholders do not trust top managers and strive to limit their authority, but not responsibility; management's authority and responsibilities are not well defined;

  - strategic goals are not clearly defined or formalized; an informal goal of a business is often to maximize short-term cash flow; a goal to attain long-term competitive advantage by following a consistent strategy is very rarely set; usually success is achieved by means of unique temporary factors such as good relations with government or access to cheap resources or assets; improvements in efficiency and business reputation are not prioritized.

- Company management:

  - middle-level managers and specialists are often not entrusted to do their work, but are heavily supervised; in general, it is very rare to find a coherent and adhered-to system of personnel evaluation;

  - participation of mid-level managers and specialists in goal setting is minimal, thus eroding their responsibility, creativeness, competence and motivation; even if there are goals, they are often not spelled out by top management;

- the remuneration of middle-level managers and specialists can be several times lower than that of top managers, which creates discontent and has a negative effect on productivity.

- Lower-level staff and workers:

  - poor definition of work responsibilities and work load;

  - poor organization of work flow and technological processes;

  - weak control of performance;

  - low wages and benefits.

Although paying better wages is important for attracting a skilled and dedicated work force, other factors are not to be neglected. Winning the loyalty of employees is also possible through improving working conditions and environments, higher safety standards than are legally required, bonus schemes, healthcare insurance, access to sport and recreation facilities, flexible hours, periodical rotation and additional training. Foreign companies have a much better track record in Russia in paying due attention to their employees, and thus enjoy a competitive advantage in hiring professional and motivated individuals.

Recruitment agencies information

According to the President of the Northwest Chapter of Personnel Consultant Association, Mr Alexei Churkin, about 150–180 personnel recruitment agencies are active on the market in St Petersburg, but only 35–40 of these have a steady flow of orders. Charges vary between 9 and 25 per cent of the annual salary of a position in question. Headhunting costs are higher, reaching 40–100 per cent of the annual salary. St Petersburg's recruitment companies include the following:

Ancor St Petersburg
maria@ancor.spb.ru
www.ancor.ru/spb/AnSpb-Index.htm
Phone +7 812 329-5770
Fax +7 812 329-5771

Boyden
info@boyden.ru
www.boyden.ru
Phone +7 812 325-8573
Fax +7 812 325-8575

Manpower
www.manpower.ru
Phone +7 812 324-4646

Ward Howell International
www.whru.com
Phone +7 812 322-9683

Staff International
www.interstaff.ru
Phone +7 812 103-4301

EMG Professionals
job@emg-prof.ru
www.emg-prof.ru
Phone +7 812 326-8097
Fax +7 812 326-8098

Kelly Services CIS, St Petersburg Branch
postmaster@kellycis.spb.ru
www.kellycis.spb.ru
Phone +7 812 325-7300
Fax +7 812 325-7301

OSV Personal
person@rekrut.sp.ru
www.osv.ru
Phone +7 812 272-6279
Fax +7 812 272-2400

Avenir and Partners
stp@avenir.ru
www.avenir.ru
Phone +7 812 118-8157
Fax +7 812 118-8158

BusinessLink Personnel
blp@blp.ru
www.blp.ru
Phone +7 812 327-8996
Fax +7 812 327-8993

Lehto Consort
info@lehto.ru

www.consort.ru
Phone +7 812 327-3388
Fax +7 812 327-3393

THI Selection
spb@thi-s.ru
www.thi-s.ru
Phone +7 812 329-5710
Fax +7 812 329-5711

Part Three

Dynamic Sectors of St Petersburg's Economy

The Real Estate Market

3.1

An Overview of the Real Estate Sector

Warehouses to palaces

Alexei I. Shaskolsky, PhD, Institute for Entrepreneurial Issues, St Petersburg

Background

St Petersburg was founded in 1703, so Russia's second-biggest city is quite young by European and Russian standards. The industrious Tsar Peter the Great founded the new dynamic capital of the Russian Empire as an alternative to conservative/reactionary Moscow. The chosen location – on the marshy delta of the River Neva – brought plenty of problems to builders of the city. Tsar Peter invited European architects to build 'the Northern Venice', and through the following ages, the imperial glory of the city has been preserved. Neither time, the 900-days siege during the Second World War, with furious shelling and bombardment, nor the aggressive ambitions of modern architects and developers has ruined the pearl of the Baltic, one of the gems of World Heritage: St Petersburg.

St Petersburg is now among the largest European cities, and the historic part covers only a fraction of its vast territory of 1,439 km². So-called 'industrial belts' encircled the then city centre in the 19th century, growing continuously in the 20th century, with new residential areas growing around them after the Second World War.

In general terms, St Petersburg's real estate market is following the pattern set by Moscow, lagging three or four years behind it. Moscow's dominance in accumulating investments is undisputed: its office, retail, residential and warehouse projects are unparalleled anywhere in Russia. But St Petersburg is second only to Moscow in Russia, with huge industrial potential. It has 100 million m² of residential space, 3.2 million m² of office space, 13 million m² of industrial space and 4 million m² of warehouse space. And, in addition, it is a city whose charm has few rivals in Europe.

Residential buildings

The population of the city is 4.6 million, and residential accommodation comprises both old buildings of the 19th and early 20th centuries (still with many so-called communal flats, where several families live in one apartment and share facilities such as common kitchens and bathrooms) and relatively new construction that started in the 1950s. Of the 1.7 million apartments, more than 70 per cent have two or three bedrooms; the average size of an apartment is about 36 m². A quarter of all residential buildings were built before the Bolshevik revolution of 1917, but they comprise only about 15 per cent of the residential space.

Currently, residential construction is concentrated mostly in peripheral regions of the city, in so-called 'dormitory districts' developed in the last few decades. Reconstruction/refurbishing of the old buildings in the historic centre of the city is accompanied by a few new construction projects – with the highest-quality properties being sold at US$3,000–6,000 per m² (core and shell). Of the total, only about 5 per cent of the new apartments belong to the elite groups: about 100,000 m² of high class residential space annually. Reasonably priced high-quality apartments in the city centre can be found for about US$2,000 per m². General public/local preferences are for accommodation priced at between US$1,000–1,500 per m², but this can be found only outside the centre.

The year 2003, with 1.76 million m² of new residential space, witnessed an unprecedented upward dynamic in prices: in both Moscow and St Petersburg a 40 per cent rise was reported. Now the market has cooled and expected growth is much calmer; after allowing for inflation, it may be in the range of 10–15 per cent. Elite residential projects are more expensive, but they are oriented towards a tiny part of society (less than 5 per cent of city dwellers).

In 2004, slightly more than 2 million m² of residential space was built – the highest total since 1978. After the collapse of communism, state-financed residential construction ended quickly, and that had been virtually the only way homes were built. The construction industry recovered in the mid-1990s only because apartment buyers started advancing money to construction companies on a zero-interest basis in the early stages of construction to fund the work (due to impossibly high bank interest rates, the companies – and individuals – had been unable to obtain bank finance for building work). In 2004, only 2 per cent of residential space was financed from the municipal budget, whereas in

1978 almost 90 per cent of residential construction had been financed by the state.

Local construction companies dominate the market, with only some competitors from neighbouring Finland daring to enter the field. Yield is reported at about 15 per cent, but too much depends on location issues. Prices in economy-class residential projects range from US$950 to US$1,200 per m^2, while in elite areas the prices may be US$3,000–6,000 or more. Some elite projects are reported to bring yields of 80 per cent or more – but the market is not ready to take up all the properties at the current ambitious prices. The risk of excessive supply not supported by the cautious demand is evident. With mortgage services in their cradle, problems of excess supply are expected in most sectors. It is hoped that state support of mortgages and municipal investment in site infrastructure and related issues (roads, metro stations, etc) will partially solve the problem. More effective management of the companies involved in residential construction is also expected.

Buying, refurbishing and renting apartments is quite popular among small investors. Usually an apartment of 100–150 m^2 in the centre of the city, properly furnished, can be let to a foreigner for US$1,500–2,500 per month. Locals are renting smaller apartments in 'dormitory districts' for US$200–400 per month.

Office buildings

Non-residential real estate in St Petersburg covers 58.2 million m^2. Of that total, only about 3.2 million m^2 are office space, with A, B and C-class office buildings occupying about 0.9 million m^2. The total number of business centres in St Petersburg is about 300–350.

In terms of the amount of quality office stock per 1,000 inhabitants – about 200 m^2 – St Petersburg is lying behind Moscow (by a factor of two) and other markets in the Central and East European region (by three to five times), and even more so behind London or Brussels.

The market for office space in St Petersburg 10 years ago was dominated by administrative buildings, with obsolete floor plans and almost entirely without modern amenities. The first A-class office building, 'Atrium', was developed by Golub and Co on Nevsky Prospect, 25, in 1998, just before the August 1998 financial crisis. Rental rates for prime Western-standard offices peaked at US$700 per m^2. The White Nights and Northern Capital House business centres joined the list the same year, with vacancies reaching 50 per cent and rents declining because of the consequences of August 1998.

As the Russian economy began to recover and foreign investments became more common, the need for modern offices became more

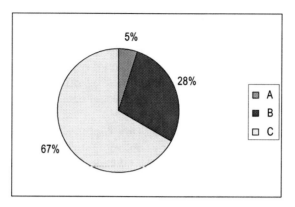

5%

28%

A

B

C

67%

Figure 3.1.1 Office space distribution in A, B and C-class business centres, 2005

crucial. Foreign and joint venture companies were competing for a limited supply of A-class office buildings, while local companies generally looked for B and C-class office space. Some five years ago, office development started to give higher returns than residential and retail construction. Some 120,000 m² of new office space was brought onto the market in 2004. Most current office development projects are B-class oriented. The year 2005 is expected to bring another 150,000–70,000 m² of new high-quality modern stock, which corresponds to the standard Western class-A and B space. Class-B projects make up 80 per cent of those scheduled for completion.

The vacancy rate has declined to 3–5 per cent, and many office buildings have a waiting list of tenants wishing to expand their space or outside companies looking for more spacious or more modern offices. A company looking for quality office space of 500–1,000 m² was a sensation a couple of years ago – but is quite common today.

Recent office development – mostly B-class office stock – is dwarfed by the Goliath of ex-administrative buildings of Soviet enterprises and research institutes that have gone with the wind; their fittings, layout and infrastructure are obsolete and inadequate. As most of the available office premises were not built for the purpose, only about 5 per cent of total office supply can be assessed as A-class (in Moscow, A-class makes up about a quarter of the office space).

The city centre has many restrictions on new development, as it is a World Heritage Site with numerous listed buildings, and the height of the Winter Palace – currently the Hermitage museum – sets the height limit for new construction. Hence, the prospect of building skyscrapers is out of question. Even out-of-centre projects currently have a height limit of 65 m. New office developments in the city centre are usually six to eight-storey projects, commonly with parking problems. Only a few developers could get permits for ten or eleven-storey buildings.

Because of these restrictions on height and on changes to façades and sometimes even interiors of the existing buildings, the periphery of the centre is becoming an adjunct to the Central Business District (CBD). Most new construction and redevelopment is taking place on the embankments of the Bolshaya Nevka, a major waterway in the delta of Neva river – the Grand Canale of the 'Northern Venice'. These embankments were occupied by industrial dinosaurs of the inelastic Soviet economy – and the buildings may remain in place even though the production lines they sheltered have become obsolete and been removed. New B-class business centres have been or are being developed in former administrative, R and D and industrial buildings of the enterprises that are gone ('Nobel', 'City Centre', 'Aquatoria', 'Times', 'Veda House', 'River House' and others), in an incomplete hotel that has been redeveloped into a business-centre ('Petrovsky Fort') and on a brownfield site (the 'Austrian Business Centre', where construction has just started).

With the current positive dynamic of market development, high-class office projects can ask not less than US$1,000–1,300 per m², with a payback period of about 5–7 years and yields of 16–20 per cent.

Buildings suitable for conversion into representative office premises are hard to find, with prices of US$1,500–3,000 per m² for centrally located properties. There have been a number of buy/sell agreements for office buildings – both those with sitting tenants and empty buildings that had been reconstructed.

Only a few office buildings were built to order, so most are available for rent. Rents used generally to be denominated in US$ but the euro is increasingly being used. Some managers nominate rents in a US$–euro median. Rents are usually inclusive of operating expenses and management fees, net of VAT (18 per cent). Fitting-out costs depend on the tenant's specific requirements, but are usually estimated at US$200–300 per m². Parking is usually a problem, so available spaces are rented at US$40–80 per month.

Although President Putin is speaking of plans to move several Federal government ministries from Moscow to his native city of St Petersburg, no behemoth projects have started, and there have been reports of problems in finding sufficient accommodation of adequate quality for them. A huge development project of 250,000 m² of office and retail space near Moscowsky railway station is in its embryo.

A genuine A-class property on Nevsky, 38, came onto the market in 2004 after the reconstruction of a listed building, with 4,500 m² of exquisite office space (estimated at 400–500 euros per m² per annum) and a boutique shopping centre. The same year brought another reconstructed gem on Nevsky, 10: cosy premises of 2,800 m², of which 1,600

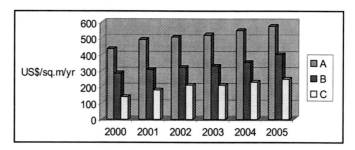

Figure 3.1.2 Rents in A, B and C-class business centres, 2000–2005

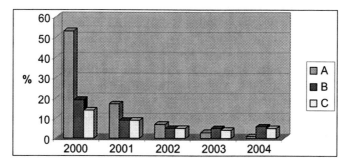

Figure 3.1.3 Vacancies in A, B and C-class business centres, 2000–2004

were leasable. Developments in 2005 include an extension of Northern Capital House, 6,000 m² of new A-class office space converted from a former car park built in the 1990s.

The low office vacancy rate is expected to persist through the years 2005 and 2006, though new ambitious projects for high quality modern stock, corresponding to the standard Western Class-A and B space, are expected to come on the market. The tight supply side is coupled with high demand, though B-class properties are entering a stage of tough competition. Rental rates are expected to increase slightly as operating expenses are rising together with construction costs; escalating supply will prevent a significant premium on letting office space in the near future. A and B-class office centres are competing with each other more and more, with-A class buildings being left with only one unquestionable advantage: their central location.

Retail premises

Retail is a mushrooming sector in St Petersburg, as in other Russian cities, and the retail market has undergone immense change since the early 1990s. After decades of total deficits and rationing, Russians are enjoying shopping conditions that sometimes rival the West. A friend who emigrated to the United States 10 years ago told me on her recent visit to St Petersburg that her Long Island supermarket is dwarfed by the one she visited here. New retail formats are attracting crowds of Russians who are voting for the consumer society with their changing consumer behaviour, following the path of the rest of Eastern Europe. Although the biggest retail changes in Russia are happening in Moscow, St Petersburg is the second logical destination for Russian and Western retail chains.

Retail premises occupy some 4 million m², which is less than 0.9 m² per person. Of the total, most shopping facilities are obsolete, atavistic, Soviet-style stores filled with dubious low-quality Chinese or Turkish produce. In that bleak retailscape, amazing new projects are growing fast, and demand far exceeds the supply. Currently about 60 shopping centres, department stores and hypermarkets are open in St Petersburg, with about 30 being built or redeveloped. Modern retail space covers about 1.2 million m², with about 270,000 m² opened last year. In 2005, from 300,000 to 400,000 m² of new shopping centres are expected. About 18 new properties are expected to open, nearly half of them hypermarkets.

About 200,000 m² of new street retail is entering the market annually on the ground floors of new residential buildings built mostly in 'dormitory districts'. Average sale prices here are about US$1,500 per m², while in the city centre sale prices for ground floor retail space in the new residential buildings are about US$2,500 and can reach US$5,000 or more.

As most of the city centre is a World Heritage site, most developments are happening in the 'dormitory districts', near metro stations and along major avenues. Some sites along Pulkovskoye or Vyborgskoye highways are becoming retail parks, with shopping centres and hypermarkets crowding in with no systematic order. In the city centre, several developments have produced phenomenal 'boutique shopping centres' with prime Western brands and prices confusing even the New Russians. Vanity has just signed a long-term lease for a whole new building of 5,000 m² in the core of the downtown area. The luxury-goods chain Mercury from Moscow has taken over one of the major department stores in the city, DLT. In 2003, a 20,000 m² Grand Palace was opened on a prime location on Nevsky with 90 boutiques – and new projects are under way.

Nevsky Prospect is still the major retail corridor, with no rivals and correspondingly high rents. In the central part of the avenue, US$1,500 per m² per year may be a bargain. A sale price for a boutique at US$10,000 per m² has already been reported. That is no surprise, with six metro stations and about 8.6 million passengers getting off at

Nevsky. Nevsky outstrips the competition, but is followed by other retail corridors, including Vladimirsky, Bolshoy at Petrogradsky district and Liteiny. Rents for prime high-street shop units are around US\$1,000 per m^2 per year. A 'cooler' space can be rented per US\$500–800 per m^2 per annum, but hot spots rarely drop beneath US\$1,000.

At the same time, most 'dormitory districts' are experiencing a deficit of retail space and residents are flocking to open markets and new hypermarkets and shopping centres that do well without the 'anchors' (the large-scale operations occupying 10,000–50,000 sq ft and generating extra consumer turnover) and other 'must-haves' of professional centres. Rents there may fluctuate between US\$350–950, with the anchors paying rates in the lower part of the scale.

Local retailers who still dominate the market are on the alert. They are trying to mark out for themselves locations that can either help them compete with the foreign retail invasion or be good properties to sell.

Various foreign retailers have taken the risk of starting projects in St Petersburg, with only a few unsuccessful entries. Those who came, have expanded. Finnish Stockmann, German Metro Cash and Carry, Swedish IKEA and Turkish Ramstore are expected to be followed by other major players. Kingfisher's Castorama is planning to open its first store of 11,000 m^2 in late 2005, to be followed by three to five other stores soon. German OBI (DIY format) and Real have announced their renting of 17,000 and 18,000 m^2 respectively in the Rainbow shopping centre, where 75,000 m^2 of total space will be completed by mid-2006.

A notable development has been local government's attempts to substitute/replace open markets and kiosk types of retail (dominant in the 1990s) with modern shopping centres. Although they occupy prime locations near metro stations, kiosks are losing ground, with vast shopping centres taking their place – and their customers.

Street retail rents are still escalating, while shopping centres may be approaching a virtual ceiling in the growth of rents – or better say retailers' revenues as every new centre has to lease more space to anchors who pay much less than the shops in the mall, invest in good architecture and stylish fittings, and pay more for the land, utilities and services.

The creation of a modern retail infrastructure in St Petersburg is under way. Many major international retailers have already understood the potential of this market and have started business in the city, setting new standards in quality goods and facilities. With growing disposable incomes, and a share of it spent in the shops that is unequalled in the West, retail here will dominate investors' minds for years to come.

3.2

An Overview of Land Development, Hospitality (Tourism) and the Commercial Real Estate Sector in St Petersburg

Vladislav Miagkov, Head of Real Estate Advisory Services Practice, Ernst & Young, St Petersburg

Land

Is it possible to purchase land on the market?

Despite the passing of numerous laws confirming the right to private property, the market for private land is practically nonexistent in Russian cities. The exception to the rule has been St Petersburg, where since 1995 there has been some success in lands sales.

The privatization of municipal land was organized in 1992 under the principle that the land beneath a building in private ownership would naturally be connected to that building. The principle that governs the purchasing of land beneath buildings (developed land) does not exclude the possibility of purchasing undeveloped land on the secondary market. Under existing laws, landowners have the right to subdivide and sell their property on the market; however, such a market has yet to appear.

Undeveloped land is usually considered municipal property and the local government has broad control over its development. The Land Code (2001) allows the local administration to sell undeveloped land directly, but only by auction and after zoning. Municipalities are not rushing to sell off undeveloped land by auction, however, preferring the old, drawn-out and costly method.

How does one acquire municipal land in practice?

In the absence of an open real estate market, developers usually use one of the following methods to obtain land:

- They find undeveloped land and convince the local administration to lease that property. After construction, the developers lease or purchase the land.

- They acquire the ownership rights to an existing building, and so acquire a long-term lease on the land that accompanies it.

The first method is often used and differs little from Soviet practices. The guiding principle here is to develop first and acquire land later – the exact opposite of accepted practice in Western countries: to acquire land first and provide collateral for subsequent development.

Local administrations often assess fees and/or require supplemental work in return for development rights. These are sometimes called 'infrastructure development fees' or 'investment conditions', and can reach US$800 per m² in the downtown area of St Petersburg. The second method of acquiring land is also widespread. Usually, a building is purchased from a private owner or leased from the city, and subsequently the property rights under/around the building are also transferred. The investor is then able to develop on that property. There are many possible variants of this method but all fall under one leading principle: the right to a piece of property follows the acquisition of ownership rights (or lease rights) to the building(s) located on that property.

The cost of utility services

The developer's task of accurately assessing a project's cost is made more difficult by the unpredictable costs involved in supplying a project with the necessary utilities. The permit process requires the developer to coordinate agreements with the utility monopolies. In some St Petersburg districts where the utility infrastructure is underdeveloped, the developer may be asked to improve unrelated infrastructure. These 'fees' can be very expensive and arbitrary. Developers are sometimes forced to enter drawn-out negotiations with the local administration and monopolies in order to retain a project's economic feasibility. The cost of connections to utility services can amount to 15–20 per cent of the total project cost (and sometimes up to 30 per cent).

The complicated task of choosing a good site is made even more difficult by the lack of access to information about infrastructure. Without this information investors cannot adequately consider project options, and well-informed economic decisions are much more difficult to make.

Despite these problems, land development in St Petersburg is beginning to evolve. Some private companies tackle these problems on a professional basis. They gather the necessary information, prepare the documentation and ready the sites for development. Developers in St Petersburg, for example, can bypass the unpleasant land acquisition problems by 'purchasing' a documented and prepared piece of property from one of these companies for anywhere from US$50 to US$1,500 per m² of land. As the demand for such services in St Petersburg grows, these businesses can be expected to actively evolve.

Leasing of municipal and state land in St Petersburg

Until recently a developer wishing to acquire the right to lease a municipally owned land plot has had to apply to the city committee on land plot procurement. Subject to certain requirements, including payment of the 'infrastructure development fee', the developer could obtain land to build on for the period of construction (about 2–3 years in general). In 2003, developers paid on average US$60–80 per m² of land to the municipal budget as infrastructure development fees in order to acquire the right to lease. The most expensive land plots of moderate size (up to 1,000 m²) were located in the CBD near Nevsky Avenue; here investors paid around US$400–500 per m². However, some developers were ready to increase their lease fee.

At the beginning of 2004 the new governor of St Petersburg gave notice of proposed changes in the procedure for providing federal and municipal land for building construction. Since then, however, the process has changed only for residential developers, a highly competitive sector. At present all sites for residential construction are distributed through open auctions, and the municipal fees for land procurement have almost doubled.

No significant changes have occurred for commercial and industrial developers in respect of providing plots of land.

The private land market in St Petersburg

At present, private companies in St Petersburg own over 3,000 sites with a total area of more than 15,000 hectares. About 40 per cent of the enterprises in St Petersburg now own some or all of the land on which they operate, having bought it from the state. Some of this land has subsequently been resold on the secondary market. Prices for land plots bought from private owners range from US$20 to US$500 per m^2 depending on their location and size. Plots with an area of over 1,000 m^2 fetch from US$10 to US$300 per m^2, depending on their location and the availability of utilities. Typical purchase prices for industrial and warehouse land plots in the 'industrial belt' outside the city centre range from US$20 to US$80 per m^2.

Demand and supply

At present the demand for private land in St Petersburg is obviously higher that the supply. When purchasing real estate facilities the buyers put great emphasis on the importance of a properly registered title to the land in order to reduce the entrepreneurial risks.

Unlike in Moscow, in the centre of St Petersburg it is hard to find a suitable site for new construction. The majority of buildings in the city centre are designated as architectural or historical monuments, and it is almost impossible to obtain permits to demolish or convert old buildings. The city centre is surrounded by the industrial belt that evolved in the 19th century. Recently, large investors have begun to purchase privatized industries in the city centre for reconstruction purposes. Generally, these are plants that have been or are about to be shut down. The investors are demolishing the low-grade buildings and using the land for residential or commercial construction.

For instance, between 2001 and 2003 a very active construction company in St Petersburg bought the premises of various inefficient enterprises and used them for residential construction at US$30–60 per m^2. In summer 2004, a private development company paid US$8 million for the property complex of an industrial enterprise, with obsolete industrial and office buildings covering in all about 20,000 m^2. The whole complex comprised a 10-hectare site, so the price came to US$80 per m^2, including the industrial buildings.

Industrial and warehouse real estate

On the real estate market, the most significant growth is currently seen in the sector of industrial and warehouse sites, as well as trading property. Since 2002, the growth rate in these sectors has begun to exceed the increase in supply, as the industrial and warehouse sector has started to outpace the trading and office sectors both in terms of sale and purchase price. This dynamic growth is due to the drastic increase in demand and the lack of good-quality supply.

The increased number of modern retail centres and the appearance on the St Petersburg market of large Western and Russian retail chains have increased demand for modern, high-quality warehouses and, especially, logistics centres. Developers who wish to construct modern warehouses have had difficulties in finding suitable land, as described in the first section of this overview. Even more important have been problems with utilities. To some extent they can overcome these problems by acquiring old industrial buildings to reconstruct as warehouses. These circumstances, together with the complicated process of obtaining long-term loans with Russian banks to finance new projects, explain why only 5 per cent of about 5 million m² of existing industrial and warehouse premises (only 250,000 m²) represent warehouses that meet international standards.

A similar situation can be seen in the industrial premises sector.

Leasing

At present the rental rates for industrial and warehouse space within the city boundaries range from US$3.5 to US$10 per m² per month (exclusive of VAT) depending on location, status and management quality. Communal services can be included in the rental rate by negotiation, as can parking space and the use of adjacent areas.

The main demand is for properties of around 300–500 m². In the warehouse sector, the most popular size is about 1,000 m², but in the city centre the most popular warehouses are small, ranging from 100 to 150 m², and are used to store small retail consignments. Large suppliers and manufacturers either use the services of the few professional logistic companies with warehouses, or have to build their own warehouses to satisfy their needs.

Few warehouses are offered for sale. Given the high demand and the complexities of new construction, owners prefer to lease and not to sell their premises.

Despite the growing demand for quality warehouse and industrial spaces, there are no Western type industrial or business parks in St Petersburg, as in other Russian regions. Over the last decade there have been some significant attempts to organize such facilities, but the projects failed because of the obstacles mentioned above.

Hotels

Russian economic development indices have been improving since 2000. The growth in economic activity is accompanied by an increase in the number of business trips and in demand for quality accommodation services. The growing prosperity of Russian citizens has led to an increase in the number of Russian tourists staying in first-class and medium-class city hotels. The growth in demand and favourable forecasts for the hotel sector have caused large-scale investments in all types of hotels.

The St Petersburg hospitality market: supply

The provision of hotels in St Petersburg has improved during the past years because of increased competition, privatization, conversion and better management. Nevertheless, although St Petersburg boasts of some 186 hotels with 18,000 rooms, only about 15 hotels offer services comparable to any international standard. Currently there are 10 first-class hotels in St Petersburg: the Astoria, Angleterre, Grand Hotel Europe, Radisson SAS Royal Hotel, Corinthia Nevskij Palace, Eliseev, Renaissance Baltic, Grand Hotel Emerald, Baltic Star and President Hotel. Five more hotels are of the medium class according to the Western classification (the Pulkovskaya, Neptun, Ramada-Dostoevsky, Moscow and Pribaltiyskaya). In the St Petersburg hospitality industry, the overall market is more stable now than four years ago, and the St Petersburg authorities have demonstrated that they realize the value of tourist activity and have established an active policy of cultivating and developing this business. Adequate accommodation for foreign guests is now considered a major priority. The structure and dynamics of hotel facilities are shown Table 3.2.1.

Table 3.2.1 Structure of commercial hotel facilities in St Petersburg (population 4.7 million)

Hotel type	Hotels			Rooms			Capacity		
	2002	2003	2004	2002	2003	2004	2002	2003	2004
First-class	5	10	10	1,169	1,620	1,612	2,332	3,194	3,180
Medium class	41	66	93	8,016	9,787	10,854	14,985	17,745	20,389
Economy class	43	54	83	2,728	2,337	2,791	5,601	4,963	6,113
Total	**89**	**130**	**186**	**11,913**	**13,744**	**15,257**	**22,918**	**25,902**	**29,682**
Corporate hotels	42	52	38	3,008	3,162	2,676	9,197	7,562	6,027
Total	**131**	**182**	**224**	**14,921**	**16,906**	**17,933**	**32,115**	**33,464**	**35,709**

Source: Tourism Committee of St. Petersburg

It should be noted that though no new hotels opened between 1990 and 2000, in the last four years the city has gained four large hotels (80–200 rooms each). In the same period, some 85 small and mini hotels opened in the city, providing 1,093 rooms (usually double) at modest prices. These small hotels are those with not more than 50 rooms, and some are like 'home hotels', with not more than 30 rooms. Almost all of them have good locations in the central business district of the city.

In all, the city has gained a total of 1,500 rooms and accommodation for 3,500 guests.

Table 3.2.2 Small hotels opening in St Petersburg, 2000–04

Year	Hotels	Number of Rooms	Accommodation
2000	3	19	38
2001	11	148	456
2002	9	135	297
2003	55	716	1,559
2004	7	75	174
Total	**85**	**1,093**	**2,524**

Demand: client segments and occupancy rates

In 2004, 30 leading hotels in St Petersburg accommodated about 1.5 million guests, including over 700,000 foreign clients. The number of foreign guests at these hotels increased by 4.7 per cent as compared with 2002, while the number of foreign tourists in the city increased by 30 per cent. The difference shows the successful take-up of new, small hotels, as well as apartments in the private sector that are furnished and offered to guests over the Internet.

Table 3.2.3 shows that the average annual occupancy of medium-class hotels has been lower than that of first and economy-class hotels since 2000, which means that the quality-to-price ratio of first-class and economy-class hotels meets the demand better than that of the medium-class sector. Thus, the market data shows that the quality of service in St Petersburg's 'medium' hotels does not correspond to their prices. Indeed, many comments by foreign citizens on the Internet show that they are generally dissatisfied with the medium-class hotels due to their excessive prices and failure to match the quality of four or even three-star Western hotels. We may conclude that this hotel sector in St Petersburg still has much room for improvement.

While corporate clients and businesspeople most often stay in the first-class hotels, tourist groups and 'incentive-tour 'participants (eg agents coming to conclude seasonal contracts) prefer medium-class accommodation. Individual guests may be found in all hotel types. Russian meeting and conference members prefer economy class.

Table 3.2.3 Occupancy rates in St Petersburg hotels, 1998–2004

Hotels	1998		1999		2000		2001		2002		2003		2004	
First-class	60.1%	−1.6	45.7%	−14.4	55.3%	+9.6	55.6%	+0.3	63.3%	+7.7	68.8%	+5.5	69%	+0.2
Medium class	45.4%	−2.1	48.0%	+2.6	52.0%	+4.0	52.2%	+0.2	61.0%	+8.8	59.6%	−1.4	62%	+2.4
Economy class	49.0%	−2.3	56.2%	+6.5	58.4%	+2.2	58.1%	−0.3	58.0%	+1.2	62.4%	+4.4	65%	+2.6

Table 3.2.4 St Petersburg hotel market segments by type of visitor (2003–04)

| | Travel segments, % of guests* | | | | | |
	Corporate	Group	Individual	Conference	Business	Incentive
Total for four prime-class hotels	26.6	17.6	35.3	7.3	6.4	4.3
Total for twenty medium class hotels	15.6	42.6	20.1	5.9	5.5	15.6
Total for six economy hotels	12	33	36.2	11	2.3	0.6
Total for 30 hotels:	**18.1**	**31.1**	**30.5**	**8.1**	**4.7**	**6.8**

Source: Tourism Committee of St Petersburg

*Corporate: guests on business trips accommodated on the terms of preliminary contracts with companies.

Tourist groups: members of organized groups of tourists accommodated under contracts with tourist agencies.

Individuals: private persons on individual visits having (or not having) made preliminary booking arrangements.

Conferences: persons invited by organizers of meetings and conferences.

Business: individual guests on business trips.

Incentive: members of incentive tours – agents of tourist operators or companies intending to conclude seasonal contracts.

Medium-class hotels
St Petersburg hotels trading as three-star accommodations let rooms from US$70 to US$220 per day. The client base of these medium-class hotels is generally made up of tourist groups (42.6 per cent) and individual visitors (20.1 per cent).

At present, investors are taking an active interest in the market sector of three-star and three-star-plus hotels that offer good-quality service and moderate prices.

Small hotels in St Petersburg
Small hotels are highly competitive and are recommended to foreign tourists by many operators. Depending on comfort and, to a lesser degree, on location, their prices range from US$40 to US$150 per day, with an average of US$50–60. In the peak season, these prices increase by at least 50 per cent, and central city locations become more

expensive as well. Most of these hotels apply a flexible pricing policy that is generally dependent on seasonality.

The number of small hotels may be expected to actively increase.

Statistics of foreign guests
According to government statistics, the number of foreign tourists in Russia in 2004 reached 2,861,000 visitors. Besides Moscow, the main tourist centres are St Petersburg, the Russian 'Golden ring' cities and the northwestern region, including Pskov and Novgorod. The greatest numbers of visitors come to Moscow (about 35 per cent of the total) and St Petersburg (over 20 per cent).

Visitor statistics in St Petersburg
As a global cultural centre, St Petersburg has a great tourist attraction potential for visitors from Russia and from neighbouring and far-distant countries. However, the city has so far made little use of this potential. Over the last two years, revenue from tourism made up 10–15 per cent of the St Petersburg budget, much less than leading European tourist centres (Paris, Rome, Venice, London).

Over the last 10 years the city has been visited by almost 2 million foreigners. In 2003, the total number of foreign visitors in the northwestern region increased by 8 per cent, stimulated by the city's 300th anniversary, and, according to the regional administration of the Federal Frontier service in the northwestern region, totalled 3.6 million people. St Petersburg has become increasingly interesting to Muscovites as well as to people of other cities and regions of Russia. It should be noted that about 70 per cent of foreign guests who enter the country through the northwestern frontier head to St Petersburg.

Table 3.2.5 shows that the number of foreign visitors varies; however, in the period 1997–2003 there has been a tendency for gradual growth. The data provided by the Tourism Committee (10 March 2005) show that the number of foreign visitors in the northwestern region in 2004 was almost unchanged from the previous year.

In the period from 1993 to 2001 the tourist flow fluctuated considerably. Since then, the number of foreign and private tourists has significantly increased, and the fastest growth has been in the sector of foreign tourists. In 2003, St Petersburg played host to 929,000 foreign visitors, 20 per cent more than in 2002. The growth rate in 2004 amounted to 21 per cent and was due to improvements in the general economic conditions in the country, as well as to global advertising of the city and the development of hotel services by reconstruction of the old lodging facilities and opening of new, mostly small, hotels. The greatest number of tourists come from Finland, then, in decreasing order, the Baltic countries, Germany, the United States, Italy, Great Britain and France.

Table 3.2.5 Entry flows in the northwestern region in 1993–2004

	Business	Tourism	Private	Total	% change from previous year
	Number of arrivals in St Petersburg				
1993	796,142	746,699	518,093	2,060,934	+ 159.0
1994	443,483	428,013	94,658	966,154	-53.2
1995	796,169	876,036	231,785	1,903,990	+97.0
1996	1,221,328	593,964	267,760	2,083,052	+9.0
1997	860,308	691,136	439,905	1,991,349	-4.4
1998	840,572	723,830	710,639	2,275,041	+ 14.3
1999	924,014	701,288	1,326,237	2,951,539	+ 29.7
2000	1,075,564	1,016,050	850,858	2,942,472	-3.0
2001	1,037,295	657,366	1,010,091	2,704,752	-8.0
2002	912,038	769,081	1,194,886	2,876,005	+6.3
2003	933,775	929,244	1,249,613	3,112,632	+8
2004	974,013	1,129,207	1,005,779	3,108,999	- 0.1

Source: Tourism Committee of St Petersburg, as of 10 March 2005

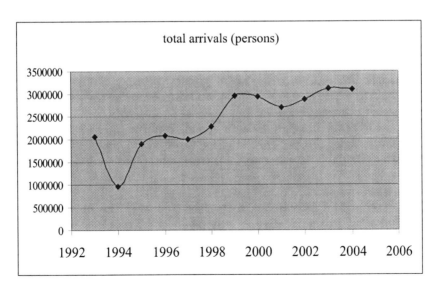

Figure 3.2.1 St Petersburg visitors statistics of 1993–2004 for all types of visitors

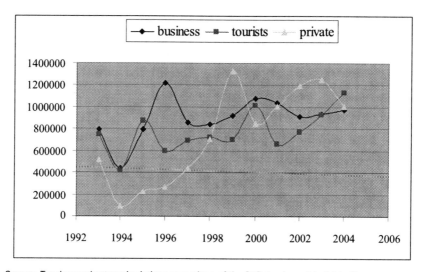

Source: Tourism and external relations committee of the St Petersburg Administration

Figure 3.2.2 St Petersburg visitors by categories (1993–2004)

St Petersburg also has a specific tourist sector: foreign tourists who travel on cruise liners and do not use city hotels. Their annual number ranges from 150,000 to 200,000. In 2004, this tourist market sector significantly increased – by 70 per cent – as compared with the previous year.

The number of foreign citizens arriving in the city on business trips is generally within the same range as the number of foreign tourists. In 2004, St Petersburg was visited by almost 975,000 foreign business-people.

The most significant increase has been in the sector of foreign tourists. A small decrease in the general number of visitors entering the northwestern region in 2004 is accounted for by the decrease in the number of private visits.

On average, foreign visitors spend from one day to two weeks in St Petersburg (58 per cent stay for three to five days, 24 per cent for one or two days, 12 per cent for a week, and 6 per cent for two weeks).

Russian tourists
We would like to emphasize the fact that over the recent years the number of Russian citizens staying in the first-class and medium-class hotels has been actively growing. This indicates the growing wealth of Russian tourists and improvements in the economic conditions of the city. These factors have led to an increased number of Russian businesspeople, first and foremost those from Moscow, visiting

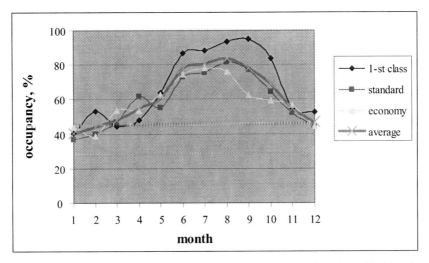

Source: Data for 2004 was provided by the Tourism Committee of the St Petersburg Administration

Figure 3.2.3 Monthly occupancy of St Petersburg hotels, 2004

St Petersburg for business development purposes. In 2003, the proportions of Russian guests in city hotels were:

- 16 per cent in first-class (four hotels with 324,702 guests in 2003)

- 51.2 per cent in medium class (20 hotels with 1,027,427 guests in 2003).

In all, St Petersburg hotels accommodated about 800,000 Russian tourists and businesspeople in 2003. The average hotel stay of a Russian tourist is 4.5 nights, whereas the average stay for foreign visitors is 2.5 nights.

Seasonality and trend of demand
The maximum occupancy of St Petersburg city hotels is observed during the 'white nights' period, which officially lasts from May 20 to July 20, with demand peaking in the middle of June. In winter months, hotel occupancy falls drastically. The monthly occupancy rates of the three hotel types (first-class, medium-class and economy-class) in St Petersburg in 2004 is shown in Figure 3.2.3.

Most European cities with tourist potential experience seasonal variations in demand for their services. However, their situation is more stable than St Petersburg's. The same may be said of Moscow, where seasonal variations in hotel occupancy among tourists are balanced by business visitors, whose numbers decrease in summer.

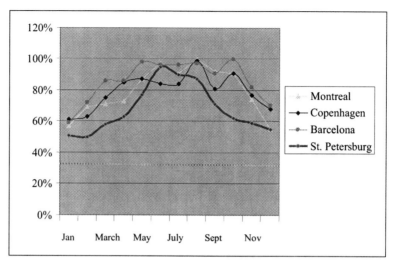

Source: BCG, RATA

Figure 3.2.4 Average hotel occupancy in St Petersburg vs three western cities, 2003

Figure 3.2.4 shows the average hotel occupancy in Copenhagen, Barcelona and Montreal compared with St Petersburg (in 2003).

From 2005, the St Petersburg Administration intends to take various actions aimed at attracting more tourists to the city and balancing the strongly marked seasonality of the tourist business in the city.

However, from the point of view of all hospitality industry players, the main task of the city administration remains ensuring the safety of guests. Apart from reducing criminal offences, this task includes citywide environmental safety issues, as well as improving the environments in medium-class hotels, which are often described by foreign gusts as 'unfriendly' (referring to their low-quality service and poor utilities and technical equipment).

The hotel market in St Petersburg

In the absence of an effective land market, new hotel construction faces difficulties in obtaining sites, especially in the city centre. The city administration has compiled a list of obsolete buildings suitable for conversion into hotels. The restrictions mentioned earlier, related to the status of historical monuments and utilities issues, significantly decrease the attractiveness of this list; however, at present almost two dozen businesspeople have announced their intention to use this opportunity to construct hotels.

In February 2005, Orient-Express Hotels Ltd acquired a majority interest in the 301-room Grand Hotel Europe, St Petersburg's leading hotel, along with full management and operational control. This sale was the most significant event in the St Petersburg hotel market in 2004–05, along with the sale by the St Petersburg Administration of its shares in eight hotels constructed 20–40 years ago. In all cases the purchasers announced their intention to redevelop the hotels and upgrade them to meet Western standards.

Table 3.2.6 Hotel sale transactions in St Petersburg, 2004–05

	Hotel	Number of rooms	Class, condition	% of shares sold	Price paid, (US$ million)	Date of transaction
1	Rossia	368	Poor condition, renovation required	60%	1.4	2000
2	Chaika	180	Poor condition, renovation required	60%	3.6	Aug 2004
3	Vyborgskaya	400	Poor condition, renovation required	60%	4.8	Aug 2004
4	Yuzhnaya	131	Poor condition, renovation required	60%	2.5	Aug 2004
5	Pulkovskaya	840	4-star, renovation required	74.9%	18.4	Feb 2005
	Deson-Ladoga	96	3-star	50%	2.4	Nov 2004
6	Pribaltiyskaya	1200	3-4-star, renovation required	49%	18.3	March 2005
7	Moskwa	735	3-4-star, renovation required	74.42%	40.1	March 2005
8	Octiabrskaya	674	3-4-star, renovation required	60%	49.7	April 2005
9	Astoria	226	5-star, renovation required	23.33%	17.6	Feb 2005
10	Grand Hotel Europe	301	Luxury 5-star, western standards, managed by Kempinsky	95%	95–100* approx.	Feb 2005

Hotel	Number of rooms	Class, condition	% of shares sold	Price paid, (US$ million)	Date of transaction
11 Kievskaya	316	Poor condition, renovation required	55%	2.2	Aug 2004
12 Tourist	113	Poor condition, renovation required	75%	4.4	Aug 2004

*According to news agencies

3.3

Regulation of the Real Estate Market in St Petersburg

Maxim Kalinin, Partner, Baker & McKenzie, St Petersburg

Introduction

St Petersburg, sometimes called the 'Northern Capital of Russia', is the largest northern city in the world and the second largest city in Russia, with huge, and so far largely unrealised, potential for investment – particularly in tourism and leisure, industry and infrastructure, residential and commercial properties.

Given current positive trends in the Russian economy, the Russian government's initiatives to improve the investment climate, the city's favourable geographical location and highly educated population, the outlook for investment in St Petersburg is extremely favourable.

In the real estate sector in particular, the city authorities of St Petersburg have, for some time, been trying to ensure greater transparency for foreign investors. Many steps have been taken to create such transparency although, while some have been successful, others need to be further improved and simplified. Nonetheless, legislation adopted by the City of St Petersburg during 2004–05, which established new regulations on investment in the city's rapidly developing real estate sector, would seem to offer some encouragement for investors.

Disposition of state property for the purposes of construction and reconstruction

The City of St Petersburg is the largest owner of real estate in the city. For obvious reasons, it has become clear that the state authorities cannot and need not manage and maintain all residential and non-residential buildings in the city. For several years the city has therefore been developing a system for granting improved rights to owners and investors in the private sector. Notable among these is the recently adopted procedure for transferring to investors rights relating to buildings (completed or under construction) and undeveloped land plots belonging to the state.

This legislation – the Law of St Petersburg No 282-43 On Procedure for Granting Real Estate Owned by St Petersburg, dated 26 May 2004 (the 'Law') – entered into force on 3 July 2004, and establishes general principles for the granting of real estate properties for the purposes of construction and reconstruction. In accordance with the Law, investors may be granted rights to real estate properties or land by means of a public tender, or through the direct grant of such property to the investor. The Law provides that decisions on the granting of real estate property for the purposes of construction and reconstruction (as well as the management of all tender terms and conditions) are to be taken by the government of St Petersburg. The Committee for City Property Management (the KUGI) is authorized on behalf of the government of St Petersburg to enter into purchase–sale agreements and land lease or investment agreements based on the results of such tenders, or on the basis of legal acts issued by the government of St Petersburg, allowing the direct grant of rights to real estate properties or land.

Following a decision of the government of St Petersburg to grant rights to real estate property, a permit for design and construction may be issued by the St Petersburg Committee on Construction and Architecture.

Public tenders

The Law establishes general principles for the conduct of public tenders. Tenders must be open to all participants and conducted in the form of an auction or competition. A tender is conducted in the form of a competition where it is necessary to establish special conditions (in addition to achieving the best price) regarding the development and ultimate use of the project. These may include conditions relating to architecture, city planning, culture or other issues of social importance.

In other cases, the award of real estate rights are made through auction, based solely on price.

Tenders are carried out by the organization specifically authorized by the government of St Petersburg to manage the organization and conduct of tenders – currently, the Fund for the Management of St Petersburg Property (the 'Fund'). The Fund's functions in this respect are to be determined by the St Petersburg government, taking into account the requirements of the Law. Deputies of the Legislative Assembly are authorized to participate in the Fund's activities during preparations for tenders, and have the right to a deliberative vote.

A competition commission has been established by the Fund to monitor all competitive tenders for real estate properties (the 'Competition Commission'). Participation and membership of the Competition Commission is determined by the Fund in agreement with the government of St Petersburg, and comprises representatives of the government of St Petersburg, the Legislative Assembly, and unions and associations of construction enterprises, each having the right to a deciding vote. The Competition Commission is responsible for reviewing all tender offers, and determines all awards.

Direct grant of real estate properties

While, in general, the direct grant of real estate property rights is not allowed, the direct grant of real estate properties without a public tender is permissible in a limited number of cases specified by the Law, including:

- the granting of land plots to parties having (in accordance with current civil legislation) the right to enter into an agreement with the government of St Petersburg on the establishment of easement for construction and exploitation of power lines, communications facilities, pipelines and other engineering facilities for the provision of essential services;

- the granting of land plots to state and municipal departments and public companies, based on the right of perpetual (indefinite) use in accordance with their charter goals;

- the granting of land plots for residential construction, subject to preliminary agreement on the location of the real estate object and subject to the transfer to St Petersburg of not less than 10 per cent of the housing fund;

- the direct grant of property rights in respect of buildings, facilities or structures where: the building is communal or is declared in need of repair; reconstruction is being carried out for the purpose of creating a religious centre, or for the fulfilment of investment activity in the spheres of culture, science, health, ecology, education, physical education or sport, or for development of hotel facilities or other tourist infrastructure.

In addition to the cases listed above, the granting of rights to land plots, buildings, facilities, structures and incomplete construction sites is possible without a public tender in accordance with certain agreements entered into by the City of St Petersburg with various bodies, including the Russian Federation, constituents of the Russian Federation, foreign governments or certain strategic investors. This category of investors represents the largest group to enjoy this concession, although the criteria for determining such 'strategic investors' were only recently established by the government of St Petersburg. Rights to real estate properties may also be awarded (without public tender) in accordance with agreements between the Russian Federation and foreign governments, or in accordance with specific federal or local investment and other programmes. Moreover, it should be noted that real estate properties may be granted where there is a sole participant in a tender that does not, as a result, take place. (The Civil Code of the Russian Federation provides that a tender is deemed to have taken place if there are at least two participants).

It is important to note certain amendments to the Russian Land Code (Articles 30.1 and 30.2) regarding the granting of land for the construction of residential buildings and complexes, adopted on 29 December 2004. Article 30.1 deals with instances where state-owned land is awarded to a private investor for the construction of one or several residential buildings, and establishes that such land may be provided only through a public tender. Article 30.2 deals with instances where state-owned land is provided to a private investor for a 'complex development for the purpose of housing construction', and stipulates that such land may only be awarded though a public tender. 'Complex development for the purpose of housing construction' is deemed to include: (i) preparation of the land-use documentation related to the construction; (ii) the construction of engineering facilities and equipment; and (iii) construction of residential buildings and other real estate objects. While Article 30.1 will take effect from 1 October 2005, Article 30.2 has already taken effect.

Strategic investment projects and strategic investors

The long awaited Government Resolution No 216 was signed by the Governor of St Petersburg on 1 March 2005 and officially published on 29 March 2005, to come into force on 8 April 2005.

This resolution includes two regulations[1] intended to introduce clear criteria and rules to be used to determine which investment projects and investment relations are to be deemed strategic. It also outlines the procedures to be used by both the city authorities and investors, in the fulfilment of such projects.

Adoption of these regulations makes clear the criteria on which projects are deemed to be considered 'strategic' in terms of their impact on the social and economic development of the city and the country as a whole, and the ability of the city to attract investment. 'Strategic investment projects' are required to demonstrate a significant improvement in the social, economic and cultural lives of the residents of St Petersburg, and to support development in the fields of investment, industry, tourism, science, culture and education, information technology, finance, transport and logistics, and other areas.

In addition to the rather general criteria above, a strategic investment project must meet all of the following five qualification requirements in their entirety:

- The project must substantially assist in the development of individual locations within St Petersburg, the city as a whole, or separate areas of the city's economy, by stimulating investment and business activity through the realization of the strategic investment project, or by stimulating economic activity in a specific area of the city's economy.

- The project must be economically viable in terms of financial recoupment.

- The project must provide total investment which amounts to (as a rule), not less than 3 billion roubles. The government of St Petersburg is responsible for determining the term over which such aggregate investment must be made.

- Where a strategic investment project is related to industrial production, use must be made of advanced technologies including energy-saving resource-saving methods.

- Where fulfilment of the project is related to the jurisdiction of a corresponding governmental executive body, the organization in question is required to make a positive decision in support of the project before it can proceed.

Strategic investors may be: individuals; legal entities; associations of companies established on the basis of a joint activity agreement but without the status of legal entities; government bodies; local self-government associations; or foreign individuals or entities engaged in the fulfilment of strategic investment projects that have particular significance for the social, economic, cultural and other development of St Petersburg.

Any decision to assign strategic status to an investment project or to an investor will be taken by the Investments and Strategic Projects Committee of the Government of St Petersburg (the 'Investment Committee'). The necessary process may be initiated by the applicant (either a potential strategic investor or a governmental executive body) on submission of an application (together with all necessary documents proving compliance with the criteria above) to the Investment Committee. The Investment Committee must, within three days, reach a decision on whether or not to proceed with the application and conduct a full analysis of the documentation received, or make clear its decision to postpone such analysis due to insufficient supporting documents. In the latter case, an applicant will have a two-month period to re-submit the remaining documents. In the event of a positive response, the Investment Committee must conduct a full analysis of the proposed documents within a one-month period, which may be extended for another month if additional information is required.

On completion of its analysis, the Investment Committee is required to rule on whether or not the project will be given 'strategic project' or 'strategic investor' status. Where the ruling is positive, the government of St Petersburg is required to adopt a legal Act confirming the status of the project.

While it is hoped that the recent adoption of these regulations will simplify regulation of major investment projects in St Petersburg, it remains to be seen how these will be implemented in practice.

Terms and conditions for investment in real estate property

The conditions relating to investment in real estate property are governed by the Law. Investment agreements must be entered into with the government of St Petersburg.

The formulation of investment terms and conditions is performed on the basis of a valuation report establishing the market value of the property concerned, the value of the rights granted under the investment agreement, and rental payments. The valuation report is completed by an independent surveyor.

Investment terms and conditions typically cover the legal form of the grant of rights to the property, and the result of investment: that is, what rights the investor will receive in relation to the property, as well as any other rights and obligations of the investor and the City of St Petersburg. For example, land plots may be granted for development under a lease, under ownership, under a right of perpetual (indefinite) use, under a right of limited use (easement), or with the right of the investor to own (for economic use or operation management) the results of the investment.

Buildings, facilities and structures that are subject to reconstruction or completion of construction are granted for the purposes of fulfilment of investment activity that will establish a new property, with the resulting right of the investor to own the final development or product of the investment.

Where the property is a land plot, the terms and conditions of the investment will include the initial price of the property or land on purchase, the amount of rental income (where the investor has entered into a lease of the land plot) or the payment to be made for use of the land plot (upon granting of the right of limited use). Where the property includes a building, facilities or structures subject to reconstruction, the cost of the right to enter into an investment agreement is also an important investment condition. In a number of cases, an obligation to complete construction (or reconstruction) of a real estate property or put the building into commission earlier than the determined date may be imposed on an investor.

Additionally, terms and conditions may be imposed on an investor relating to compensation for losses and other expenses connected with the demolition of a property. These may include an obligation to compensate for the consequences of movement of a structure, or alterations to transport facilities or telecommunications and engineering equipment, and may also include an obligation to provide alternative accommodation to residents or other tenants evicted from the property under development.

In addition to the standard investment terms and conditions relating to the granting of rights to property, additional terms and conditions provided for in the Law may be imposed by the KUGI.

The simplified 'short-set' procedure for the granting of land plots

Currently, the granting of land plots for development in St Petersburg is performed through a simplified scheme pursuant to Government

Resolution No 405 of March 16, 2004. This procedure is used because it is, at the moment, impossible to realize a number of provisions of the Law.

The essence of this scheme is that certain investors may acquire a land plot under a six-year term lease; however, these land plots are unprepared for construction and the investors are therefore obliged to undertake all the necessary work to determine whether or not the land in question is viable for development, to secure public support for the project and to guarantee certain conditions for the maintenance of communications facilities relating to it. Where investors conclude construction at the end of the six-year term they have the right to extend the lease agreement for up to 49 years.

Of course, investors taking part in tenders under this simplified procedure take the risk of the land plot being considered unsuitable for construction (or for the purposes for which the investor was planning to use the land), and of incurring potentially significant losses as a result. Therefore, following an official statement by the St Petersburg Administration, it is anticipated that land plots prepared for construction will be made available for investment by the end of this year, and the 'long-set' scheme should become the basis for local policy in 2006.

The private property market

Russian legislation provides for the possibility of private ownership of real estate properties, including land. Following the privatization processes of the mid-1990s, an active market in private real estate has developed in the city. This market covers all forms of real estate property, including industrial, commercial, residential, retail, and, quite often, land plots. These may be offered by their owners for sale or on other conditions.

When dealing with a private owner, an investor must carry out a careful due diligence of the property, covering both legal issues and land use regulations, to ensure that the property may be reconstructed and used for the intended purposes of any proposed investment project. Russian civil legislation generally gives the parties freedom of contract. Since rights to the real estate are subject to state registration however, investors should pay close attention to the wording of such agreements to ensure they are appropriately registered by the state authorities so as to secure the rights of the investor.

Note:

1 The 'Regulation on Strategic Investment Projects of St Petersburg and Strategic Investors of St Petersburg' and the 'Regulation on the Procedure for Interaction of Government Executive Bodies of St Petersburg for the Purposes of Realization of Strategic Investment Projects in St Petersburg'

Practical Steps and Guidelines for the Acquisition of Residential Property in St Petersburg

Paul May, General Manager, City Realty

Introduction

The residential real estate market in St Petersburg has proven extremely attractive to both foreign and local investors over the past three years. The market itself is quite specific, differing in many ways from residential markets in the West. The differences are mainly due to the former state ownership of all property during the Soviet period and the strong social protection system covering the original occupants of the property. The market also has its own peculiarities, such as communal ownership of apartments. This article will attempt to give a little background on the market specificities as well as take the reader through the practical steps of the purchasing process.

Background

St Petersburg was built specifically to be the capital of the Russian Empire. From its birth, one of the urban planners' most important tasks was to accentuate the city's beauty and grandeur. Today, the city centre still retains much of its original design; it is full of pre-revolutionary buildings with magnificent facades as well as exquisitely landscaped parks and a large system of canals, creating an architectural harmony that is quite unique and making St Petersburg one of the most beautiful cities in the world.

There has been growing attention to St Petersburg by international investors over the past few years. This can be attributed to St Petersburg's geographical and social/cultural position as Russia's most Western city. It is also a vibrant centre of 5 million with a well-educated work force. Compared with Moscow, it is a city in which foreigners feel a bit more comfortable and a bit more at home.

Residential property investment climate

Prices of residential real estate have grown by approximately 80 per cent over the past 2.5 years. Growth was largest in 2003 and the first half of 2004, with a compound annual growth rate (CAGR) of approximately 35 per cent. Since June 2004, prices have levelled off with slight price drops in the outlying residential regions of the city and lower growth rates in the city's centre. The explosive growth was initially due to the high levels of foreign currency pumped into the Russian economy from the oil industry, combined with the general consensus of the market being undervalued when compared with its peers in Moscow or other eastern European capitals. Both foreign and local investors moved money into the city, buying massive amounts of residential property and driving the prices upward. The recent slowdown of the market may be attributed to a heavy reliance among late and speculative investors (2004) on barter instead of cash as a means of purchase funding, especially in the primary real estate market. Another factor has been the general 'catching up' of the market to a more stable value that is more in line with discounted cash flow forecasts when taking into account the city's and Russia's own risk and return profile in calculating discount rates.

This said, prime property in the centre of the city is continuing to grow at a healthy rate, and average prices for central property are still well below levels in Moscow or other major European cities. It is also encouraging to see that even after the exceptional growth rates of 2003 and 2004, no 'bubble has burst': in other words, there has not been a sudden drop in property values.

There are three typical types of investments popular in the residential market:

- long-term investment to capture value from both rental income and property appreciation;
- investment in businesses linked to residential property;

- investment by Western companies and company employees.

Long-term investment

These investments usually entail the purchasing of centrally located apartments for the purpose of renovation and then rent. Property in this category ranges from small, two-room apartments to large, communal flats. Most of the property purchased requires major renovation. Returns are made from rental income as well as from the overall appreciation of the property itself. The residential rental market in the city is quite healthy, driven in large part by increases in the city's business activity. Annual returns from 12 per cent to 20 per cent are typical in this type of investment.

Investments in businesses linked to residential property

Although this category is really part of the long-term category stated above, I have separated it due to its current popularity and relevance to today's market. Since 2003, a large number of foreign and local investors have opened small hotels in buildings that were formerly apartments. This trend can be seen as an organic reaction to the city's underdeveloped tourism and hotel industry. Plainly put, there are simply not enough hotels in the city to meet the growing demand of tourists and business people visiting St Petersburg. Investors usually purchase at least one if not more communal apartments in the same apartment building and convert the space into a small hotel, usually containing between five and 15 rooms. The typical return for this type of investment is between 20 per cent and 30 per cent annually. This investment, like other long-term investments, is built upon expectations of rental returns and property appreciation. However, it is more complex in that it deals with running a business requiring operations (management) and advertising in an environment that is still highly seasonal.

Investment by Western companies and company employees

Many foreign companies and their Western employees have started to purchase the apartments in which they live, rather than renting. With return on investment typically lower than five years, this variation can be quite attractive in terms of current cost savings and future property appreciation.

Specificities of the St Petersburg market

As mentioned in the introduction, the St Petersburg market is quite different from markets in the West. Below is a list of some of the major differences along with a short explanation of each.

Legality or 'cleanliness' of title ownership

Because of the sudden emergence of a secondary real estate market after the collapse of the Soviet Union and the shift from state owner-ship to private ownership, most properties on the market are not 'ready for sale' as you might find with properties in the West. For many sell-ers, this is the first time that apartments have been put on the market for sale. A typical list of problems follows:

- An apartment may not be fully privatized (still partially owned by the state), requiring the privatization of all or parts of the apartment before sale can be facilitated.

- Different people who do not actually live in the property may still be registered there, requiring their re-registration at different ad-dresses to eliminate the chance that they may claim rights to the title after the sale. Registration is a relic from Soviet times when it in many ways substituted for a person's 'right to property' as opposed to actual ownership (all property was state owned).

- Minors may have been moved out of the apartment illegally to make room for the sale. This creates a serious risk for the buyer that such a minor may eventually claim rights to the property.

- Mentally ill people may live in the apartment. They may not be legally responsible for their actions and may be able to contest a sale at some point in the future.

- Prisoners or former prisoners, citizens of former Soviet Republics or now 'stateless' people and other people in similar conditions may be registered in the property.

- The property's may be classified as a state architectural monument.

Due diligence on the history of the apartment and its current and for-mer inhabitants must be conducted thoroughly by the buyer or his or her real estate agency to limit the risk of claims to the title after pur-chase. Some of the problems listed above can be resolved during the purchasing process, but others may not. This is what is meant by not ready for sale. The checks not only include the State Bureau of Regis-tration archives but also may encompass Police and Security Services archives, the Municipal Department of Education, the Committee for State Inventory and Protection of Monuments, the Committee of Land Resources, the Regional Interdepartmental Commission and more.

Communal apartments

Communal apartments are a leftover facet of Soviet life. A large portion of the apartments in St Petersburg city centre are still communal. They are usually large apartments built before the 1917 revolution in which several families live together in one apartment, each owning one or two rooms. They share a communal kitchen and bathroom. Usually the only way to transform a communal apartment into a regular apartment is by purchasing all of the rooms in the apartment from their current owners. This is usually done step by step. The buyer first buys a piece of property for each family in the buyer's own name. When this is completed, the buyer trades these properties for the rooms in the apartment, thereby purchasing the entire apartment. This process can be quite long and entails some risk. The usual time frame for the purchase is from four to eight months but in some cases, if the owners decide to start playing speculative games, it can take much longer. For this reason, communal apartments are usually less expensive than apartments owned by single owners and can often be a good investment.

Condition of the housing stock

The housing stock of St Petersburg may be in rather poor condition due to the lack of state investment in residential housing services over the past 20 years. What this means for the investor is leaky pipes and low water pressure, poor and insufficient electrical systems, weak structural elements requiring reinforcement (weak floor beams, etc). This, along with the history of state ownership of property coupled with other historical elements (serfdom, the slow emergence of a middle class, the speed of urban industrialization during the beginning of the last century and early Soviet period) has also had a psychological effect on the inhabitants of city property and the way in which they view 'common' areas of apartment buildings. The entrances, stairwells, basements and attics of the city's residential property can visually be in quite alarming condition: dirty, dilapidated, poorly lit and poorly secured. This situation is changing, mainly through the initiative of private owners. Another difference from Western markets is purely demographic. Due to the rapid privatization and restructuring of Soviet society, there is little in the way of 'neighbourhoods' as defined by common income, social level, cultural dispositions. In prime central locations, an apartment building may still consist of flats owned by rich, 'new' Russians, foreign business people, alcoholics, poor families living in communal apartments and unprivatized apartments. This situation is changing but is definitely a peculiarity of the market that the investor must consider before purchasing.

Purchase settlements in cash

Around 95 per cent of residential purchases in Russia are made in cash. This is due in part to many Russians' mistrust of the banking system, schemes for tax avoidance and the current lack of mortgage programmes offered by Russian banks.

The purchase process

The purchase process can be broken down into the following steps:

- property selection;
- title research;
- structuring the agreement, purchase and registration.

Property selection

First, it is important to find a good real estate agency. Besides our agency, City Realty, there are a number of others that assist foreigners with purchases including Alexander Nedvizhimost and Talan. A business directory or the local English language newspaper, *The Saint Petersburg Times*, www.sptimes.ru, are good places to start when searching for firms. When selecting a real estate agency, it is best to find one with which you feel comfortable. The city has over 400 agencies but few have the resources necessary to work with international clients, mainly due to language constraints. It is also best to make sure that the agency that you are working with will represent your (the buyer's) interests alone rather than the interests of the seller. This is important when factoring in the amount and quality of research necessary to ensure that the property title is clean. An agency with divided interests may pay more attention to merely closing a sale than to finding a property that matches the requirements of the buyer.

Below is a list of items that are important when selecting a property. Property selection depends heavily on the purpose of the purchase (to live in full time, occasional occupancy, to rent out as an investment, to make an investment for the short or long term). Regardless, the most important points to look for are as follows:

- Location: near to historic buildings or monuments, metro stations, parks, river or canal embankments, shopping centres, kindergartens and schools.

- Building condition: old building (with or without capital renovation), a building after reconstruction, the material of which the building is constructed, (bricks, concrete panels, etc), the year when the building was built or renovated, the condition of the attic and cellar, the condition of the pipes and electric wiring, and so on.

- Entrance: stairwell condition and entrance. Apartments with entrance from the street or from a clean, renovated courtyard are preferred.

- Views and noise: views of water, historical monuments or a beautiful building are in high demand and cost more. Sometimes it may be better when the windows face a quiet, green courtyard. Prices are usually lower if the windows face a dark, small courtyard.

- Apartment layout: apartments whose windows look out from two sides of a building are preferred; the type of bathroom (separate or combined, the price is lower if there is no bathtub in place); ceiling height.

- Floor: in general, the ground and top floors are less expensive, but if the ground floor can be used for commercial purposes, the price may actually be higher than for other floors.

- Apartment condition: renovated or not.

- Safety: security, parking.

- How quickly the property can be purchased.

- Legal transparency.

The more positive points the property has to it, the higher the price.

Title research

Once a property has been selected on the basis of the physical attributes listed above, the next and arguably most important stage of the selection process occurs: research into the property history and legal status of current ownership. As mentioned above, the time and effort needed to make the proper checks into the legality of the potential purchase is one of the major differences between purchasing property in the West and in Russia.

The decision to purchase the selected property should only be made after a positive recommendation from the agency conducting the title research. Where the legality of the property is in question, it is best to select a different property. To learn more about this, the steps and the organizations involved in title research are described at the beginning of this article.

Structuring the agreement, purchase and registration

When a property is finally selected and the initial results of the title research appear to be positive the next steps usually follow:

- A deposit is typically made to the real estate agency (usually 5 per cent of the purchase price) that will be used for a down payment to the owner of the property or his/her representative in order to secure the property. If on further inspection of the legal papers associated with the property, the agency gives a recommendation not to buy the property, the buyer will receive the deposit back in full.

- When the exact date of the transaction is fixed, the buyer must be prepared to have the required purchase amount available in cash. Approximately 95 per cent of all transactions in Russia take place using cash. The cash is usually deposited on the day of transaction in a bank safe. This only allows simultaneous access to the buyer and the seller or their representatives, thus limiting the risk that the property is transferred without payment or that payment is made without transfer of the property. This safe deposit box is similar to the escrow account used in Western real estate transactions. The bank where the safe is kept, and/or the agent representing the buyer, becomes the third party ensuring that the funds are not moved until all requirements of the buyer and the seller have been fulfilled (title registration, etc).

- The control of the safe is governed by the conditions of a contract set up between the bank, the buyer and the seller. The buyer is the owner of the money until the purchase contract is signed with the seller and the apartment is registered with the state. Parties usually split the bank service fee (up to US$60).

- The parties then sign and notarize the main purchase contract and send it to the state registry. The buyer will usually pay a notary fee (1.5 per cent of the contract cost) and always pays the state registry fee (about US$20). The buyer can also sign a contract without using a notary but it is strongly recommended that the agreement be notarized to avoid problems in the future. Currently, the legal period for the State Registration Bureau's inspection of the purchase/sale agreement is 10 days.

- The buyer and seller may agree to write an arbitrary property price (for example the property's book value or any other price that the parties agree upon) into the contract if the seller wants to avoid paying a large sales tax or if the buyer wants to reduce the notary fee. However this price must not be less then inventory value (book value).

  For example:

  Real (market) price – US$80,000
  Inventory value (book value) – 450,000 roubles (US$15,000)
  Contract cost using market price – US$80,000
  Notary fee using market price – US$1,200
  or
  Contract cost using book value – US$15,000
  Notary fee using book value – US$225

- The seller usually receives his money from the bank according to the following schedule:

  - 50 per cent after receipt of the new, state registry certificate

  - 40 per cent after the cancellation of every tenant's registration

  - 10 per cent after the apartment handover act has been signed.

The time needed to complete the purchase process varies widely, depending on the type of property selected (communal or single owner) and the legal status of the current ownership. The purchase period for an apartment with only one owner can be as short as three or four weeks including the selection period, while a deal involving a communal apartment may take from four to 10 months. There are frequently deals where an owner will require not only cash for his or her property but additional property as well. Such a transaction will typically take from six to 10 weeks.

Post-purchase concerns

The main post-purchase concerns for foreign owners are taxation on income generated in Russia and concerns over the safety of their investments.

There are no restrictions on foreigners purchasing residential property in Russia. Under both the Russian Constitution and the section of the Russian Civil Code governing property ownership, any physical person, whether Russian or foreign has equal ownership rights and protection by law. Rights are typically upheld if the foreign owner has followed Russian law during and after the purchase: payment of income taxes if the apartment is used to generate income and so on.

Social protection law is still quite strong in Russia, adding to the security of property ownership by individuals.

From a taxation standpoint, it is preferable to earn money from a property, for example rental income, as a private individual with residence in Russia or as a sole proprietor rather than as a legal entity. If the owner lives in Russia for 182 days or more, he or she will be considered a resident of the Russian Federation and will be taxed on rental income at a rate of 13 per cent of this income. This is considered a personal income tax. Owners who live in Russia for less than 183 days will be required to pay a non-residential tax on income generated in Russia of 30 per cent of the rental income.

Owners who register as sole proprietors can opt to pay 6 per cent on the total revenue generated by their proprietorship or 15 per cent of the net income generated (the difference between documented revenues and expenses). No VAT need be paid in either case. The drawback to registering as a sole proprietor is that the proprietor must register with the tax authorities and create tax reports and submit them to the state four times a year; this requires accounting and the use of an accountant. A further point to note is that sole proprietor registration can only be adopted for businesses that generate less than 15 million roubles in revenue per year (approximately 410,000 euros).

A legal entity (company) following regular Russian accounting,[1] will be required to pay 18 per cent VAT on property revenues as well as 24 per cent profit tax on income generated from a property. A legal entity can also apply for simplified accounting and taxation status. The rules for this are exactly the same as those for the sole proprietor listed above. The company can adopt to pay 6 per cent on the total revenue generated by operations or 15 per cent of the net income generated (difference between documented revenues and expenses). Similarly to the rules for sole proprietors, VAT is not charged in either cases, but the simplified system can only be adopted for businesses that generate less than 15 million roubles per year.

Note

1. Companies in Russia can opt to use one of two systems of accounting. The simplified accounting method is either a flat 6 per cent tax on revenues (not profit) or 15 per cent on revenues minus costs. No VAT is due on simplified accounting bills. The company cannot collect or charge VAT. The simplified method can only be used for companies that have revenues of less than 15 million roubles per year (US$500,000). The regular accounting method is what most companies use. It is in the form of profit taxes paid on revenues minus costs, and VAT is applicable.

St Petersburg Real Estate Sector

Due diligence and acquisition case studies

Beiten Burkhardt

The purpose of this chapter is to familiarize foreign investors with the peculiarities of acquiring real estate in St Petersburg. The paper consists of two sections. The first (acquisition case studies) is devoted to issues of how and for what purposes foreign investors may acquire real estate in St Petersburg. The second section (due diligence case studies) describes typical legal risks that arise during real estate acquisition.

Acquisition case studies

Foreign investors are most frequently interested in acquiring the ownership rights to or lease of land plots, buildings or apartments. No significant restrictions on acquisition of real estate by foreigners exist in Russia (see Case 1, below).

Real estate located in St Petersburg may be either privately owned or owned by St Petersburg. As a regional subject of the Russian Federation, St Petersburg is entitled to manage real estate owned by the city.

As mass privatization of land only began in 2002 (after the Russian Federation Land Code's entry into force), most land plots located in St Petersburg are owned by the city and are provided to investors in accordance with the provisions of federal and regional legislation on land privatization (see Cases 2 and 4, below).

St Petersburg continues to own a large number of unfinished buildings and buildings requiring reconstruction, which investors are frequently interested in acquiring in order to open shops, hotels or business centres. The procedure for acquiring buildings owned by St Petersburg is governed by St Petersburg regional investment legislation (see Case 3).

Land plots and buildings privately owned by legal entities may be acquired either as real estate objects or by acquiring shares or ownership interests in the share capitals of the legal entities that have the rights to the real estate objects (see Case 5, below).

The overwhelming majority of apartments in St Petersburg are privately owned. When acquiring apartments, clients frequently ask whether apartments may be used not only for residential purposes but also as offices (Cases 6 and 7).

Case 1

Mr Smith owns a shoe manufacturing company registered in England. He would like to build a factory in Russia in order to increase the competitiveness of his factory's products on the Russian market. His Russian business partner, Mr Ivanov, offered to sell Mr Smith a land plot for the factory. Mr Smith told Mr Ivanov that he was prepared to lease the land plot from him for 50 years, as he presumed foreign individuals and legal entities do not have the right to acquire ownership rights to land plots in Russia. Is Mr Smith right?

Mr Smith is not right. As a general rule, foreign individuals and legal entities have the right to acquire the ownership rights to or lease of land plots and other real estate objects on a par with Russian individuals and legal entities. Russian legislation only establishes restrictions on acquisition of ownership rights to land plots by foreigners in respect of border territories, agricultural land and land not allowed on the market:

- Under Article 15 Point 3 of the Russian Federation Land Code dated 25 October 2001 (hereafter the 'Land Code'), foreign individuals and legal entities may not acquire ownership rights to land plots located in border territories, the list of which is to be established by the President of the Russian Federation.

- Under Article 3 of the Federal Law 'On Turnover of Agricultural Land', foreign individuals, and legal entities in whose share capitals the share of foreign individuals or foreign legal entities exceeds 50 per cent, may hold only lease rights to agricultural land.

- Finally, under Article 27 of the Land Code, Russian and foreign individuals and legal entities may not acquire ownership rights to land occupied by wilderness areas and national parks, as well as areas occupied by elements of the Russian Federation's military forces and the Russian Federation Federal Security Service, and other installations essential for state security.

Case 2

Mr Smith did not like Mr Ivanov's land plot. After a long search, he found an alternative located on the outskirts of St Petersburg that is suitable for construction of the factory. The land plot, however, 'does not have an owner'. Can Mr Smith acquire the ownership right to this land plot from the state?

Under current Russian Federation legislation, Mr Smith has the right to acquire the ownership of the land plot for construction of the factory (see section on 'Acquiring ownership rights' below). In practice, however, the state and municipalities tend to provide investors with rights to lease land plots for construction purposes together with rights to privatize the plots once the construction work is complete (see section on 'Granting lease rights' below). This practice is primarily connected with the state's intention to prevent land from being acquired for further speculation.

Acquiring ownership rights to state-owned land plots

The granting of ownership rights to land plots for construction purposes to investors is governed by the Land Code and the St Petersburg Law 'On the Procedure for Providing Real Estate Objects Owned by St Petersburg for Construction and Reconstruction', dated 17 June 2004 (hereafter the 'Law on Provision of St Petersburg Real Estate').

In accordance with Article 30 Point 2 of the Land Code together with Article 4 Point 4 of the Law on Provision of St Petersburg Real Estate, ownership rights to land plots for construction are granted only at auctions or by tender. A tender is conducted when the conditions for using the land plot need to be established by the land plot owner.

Auctions are conducted to sell formed land plots that have undergone cadastral registration. Formation of a land plot includes, in particular, the preparation of a draft of the land boundaries, determination of its permitted use, and establishment of the technical conditions for connecting buildings or other constructions to engineering networks. In St Petersburg, formation is mostly performed by the City Planning and Architectural Committee and by specialized companies.

Cadastral registration results in assignment of a cadastre number to the land plot and preparation of the plot's cadastre card. The card is a plan showing the main graphical and textual information about the land plot, in particular its area, location, permitted use and cadastre number. Only land plots that have undergone cadastral registration may be subject to sale (and lease). At the moment, cadastral registrations in St Petersburg are performed by the Land Resources and Planning Committee (hereafter the 'LRPC').

After formation and cadastral registration of a land plot, the government of St Petersburg, or a state body authorized by it, adopts a resolution to conduct an auction. The St Petersburg Property Fund is responsible for organizing auctions.

Auction results are executed by a protocol signed by the organizer and winner of the auction. A land plot sale and purchase agreement is signed on the basis of the protocol. For St Petersburg, the agreement is signed by the City Property Management Committee (hereafter the 'CPMC').

A purchaser's ownership right to a land plot becomes effective when it is registered in the Single State Register of Rights to Real Estate and Transactions Therewith (hereafter the 'Register of Rights to Real Estate'). Currently, registrations in St Petersburg are performed by the Main Administration of the Federal Registration Service for St Petersburg and Leningrad Oblast (hereafter the 'Federal Registration Service').

Granting lease rights to land plots for construction purposes

Under provisions of the Land Code, Mr Smith may also lease a land plot from the city of St Petersburg and, upon completion of construction and registration of the ownership right to the factory building in the Register of Rights to Real Estate, privatize the plot under the building. Under Article 36 of the Land Code, legal entities owning buildings, structures or constructions located on state-owned or municipally owned land plots have the exclusive right to privatize such plots.

Granting lease rights to land plots for construction purposes is provided for by Article 30 of the Russian Federation Land Code. Land plots for construction purposes are granted for lease without conducting auctions, subject to preliminary approval of the locations of the structures. If there is no preliminary approval of the locations, land plots for construction purposes are granted for lease only through auction.

Prior to concluding a lease agreement, formation and cadastral registration of the land plot must be completed (as detailed in the previous section).

In St Petersburg, when granting a land plot for construction for lease to an investor, an agreement for lease of the land plot on investment conditions is concluded between the government of St Petersburg and the investor. A lease agreement on investment conditions usually stipulates the rent amount, deadlines for completing construction, the investor's rights to the real estate object constructed by the investor (ownership, current management), the consequences of non-fulfilment of investment conditions (non-fulfilment is, as a rule, the basis for refusal to register the ownership right to the constructed real estate object).

Land plot lease agreements concluded for more than one year shall enter into force not at the date of signing but when registered in the Register of Rights to Real Estate.

Case 3

English company C wants to open a hotel in St Petersburg. In one of the city's historical districts the company has found an unfinished hotel building owned by St Petersburg. On what conditions may English company C acquire the unfinished hotel building?

Under the general rule established in Article 3 Point 2 of the Law on Provision of St Petersburg Real Estate, real estate owned by St Petersburg is granted through auction (see section on 'Acquiring ownership rights'). If real estate objects are buildings subject to reconstruction or completion of construction works, the subjects of the relevant auctions are rights to conclude investment agreements. An investment agreement provides for the rights and obligations of St Petersburg and the investor in respect of reconstruction or completion of construction of a building.

Exceptions to the general rule are provided for in Article 5 Point 2 paragraph 4 of the Law on Provision of St Petersburg Real Estate, according to which buildings classified as objects of the hotel and tourist infrastructure may be granted to investors on the basis of investment agreements with the government of St Petersburg without the need for auctions. In St Petersburg, auctions are also not required for granting dormitory buildings, dilapidated buildings, religious buildings such as churches and cathedrals, and buildings intended for activities in the fields of science, public health, ecology, education, physical culture and sport.

At the moment, no standard form of an investment agreement for granting unfinished buildings to investors who will complete construction has yet been developed. An investment agreement establishes, in particular, the conditions the investor must fulfil in order to obtain the ownership right to the building once the construction work is complete, as well as the cost of the right to conclude the investment agreement. The ownership right to a finished building may be registered in the Register of Rights to Real Estate only after fulfilment of all conditions of the investment agreement.

In addition to the Law on Provision of St Petersburg Real Estate, when executive authorities of St Petersburg grant buildings for reconstruction and completion of construction to investors, they are also guided by the Regulation on the Procedure for Decision-Making on the Provision of Real Estate Objects for Construction and Reconstruction, approved by Resolution of the government of St Petersburg, No 1592 dated 21 September 2004, (hereafter the 'Regulation on Provision of Real Estate Objects for Construction and Reconstruction'). In order to conclude an investment agreement for completing the construction of the building, English company C must file the relevant application to the St Petersburg State Enterprise 'Management of Investments' (hereafter the 'Management of Investments'). The Management of Investments coordinates the consideration of the application by various St Petersburg executive authorities, and prepares a conclusion as to whether the engineering and city-planning documents prepared by the investor comply with the requirements of the Regulation on Provision of Real Estate Objects for Construction and Reconstruction. On issuance of a favourable conclusion, the government of St Petersburg prepares a resolution to grant the real estate object to the investor, laying out the investment conditions, on the basis of which resolution the CPMC signs the investment agreement.

Case 4

German company Z wants to open a shop in St Petersburg. For this purpose it has been offered a building of a former weaving factory. When the head of company Z found out that the seller of the building is not the owner of the land it stands on, he refused to buy the building. In his opinion, the owner of the land plot should also own the building situated on it, as the building is inseparably attached to the land plot. Is he right?

The opinion of the head of company Z is incorrect. In contrast to legal regimes in other countries (for example, Germany), in Russia land plots and buildings are distinct real estate objects. Therefore, in Russia a land plot and a building situated on it may be owned by different parties.

Under Article 552 Point 3 of the Russian Federation Civil Code (hereafter the 'RF CC'), the owner of a building situated on land that he or she does not own can sell the building without the consent of the owner of the land plot, provided that this does not contradict the conditions for using the land plot established by the lease agreement. Therefore, prior to signing a building sale and purchase agreement, it is essential for company Z to check the lease agreement between the land plot's owner and the seller of the building for any prohibitions established on sale of the respective building.

If sale of the building is not prohibited by the lease agreement between the owner of the land plot and the seller of the building, then company Z will also acquire, together with the ownership right to the building, the right to use the land plot on the same conditions as the seller.

The Land Code contains a number of provisions aimed at both eliminating and preventing situations where a land plot and a building are owned by different parties.

As mentioned above (in the section on 'Acquiring ownership rights'), the owners of buildings situated on state or municipally owned land plots have the right to privatize them. Furthermore, owners of buildings situated on land belonging to other people have the right of first refusal on purchase of the respective land plots in case of sale thereof.

As a general rule, the Land Code prohibits the sale of buildings separately from land plots or of land plots separately from buildings if they are owned by the same party.

Case 5

German company Z would like to avoid the complicated procedure of registering the ownership right to the building in the Russian Register of Rights to Real Estate and Transactions Therewith. Is it possible to acquire the legal entity that owns the building?

Company Z may acquire 100 per cent of the shares or ownership interests in the legal entity that owns the building (land plot) and, therefore, avoid the procedure of registering the ownership right.

However, company Z should take into account that acquiring ownership interest in a Russian limited liability company (hereafter 'LLC') will involve making amendments to the Articles of Association of the acquired LLC relating to the change of the owner, and state registration of these amendments with the tax authority at the LLC's location. Company Z will not be a participant of the LLC owning the building (at least where third parties are concerned) until the amendments to the Articles of Association have been formally registered.

From the organizational point of view, the procedure for state registration of amendments to an LLC's Articles of Association is no less complicated than the procedure for registering the ownership right to a land plot. However, it is less time-consuming. While a tax inspectorate registers amendments to Articles of Association within five business days, the Federal Registration Service takes up to a month to register a purchaser's ownership right to a real estate object.

When acquiring shares in a joint stock company, company Z should bear in mind that ownership rights to shares acquired under a sale and purchase agreement commence when an entry is made in the company's shareholders register to show the transfer of the ownership rights to the shares to company Z. An entry on the transfer of the ownership rights to the shares shall be inserted immediately after the submission of all necessary documents.

In practice, sellers frequently offer shares or ownership interests in companies that own buildings in order to circumvent value-added tax. Under Russian legislation, transactions for the sale and purchase of shares or ownership interests in companies' share capitals are not subject to value-added tax. As of 1 January 2005 value-added tax does not apply to sales of land plots, either. Such offers should be treated with caution, however, as in acquiring ownership interests (shares) in a company owning real estate, the purchaser, first, also 'acquires' the risks connected with the company's previous activities, and second, may be obliged to withhold taxes from the selling price.

Case 6

German entrepreneur Mr Müller has owned an apartment in the centre of St Petersburg for two years. The apartment is on the second floor of a block of apartments. Mr Müller would like to establish a subsidiary of his German company in Russia. As he would like to save money by not renting an office, he has decided to have his firm registered at the address of his apartment. Is this lawful?

The registration and location of a legal entity's business premises at an apartment is unlawful. These actions contradict Article 288 Point 3 of the RF CC, according to which an owner may use his/her apartment as an office only after conversion of the apartment into non-residential premises.

Mr Müller should also take into account that, as a consequence of converting his apartment into non-residential premises, it formally can no longer be used for residential purposes. In practice this means that all the people residing at the apartment would have to de-register from it and register at a new residential address.

Case 7

Despite searching intensively, Mr Müller has failed to find a suitable office for the Russian subsidiary of his German company. He consults his lawyer as to whether it is possible to register his apartment as non-residential premises.

At the moment, issues of converting residential premises into non-residential premises are governed by the new Russian Federation Residential Code (hereafter the 'RF RC'), which entered into force on 1 March 2005. Under the provisions of Article 22 of the RF RC, converting Mr Müller's apartment into non-residential premises is possible subject to the following requirements:

- The apartment must be on the first floor of the building, or the premises situated directly beneath it must also be non-residential.

- The apartment must be accessible without the use of facilities providing access to other residential premises (stairs and landings), or it must be technically possible to provide separate access to the apartment. Thus, for example, if Mr Müller's apartment was situated on the first floor, following its conversion into non-residential premises a separate entrance from the street would have to be constructed.

- The apartment must be fully, not partially, converted into non-residential premises. Furthermore, no permanent residents may continue living there.

- Mr Müller's ownership right to the apartment must be free from any rights of third parties. Thus, for example, if Mr Müller has pledged the apartment, the pledge must first be lifted.

Subject to the above requirements, and following the submission of all necessary documents, Mr Müller's apartment will be converted into non-residential premises.

Under the new RF RC, a decision on conversion into non-residential premises must be made by a local authority. In St Petersburg this authority is the administration of the municipality in which the apartment is situated.

In St Petersburg, decisions on conversion into non-residential premises are made directly by the Governor of St Petersburg (Article 14 Point 2 of the RF RC and Article 3 of the Law of St Petersburg 'On Procedure and Conditions for Converting Residential Buildings and Premises into Non-residential Buildings and Premises', No 69-21 dated 28 April 1997).

Due diligence case studies

Due diligence is primarily aimed at examining a seller's ownership rights to real estate (see Case 1 below). In the case of real estate acquisition, the examination covers the existence of possible corporate risks (Cases 2, 3 and 4) as well as the possible uses of the real estate object (Case 5). Furthermore, as a rule, within the framework of a due diligence a check is made as to whether registration of the ownership right to the real estate object has been performed by a proper state authority (see Case 6) and whether the real estate object has been encumbered in any way (see Case 7).

The situations described in Cases 1, 2, 3 and 4 apply to acquisitions of both buildings and land plots.

Case 1

The management of company Z is not willing to spend time on due diligence on the seller's ownership right to the building (as the seller has provided company Z with an excerpt from the Register of Rights to Real Estate verifying the seller's ownership right to the building). Furthermore, the management of company Z has learned from the Law 'On State Registration of Rights to Real Estate and Transactions Therewith' that the authorities responsible for registering rights to real estate check the validity of documents submitted by applicants, the respective rights held by the individual or authority that prepared the documents, and the existence of previously registered rights. Is this position wise?

The position taken by the management of company Z is unwise for two reasons. First, although the state registration of the ownership rights in the Register of Rights to Real Estate is the only evidence of such rights, information in the Register is not 'publicly credible'. This means that even if the seller provides an excerpt verifying his/her ownership of the building, company Z cannot be sure that it is acquiring the building (land plot) from the lawful owner. Consequently, the excerpt does not guarantee that the right to own the building acquired by company Z may not be contested by third parties that owned the real estate object in the past.

Due diligence allows for two methods for evaluating the risk of possible claims from former owners of the building against company Z:

- examination of all transactions for transfer of the ownership right to the building, including its privatization;

- examination of all transactions for transfer of the ownership right to the building that were performed prior to acquisition by the seller.

If the due diligence determines that the building (land plot) was privatized in conformity with current legislation and that all subsequent transactions for transfer of the ownership right are lawful, no claims by former owners of the building (or land plot) are likely to succeed, and they are therefore not to be expected.

Due diligence on all transactions for transfer of the ownership right to the building that were performed prior to acquisition by the seller makes it possible to determine whether company Z will be a bona fide purchaser of the real estate object. Under the general rule provided for by Russian legislation, a bona fide purchaser of a real estate object becomes the owner thereof as of state registration (Articles 223, 302 of the RF CC).

The second flaw in the thinking of company Z's managers is that the examination of documents by the Federal Registration Service is of a rather technical nature. The purpose of examination is not to cover all possible legal risks connected with the acquisition of the real estate object. As a rule, the scrutiny is limited to verifying the completeness and authenticity of the documents required for inserting an entry on the transfer of the ownership right to the real estate into the Register of Rights to Real Estate.

Case 2

Russian company LLC Y has sold, under a sale and purchase agreement, its building in St Petersburg to American company X. For LLC Y, the sale and purchase agreement was signed by Mr A as its general director. Three months after registration of the transfer of the ownership right to the building to American company X, the Russian seller filed a claim to invalidate the building sale and purchase agreement and to regain the building it had sold. LLC Y claims that by the time of the signing of the sale and purchase agreement Mr A's powers as general director had terminated. As evidence, LLC Y has submitted the minutes of the General Participants Meeting, according to which on the day preceding the signing of the agreement Mr A's powers terminated and another general director was elected to replace him. Company X refers to the fact that, according to the excerpt from the Single State Register of Legal Entities, Mr A was the general director of LLC Y at the moment of the signing. Can LLC Y's claim against American company X be successful?

LLC Y's claim can be successful and will be satisfied. LLC Y can prove that Mr A's powers as its general director had terminated by the time he signed the building sale and purchase agreement. Company X may not refer in court to the content of the Single State Register of Legal Entities as it was on the date of the signing of the agreement, as the information contained therein is not 'publicly credible'.

In Russia, the general director is the head of the company. He or she is entitled to conclude transactions on behalf of the legal entity without a power of attorney. The general director is elected by resolution of the company's General Participants (Shareholders) Meeting for the period established by the Articles of Association. The general director's powers automatically terminate following the lapse of the stipulated period of time.

The powers of the general director of a commercial company are verified by the minutes of the General Participants (Shareholders) Meeting on his/her election, and by the company's Articles of Association. By referring to these documents, company X could easily have established that Mr A's powers as LLC Y's general director would have terminated by the time he signed the building sale and purchase agreement. The purchaser could have requested to see the minutes of the resolution of LLC Y's General Participants Meeting to re-elect Mr A or appoint a new general director and thus avoided the problem.

Under Russian Federation legislation, a claim to invalidate a building sale and purchase agreement, and to enforce the consequences of the invalidity of the transaction, must be filed to a state arbitration court at the location of the real estate. This rule is mandatory and may not be changed by the parties' agreement.

An arbitration court's ruling in favour of LLC Y would serve as the basis for its registration as the owner of the building in the Register of Rights to Real Estate.

Case 3

The same conditions apply as in Case 2, but here LLC Y claims that the agreement is not valid as the general director concluded it without the approval of the company's General Participants Meeting. The approval of the General Participants Meeting was required as the value of tho building exceeds 25 per cent of the total value of the company's assets. Can LLC Y's claim against company X be successful?

LLC Y's claim will be satisfied if the company proves, on the basis of its accounting reports data, that the value of the building actually exceeds 25 per cent of the value of all the company's assets.

Under Russian legislation, transactions connected with the sale by an LLC or a joint stock company of assets valued in excess of 25 per cent of the value of all the company's assets are considered large-scale transactions and, as a general rule, require the approval of the General Participants (Shareholders) Meeting.

In order to verify whether a sale of a building is a large-scale transaction, the latest version of the seller's Articles of Association and the accounting reports for the latest reporting period that preceded the building's sale should be inspected.

As a result of due diligence, company X might have determined that the sale of the building was a large-scale transaction for LLC Y. Company X might then have requested approval of the building sale and purchase agreement by LLC Y's General Participants Meeting. By acting so, company X might have avoided the problem.

Case 4

Company X managed to acquire the ownership right to the building only because it offered LLC Y a higher price than the other potential purchaser, Russian company B. As company B was unwilling to drop the idea of acquiring the ownership right to the building (land plot) in question, it informed the Russian Federation Federal Antimonopoly Service (hereafter the 'FAS') of the transaction between companies X and Y in hope that the FAS would terminate the building sale and purchase agreement. Can the FAS contest company X's ownership right to the acquired building?

Under Article 18 Point 9 of the RSFSR Law 'On Competition and Restriction of Monopolistic Activities in Commodities Markets', No

948-1 dated 22 March 1991, (hereafter the 'Law on Competition'), a court may invalidate a transaction contested by the FAS if the transaction violates antimonopoly legislation. The claim must be lodged within one year as of the moment the FAS became aware of the transaction. A court ruling invalidating the building sale and purchase agreement serves as the basis for registering LLC Y as the owner of the building. Until a court issues a ruling in favour of the FAS, the transaction is considered valid.

In practice, the Federal Registration Service may refuse to register the ownership right to real estate, if the sale and purchase agreement was concluded without the FAS's prior consent.

Under Article 18 of the Law on Competition, in the version that came into force on 22 March 2005, acquisition of real estate by an economic entity (hereafter the 'purchaser') from another economic entity (hereafter the 'seller') is subject to the FAS's prior consent, if:

- the balance value of the property being alienated exceeds 10 per cent of the balance value of the seller's fixed production assets; and

- the aggregate value of the assets of the purchaser, the seller and parties directly or indirectly controlling the seller exceeds 30 million minimum wages as established by federal law (at the moment of publication, approximately US$108,546,000).

Until 22 March 2005, the FAS's prior consent was required if the aggregate balance value of the assets of the purchaser and the seller exceeded 200,000 minimum wages as established by federal law (at the moment of publication, approximately US$723,638).

Case 5

The land plot that Mr Smith hopes to use for construction of the factory is, according to the excerpt from the Register of Rights to Real Estate and the cadastre plan, classified as 'settlement land for agricultural purposes'. Might this be an obstacle to construction of the shoe manufacturing factory?

One of the goals of due diligence on a real estate object is to determine the types of permitted use thereof. The information on permitted use of a land plot is provided in its cadastre card.

Regarding designations, the Land Code divides all land plots into seven categories. Industrial land and settlement land may be used for construction of factories.

In St Petersburg, the overwhelming majority of land plots are classified as settlement land. Whether a land plot located in St Petersburg and classified as settlement land may be used as a site for a factory depends on which territorial zone the land plot belongs to. Under Article 85 Point 1 of the Land Code, city-planning rules may assign settlement land to one of the following territorial zones:

- residential;

- public and business;

- industrial;

- of engineering and transport infrastructures;

- recreational;

- agricultural;

- of military objects.

As the land plot chosen by Mr Smith is classified as settlement land and assigned to the agricultural territorial zone, the shoe manufacturing factory may not be constructed on it. Under Article 85 Point 1 of the Land Code, land plots in agricultural territorial zones are intended only for agricultural production. In order to have a shoe factory constructed on such land, it is necessary to change the land plot's functional designation: in other words, to 'convert' the land plot from an agricultural territorial zone land plot into an industrial territorial zone land plot.

In St Petersburg, the procedure for changing land designations is governed by the Law 'On Regulating the City-Planning Activities in St Petersburg'. Under this legislation, assignment of a land plot to a particular territorial zone is established by city-planning rules. City-planning rules form a part of the St Petersburg Construction Development Rules, which have the effect of a law. (At the moment of publication, however, the St Petersburg Construction Development Rules have not been established.) Therefore, as a general rule, changing a land plot's functional designation requires a new law.

However, an exception is provided for land plots that are located in territories for which no city-planning rules have been enacted. Until 1 January 2006 the permitted use (functional designation) of these land plots is established by temporary city-planning rules. Temporary city-planning rules are to be established in St Petersburg not by the Legislative Assembly but by the City-Planning and Architectural Committee of the government of St Petersburg.

Case 6

Russian LLC W would like to sell a land plot to Mr Smith. LLC W has provided Mr Smith, inter alia, with the Certificate of Registration of the Ownership Right to the land plot, which was issued on 20 October 1996 by the LRPC. Mr Smith is concerned that LLC W is not the owner of the land plot (building), as the ownership right thereto was not registered by the Federal Registration Service.

Mr Smith's concern is unfounded. The state body responsible for maintaining the Register of Rights to Real Estate in St Petersburg has changed several times. From the beginning of 1995 until 17 July 1998, state registrations of rights to real estate in St Petersburg were performed by the LRPC. This authority was vested in the LRPC in accordance with Order of the President of the Russian Federation 'On the State Land Cadastre and Registration of Documents on Rights to Real Estate', dated 11 December 1993.

From 17 July 1998 until 31 December 2004, rights to real estate in St Petersburg were registered by the State Enterprise of Justice 'City Bureau for the Registration of Rights to Real Estate' (hereafter the 'CBR'). The CBR was subordinate to the government of St Petersburg. It was established on the basis of Article 3 Point 2 of the Law 'On State Registration of Rights to Real Estate and Transactions Therewith'. Under this law, establishment of the bodies responsible for the registration of rights to real estate was vested in the regional subjects of the Russian Federation.

Since 1 January 2005 registrations of rights to real estate and transactions therewith have been performed by the Main Administration of the Federal Registration Service for St Petersburg and Leningrad Oblast. The Federal Registration Service is subordinate to the Russian Federation Ministry of Justice.

The Federal Registration Service was established within the framework of ongoing administrative reforms on the basis of Order of the President of the Russian Federation 'On the System and Structure of the Federal Executive Authorities', dated 9 March 2004. The goal of establishing the Federal Registration Service is to form a unified system of the state authorities responsible for the registration of rights to real estate throughout the Russian Federation.

Case 7

American company N is interested in acquiring a building in St Petersburg that is owned by a Russian legal entity. According to the excerpt from the Register of Rights to Real Estate, the building is a 'revealed object of cultural heritage', which is encumbered with the obligation to preserve it. The management of company N would like to know whether this could be an obstacle to acquiring the ownership right to the building on the basis of a sale and purchase agreement.

Under Article 48 Point 1 of the Federal Law 'On Cultural Heritage Objects (Historical and Cultural Monuments) of the Peoples of the Russian Federation', No 73-FZ dated 25 June 2002, (hereafter the 'Law on Monuments'), cultural heritage objects, regardless of the category of their historical and cultural significance, may be either state or privately owned. On this basis, the mere fact that the building is an object of cultural heritage does not prevent acquisition of the ownership right to it by company N. However, the management of company N should take into account that, under Article 48 of the Law on Monuments, upon state registration of the agreement for the sale and purchase of this building company N will assume all obligations of the former owner to preserve the cultural heritage object, which will encumber the ownership right to this object. In particular, restrictions will apply to repairing the building and re-planning its layout.

Manufacturing and Natural Resources

The Market for Engineering Services

Igor Yegorov, BISNIS Representative in Northwest Russia

Introduction

Economic growth in St Petersburg and northwest Russia is supported by rising fixed capital investment, which reached US$1.5 billion in the Leningrad Region (which surrounds St Petersburg) in 2003 and US$3 billion in St Petersburg itself. In 2004 these figures are expected to increase further. Whereas over 70 per cent of fixed capital investment in St Petersburg goes into the real estate market, the Leningrad Region has recorded increasing industrial investment in new construction, equipment, technology and renovation. It is important to note that, depending of the sector, 65–80 per cent of fixed capital in the region is depreciated. This fact indicates a high, ongoing demand for capital investment, thus supporting the need for quality engineering services in a wide variety of industries.

This paper focuses on the engineering services market in St Petersburg and the Leningrad Region. It first presents a brief overview of investment activity in the region, because the volume of investment is closely correlated to the size of the engineering services market. The size of the market can be approximately estimated as a share (usually 3–7 per cent) of capital investment volume. The supply of engineering services in St Petersburg – market players and their strengths and weaknesses – is also discussed, as well as factors that should be carefully considered by foreign engineering companies hoping to enter the market. This chapter is divided into the following sections:

- an overview of investment activity in St Petersburg and the Leningrad Region;

- the size of the engineering services market;

- the engineering services market in St Petersburg;

- market entry strategies.

An overview of investment activity in St Petersburg and the Leningrad Region

The economy of St Petersburg and the Leningrad Region has been steadily growing over the past three years. For example, in the first nine months of 2004, the index of industrial production in St Petersburg increased by 13.9 per cent, while in the Leningrad Region it grew by 11.2 per cent. Around 86 per cent of all industrial production in St Petersburg is concentrated in four sectors: machine-tool building and metalworking, food processing, power generation and metallurgy. The neighbouring Leningrad Region is overtaking St Petersburg in industrial development as it is in close proximity to the city and has sufficient space to develop large projects. The key industries of the Leningrad Region are food processing, oil processing and transportation, chemicals and petrochemicals, forestry, wood pro-cessing and pulp and paper, metallurgy, metalworking and engineer-ing, and production of building materials. While oil processing and petrochemical industries are confined to a limited number of compa-nies, food processing, metalworking and machine-tool manufacturing, and wood processing are much more diversified. For example, approx-imately 770 enterprises are active in the wood processing sector of the Leningrad Region, including 80 large (in Russian terms; a large firm in Russia would correspond to a relatively small company in other countries, such as the United States) logging companies, 20 furniture manufacturers, 20 saw mills, and so on. There are currently 62 medium and large companies working in the machine-tool building sector of the Leningrad Region. The building materials industry is represented by 35 medium and large companies. There are between three and 10 large companies in each of such important sectors as petrochemicals, chem-icals and metallurgy as well.

According to the State Statistical Committee, industrial growth in the Leningrad Region in 2003 reached 120.3 per cent compared with the previous year. Total investment in the region over that period grew by 36 per cent compared with 2002 and amounted to RUB 44 billion (US$1.5 billion). The total capital investment in the first quarter of 2004 increased 1.4 times, to RUB 17.4 billion (US$600 million) in com-parison with the same period of the previous year. The most important investment projects in early 2004 included an electrical substation, the first stage of a plant for production of wall plates, a stone crushing plant, a polystyrene production plant, the first stage of a plant for producing aluminium cans, a sawmill, a furniture production line, a pedestrian bridge and various other projects. Extrapolating from this, one can confidently predict that for 2004 as a whole, capital investment in the Leningrad Region may reach US$2–2.4 billion. Investment in fixed capital in the Leningrad Region is forecast to increase by 30 per cent in 2005 compared with 2004. In particular, foreign investment is expected to increase by 11 per cent to US$300 million, including construction of new plants and expansion of existing ones. It is clear that the main market for engineering services is in the Leningrad Region around St Petersburg, as industrial enterprises and plants mainly build there (the city does not have enough space for construction of large plants).

Investment in fixed capital in St Petersburg amounted to RUB 90 billion (US$3 billion) in 2003. In the first half of 2004, large and medium-sized industrial enterprises in St Petersburg spent RUB 7.1 billion (US$245 million) on investment projects. This represents less than 25 per cent of total investment in St Petersburg over that period. The food processing industry is the leader in terms of investment share. In 2003 alone, food processing companies in St Petersburg invested RUB 8.5 billion (approximately US$280 million) in production, half of the total investment in St Petersburg's industries in that year. This investment may have been used for anything ranging from the purchase of land, buildings and premises to the acquisition of equipment or major refurbishment of capital equipment and/or property. In the first half of 2004, food-processing companies invested RUB 2.5 billion (US$86 million). Overall, the largest share of investment in St Petersburg (unlike the Leningrad Region) is directed into the real estate market, both commercial and residential, in such projects as development of trade centres, office buildings, warehouses and dwelling houses. For example, in the single year 2003, large retail chains alone poured an estimated US$300 million into construction of trade centres, making up 60 per cent of investment in commercial real estate. According to some estimates, total investment in real estate in St Petersburg in 2004 may exceed the US$1.8 billion reached in 2003 by 25 per cent, with more than 60 per cent of that amount invested in residential property. There is also some infrastructure investment in the city, mainly in road construction (ring roads), the flood protection barrier, a water treatment plant, port facilities and, to a lesser extent, rail transport.

To give an idea of the nature of the recent investment projects that have been announced in 2004, a sample list of the most prominent projects is provided:

- The mineral fertilizers terminal in the St Petersburg seaport is to be expanded by 9 ha. The US$13 million project envisions construction of new warehouses, an unloading facility and installation of other equipment. The cost of the fertilizers terminal project has already exceeded US$80 million.

- Lukoil's oil transhipment terminal in the port of Vysotsk outside Vyborg (in the Leningrad Region) has been expanded. The initially planned capacity of the terminal has been increased by 65 per cent, raising the cost of the project from US$170 million by an extra US$225 million. The design, delivery and construction works are being jointly carried out by American company Fluor Corporation and LUKOIL-Neftegazstroy.

- Svetogorsk (International Paper's subsidiary) built a solid waste facility at a cost of US$2.5 million, and new production premises at a cost of US$17 million. Projects totalling more than US$100 million are being prepared.

- Finnish company Elcoteq Network Oy will assemble integrated circuits for the telecommunication equipment manufactured by Husqvarna and Ericsson. The new facility will employ 1,000 people, and the investment in the new operation is announced to be US$100 million.

- Merloni TermoSanitari Rus Ltd, a Russian subsidiary of the Italian MTS Group, is starting assembly of ARISTON water heaters in November in the Vsevolozhsk District of the Leningrad Region. The current capacity of the assembly line is 500,000 heaters per year. However, since demand for water heaters in Russia is steadily rising, MTS has decided to double production capacity over 18 months to a million heaters per year. This requires an increase of investment from 30 million to 45 million euros. Merloni also plans to attract more local suppliers of components for its Russian production.

- The Swedish concern Electrolux AB intends to open a factory in St Petersburg in 2005. The plant will assemble 250,000 Zanussi and Electrolux washing machines per year. Later its output may be increased fourfold.

- The Finnish company Nokian Tires has started building a car tyre plant in the Vsevolozhsk district of the Leningrad Region. The first stage of the plant is scheduled to be launched in the third quarter of 2005. The new plant's production capacity will be a million tyres per year, increasing to eight million over the next decade. Investment is partially financed by a loan from the European Bank for Reconstruction and Development, and the total investment is said to be 52 million euros.

- Severstal Steel Mill's total investment in Izhorsky Pipe Plant will amount to US$100 million, equipping it to produce 450,000 tons of large-diameter pipes a year. An additional investment of US$25 million at a later stage would bring the annual output to 800,000 tons.

The size of the engineering services market

The suppliers of engineering services in northwest Russia are concentrated in St Petersburg, due to the city's scientific and research potential, although demand for such services is more evenly spread across the northwest. St Petersburg and the Leningrad and Vologda Regions are the core industrial regions, but all the other regions require modernization of their industries too. Examples include port infrastructure in Murmansk and Archangel, wood processing in Komi, Karelia and Archangel, and food processing and manufacturing in Novgorod and Pskov. St Petersburg, however, represents 30 per cent of the northwest's industrial production, Vologda Region 17 per cent and the Leningrad Region 14 per cent.

Demand for engineering services is closely correlated to the volume of reconstruction, modernization and new construction, which is largely captured in official reporting as fixed capital investment. Hence, the size of the engineering services market can be roughly estimated as a share (3–10 per cent, depending on the project in question) of the total fixed investment. However, it is difficult to evaluate the size of the engineering service market in St Petersburg and the Leningrad Region due to the lack of reliable statistical information on total investment, including fixed capital investment. There are official figures, but they can be considered deficient for two main reasons. First, the authorities pay little attention to industrial development and industrial policy, and there is thus no official pressure for reliable information and improvement of accounting methodology. Second, there is corrupt accounting by companies, partly because they tend to understate profits, but also because of Soviet accounting principles still used in Russia. It is hardly necessary to say that accounting principles inherited from the Soviet times significantly deviate from Western accounting principles, and from the reporting standards required in a market economy.

For example, the positive statistical reports of growing investment figures in St Petersburg largely reflect surging real estate prices (although new construction is also taking place). Many individuals and companies (or their shareholders) are buying real estate in order to resell it in the future, or to capitalize on growing market valuations, which are seen to be rising indefinitely. To a certain extent, the current situation can be compared to the mid-1990s, when manufacturing companies and banks were buying government's debt securities (GKOs) because these gave the most profitable return on financial resources. Real estate is for the moment a similar vehicle, producing delusive capital gains. The growth of real estate valuations (spurred by global credit growth) has made real estate investments seem very attractive. However, it has also become hard to tell from looking at official statistics whether the increase in reported investment stems from spending on projects such as plant modernization and new equipment, or just from speculative buying of real estate assets. Since the Leningrad Region is not experiencing a real estate boom similar to the city's, investment statistics in the region reflect the real situation better, although there are problems there too.

For example, according to information obtained from industry experts, the actual construction cost of one square foot of a residential brick and solid-cast building in St Petersburg is currently in the range of US$380–580 (depending on location, etc). However, construction firms publicly announced their costs to have amounted to US$88 on average in 2004 (rising incredibly from US$45 reported in press a year earlier). The cheapest new apartments in St Petersburg tend to cost about US$1,000 per square foot, but most fetch around US$1,100–1,500. For industrial and commercial real estate the situation is similar, although prices may be less overblown as companies generally have greater real-cost awareness and negotiation power than individuals. The degree to which firms are able to pass inflated capital costs (including construction costs) on to consumers depends on how far there is a monopolistic situation in the industry. In general, it is in the interest of manufacturing companies to overestimate costs 'on paper' as a way to avoid profit taxes, and to manage a 'hidden' transfer of part of the revenue to the shareholders' pockets that is not reported as a profit (suppose, for instance, that the shareholders own two companies, one supplying building materials to the other which is a construction company; if the latter buys goods at inflated prices from the former, the costs can be passed on to the end-buyer, while the shareholders make a significant profit from the transaction). There are plenty of tricks in every industry that help managers inflate the costs reflected on the balance sheet. In short, all these statistical problems add to the difficulty of correct market size evaluation.

Despite these difficulties, an approximate estimate of the size of the engineering market is still possible. Fees paid to engineering companies usually amount to 3–7 per cent of the total investment project cost (rising to as much as 10 per cent for certain projects). The fixed capital investment figures in St Petersburg and the Leningrad Region mentioned earlier give a conservative forecast of approximately US$3 billion in 2004 for St Petersburg and US$2 billion for the Leningrad Region. On this basis, the market for engineering services can be estimated as 3–7 per cent of those sums: that is, in the range of US$90–210 million in St Petersburg, and US$60–140 million in the Leningrad Region. To get an estimate of northwest Russia as a whole, one should add 35–40 per cent to the combined figures for St Petersburg and the Leningrad Region.

Since the market for engineering and architectural services in the residential housing sphere in St Petersburg may be very hard to assess, the size of the industrial engineering services market in the city can be more accurately estimated as merely a share of industrial investment (approximately US$600 million this year): some US$20–50 million. It is important to keep in mind that the capital depreciation level has reached 65–80 per cent on average in Russian industry, so the demand for quality engineering services is going to be very significant over a prolonged period of time, as is the demand for modern equipment, technology and materials.

There is a lot of potential for market growth that is not being realized due to lack of quality engineering firms able to provide services at a reasonable price. The variation in the prices of engineering services in St Petersburg is quite significant, and the quality of work also varies widely. For example, a large Russian company paid a design firm several million dollars to design its logo, without getting the result it wanted; it eventually bought the logo from a private designer for just a few thousand dollars. Lack of competition in the market leads to a relatively low quality of available supply. Another important consequence of the virtual absence of foreign engineering firms in St Petersburg (one that is easily overlooked) is the rather limited access of local companies to small and medium foreign equipment manufacturers.

Engineering services in northwest Russia are required in such sectors as:

- Capital-intensive industries:

  - the pulp and paper industry;

  - wood processing;

  - road construction, at federal as well as regional and municipal levels;

  - building materials manufacturing;

  - metallurgy;

  - ports and port facilities;

  - chemicals and petrochemicals;

- automotive components manufacturing;

- power generation;

- mining complexes;

- utilities.

• Less capital-intensive industries:

- food processing;

- logistics, warehouses and terminals;

- hotels;

- consumer products manufacturing;

- trade, entertainment and sport centres.

The engineering services market in St Petersburg

In Soviet times, engineering and project design work was organized in a system of sectoral scientific-research institutes, design institutes, bureaux and laboratories, which specialized in their respective industries, and combined applied research, engineering, design, management and implementation capabilities. Usually a sector-specialized design institute was able to act as a general designing contractor, working with a number of other institutes and design organizations to coordinate the complex process of project design, planning and implementation. Most of the engineering companies active now in St Petersburg are privately owned firms created by top executives of the former Soviet sectoral scientific-research and design institutes. These companies usually draw on the experience and status of their parent institutes to offer engineering solutions to their clients.

Some of the old scientific-research and design organizations in St Petersburg that still offer project design services, either through a subsidiary or directly, are:

• Gidrotekh, ZAO (subsidiary of LenHydroProekt) – hydrotechnical constructions;

• NIIHIMMASH (www.niihimmash.com) – gas fractionation installations, etc.;

• Giprobum-Engineering (www.giprobum.spb.ru), subsidiary of Giprobum – lumber industry;

- DORSERVICE (www.dor.spb.ru) – Construction and repair of roads and housing and public utilities structures;

- Leningradskiy Promstroyproekt ZAO – industrial projects design, town planning;

- LENNIIPROEKT (www.lenproekt.com) – comprehensive design of residential and public buildings;

- Transmashproekt OAO (www.tmproj.ru) – process design of production facilities and public buildings, networks design, etc;

- LENMORNIIPROEKT (www.lenmor.ru) – engineering and consulting firm, specializing in port construction;

- Lengiproinzhproekt (www.lgip.spb.ru) – comprehensive planning of engineering constructions, networks and utilities. The institute designs water treatment plants, canal systems, tunnel collectors, bridges, overpasses, viaducts, embankments, utilities, electricity supplies, cable networks, urban transport systems, etc;

- AO Harris Group International Project and Construction Services (www.aohgi.spb.ru), one of the very few engineering companies independent of Soviet-era design institutes, which was established in St Petersburg in 1996 in partnership with the US-based Harris Group, but has now separated from its US founder.

Those engineering companies in St Petersburg that have branched out from old design organizations face a number of problems which, looking into the future, they will have a hard time resolving. First of all, the design, technological and process engineering solutions offered by most of the engineering companies in St Petersburg are starting to lag behind worldwide technological trends and innovations. Local engineering companies have relied heavily on knowledge and expertise accumulated during Soviet times, and it is now becoming increasingly obvious that many do not have necessary skills to propose up-to-date plant design and engineering solutions in many industries. This also pertains to testing and design technology, as design methods, equipment, software and management practices do not meet modern requirements.

Second, most of the local engineering firms can no longer offer the comprehensive packages that their parent institutes could: complex project design, approval and implementation services, pre-feasibility studies, budgeting, planning, vendor relations (procurement process, delivery, installation, commissioning), financial arrangements, implementation and start-up. It is especially important to note that few local engineering firms offer services to organize the equipment and service procurement process and set up financial arrangements. The general pattern is that the project initiator first identifies an equipment vendor, and asks the engineering company to draw up an approvable design and implementation plan. This limits the access of local companies to modern technology and equipment at competitive prices. The practice of offering full engineering services with an option of procurement, construction management and commissioning (EPCM and EPC) is not common among local engineering companies.

Third, many local engineering firms do not understand the crucial importance that investment in employee and customer relations has for the future of their businesses. This means that customers are not confident of an ongoing quality of service, and that employees are not getting adequate training or remuneration, or a good working environment. For foreign investors, as well as for Russian domestic investors, a proven, reliable market reputation will mean a lot. An established international engineering firm will quickly be able to attract talented staff and solid orders.

Market entry strategies

Evaluation of various strategies available to foreign engineering companies willing to enter the local market should be based on a number of considerations. The most important factors to consider in current market situation in St Petersburg and the Leningrad Region are briefly described below.

Brand name

A well-known and established brand name is a clear advantage for a foreign company wishing to enter the market, which it should seek to capitalize upon. By bringing forth and sustaining market reputation, a foreign company will quickly be able to gain a solid footing in the local marketplace.

Quality and price control

A foreign engineering company entering this market should pay particular attention to establishing solid quality control guidelines, and to conducting a responsible pricing strategy, thus assuring customers that they are charged reasonable fees for work of excellent quality.

Vendor relations

It is difficult to see how the potential for increasing sales of imported technology and equipment in northwest Russia could be exploited if foreign engineering firms are not active in this market. Many innovative technological solutions and materials are simply not available for consideration to Russian enterprises because they are not represented in the market. They are thus not incorporated in any process design and planning decisions. In addition, many Russian companies want to have second-hand equipment incorporated in the production process design from the very start, while only the most crucial equipment will be new.

Licensing

There are a number of Russian statutory requirements, licences and permits that need to be adhered to/obtained by an engineering firm before it can start offering its services. Different types of engineering and design work require licences from different organizations. Gosstroy, for example, issues licences for design of foundations and buildings, process engineering in various industries, design of internal and external networks (heating, ventilation, air-conditioning, water supply, sewerage, electricity, etc), design of engineering utilities, environmental impact analysis and other services. Special licences are needed in such fields as mining production design, gas units design, chemically-dangerous operations, steam and hot water networks, electricity distribution networks, renovation of historical monuments, design of facilities that require the use and handling of explosive or toxic substances and/or mixtures, environmental safety assessment of the materials, processes, and equipment for industrial facilities in the Russian Federation, design of hazardous process systems and many others.

Personnel

A decisive factor for long-term success is acquiring and maintaining an excellent team of professionals. Offering various financial and non-financial incentives should be an integral part of the personnel strategy. Training of junior staff to support and, in the future, replace older employees should also be considered as an option. The personnel of the local office are by far the most significant ingredient of success, because even the most innovative and efficient engineering solution must be approved by local authorities and properly implemented by local contractors. It will be the job of the local office to ensure that this happens in a timely and efficient manner.

Knowledge of local legislation

Russian design and building norms and standards still differ very significantly from Western standards. Crucial to success in adjusting design and process engineering solutions to the Russian market are, first, knowledge of Russian building and technological norms and standards, and second, experience of going through the sequence of investment process steps and approval procedures (as described in local investment laws).

Remote design

A possible way to ensure quality and to cut operating costs is remote design of some parts of project documentation. In such an arrangement, an office in St Petersburg would be responsible for customer relations, compliance with local regulations and standards, project documentation approval and construction authorization and permits, and similar work, whereas feasibility studies, basic and detailed engineering (and marketing studies for export-oriented projects) would be partially carried out at the headquarters in the foreign company's own country. Standard process designs and construction/architectural solutions developed in another country will have to be adjusted to Russian norms and regulations. There is a lot of work that can be carried out locally more efficiently, such as pre-feasibility studies, concept-level proposals, business planning and detailed cost estimates, project documentation approval, construction permits and commissioning. Of course, the detailed breakdown of work between an international parent company and Russian subsidiary is a matter of corporate decision, which should be based on scrupulous and thoughtful process analysis.

3.7

The Electrical Energy Sector

Gregory Kharenko, Acting Head of Investor Relations, and Larissa Semenova, Public Relations Director, JSC Lenenergo

Historical note

At the end of the 19th century, electric power became a precondition for progress, and St Petersburg was a pioneer in the industrial production of electric power at that time. The 1886 Society for Electric Lighting, established by Karl Siemens, was approved by a statute passed on 16 July 1886, a date that is now considered to mark the creation the first Russian power system, which is now the open joint-stock company for power and electrification 'Lenenergo'. That was how the 'electric era' began in the history of Russia, when the best engineers and managers of the country worked in the power system of the northern capital.

JSC Lenenergo: company structure and power generating capacity

The open joint-stock company Lenenergo is a major power system of the Russian northwest and one of the largest in the Baltic region. The company provides services over a territory of around 85,300 km^2 (which is several times the size of whole countries such as Belgium, Denmark or Albania) with a population of about 6.2 million, including St Petersburg with a population of 4.5 million (and about 1,400 km^2) and Leningrad Oblast with a population of 1.7 million (83,900 km^2).

Lenenergo consists of over 20 structural divisions: thermal power plants, hydropower plants, enterprises of electric networks, heating grids and general system enterprises. On 1 January 2005, Lenenergo's total workforce stood at 12,500 employees.

The company comprises 15 power generating enterprises: six hydropower plants, eight thermal power plants and 1 GRES natural gas power plant. The estimated electric power of the plants comprising Lenenergo complex is around 3,227 MWt, and heat power is about 11,880 Gkal/hour. One major competitive advantage that the company enjoys is the high proportion of hydraulic generators, which represent 20 per cent of its overall generating capacity, and are the cheapest and most efficient electric power source available.

During the heating season, which on average lasts 230 to 240 days per year, Lenenergo is a strategic supplier of heat power to St Petersburg. About 80 per cent of the company's generating capacity functions in heat-extraction. The length of the heating grid is over 750 km, and its heating pipelines have a diameter of between 500 and 1,000 mm. The overhead power line stretches for 40,000 km, and cable power lines for over 15,000 km.

Through its own generation of power and the activity of the Federal Wholesale Market of Electric Power (FOREM), the company provides 100 per cent of St Petersburg's and Leningrad Oblast's requirements for electric power.

Due to the geographical closeness of Finland and the Baltic states, Lenenergo is able to direct its output to the international electric power market. It is one of the few Russian power companies that exports electric power to Western countries independently.

Corporate structure and company objectives

RAO UES of Russia is the company's major shareholder, but Lenenergo is unique in the power sector in having a Western company, the Finnish corporation Fortum Power and Heat Oy, as a strategic shareholder (with 30.71 per cent of its shares). The presence of foreign companies among the shareholders has produced significant benefits in terms of internal corporate procedures and rules of corporate governance, and this is especially critical at a time when power industry faces restructuring.

At the end of December 2004, the market capitalization of Lenenergo was US$727.08 million. One kilowatt of Lenenergo's installed capacity is estimated at over US$200 (based on the ratio between the company's market capitalization of US$727 million and its installed capacity of 3,227 MWt) – this is one the highest levels in Russia.

The scale of Lenenergo's activity and its exclusive market position involve a high level of responsibility to shareholders, employees, consumers, suppliers and society as a whole. Lenenergo is a company that sees its key purpose as a reliable and uninterrupted supply of high-quality, ecologically clean power to consumers. Its goal is to achieve stability of operations, improvements in its financial position, modernization of its technical base and increased investment attractiveness. These objectives are set against the backdrop of maintaining the positive dynamics of the company's capitalization and acting in the interests of state and society. 'We must be a leader, catch up with modern developments and be responsible to our clients – that's our task and that's how we'll succeed', says Andrey Likhachev, General Director of JSC Lenenergo. The basis for this success is a highly efficient management team and well-qualified employees who are committed to the general development goals of Lenenergo.

Lenenergo: an overview of recent corporate history

Today Lenenergo is a stable and dynamically developing company, and one of the leaders in power sector, although five years ago many market analysts forecast bankruptcy. In the middle of 1999, about one third of RAO UES's affiliates were making losses, and seven were in a very difficult financial condition; Lenenergo was one of these. The losses the company was suffering were exacerbated by the tariff-charging policy of the St Petersburg Administration and the use of a barters scheme instead of actual payments.

All this ceased in December of 1999, when a new team of managers, led by General Director Andrey Likhachev, arrived at Lenenergo and set to work to optimize the company's activity, increase its profitability and steer it away from bankruptcy. The team had not only to save the power system from crisis by rearranging its financial and industrial activity, but also to create a corporate governance system that would win the trust of the shareholders and potential investors. At that time, market capitalization of Lenenergo was only about US$60 million.

The year 2000 was a critical one for the company. In July 2000, Lenenergo was one of the first companies in Russia to adopt a Memorandum of Corporate Governance. Lenenergo's specialists, together with the International Finance Corporation (IFC), developed a Corporate Governance Code that became an instrument to protect investors' and shareholders' interests. In 2000, the company broke even for the first time, and in 2001 recorded profits of 1,005 million RUB. This allowed Lenenergo to pay dividends to shareholders for the first time in many years. At the same time Lenenergo together with JP Morgan Chase Bank launched a programme of sponsored American Depositary Receipts. The practice of issuing financial reports in accordance with international accounting standards (IAS) began to be incorporated into the company.

All these steps were evaluated positively by independent business experts. The financial analysts of Brunswick UBS Warburg, named Lenenergo the best management team in the Russian power industry, on the basis of its results in 2000. The following year, the company was included for the first time in the *Financial Times'* listing of the hundred leading East European companies in terms of market capitalization, leading Andrey Likhachev to comment:

> At the very least, our company plans to retain a stable position in the ratings of the hundred leading European companies generated by the *Financial Times*. At best, we plan to move into to the ranks of the 200 major European companies and 500 top companies of the world.

Industry-wide achievements and corporate recognition

In March 2001, according to the research of the Institute of Corporate Governance, Lenenergo took third place in the rating of major Russian companies for overall good practice in corporate governance.

The enterprise has won numerous national and international prizes. In 2001 and 2002, it won the all-Russian competition for 'Best Russian Enterprises' in as 'The Most Dynamically Developing Company' and for 'Irreproachable Business Reputation of Company Management'. Lenenergo General Director Andrey Likhachev was also named 'The Best Entrepreneur of 2001'.

In June 2002, Lenenergo was named the 'Leader of Corporate Governance in Russia' by *Euromoney* magazine (London), a leading magazine in the financial sector. In September that year, a gold medal for the irreproachable business reputation of the company was awarded to the General Director of Lenenergo. This award was established by the Russian-Swiss Business Club, the Higher Geneva Institute of Business and Management (INSAM), the Swiss Association GRM CONSULT and the international consulting company Tecnomic Consultants SA.

In December 2002, Lenenergo received a national award for 'Company of the Year 2002' in the 'Best Management' category. In addition, General Director Andrey Likhachev was named as a 'Face of St Petersburg' in the 3rd all-Russian competition, 'Faces of the Year'.

Lenenergo's annual report for 2001 won the annual report competition held by RTS; it was ranked as 'The Best Annual Report of 2001', and as having the 'Best Level of Information Presentation'. In December 2003, Lenenergo was the winner of the 'Russian Leaders of Corporate Governance 2003' competition, in the 'Annual Report' category. The Annual Report of JSC Lenenergo for 2003 also won the first prize in the category 'The Best Idea and Design' in the contest of annual reports and websites of power industry companies.

In March 2002, the international rating agency, Standard &Poor's (S&P) awarded JSC Lenenergo a rating for corporate governance of 5.7, the highest rating in Russia at that time. In July 2003, this was increased to 5.9 and in May 2004 it reached 6.0.

The achievements of the company's management have been acknowledged widely by the investment community, as the increase in Lenenergo's capitalization and the presence of Western capital in the company's shareholder structure confirm. On numerous occasions, Lenenergo has been acknowledged as a company that actively promotes and incorporates the corporate governance principles adopted by the worldwide business community. The role of these principles has become increasingly important from the viewpoint of branch restructuring, and also within the company as a whole. In 2003, *The Banker* magazine awarded Lenenergo the highest rank in the rating of leaders among Russian enterprises in respect of introduction of corporate governance.

The unanimous re-election of Andrey Likhachev as General Director of Lenenergo, at a Shareholder Meeting in May 2004, was just another confirmation of the efficient and successful activity of the company's management.

Successful financial indicators and stable economic activity allowed Lenenergo to take its place among the three leading companies in the Russian power sector in terms of investment attractiveness, and to present itself confidently both on the domestic and international markets. All these achievements enabled the company to overhaul its equipment as well as to carry out new construction, using not only its own funds but also loaned capital.

In April 2004, Lenenergo placed its first bonds to the amount of 3 billion RUB with a 3-year circulation period on the Moscow Interbank Currency Exchange (MICEX).

The TPP-5 project

In November 2004, the company received a loan of €40 million from the European Bank for Reconstruction and Development (EBRD). It was a sign of the increased trust in Lenenergo and the high regard in which its activities were held by the investor community. These funds have been directed towards the completion of a new district heat power plant installation (TPP-5). This will provide a guaranteed heat supply to the inhabitants of the southeastern part of the city. TPP-1 is the first heat power plant constructed within Lenenergo according to the GOELRO plan. This is one of the oldest power generating units of Lenenergo's system. The plant has to provide the heat supply for over half a million St Petersburg citizens.

The new TPP-5 block is one of the most important projects of Lenenergo's investment programme. This project is unique in Russia in a number of ways. This is the first new power generating facility produced in Lenenergo's system for the last quarter of a century. It is also the first case in the history of contemporary Russia where a new, modern power generating facility is to be constructed near an old plant. It represents the start of an ongoing process to meet the need to replace outdated equipment that can no longer function effectively; after the start-up of the new TPP-5 installation, the old production plant complex will be decommissioned.

The new TPP-5 block meets all contemporary environmental requirements. One of the main benefits of replacing outdated equipment is that it will end the pollution of the River Neva.

The total cost of constructing the new TPP-5 block is €60 million. Lenenergo has provided €20 million of this from its own funds, and €40 million has come from the EBRD.

Modernization of the power complex

Today, Lenenergo pays close attention to the issues of stable development and the modernization of the power complex. In the last few years the company has carried out a campaign unprecedented in its scope on equipment overhaul. Such activities have not been undertaken in the region for decades.

Science 2002, the power company, has addressed a programme of replacing outdated pipelines in Lenenergo's heat supply zone. Nearly 40 km of heat pipelines were replaced in 2003, and in 2004, Lenenergo's heating department specialists replaced over 32 km of heat supply lines in St Petersburg and in the town of Kirovsk in the Leningrad Oblast. This compares with 18 km of heat supply lines refurbished in 2001, and only 12 km in 2000. Altogether in St Petersburg over 110 km of heat supply lines have been replaced and repaired since the commencement of the programme.

Similar large-scale refurbishments are also being carried out on the generating facilities and the electric power network complex. In 2004, Lenenergo's specialists repaired and refurbished 315.6 km of the power network in St Petersburg and Leningrad Oblast.

The total cost of this repair campaign amounts 1.8 billion RUB. It has improved the reliability of electric and heat power supplies during the autumn/winter high demand period. For the second year running, the power system has experienced almost no emergencies.

Since 2002, there has been an active and ongoing process of new facility construction in St Petersburg and Leningrad Oblast. A new substation, Sosnovo, was commissioned in Priozersk region at the end of 2003. The Port substation that opened in June 2004 will provide a stable and uninterrupted electric power supply to Ust-Luga commercial seaport. Construction work is nearly completed at other large facilities in Leningrad Oblast, such as the Vozneseniye substation in Podporozhye region. In February 2005, St Petersburg witnessed the official opening of substation No 542. This is one of Lenenergo's most important investment projects in the last few years. The new substation was designed to increase electricity deliveries and improvethe reliability of downtown consumer power supplies.

The 'Programme for reconstruction and development of engineering provision sources and engineering networks in the JSC Lenenergo electric power supply period for 2005–2010' was approved by the St Petersburg government on 13 July. This was one of the most important events for the company during 2004. The programme was the result of the joint activities of Lenenergo's specialists, the city Administration and expert bodies. Lenenergo's management aims to create a united regional engineering infrastructure development plan. In the process of developing this document, many contradictions have been eliminated and new principles and methods have been developed. This will have a great impact on the development of the whole power system, as well as on its separate structures, which will be integrated into a unified power network system.

The programme of power source development clearly defines where, when, and with what funds the construction and reconstruction of power plants, substations, and networks will be carried out. The combined costs of the programme up to 2010 are estimated at 45.235 million RUB; 17.575 million RUB of this will come from Lenenergo's own funds, while the St Petersubrg city government will contribute 4.565 million RUB from its budget.

Financial indicators

The financial indicators of the company are constantly improving. Consolidated sales in 2004 comprised 30.189 million RUB (up from 26.623 million RUB in 2003 and 22.513 million RUB in 2002). In 2004 net profit was 840 million RUB in comparison with 219 million RUB in 2003. The total assets increased by 10.7 per cent to 54.498 million RUB.

Capital investments in 2004 comprised 5.334 million RUB, an increase of 1.9 times over 2003.

The ongoing restructuring of Lenenergo

Today, Lenenergo is in the process of restructuring. This is a new stage of development aimed at adapting power system activity to market conditions. The main procedures of company restructuring are to be implemented in 2005 and will result in the foundation of separate generation, electric network, power delivery and administrating companies.

The main goal of the restructuring plan is to separate competitive and monopoly types of activity. The essence of the first stage of restructuring is to create conditions for developing market relations in the competitive sectors of the power system. For this purpose, a monopoly power transmission network will be separated from the potentially competitive generation and sales elements. The aim of this reform is to create a competitive market for electric power, attract investments into modernization and technical re-equipment, increase capacity and improve the quality and reliability of the power supply. The process of reform, which will have several stages, is to be finalized in October 2005 when new companies and new control mechanisms will be formed. The new configuration of the company will make it possible to provide significant growth in the near future.

Today, the decision on the foundation of TGC-1 has already been taken. The generating assets of TGC-1 will be consist of JSC Lenenergo, JSC Karelenergo and JSC Kolenergo (but not the Murmansk and Apatit thermal power plants). The structure capital of TGC-1 will be 10 million RUB divided into one billion common shares. The Karelenergo's share of TGC-1's structure capital will be 12 per cent, Kolenergo's 25 per cent and Lenenergo's 63 per cent.

With a significant part of the hydro-generating assets, which comprise nearly half of the company's installed capacity, and an advantageous geographic location, TGC-1 will be able to take a leading position among the territorial generating companies of Russia. 'I am sure that TGC-1 will become the best in the country; due to the structure of its assets, no one can compare with it', stated General Director of Lenenergo, Andrey Likhachev.

The position of the company in the northern latitude offers extremely profitable opportunities for heat power sales. The dynamic development of the northwestern region and the consequent increase in demand for electric power will provide a constant growth of sales. TGC-1 will also have an advantage over other generating companies as it is operating beside the Finnish border, which gives great opportunities for international trade.

All this will create the preconditions for a future increase in TGC-1's capitalization. After several years' activities, experts predict that the capitalization of TGC-1 will be approximately US$2 billion.

The main goal of management during the restructuring is to maximize publicity and transparency at every phase. The managers of the power system are confident that the newly created structures will preserve the principles and practices of corporate governance that are characteristic of Lenenergo today. The current Lenenergo management team headed by Andrey Likhachev will form the basis of TGC-1's management.

The power industry is one of the foundations for the normal functioning of any city and an integral component for the development of the state economy. The day-to-day tasks facing Lenenergo today are the construction of new power supply facilities; technical re-equipment; and the reconstruction and refurbishment of generating plants, electric and heat networks, using highly efficient modern technology. The future of Lenenergo lies in responsibility, dedication and progressive improvement.

Services

3.8

Development of the Transport System and Road Sector in St Petersburg

S.D. Vorontsova, Senior Deputy Director, Research and Design Institute of Regional Development and Transportation, St Petersburg, Russia

St Petersburg has a uniquely favourable economic and geographical position, lying as it does in immediate proximity to developed European countries, on the coast of the Gulf of Finland of the Baltic Sea, at the mouth of the River Neva (which provides access to a huge lake and river system), and linked to the major water basins of European Russia by rivers and canals. Since St Petersburg became part of the globally connected economic and socio-cultural system, its role as a bridge between Russia and the West has become more important. The city provides a link between the major markets of central and eastern Europe, the Baltic region and CIS-countries.

St Petersburg is a vital element in the transport system of Russia. Due to its advantageous geopolitical position, its closeness to the European countries, and developed transport infrastructure, the city has become a major centre for international freight handling. Two Euro-Asian transport corridors – 'North–South' and 'Transsib' – and the Pan-European Transport Corridor IX cross the area of St Petersburg, providing Russia with an outlet to Western Europe (see Figure 3.8.1). Moreover, the city is the most important Russian Baltic port and a leader in handling dry cargo, including containers. The Volga–Baltic waterway crosses the St Petersburg area. In addition there is an advanced network of airlines, roads and railroads. All this makes

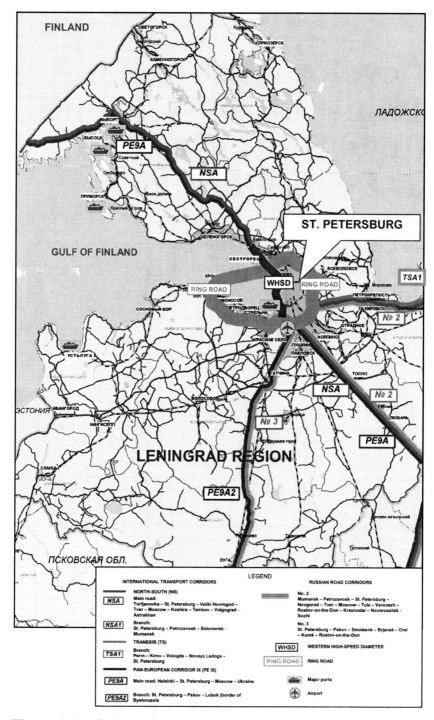

Figure 3.8.1 St Petersburg and the Euro-Asian transport corridors

St Petersburg a strategically vital area in terms of Russia's economy and national security (Figure 3.8.2).

The total freight transport volumes in St Petersburg exceed 270 million tons per year, 30 per cent being foreign trade. The transit freight flow through St Petersburg is over 100 million tons per year.

Transport is one of the most dynamically developing industries St Petersburg specializes in. The transport sector is a leader in attracting investment, and in input to the gross value added and employment provision, as the following figures show:

- The total cost of major and mid-sized transport companies' services in 2003 amounted to 56.2 billion roubles (RUB).

- The transport industry includes 7,800 companies, employing 190,600 people (8 per cent of all employment in St Petersburg).

- The transport and road sectors account for 9.4 per cent of the gross regional product.

- Export and import of transport services (including storage services) in St Petersburg in 2003 totalled US$682.5 million. Export of transport services (including storage services) accounted for US$567.7 million or 70 per cent of total exported services in St Petersburg.

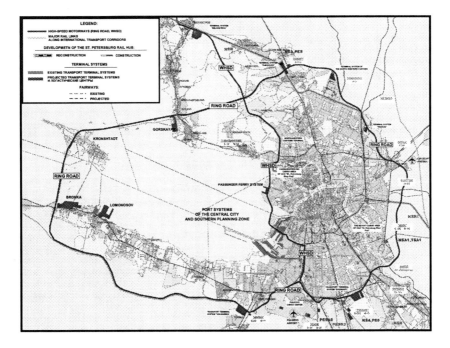

Figure 3.8.2 St Petersburg's key geographical location

Imports of transport services (including storage services) amounted to US$116.4 million, or 41 per cent of total imported services.

- Taxes and other transport sector revenues provide 12 per cent of all city budget revenues.

- In 2003, the transport sector received nearly 20 per cent of the total investment in St Petersburg.

- Household costs related to car, fuel and spare parts purchase amount to 40–42 billion RUB per year.

St Petersburg is the only Russian city listed among the world top 10 tourist attractions. Two-thirds of foreign tourists coming to Russia visit the city on the Neva. Every year, St Petersburg receives about 4 million guests from 175 countries of the world and other regions of Russia, both tourists and those arriving for other purposes. Most tourists arriving in the city use rail, air, river and road transport. External transport modes carry over 10 million passengers per year.

The key objectives of transport policy in St Petersburg are: 1) to promote economic growth and improvement of the residents' welfare by providing safe, high-quality transport services to meet the needs of the economy, population and state; 2) to create an internationally competitive multi-modal transport centre in St Petersburg. The most important goals are:

- to improve the competitiveness of the city transport sector and its role as a key centre of foreign trade, transit cargo handling and passenger transport;

- develop and implement activities to improve the infrastructure of all transport modes operating on international north–south and west–east transport corridors within St Petersburg and its suburban zone, as well as of storage terminals, and to organize streamlined customs processes for international freight;

- provide for sustainable development of the transport sector to meet the ever-growing demand for passenger and freight transport in order to achieve the highest possible quality in transport services and reduce operating and time costs;

- renovate transport assets, and improve their competitiveness on both domestic and international transport service markets;

- improve the investment climate to attract private investment by means including large-scale adoption of new financing tools, such as public–private partnership (PPP) and private finance initiative (PFI);

- improve the integration in management of the city transport system;

- introduce advanced navigation technologies;

- increase budget revenues from transport companies and various actors supporting their activities;

- improve safety and sustainability of the transport sector;

- reduce adverse impacts of transport on the environment.

The priority of the St Petersburg transport policy is to improve coordination in development of all transport modes – sea, rail, river, air, pipelines and road transport as well as the road network – in order to improve competitiveness of the transport system of the city.

Sea transport and the main seaport of St Petersburg

St Petersburg was founded as a second, sea-facing, capital of Russia. There is the main seaport of St Petersburg, whose cargo turnover in 2004 amounted to 51.2 million tons. The total cargo turnover of the port is the biggest of all the Baltic ports, and the second biggest in Russia after the port of Novorossiisk.

St Petersburg is the leading dry-cargo handling port in Russia, accounting for over 25 per cent of all export/import dry-cargo handling in Russian ports. In recent years, there has been a steady increase in cargo turnover in the port of St Petersburg. Between 1990 and 2004, its cargo handling volume increased by 500 per cent (Figure 3.8.3).

St Petersburg seaport is one of the most dynamically developing Russian ports. Recently its container terminal has been enhanced, oil terminal capacity extended, special new berths created for general cargo reloading, and a mineral fertilizer transfer terminal built.

The fastest growth rate is in container cargo flows. At present, the port of St Petersburg handles 55 per cent of all international container cargo transported by sea in the Russian Federation. The main seaport of St Petersburg has become an absolute leader in highly remunerative container cargo handling not only in Russia but also in the whole Baltic region. The annual growth of container handling is 20–30 per cent. Over the last four years alone, the percentage of container cargo has increased from 10 per cent to 18 per cent of the total cargo flow through the port. St Petersburg port operates 13 regular container lines, providing links to the ports of England, Belgium, Germany, Spain, Netherlands, the United States and France.

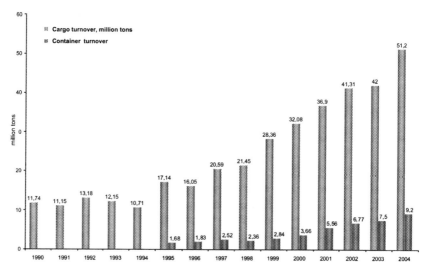

Figure 3.8.3 Cargo turnover in the main seaport of St Petersburg, 1990–2004 (million tons)

According to the forecast presented in the Concept to the Master Plan for Development of St Petersburg, the cargo turnover of seaport systems will increase to 90–135 million tons by 2025, the share of containers being 52 per cent.

Significant flows of foreign tourists arrive in St Petersburg by sea. Nowadays, cruise navigation in the port is already one of the key sectors of the city's tourist business, and brings in significant revenues. Figure 3.8.4 shows the development of sea cruise transport in the port of St Petersburg. Over the period from 1998 to 2004 the number of cruise liners calling at the port increased by the factor of 2.4 (up to 462), and the number of tourists by three times (320,000). A ferry service between St Petersburg, Helsinki and Tallin has established regular sea communications between the three sea capitals of the Baltic region. There are projects for new ferry routes between St Petersburg and Stockholm, and St Petersburg and Rostok.

In the future, a significant increase in passenger transport in St Petersburg is expected as a result of the development of cruise navigation, renewal of previously operating ferry routes and introduction of new ones to link the city to the nearest European countries. According to the forecasts, by 2010 the number of tourists arriving in St Petersburg by sea will be between 600,000 and a million, and by 2025 2–3.3 million. In this context, one priority project for the city is the construction of a passenger ferry system in the western part of Vassilievski (Basil's) Island. On the Gulf of Finland, a land area of 350 hectares is to be used to construct six passenger ferry berths, as well

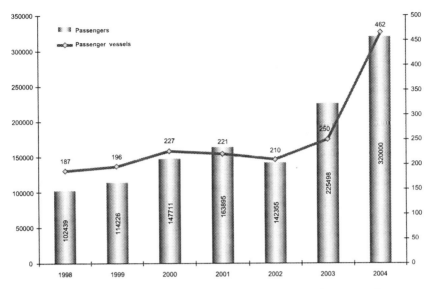

Figure 3.8.4 Development of seaborne tourism in the port of
St Petersburg, 1998–2004

as a complex of buildings and structures for receiving and servicing
1.2 million passengers per year, along with their motor transport.

The priority goals for developing port activities in St Petersburg are:

- to increase turnover of the main seaport of St Petersburg through
  construction and reconstruction of specialized terminals, and to
  reorientate the port towards environmentally safe and high-profit
  cargoes, particularly containers;

- develop port capacities on the coast of the Gulf of Finland, near the
  flood control facilities (Lomonosov, Bronka, Baza Litke, Gorskaya)
  in order to increase the turnover of the port and partially divert the
  cargo flow from the centre of the city;

- construct a second sea canal, and deepen and widen the main sea
  fairway to provide for big ocean-going ships calling at the port;

- create rear container terminals to relocate the cargo operations from
  the port zone;

- improve the coordination of sea transport and other transport
  modes;

- provide for safety of navigation, port operations and environment.

Rail transport

The St Petersburg rail hub is one of the biggest in Russia. It provides for suburban and long-distance passenger transport as well as a major portion of mass freight transport both in Russia and to central and eastern Europe, the Baltic region and CIS countries. The hub is made up of 10 radial railway lines, linked by the tracks of the northern semi-ring. The rail company servicing the area of St Petersburg is Octyabrskaya (October) Railways.

In 2003 total freight turnover of the St Petersburg rail hub amounted to 103.3 million tons, of which transit cargo made up 54.7 per cent. Nearly 19 million tons of cargo per year that goes through the port systems of St Petersburg is conveyed by rail. Up to 25 per cent of rail transport is for direct links to the EU, Baltic countries and Belarus. Rail-transported exports are oil, timber, metals, mineral fertilizers, ore and coal.

The St Petersburg rail hub comprises 100 stations, among which there are five main stations, eight freight stations with freight yards, and two marshalling yards. Rail transport is hugely important for St Petersburg. The railways convey about 8 million passengers per year on long-distance links, are used for part of intracity and a significant portion of suburban trips, deliver cargo to the main seaport of St Petersburg and carry exports and imports for the city's enterprises.

In the local freight turnover of St Petersburg, more is brought in than goes out due to: 1) the city's lack of material resources; 2) the large-scale delivery of raw materials and fuels; 3) the main seaport of St Petersburg receiving a lot of export cargo; 4) the import of building materials as well as industrial and food products.

One important event in terms of rail transport development was the development of the new Ladozhski Vokzal (Ladozhski Rail Station), which is to become the second biggest terminal (after Moscow) for the arrival and departure of local and long-distance passenger trains.

In 2008 a new high-speed link is to be introduced between St Petersburg and Helsinki, the projected travel time being 3–3.5 hours. This project would improve the competitiveness of rail communications and allow an increase in passenger flows as passengers switch to rail from other transport modes.

The rail transport volume in St Petersburg is expected to grow, because of increases in production, seaport turnover, the percentage of cargo delivered to/from the port by rail and a growing demand for rail transport resulting from the increasing economic activity and prosperity of the residents.

According to the forecast in the Concept to the Master Plan for Development of St Petersburg, by 2025 the total rail freight turnover will amount to nearly 250 million tons, of which 130 million tons will be local turnover, including 93 million tons for the port stations. Long-distance passenger departures will increase to 14.5 million passengers by 2025.

To meet the rail transportation demand in St Petersburg hub, there are plans to:

- construct a rail bypass around St Petersburg in order to divert the transit rail traffic from the city bounds;

- relocate the marshalling station Sortyrovochni-Moscowski beyond the city bounds and construct a new marshalling yard at the southern rail approaches to the city;

- relocate step-by-step the freight yards of rail stations now situated in the central zone of the city;

- reconstruct the freight stations Avtovo, Novy Port and Predporto-vaya to allow a smooth service for the main seaport of St Petersburg;

- construct a freight rail bypass around the southwestern coastal zone to accommodate the increasing freight flows through the port rail stations Oranienbaum and Bronka;

- establish a rapid Helsinki–St Petersburg–Moscow link through the Ladozhski Station;

- set up advanced transfer terminals for cargo handling.

Inland waterways (river transport)

The main arterial waterway in the area of St Petersburg is the Volga–Baltic (Volgo–Baltkiiski) waterway that links the Volga to the Baltic Sea and – through the White Sea–Baltic (Belomoro-Baltiiski) canal – to the White Sea.

The inland waterways of St Petersburg that make part of the single deep-water system of European Russia are the River Neva and its tributaries, their total length being 44 km.

Baltic-oriented cargo traffic has become the greatest element of shipping along the Volga–Baltic waterways. The key exports are oil and oil products, timber, coal, and metals from the central and north-eastern regions of Russia; the imports are equipment from Western countries. These goods are conveyed by river vessels, most of which are specialized vessels of the 'seagoing–river' type.

The St Petersburg river port consists of two cargo areas: the Nevski and the Vassileostrovski. The passenger port serves cruise vessels.

Over the period from 1990 to 2003, river cargo transport in St Petersburg increased from 10.9 million tons to 16.1 million tons (almost 50 per cent), while the proportion of international traffic increased from 32 to 67 per cent. Oil products account for 28.7 per cent of all river transport by volume, and sand from the Gulf of Finland for 34 per cent.

In 2003, passenger traffic on river transport totalled 1.4 million, with suburban and intracity links accounting for 87 per cent and tourists for 13 per cent.

Since 1990, traffic on external tourist links has increased more than threefold and in 2003 reached 180,000, with foreign tourists making up 75 per cent of the whole. The main tourist routes are: St Petersburg–Moscow, St Petersburg–Valaam Island, St Petersburg–Kizhi, St Petersburg–Mandrogi.

In the future, cargo transport is forecast to grow both on the Volga–Baltic waterway as a whole and in St Petersburg. The growth will result from the increased export of timber and building materials, ferrous metals and fertilizers, as well as transit cargo traffic through the international north–south transport corridor. According to the forecast, by 2010 inland waterway cargo transport in St Petersburg may reach 28–29 million tons, and by 2025 may be between 33 and 42 million tons. This includes Baltic-bound cargoes, which are expected to double from their present level and reach 16-20 million tons. However, bottlenecks caused by bridges over the River Neva, which can only be raised for short periods to allow shipping to pass, mean that the part of the city within the city bounds will not be able to meet the increased transport demand. To solve this problem, a proposal is now under consideration to create a new canal between Lake Ladoga and the Gulf of Finland. This would be a solution to the Volga–Baltic waterway capacity problem.

According to forecasts, cruise traffic will double by 2025. Therefore the priority tasks are: 1) to build a new river station to meet the needed accommodation capacity of 30 vessels and more; 2) reconstruct the passenger terminal and organization of tourist links to European countries.

The priority goals of inland waterways development are to:

- increase the capacity of the Volga–Baltic waterways, dredging to guarantee the passage of river vessels;

- extend the period for which bridges can be raised for shipping in order to increase the waterway capacity;

- construct a shipping canal between Lake Ladoga and the Gulf of Finland to provide for smooth operation of the water section of the international north–south transport corridor;

- reconstruct and develop the Vassileostrovski and Nevski cargo areas;

- construct a new river station;

- create mechanisms to involve commercial organizations in financing rehabilitation and reconstruction of waterways;

- acquire dual-purpose 'river–seagoing' vessels for foreign trade;

- construct a new shipping fairway as an extension to the existing ones from the Petrovski Canal up to the northern Kronshtadtski Fairway in order to provide for smooth passage of the dual-purpose 'river– seagoing' vessels bound for Europe;

- maintain the safety of navigation and smooth operation of water development facilities;

- introduce cargo transfer capacities for handling cargo in large-capacity containers.

Air transport

Pulkovo airport in St Petersburg, the second airport in Russia and the biggest in northwest Russia, has regular links to almost 60 cities in Russia and the CIS countries, and to more than 40 other cities. In 2004 passenger departures from Pulkovo airport on all airlines totalled 4.3 million passengers, with 48 per cent travelling on domestic routes and 52 per cent on international ones. Pulkovo's own fleet was used to convey 2.7 million passengers, half on domestic and half on international routes.

Pulkovo airport has two terminals: Pulkovo-1, which serves mostly domestic flights and those bound for CIS countries; and Pulkovo-2, a solely international terminal. The capacity of the Pulkovo-1 terminal is 1,800 passengers per hour, while Pulkovo-2 can handle 1,200 passengers per hour.

The reconstruction of the Pulkovo-2 terminal was completed in 2003, giving increased capacity and improved passenger service. The new terminal meets all standards for international airports. In 2005 its capacity is to increase from the current 1.5 million passengers to 3 million passengers per year, and by 2010 it will be able to handle up to 4.5 million passengers per year. By 2015 the total passenger traffic through Pulkovo airport is expected to reach 4.2 million passengers per year, rising to 7.5 million by 2025.

Airfreight at Pulkovo airport is handled by ZAO 'Gruzovoi Terminal Pulkovo' (the Pulkovo Freight Terminal). In 2003 the terminal, which is equipped to international standards, handled 24,100 tons. It is located beside Pulkovo airport, between the passenger terminals Pulkovo-1 and Pulkovo-2, thus allowing the on-land handling of foreign, Russian and charter cargo on two platforms. It is planned to increase the design capacity of the terminal to 100,000 tons per year. The management of the terminal plan to implement Phases 2 and 3 of the terminal, their capacity being 30,000–35,000 tons each.

The priority goals of air transport development are as follows:

- to extend air communications and increase air traffic between regions of Russia and other countries;

- construct a hotel and business centre with parking lots and approach roads;

- promote air fleet renovation and implement lease programmes for acquisition of new aircraft to meet international requirements;

- develop the Pulkovo cargo centre;

- enhance the technical capacity of the air traffic control system to meet current international requirements.

Road transport

According to GIBDD (Traffic Safety Authority) data, over the period from 1990 to 2003 the number of motor vehicles in St Petersburg increased by 2.9 times – from 376,300 to 1,100,800 vehicles (Figure 3.8.5). The increase was fastest in private car ownership. Between 1990 and 2003 the number of individually owned private cars increased by 3.5 times, while the car ownership rate grew by 3.6 times (Figure 3.8.6). Fluctuations in the number of vehicles and the car ownership rate are the result of some vehicles being re-registered in the Leningrad Region, where vehicle tax rates were much lower than in St Petersburg.

The proportion of cars and lorries remained largely unchanged during that period: cars accounted for 88 to 90 per cent, and lorries for 9–10 per cent. Cars are very important in terms of intracity passenger traffic, and account for nearly 50 per cent of total passenger travel in the city.

At present, a bus-manufacturing plant, Scania-Peter, is operating in St Petersburg; its production capacity is to increase from 100 to 350–400 buses per year. The Ford-Focus car plant, which operates in the town of Vsevolozhsk a few kilometres away from St Petersburg, plans to increase capacity to 25,000–30,000 cars per year in the immediate future, and in the longer term to 100,000 cars per year. The Finnish concern Nokian will soon start construction of a modern

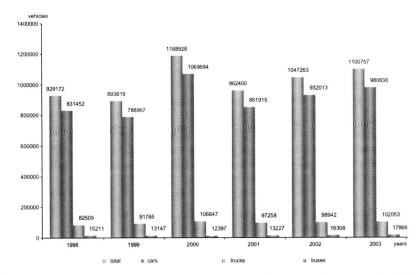

Figure 3.8.5 Number of motor vehicles in St Petersburg, 1998–2003

tyre-producing plant; thus one might say that one successful investment project attracts new investors.

In 2005 the Japanese Toyota Motor Corporation will start construction of an assembly plant for Toyota Camry cars. The plant will be located in St Petersburg's Shushary industrial area and is scheduled for
2007. The designed capacity is 50,000 cars per year. Other possibilities for assembly production development in St Petersburg are being

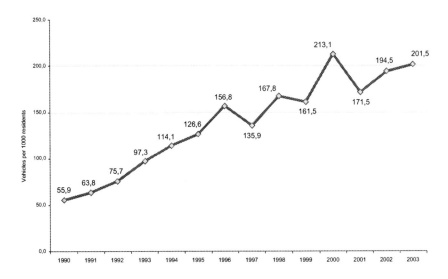

Figure 3.8.6 Levels of car ownership in St Petersburg, 1990–2003

discussed with foreign companies. According to the forecast, in 2010 there will be 1.1–1.3 million privately owned cars in St Petersburg, and 2.1–2.3 million in 2025. The car ownership rate will increase from 202 vehicles per 1,000 residents in 2003 to 250–300 per 1,000 in 2010 and 450–500 per 1,000 in 2025.

Freight transport provides regional and interregional links and carries goods abroad. The extent of use of road transport has widened significantly, as its prices can compete with those for rail services. Road transport carries small loads of high-value and/or perishable goods for long distances, and makes many medium-distance (200–1,000 km) and virtually all short-distance deliveries.

Calculations show that in 2003 the road transport of goods for St Petersburg's economy totalled about 102 million tons. These were made up as follows:

- building-related goods 58 million tons;

- industrial goods 34 million tons;

- consumer goods 10 million tons.

According to the 2025 forecast, the amount of road freight supporting St Petersburg's economy will grow by a factor of 2.6 as a result of increased production and construction, and the development of tourism and services. Capacity will reach 270 million tons while the lorry fleet will increase by 90 per cent to 195,000 vehicles.

A variety of St Petersburg enterprises are oriented towards international freight transport, because northwestern Russia conducts more of its foreign trade by road than most regions of the country, accounting for 20 per cent of all Russian imports delivered by road and for 52 per cent of exports. Over 7 million tons of goods are brought by road across the Finnish border each year, most of which is bound for St Petersburg.

Given the role of St Petersburg as a transport distribution centre, the through traffic by road is forecast to increase significantly. With the expected growth in foreign trade operations, by 2025 the amount of freight traffic crossing the city in the direction of road border-crossings will increase by 4.5–4.6 times.

Freight going through St Petersburg to neighbouring regions of northwest Russia is expected to grow by a factor of 2.1–2.2 by 2025, to reach 16 or 17 million tons.

Road transport works in conjunction other transport modes. Thus, some 80–85 per cent of all freight within St Petersburg involves at least two modes.

The priority tasks for development of road transport are as follows:

- to divert through traffic onto the Ring Road;

- establish freight transport collector areas for waiting and rest;

- carry out staged development of the network of cargo handling and develop terminals and multi-modal terminal systems offering the whole range of customs and forwarding services;

- support Russian carriers in the international transport market;

- develop roadside service facilities to improve conditions of transit and interurban transport.

- improve traffic safety.

Terminals and logistic systems

The special status of St Petersburg as a major transport centre is an incentive to develop logistic activities. At present, 2.6 m^2 of terminal facilities are used in foreign trade operations. Port terminals account for 77 per cent of the capacity (2.0 million m^2). Domestic terminals also serve foreign trade traffic, offering storage, reloading and customs services (many such terminals have zones operating as temporary storage facilities). The total area of such terminals is 614,000 m^2, including 181,000 m^2 of warehouse space (30 per cent).

Most logistic systems are located within or near the port area, as well as near the Kirovski Zavod and the Northern Wharf, and in the industrial zones – Predportovaya, Parnas, Rybatskoje – around Sofiiskaya St. At present, the company Inkotek is setting up a logistic terminal based on the biggest St Petersburg storage system, Interterminal (11.5 hectares), located in the Parnas industrial zone; the Dekort company is implementing a terminal-storage facility in the non-residential zone of Beloostrovskaya; the Nevatransterminal company works in the area of Shushary settlement. There are also various other projects.

For the future, a rapid development of freight terminals and logistic centres is envisaged in the zone of St Petersburg's ring road. In addition, there will be transport distribution centres in St Petersburg to serve regions of northwestern Russia.

Urban streets

Thirteen radial federal and regional roads converge in St Petersburg. The federal roads have an important long-distance influence, linking

St Petersburg to other regions of Russia and foreign countries. They also serve regional and suburban transport, which explains the heavy traffic all along the roads. Together, they make up Russia's European road network. Federal roads that provide access to St Petersburg are: the Scandinavia road (St Petersburg–Vyborg–State border), the Kola road (St Petersburg–Murmansk), the Russia road (Moscow–St Petersburg), the St Petersburg–Pskov road and the Narva road (St Petersburg–Narva). Regional roads leading from the city mostly serve regional transport, although some of them also affect zones within the suburban area of St Petersburg.

The heaviest international traffic is between St Petersburg, the Leningrad Region and Finland. The Scandinavia road crossing the Leningrad Region is a section of the Pan-European Intermodal Transport Corridor IX and is virtually the only first class road outlet from northwestern Russia to Europe. The road forms part of the route crossing Finland, Sweden and Norway, and is important for foreign trade operations between Russia and EU countries.

The road network is a vital element in the transport system in St Petersburg. Its efficiency and sustainable development are prerequisites for economic growth and improvement of living conditions. Therefore one important task at the moment is to develop an integrated road infrastructure as a component of the single transport network of St Petersburg in order to improve the efficiency of St Petersburg's transport system.

Urban street networks link economic activity centres as well as major transport hubs such as the seaport, Pulkovo airport, freight terminals, river port facilities and rail stations, making it possible to create a modern intermodal transport system and so optimize the working processes of different transit modes and provide reliable and efficient traffic handling.

The priorities of road construction in the city are laid down in the Concept for Improvement and Development of the Road Sector of St Petersburg in 2000–08 and the Master Plan for Development of St Petersburg up to 2025. According to these documents, the priority goal for development of the St Petersburg street network is to: introduce high-speed motorways and non-stop arterial roads; divert freight transport from residential zones; provide for easy transport links between peripheral districts as well as links to stations, ports and external roads; and redistribute traffic flows in all planning zones of the city to the best advantage.

High-speed motorways will be vital for the general improvement of the street network's capacity in St Petersburg. These motorways will be the St Petersburg Ring Road, the Western High-Speed Diameter and a section of the arc motorway from Pr. Stachek to Pr. Energetikov.

A map of the projected development of high-speed motorways and freeways, laid down in the Master Plan for Development of St Petersburg up to 2025, can be seen in Figure 3.8.7.

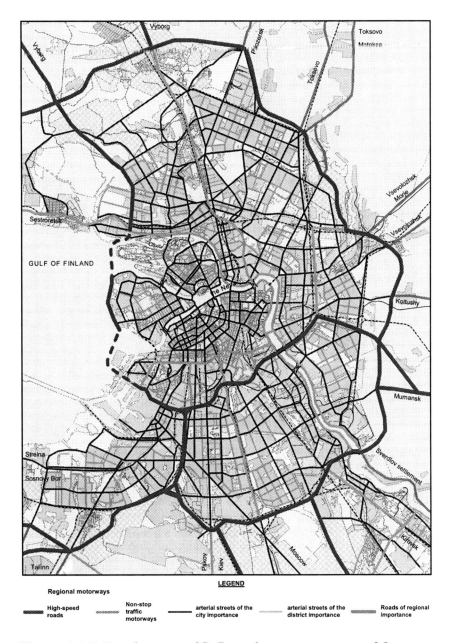

Figure 3.8.7 Development of St Petersburg motorways and freeways

At present, the St Petersburg Ring Road is under construction, its total length being 140 km. The eastern half of the Ring Road is to be introduced in 2005 and the project, including flood control facilities, is scheduled to be fully completed in 2008. For St Petersburg, construction of the Ring Road was a catalyst of the road sector development. In order to make that bypass efficient, a great range of construction projects had to be undertaken to link the new motorway to the city's street network, and a number of city roads, and facilities had to be reconstructed and repaired to serve as access to the Ring Road.

Another large-scale project is the Western High-Speed Diameter (WHSD), whose total investment amounts to US$2 billion. This will be a tolled urban motorway from the southern link to the Ring Road near the Predportovaya station through the seaport and Vassilievski Island up to the federal Scandinavia road. The WHSD will be built as a PPP scheme (ie with private investors involved). So far, a few potential investors from Europe and Japan have expressed an interest in it. The aim of the project is to introduce a high-speed motorway serving passenger and freight traffic at the busiest locations between the southern, central and northern districts of St Petersburg, and linking the city transport hub (including the main seaport) to the federal road network of Russia. The WHSD is to be linked to the tolled motorway Moscow–St Petersburg that is being developed pursuant to the order of the President of Russian Federation. Construction is to commence in 2005.

There is a plan to design a high-speed motorway from Pr. Stachek to Pr. Energetikov via a new bridge across the River Neva. This would allow transport to flow between the southern and eastern districts of the city, relieve the Obvodny Canal (Bypass Canal) and the Central Arch Motorway, and link the WHSD to the eastern road exits from the city. An economic feasibility study fn the project has been developed.

The creation of a high-speed road system in the city would provide a basis for a core framework for development of the St Petersburg area as a key transport distribution centre of Russia, providing for the heavy transport flows between the main transport hubs of the city and their outlet to federal and regional road networks.

Non-stop motorways will enhance the urban high-speed network without making a separate road system. Their purpose is to divert the through traffic from the centre of the city and so relieve several main streets of St Petersburg. The motorways are aligned along the banks of rivers and canals as well as along railways.

One non-stop motorway now under active development runs along the right-bank embankment of the Neva. Furthermore, Vitebski Pr. is to be enhanced to become a non-stop motorway. The left-back embankment of the Neva from the Obvodny Canal (Bypass Canal) up to Troitsky Bridge is to become a semi-non-stop motorway with mostly uninterrupted traffic.

Measures to improve the arterial network of the city include the completion of existing arc links and the creation of new ones in the central and peripheral districts. These will divert the through traffic from the historic centre of St Petersburg. Construction is also needed to cover gaps in the network and increase the capacity of existing routes (overpasses, underpasses, interchanges, pedestrian subways, etc).

One important task is to provide the seaport and other transport terminals with high-quality road links.

To enhance the capacity of the street network the following measures are planned:

- completion of non-stop motorways on the embankments and delta of the River Neva in order to improve access to the central districts of St Petersburg and divert some traffic from the overloaded arterial streets of the city centre;

- integration of existing street network sections into the arterial network of the city centre in order to provide back up to major arterial streets;

- increase in density and binding (connections between motorway sections) of the motorway network in the city centre, reconstruction of bridges, introduction of interchanges to enable non-stop traffic at the intersections.

The public transport system of St Petersburg will also be further developed, beginning with the underground system and other rapid transit modes. The City and major international companies are planning cooperative projects to develop a light rail system, 'Elevated Express', and a rapid tram system.

Achievement of these goals would allow improved transport services, and growth in passenger and freight transport and international cargo handling. The transport work, in its turn, would lead to increased GDP, generate higher budget revenues at all levels, stimulate other industries and create favourable conditions for the socio-economic and urban development of St Petersburg.

3.9

Building and Construction

Alexei I. Shaskolsky, PhD, Institute for Entrepreneurial Issues, St Petersburg

Introduction

St Petersburg was founded in 1703 by Tsar Peter the Great, who wanted to build a European capital as a political challenge to the then-conservative, orthodox Moscow. European architects that he invited introduced the French, Italian and German cultural heritage into city plans, palaces and mansions, making St Petersburg the most European of all Russian cities. As a cosmopolitan capital city throughout the 18th and 19th centuries, St Petersburg preserved most of its imperial architectural ensembles and well-proportioned buildings despite the 900-day Nazi siege and Soviet negligence. The core of the city centre, with magnificent palaces and museums and the grandeur of the River Neva and its bridges, is second to none in Northern Europe – and perhaps in the whole of the Old World.

The territory of St Petersburg is 143,000 hectares. The historical part, with its world-famous palaces and architectural ensembles, covers less than 1 per cent. The 'greater city' includes several suburban districts with parks, forests and farmland.

Alongside the unique central city historical heritage there are the suburban 'summer' palaces of the tsars and aristocracy, whose ambitions matched the royal Europeans in luxury. There are nearly 8,000 listed buildings in St Petersburg, half of them of national importance. Many need renovation, and some palaces both in the city and in the suburbs desperately need investors. As the state and municipal budgets are unable to finance their restoration, the policy of privatizing listed buildings, until recently an anathema, is currently the official position of the governor of the city, Russian ministry of culture – and growing number of legislators.

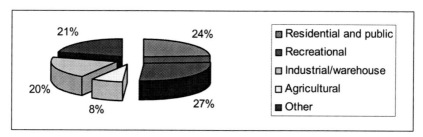

Figure 3.9.1 Land use in St Petersburg

Most of the city was built after the Second World War. The so-called 'dormitory districts' were started in late 1950s by the government of Nikita Khrushchev, who was the first Soviet ruler to start mass residential construction. Practically all the residents of what was then Leningrad were living in so-called communal apartments, where several families shared a common kitchen, toilet and bathroom (if there was one). One room per family was normal. Although the new apartments that Khrushchev started to build were small, a new phenomenon of single-family apartments had arrived.

Mass residential construction – practically all of it financed by the state – continued during the Brezhnev era. However, most of the people still lived in communal apartments (Leningrad was called 'the communal capital of Russia'). There were two main reasons for that. First, there was not enough residential space in the city for much new construction – and the population of the second most important industrial centre of the country was growing fast. Second, the residential space inherited from Imperial past was too spacious; not only the aristocracy but even families of workers in tsarist times had a considerable number of rooms in their apartments. I remember visiting a 17-room communal apartment in a neighbouring house that was built in the early 20th century; no Soviet family, including party bosses, could expect to have such a home.

The dormitory districts built between the 1960s and 1990s now house about 3 million of the 4.6 million population of the city.

Of about 100 million m² of residential space that now exists in St Petersburg, more than 90 per cent is high-rise, while single family homes make up less than 4 per cent of the total. There are no skyscrapers in the city; buildings in the city centre are mostly of 5 or 6 storeys, while new out-of-centre construction rarely goes far beyond 16 storeys. Many single-family homes in the suburbs are obsolete wooden 'Uncle Ivan's cabins' with outside toilets. At the same time, new low-rise settlements, both within the city limits and in the suburbs, are among the most striking examples of a rising affluent class able to pay

US$300,000–500,000 for a home, a price that was absolutely unimaginable for a Russian only 15 years ago.

In 2004 more than 2 million m² of residential space was built in St Petersburg – the highest rate since 1978, when it reached 2.3 million m². An ambitious 3 million m² per year is projected by 2008. In five years, the rate of new construction in St Petersburg had doubled. Some 90 per cent of the new residential space is bought by citizens of St Petersburg.

Table 3.9.1 Residential construction in St Petersburg, 2004

Construction	Sq. m	Number of buildings	Number of apartments
New construction	1,863 937.7	158	26,235
Reconstruction	88,930.3	24	980
Single-family homes	79,104.6	342	344
Total	2,031,972.6	524	27,559

Note: Single-family homes (detached and semi-detached town houses) are listed separately from other kinds of construction.

It is worth noting that only 2 per cent of the residential space in St Petersburg was built by the municipality; in other words, 98 per cent of all residential construction is financed privately. This is impressive evidence of consumer potential, because mortgage financing is virtually in its cradle, although federal and local governments are trying to find ways to foster it. The declared plans of the city government are for 10 per cent of new residential space to be built by municipal financing.

The five-storey residential buildings dating from the 1960s need reconstruction as their materials and layouts are becoming increasingly sub-standard and dilapidated. The city government had started a programme to renovate these houses (roof repairs, building insulation, modernized heating systems, new window frames, etc).

Non-residential construction in St Petersburg in 2004 resulted in about 900,000 m² of commercial and other space in 227 new buildings, including 45 office buildings, 7 hotels, 57 retail properties, 36 industrial/warehouse buildings and 33 petrol stations. Some 190,000 m² of ground floor space in new residential buildings, built mostly in dormitory districts, also came onto the non-residential market.

New shopping centre projects are becoming more Western-looking, and a growing number are being developed by Western chain operators. Retail parks with numerous retail and entertainment facilities are being developed, and in both the city centre and dormitory districts shopping centres that sell international produce are leading the populace into the world consumer society. Office buildings of A and B class have no vacant space – and new projects are introduced to a market that seems to be almost infinitely elastic, with demand so high that practically all the new entries are immediately snapped up.

Urban development plans

The future of St Petersburg's urban development is currently a hot topic both in the media and among the political/business elite. Among the factors seen as most important for the city's future are tourism, art and culture, science and education, financial services, transport and logistics. The city's architectural heritage and location – so close to the European Union border – is a long-lasting advantage that is potentially worth more than oilfields.

The current ratio of residential space to population is less than 22 m^2 per person. The medium-range plans of the city government aim to provide 30 m^2 per person, which is considered a decent level by European standards. Growth in per capita commercial space, hotel rooms, parking spaces is also oriented towards European rates.

Most of the residential and related development is zoned in north-western, northern and southeastern parts of the city. There are 856 ha of land available there, and space for 13 million m^2 of housing developments by 2010. The city government has decided to reclassify agricultural land as available for urban use, thus expanding the city territory into its suburban areas. Other sources of new space for development are industrial areas near the city centre that have evident potential for residential and commercial use.

In the end, however, higher-density development in the central districts is inevitable – though very unpopular. There are quite frequent public protests against new construction. Some 690,000 people live in the city centre, and urban regeneration plans aim to add some 150,000–180,000 more so as to prevent the central districts being dominated by office and commercial build-up.

The 19th-century industrial development resulted in most of the river's embankments outside the city centre being dominated by industrial enterprises. As the Soviet economy was resistant to market forces, no redevelopment occurred in these areas until recently. The same can be said about industrial enterprises in prime locations of the city centre. Under the current city government plans, these enterprises will have to make way for residential and commercial properties. Business is actively redeveloping the sites of inefficient enterprises in prime locations, demolishing obsolete, dilapidated buildings to build residential properties or reconstructing administrative/R&D buildings into business centres.

St Petersburg's city government has just adopted a system of building-height permits and building restrictions designed to preserve the architectural integrity of the original city, its landscapes, panoramas and views. The city centre is now subject to tighter building regulations that are likely to be more efficient in saving one of the best examples of European architectural ensembles of the 19th and early 20th centuries.

Major development projects

Of all investment in the economy of St Petersburg, some 36 per cent goes into construction. In contributions to the city budget, tax revenues from the construction sector rank third, after industry and retail services.

The current city government is deliberately promoting several investment projects that previous city governments did not dare to push through. The impressive list of ambitious multi-million projects includes the examples outlined below.

Ferry passenger terminal

This is to be built on Vasilievsky Island, and entails the construction of six berths with a total length of 1,710 m, and terminal and support buildings with the capacity to handle 1.2 million passengers per year. A reclaimed area of 350 ha, created with a hydraulic fill layer made up of the sand from the bottom of the Finnish Gulf, will be used for a new residential and commercial district. The costs are estimated at US$1 billion. Construction is to start in 2005 financed by the state budget, but most of the capital is expected to come from investors.

The Western High-Speed Highway

This is an extension of the so-called Ring Road (which so far is an Eastern semicircle) to complete the circular highway around the city. A 46-km highway will connect the practically finished eastern semicircle of the Ring Road (to be completed in 2005) from the Scandinavia highway on the north of St Petersburg to its southern suburb. As costly tunnels and bridges will be needed to solve complicated engineering and property problems, the total cost is expected to be US$1.9 billion. Private investments are expected to make a major contribution to the project's budget.

The Western High-Speed Highway would supplement a new highway that is built above the dam in the Finnish Gulf that connects its northern and southern shores (through the town Kronstadt situated on an island in the Gulf), which is to be completed by 2008. It is designed to prevent floods in St Petersburg.

Baltic Pearl

This is a Chinese investment project worth US$1.25 billion aimed at developing 180 ha on the southwestern side of the city, near the Gulf of Finland. A Shanghai consortium of investment and development companies, retailers and hotel operators are supported by the city administration and may start the construction of about 1 million m² of residential and commercial space in 2005.

The New Holland project

This is a US$600 million venture to reconstruct a historic complex on an island just outside the city centre. The existing 52,000 m² of historic buildings are to be renovated, and about 180,000 m² of new non-residential space should be ready by 2009. With a new office, hotel, retail and entertainment complex, this may become a landmark in the renovation of depressed territories.

Moscowskaya Tovarnaya

This railway cargo terminal is a 24-ha plot just beyond Moscowsky Railway Station – a backyard of the city's main passenger terminal. Its warehouses are inappropriate for their central location and are finally destined to be relocated to the southern outskirts of the city, freeing some 300,000 m² of office, retail and residential space in close proximity to Nevsky prospect.

The Orlovsky tunnel

A 1.5-km auto route is to be built under the River Neva, the first of eight such tunnels that the city government plans to build by the year 2025. This one is scheduled to open by 2008, will cost US$350–400 million and is expected to be crossed by 40–60,000 automobiles per day. The first all-season bridge across the Neva that was open 24 hours a day was built only recently. It has always been difficult to cross the Neva, which cuts through the city: every night bridges were raised to allow shipping through – a charming sight for spectators but a curse for those who needed to reach the other side.

Northern Valley

A new development site of more than 500 ha on the northern outskirts of the city may become one of the major residential construction sites. It has space for some 1.5 million m^2 of residential development. The city is to build the off-site infrastructure and sell land plots for development at auction.

Sites for development can be bought (rented) from the municipality or from private freeholders. Under the law, a site for development can be acquired at an auction organized by the Property Fund of St Petersburg, a municipal body that is in charge of selling state-owned and, currently, private properties. Sites for a few specified purposes (like hotels, educational establishments, cultural, sports, health care facilities) can be acquired without auctions, as the city is promoting social projects and areas. A total area of about 5 million m^2 of plots for development is being prepared for auction by the city government. According to the General Plan of the city, some 70 million m^2 of residential and non-residential space can be built within the city limits.

3.10

The Retail Sector

Alexei I. Shaskolsky, PhD, Institute for Entrepreneurial Issues, St Petersburg

Introduction

Retail is still the fastest developing business sector in Russia. After so many years of queues for every daily need from toilet paper to footwear or furniture, Russians are enjoying shopping facilities that are quickly drawing them into the consumer society. With 70 per cent of income spent on goods and services (while housing, health care, education and similar services are still mostly provided by the state) and growing disposable incomes, Russians are customers whom international retailers cannot ignore. Retail's share in gross domestic product is 2–2.5 times greater than in the West.

Although local salaries and wages are still lagging far behind western and even eastern Europe, the high proportion of the family budget spent in stores is a temptation for a growing number of Western retail operators. A young Russian buying Swiss watches at Harrods for £1,500 is planting ideas about opening an outlet closer to his or her home.

Retail is a mushrooming business in St Petersburg, as in other Russian cities. The retail market has undergone immense change since the early 1990s. After decades of shortages and rationing, Russians are enjoying shopping conditions that sometimes rival those in the West. A friend who emigrated to the United States 10 years ago told me on her recent visit to St Petersburg that her Long Island supermarket is dwarfed by the one she visited here. New retail formats are driving crowds of Russians to vote with their feet for the consumer society through their changing consumer behaviour, following the path of the rest of eastern Europe. Although the greatest retail changes in Russia are happening in Moscow, St Petersburg is the second logical destination for Russian and Western retail chains.

Retail premises in St Petersburg occupy some 4 million m², which is less than 0.9 m² per person. Most shopping facilities are obsolete, atavistic Soviet-style stores filled with dubious Chinese or Turkish reproductions of branded products. In this bleak retailscape, amazing new projects are growing fast, and demand far exceeds supply. Currently about 60 shopping centres, department stores and hypermarkets are open in St Petersburg, with about 30 being built or redeveloped. About 270,000 m^2 of modern shopping centre space was opened in 2004. In 2005, another 300,000 to 400,000 m^2 is expected. Some 18 new retail centres are expected to open, nearly half of them hypermarkets.

Macroeconomic trends

St Petersburg is second largest Russian city, and has a population of 4.6 million. Although its population is declining, per capita incomes are growing and the city government predicts that by 2008 the median monthly income will exceed US$550 (today's is US$360). Retail turnover in St Petersburg grew by 25.1 per cent in 2004, with 38.6 per cent spent on food and 61.4 per cent on non-food items.

Although St Petersburg has no oil or gas resources, in the six years since 1999 industrial output has grown faster there than in Russia as a whole. Even so, St Petersburg does not enjoy Moscow's affluence. Although President Putin is trying to move some ministries (and more important, some leading taxpayers) from Moscow to his native St Petersburg, the purchasing power of the population in St Petersburg can hardly be compared with Moscow, where retail turnover is about seven times bigger.

Foreign investments in St Petersburg and the adjoining territory of the Leningrad Region are growing fast, with the recent success story of Toyota a clear indication of Western belief in the consumer capacity of Russian market.

A steady growth in disposable incomes in the city coupled with relatively low inflation has brought about an explosion in consumer spending that provides a solid foundation for future retail developments. The country's positive macroeconomic outlook, the successful development of St Petersburg's economy and the projected national and local GDP growth have fuelled a burgeoning retail market that is absorbing practically all new entries (with just a few unsuccessful examples). There are few vacant premises (5 per cent or less), and successful centres have a waiting list of tenants that want to expand or join the sector.

Experts believe that the growth in large food retailers will continue, with only minor competition. Finnish Super Siwa, a deli supermarket, is doing well although two local chains – Lenta cash-and-carry and O'Key hypermarket – have opened opposite it. By an odd coincidence, these three were already operating alongside each other in two different locations in the city in the northern and western parts. But an even more exuberant grouping of no fewer than five enterprises seems to be developing in the south, near Pulkovo airport, where a successful Lenta was joined in May 2005 by its German counterpart Metro, with O'Key, Paterson and a new local chain Carrousel that will be competing for customers within walking distance. It is curious that the hypermarkets, which only appeared some five years ago in St Petersburg, seem to flock together in particular location, even though vast areas of the city still lack such facilities.

Major retail trends

Retail in St Petersburg is shaped by the same determining factors in the industry's development as in Moscow, although new formats and operators arrive in Moscow first (the lag between the two cities is estimated at 2–3 years). Moscow is experiencing an enduring retail boom, and the St Petersburg retail landscape is successfully replicating it. Major European companies have been opening their stores in Moscow, and St Petersburg is a logical next stop. The largest companies understand the importance of establishing themselves in St Petersburg and the regions ahead of their competitors. Several Russian retail chains are rapidly reaching the stage of maturity, with foreign retail giants at the gates.

Foreign operators in the market are no longer seen as strangers, with the German cash-and-carry firm, Metro, followed by the Turkish hypermarket operator, Ramstore, and the Swedish furniture retailer IKEA. An ambitious new project has been started by Vinci Construction Grand Projets from France: a 75,000 m² mall, the Rainbow, with German retailers DIY OBI and Real hypermarket renting 17,000 and 18,000 m² respectively. Its grand opening is scheduled for 2006.

As most of the city centre is a World Heritage site, most developments are happening in the 'dormitory districts', near metro stations and along major avenues. Some sites along the Pulkovskoye or Vyborgskoye highways are becoming retail parks with shopping centres and hypermarkets crowding together in an unprecedented fashion. In the city centre, several developments have produced phenomenal 'boutique shopping centres' with prime Western brands and prices confusing even for New Russians. Vanity has just signed a long-term lease for a whole new building of 5,000 m² in the downtown centre. Luxury-goods chain Mercury from Moscow has taken over one of the major department stores in the city, DLT. In 2003, a 20,000 m² Grand Palace was opened on a prime location on Nevsky with 90 boutiques, and new projects are underway. Nevsky, 38 – two stories of boutiques with an office complex above – is another gem of this famous prospect's luxury shopping.

A true retail treasure is Bolshoi Gostinny Dvor (BGD), a huge area in the core of the city centre to be developed when the necessary permits and owner's decisions have been agreed. At present only the listed buildings on its perimeter are used for shops, but there are plans to build several hundred thousand square metres of retail and entertainment facilities inside the famous façade.

A huge mixed-use retail and office centre development near Moskovsky Railway Station may bring a further 300,000 m^2 to the market in 2009–10. A 30,000 m^2 centre is under development just across Nevsky and another retail area is under construction next to the five-star Nevsky Palace Hotel.

Nevsky Prospect is still the unrivalled retail corridor – and has rents to match. In the central part of the avenue, US$1,500 per m^2 per year may be a bargain. With six metro stations and about 8.6 million passengers alighting at Nevsky, that is no surprise. A sales price for a boutique of US$10,000 per m^2 has already been reported. Nevsky outstrips all competition, but is followed by other retail corridors such as Vladimirsky, Bolshoy in the Petrogradsky district and Liteiny. Prime high-street shop rents are in the area of US$1,000 per m^2 per year. A less favourable space can be found for US$500–800 per m^2 per annum, but rents in the hot spots rarely drop beneath US$1,000.

At the same time, most dormitory districts have a shortage of retail space and residents are flocking to open markets and new hypermarkets and shopping centres that do well without the anchors (the major tenants who occupy large premises and generate extraordinary consumer streams) and other 'must-haves' of professional centres. Rents there may fluctuate between US$350 and US$950, with anchors paying the lower rates – and sometimes even less.

There have been noticeable attempts by local government to substitute/replace open markets and the kiosk type of retail outlet (dominant in the 1990s) with modern shopping centres. Although they occupy prime locations near metro stations, kiosks are losing ground, with vast shopping centres taking their place – and their customers.

Although the shopping-centre sector is adding some 300,000 m^2 of new space annually, street retailers still occupy the majority of shopping space. About 200,000 m^2 of new street retail is entering the market annually on the ground floors of new residential buildings, built mostly in dormitory districts. Average sale prices here are about US$1,500 per m^2, while in the city centre, sale prices for ground floor retail space in the new residential buildings are about US$2,500, and can reach US$5,000 or more.

Street retail rents are still escalating, while shopping centres may be approaching a virtual ceiling in rental growth, or more accurately in the increase in retailers' revenues, as every new centre has to lease more space to anchors (which pay much less than the shops in the mall), invest in good architecture and stylish fittings, and pay more for the utilities and services.

The still-dominant local retailers keep a sharp eye on the market. They are trying to establish themselves in locations that can either help them compete with the foreign retail invasion or make good profits from the sale of their properties.

Foreign retailers are increasing their presence in St Petersburg, with only a few unsuccessful entries. Those who come, generally expand. Finnish Stockmann, German Metro Cash & Carry, Swedish IKEA and Turkish Ramstore are expected to be followed by other major multinationals. Kingfisher's Castorama is planning to open its first store of 11,000 m² in late 2005, soon to be followed by three to five other stores.

Northern Mall is a Promocentro Italia shopping centre, whose first stage of development is to be opened in mid-2006 on a 50-ha site on the northern outskirts of the city, near the Outer Ring Road. German Real is investing 30 million euros in the project and will own 17,000 m² of its premises. The first 35,000 m² superstore will open in 2006. Total investment in this complex is estimated at 180–200 million euros. The site has sufficient space to develop a grandiose retail park with up to 500,000 m² of retail and entertainment premises.

Although the Adamant chain, with its 11 shopping centres covering 318,000 m² in prime locations, is an unquestionably dominant force in the St Petersburg market (planning to add some 430,000 m² more by the year 2007), Sennaya shopping centre is considered by most experts to be the most professional such operation in the city. The stylish Pik shopping centre of over 30,000 m², with a shopping mall, multiplex movie theatre and a number of restaurants and cafes, has opened next to Sennaya. There have been no complaints about consumer drain: rather, it has proved a consumer draw.

Among the major food market players are Liat-Dixie, Agrotorg and Lenta. They are competing with foreign chains that are becoming serious about Russia's second capital.

A newcomer to the market, Macromir, is building a new chain of retail and entertainment centres and themed parks. It is scheduled to open about 450,000 m² of new retail space at prominent locations near metro stations and/or on major thoroughfares by the end of 2007.

Another recent entry is Gulliver, with its 60,000 m² of retail and entertainment space, shopping malls, food courts, bowling alleys, movie theatres and two anchors: the Ramstore hypermarket and a 10,000 m² electronic store, Matrix.

The biggest retail and entertainment complex, the 73,000 m² Grand Canyon, is expected to open soon in the northern part of the city.

Together with the existing complex, Lider, it will occupy 150,000 m^2. Anchors are Ramstore, electronic hyperstore M.Video and the multiplex Cinema-Park.

Several successful Russian chains are going public or being sold to foreign operators. The most successful grocery discount chain Pyaterochka (460 supermarkets in Russia, Ukraine and Kazakhstan) has established itself on the London Stock Exchange with Global Depositary Receipts on 30 per cent of Pyaterochka Holding that is expected to bring US$598–735 million. The British retailing store Dixons has signed an option to buy Eldorado – a major electronic Russian chain – for US$1.9 billion by 2011 (Eldorado's turnover in 2004 was US$2.5 billion).

Future outlook

Retail is mushrooming in both Moscow and St Petersburg, although the rest of Russia (except a few major cities) lacks most of the pleasures of modern shopping. The present trends of retail industry in St Petersburg are expected to continue, with accelerating sophistication and a diminishing proportion of kiosks and open markets. Municipal policy favours modern big-box retailing and is deliberately squeezing out old-fashioned small-scale retailers from the city. The turnover of kiosks and open markets has dropped to below 13 per cent of total retail sales.

Shopping centres are becoming more professional, with food courts and entertainment becoming a necessary component for any new project. The time has gone when the word 'anchor' in Russia was purely a marine term; now anchors and big-boxers are carefully selected – and the choice is expanding.

Department stores have seen better days. There is no evidence that local department stores, once the unquestioned market leaders, will revive. Perhaps foreign operators (Finnish Stockmann, BHS and some other international leaders are mentioned) will fill the niche.

Entertainment is also booming. Multiplexes and bowling alleys are not enough: themed shopping centres are on the way, with Neptune's 28,000 m^2 (to be extended to 68,000 m^2) hosting the clone of a famous Singapore oceanarium to be opened by October 2005. Pieter/IB-Group, Neptune's management company, has successfully launched the Sennaya shopping centre, the most professional in the city. Rodeo Drive and Grand Canyon are paying tribute to the founding fathers of themed shopping centres, reflecting a new stage of maturity in the industry. International entrants will bring the most up-to-date expertise and make the retail landscape in St Petersburg more competitive and efficient.

Conclusion

The impressive, as-yet unrealized growth potential within the retail sector in St Petersburg is the reason for the optimism that both developers and operators share. People are exploring new retail formats once seen only in Hollywood movies, flocking to hypermarkets and discounters, DIY stores and cash-and-carry. Replicas of Western shopping centre/hypermarket/supermarket subcultures are opening in new buildings or brownfield redevelopment, and self-service retail is booming. At the same time, unsophisticated companies or shopping centres built years ago that lack dynamism and fail to remodel themselves and redevelop are experiencing escalating problems with tenants and rent decline.

The 'wee-box' retailing that was most popular in the mid-1990s and early 2000s, when tiny 8–15 m^2 shops were packed in galleries with narrow walkways, no anchors and few cafeterias, are giving ground to professionally managed, spacious, anchored malls with entertainment and food courts. The cosmopolitization of ex-Soviet shopping is in full swing, and archaic formats and practices stand no chance in the move towards Western consumer standards.

3.11

The Market for Fixed Telecommunications

Anastassia Bogatikova, Senior Marketing Specialist, ZAO PeterStar

Economics of Russia: development of the telecommunications industry

At the beginning of 2004, a new stage of development began, resulting from legislative control reforming the communications industry. The Federal Law 'About Communications' that took effect in 2004 was a key event for the industry. Although throughout 2004 government regulations were being formulated, outlining the procedure for applying the law, most regulations were not approved until the beginning of 2005. Nevertheless, 2004 was quite successful for the industry. The growth of the information and communications technology (ICT) market was more than four times greater than the economic growth rate. According to the Russian Minister of Information Technologies and Communications, in 2004 the revenue from the communications services market reached 540 billion RUB, 37 per cent up on 2003.

At the same time, operators' revenue from telecommunications services exceeded 500 billion RUB, and from postal services 34 billion RUB. The volume of Russian IT services and the technologies market was valued by the Minister at 255.6 billion RUB, an increase of 20 per cent over 2003. The ICT share of Russia's gross domestic product has grown 1.5 times during the last four years, from 3.2 per cent to 4.9 per cent. In 2004, enterprises in the industry invested over US$4 billion in fixed assets development, 25 per cent more than in 2003.

In 2005, the volume of capital investment is expected to be around US$5 billion. Foreign investments in 2004 doubled to about US$1.5 billion. It should be noted that the industry's basic dynamics are determined by the development of mobile communications, and the majority of investment goes into this sector. According to Renaissance Capital analysts, this trend will continue for several more years. According to Troika Dialog analysts, the revenue of cellular operators will increase by at least 40 per cent in 2005, while that of traditional operators is unlikely to increase by more than 22 per cent. Overall, the industry is expected to grow by 30–35 per cent.

The development of certain industries depends directly on the existing needs of the industry's entities, which change along with the country's common prosperity. The growth of gross domestic product (GDP) in 2001 was 5.1 per cent; in 2002 it was 4.7 per cent, and in 2003 it reached 7 per cent, remaining at 7 per cent in 2004. Such continuous GDP growth over several years resulted in an increased purchasing capacity. The number of mobile phones now exceeds the number of fixed ones in the country. Wireless and fixed communications operators were increasingly diversifying their range of services. As the list of additional telecommunications services expanded, equipment suppliers also increased their turnover. Increased purchasing capacity resulted in great demand for many services that had not previously been widespread, together with the creation of a whole range of telecommunications services new to Russia.

One sector of the telecommunications industry is the fixed communication market. Fixed communications operators continue to achieve stable development. Despite changes in the pattern of consumption in favour of new services, fixed communications remain standard for both business and the population in general.

Russia is one of the most 'talkative' nations in the world (in 2003 the average duration of total telephone calls through traditional systems was 893 minutes per line, and in 2002 it was 727 minutes). The high potential of the fixed communication market in Russia contributes to the growth of these figures. Based on the results of 2004, iKS-Consulting analysts value the fixed communication market in Russia at US$8.9 billion. This takes into account local, national and international communications services, telematics and data services, and intellectual and Internet working services.[1] Compared with 2003, this sector has increased by 41 per cent. The number of fixed telephone users has also increased by 2.2 million, totalling 38.2 million people.

Nevertheless, the level of installation of traditional and cellular telephones that exists in Russia as a whole is inadequate, a result of the lack of uniformity in telephone installation in the regions. The basic indicator of the penetration and development level of fixed telephony services is represented by telephone density (the number of basic telephone lines per 100 residents). According to the 2004 results, this penetration in Russia was 24 per cent (ranking the country ninth in the world). Despite the fact that the Russian fixed communications network is among the ten largest national networks in the world, in terms of the number of fixed communication lines and the level of penetration of traditional telephony services, the country remains not only behind the developed telecommunications markets but also behind Eastern Europe.

The uneven coverage of telephone systems in the regions means that there is potential for increasing the subscriber base and the further development of telecommunications companies. This is why most operators, both mobile and fixed, together with investors, shifted attention from the central markets of Moscow and St Petersburg to the regions in 2003 and 2004. According to iKS-Consulting, the unrealized potential of regional markets could reach 10–15 per cent of revenues earned. However, the potential demand for communication services depends on the development of regional economies, in particular on the development of small and medium-sized businesses.

The St Petersburg economy and the development of St Petersburg's telecommunications industry

The creation of information and communications infrastructure may be considered the most important factor in the expansion and growth of business and the intellectual activity of society as a whole. The development of telecommunications services is a prerequisite for creating an efficient business infrastructure, establishing a favourable investment climate, solving employment problems and developing up-to-date information technologies.

The Northwest Federal Okrug (region) is one of the Russian Federation's largest industrial regions (producing over 10 per cent of Russia's GDP), and one of the most developed telecommunications markets in Russia (about 16 per cent of revenue).

In terms of revenue earned in 2004 from the provision of fixed communications, data and Internet services (valued at US$8.5 billion), the Northwest Federal Okrug ranked third after the Central Okrug (46.2 per cent) and the Privolzhsky Okrug (13.10 per cent). Its share was 10.1 per cent (US$0.86 billion), with most revenue coming from mobile communications. The share of St Petersburg's revenue in the industry amounts to 7.2 per cent. As a rule, St Petersburg is consistently second after Moscow in terms of all the main indicators of the industry.

The telecommunications industry is one of the most profitable and dynamically developed of St Petersburg's industries. According to the Administration on State Communication Supervision for St Petersburg and the Leningrad Oblast, by May 2003 753 licences had been issued in the region for the provision of various telecommunications services, 15 per cent more than the figure in mid-2002 (655 licences).

Table 3.11.1 St Petersburg revenues

Communication (US$ billion)*	2004 vs 2003 (% change)	Incl. telecommunications (US$ billion)*	2004 vs 2003 (% change)
1,375,448	131.9	1,318,691	132.4

* This indicator is calculated at an average US$ exchange rate for a period of January–March 2004.

According to iKS-Consulting, the level of fixed communications development in St Petersburg and the Leningrad Oblast in 2003 reached 37.6 per cent, with 2.4 million subscribers. In Moscow, this indicator was slightly higher and reached 40.2 per cent, with 6.8 million subscribers. The level of fixed communications development is determined by the population and the level of telephone density (the number of basic telephone lines per 100 residents). In 2003, the population of St Petersburg was 4,943,900 and the level of telephone density reached 42 per cent.

In 2003 the telecommunications market of St Petersburg and Leningrad Oblast reached US$1,088 million – approximately US$137 per resident, bringing the region into second place after Moscow. The revenue from all types of telephony services (including phone cards) in St Petersburg reached US$266 million. The revenue from the data services and leased channels market for the same year amounted to US$24 million, and that of Internet access services, US$44 million. The main revenue for operators is derived from rental fees and national/international traffic.

Over recent years, the growth in business lines has substantially increased in St Petersburg. In 2001, there were around 18,000 lines, in 2002 there were 25,000, and in 2003 alternative operators connected 37,000 lines.[2] According to information submitted by the Northwest Media Group, in 2003 the growth in subscriber lines for the leading operators averaged 11.2 per cent between September 2002 and September 2003, compared with growth of 7.4 per cent for the same period in 2001/2002.

As a result of activities during the first nine months of 2004, the number of fixed communications subscribers reached 2,546,000. Regarding the long distance communications market, St Petersburg and the Leningrad Oblast is second after Moscow, with revenue of US$120 million from 7,943,000 people.

A significant advantage of the telecommunications industry – last year's leader in terms of growth – over other industries is the fact that, in contrast to the others, this industry grew while increasing the volume of services and periodically cutting tariffs rather than by increasing the prices of its products (as in the oil producing and fuel industries, as well as metallurgy) and the tariffs for services.

The strengthening of the rouble against the dollar (by 7.3 per cent in 2003) also benefited the telecommunications companies. Since the revenue of many companies is based on rouble tariffs, their income in dollars increased, and it is dollar income that must be used in revenue reports. As forecast by the Finance Group, NIKOIL, due to the strengthening of the rouble, revenue will continue growing by approximately five per cent over the next three years.

Fierce competition among operators in the communications market forces them to invent various ways of obtaining extra income and cutting costs. Extra income is mainly attracted by expanding the range and quality of services, as well as providing package services. The fixed communications operators, together with intellectual services providers (mainly Moscow companies), are gradually enabling their subscribers to access intellectual services. As a rule, these are enquiry and information services, quiz programmes, chat rooms and other services. In addition to cooperating with other companies, the operators aim to offer their customers the widest list of enquiry and information services from their own call centres.

At the same time, growing competition amongst the operators of fixed and mobile communication forces them to cooperate in the provision of attractive additional services to their own subscribers. Telecom operators such as Golden Telecom and Equant, together with Vympelcom, provide their customers with a service called 'Fixed Mobile Communication'.

At present, there is a tendency on the St Petersburg telecommunications market for the communications operators to actively develop their own infrastructure. The operators attempt to offer services through their own multi-service networks in order to reduce the costs incurred by leasing resources from other operators. This allows them to make their pricing policy more flexile and independent of fluctuations on the resource lease market. Some companies such as PeterStar and Golden Telecom, as well as Equant, Eurasia Telecom and Eltel, have constructed their own MetroEthernet (high speed data transmission) networks.

In order to cover all districts of St Petersburg and its suburbs, companies have not only constructed fibre-optic networks. PeterStar, Metrocom, Golden Telecom, Linia Svyazi and Wellcom provide their subscribers with narrowband wireless services (WLL). Wireless networks based on broadband access technology are also being actively constructed. In 2003, the PeterStar company, one of the largest players in the St Petersburg telecommunications market, launched a broadband wireless access system to provide high-speed Internet access, create corporate networks, and deliver wireless telephony services. The data speed on the network is up to 10 Mbps. The company's wireless network covers the whole city of St Petersburg, its suburbs and the largest settlements of the Leningrad Oblast.

Wi-Fi technology implementation has been launched quite dynamically, though not as quickly as in Europe. PeterStar and Quantum provide wireless Internet access services on the basis of their own Wi-Fi networks. At the moment, there are in all more than 40 hot spots (Internet access points, usually in public places such as cafes, airports or hotel lounges). PeterStar has arranged about 17 hot spots in St Petersburg, and Quantum about 20 more. In order to make Internet access more convenient for their users, the companies allow roaming between their networks.

Competition encourages companies to expand beyond one region to develop their business. Telephones in large cities such as Moscow and St Petersburg have already achieved adequate coverage, but in the regions communication services are still deficient or expensive. Moreover, regional economies are still growing, and there is substantial potential for the future development of alternative operators. Expanding into the regions will become an important way of increasing profits.

Companies expand their market presence either by acquiring companies or by constructing their own nodes. Golden Telecom – a Russian alternative operator – expanded intensively in 2002–2003 by means of acquisitions. They purchased Sovintel and Comincom/Combellga. PeterStar started to expand actively in 2003–2004. Nodes were opened in Moscow, Veliky Novgorod, Petrozavodsk and Vyborg, and companies were acquired in Pskov, Murmansk, and Kaliningrad.

The structure of St Petersburg's telecommunications market

The basic services of both traditional and alternative fixed communications operators in St Petersburg are almost identical: telephony services, data and Internet access services. At the same time, alternative operators possess a wider technological base for rendering such services.

About 50 companies provide local, national and international telephone communication services in St Petersburg. The corporate market is growing at 20 per cent per year on average. There is more and more demand from corporate customers for modern services, which in turn are proving highly remunerative for the providers.

In 2003, the revenue of the fixed communications market providing services to business customers (excluding backbone providers[3]) was approximately US$260 million, 188 per cent up on the figure for the middle of 2002. Of this, US$188 million was from Petersburg Telephone Network (PTN) services, while the rest was divided among the city's alternative operators.

Subscribers are able to connect to both analogue and digital lines, which may use copper or fibre-optic cable or wireless technology.

Increasingly, operators are issuing prepaid phone cards as a method of attracting more clients to their national and international services. Phone cards represent one of the most dynamic developments in the telecommunications business in St Petersburg. In a single year – from September 2002 to September 2003 – revenue from the cards of all St Petersburg's operators amounted to US$6.3 million. Compared with 2001/2002, the volume of sales had practically doubled. In addition to traditional telephony services, IP telephony services have been intensively developed, mainly provided through prepaid cards.

Over 30 companies offer data and leased-circuit services in St Petersburg and the Leningrad Oblast. This market segment is one of the most competitive and dynamically developed. In 2003, the revenue of the data services market exceeded US$25 million. The overwhelming majority of data channels leased by St Petersburg operators are from local channels (88 per cent). National channels account for 10 per cent and international channels 2 per cent of the whole market.

Internet access services are furnished in the form of dial-up and leased-circuit access. An important trend of the dial-up market is towards consolidation: the leading players control a substantial market share that continues to increase, and the number of small providers has declined. Moscow operators have developed their business more actively. In 2003, Elvis Telecom entered the St Petersburg market and purchased the substantial subscriber base of Zebra Telecom. By the end of 2003, aggregate receipts from the dial-up services of St Petersburg's Internet service providers (ISPs) had amounted to US$27million.

Revenue from the dial-up access services market in St Petersburg amounted to US$25 million by September 2002, an increase of 0.8 per cent over the previous year (while the subscribers base increased by 53 per cent).

St Petersburg providers have expanded the capacity of their modem pools (quantity of numbers used for dial-up access to the Internet). By September 2002, the modem pool capacity had increased by 133 per cent in total, compared with growth of 75 per cent in 2001. At the end of the second quarter of 2002, the hardware of all St Petersburg ISPs ensured on aggregate 13,000 concurrent modem connections. By the beginning of 2004, the modem pool capacity had increased by 128 per cent in total, and the total number of concurrent modem connections provided by the ISPs had reached 27,500.

On the Internet leased-circuit access market, high-speed channels (over 2 Mbps) are in great demand. Of all connections, 82 per cent are from high-speed channels used for creating corporate networks, with only 6 per cent using slow-speed channels (up to 128 Kbps), and 9 per cent using medium-speed connections (up to 2 Mbps).

The main players of St Petersburg's telecommunications market

The St Petersburg telecommunication services market is traditionally divided into two main sectors, served by traditional and alternative operators. These are business customers and individuals.

In addition to OAO Northwest Telecom, a natural monopoly in the field of communications which, according to information provided at the end of 2004, occupies about 70 per cent of the whole fixed communications market of St Petersburg (including domestic customers), the key market players are the alternative operators, PeterStar, Golden Telecom, and Metrocom, occupying 16 per cent, 4 per cent and 4 per cent of the market respectively. The remaining 6 per cent is distributed amongst Equant (2 per cent), Smart Telecom (1 per cent), West Call (1 per cent) and other operators.

While PTN remains a leader in terms of connecting and servicing the residential market, of which it has over 90 per cent, its position in the corporate sector is more modest. Alternative operators are traditionally stronger in this market as they initially entered the market with the intention of providing services to organizations rather than individuals.

NWT values its share on the St Petersburg corporate connections market at approximately 50 per cent. The remaining 50 per cent is divided among PeterStar, Metrocom, Golden Telecom, Petersburg Transit Telecom, and Equant. Figure 3.11.1 provides a breakdown of local lines by St Petersburg's alternative operators.

The main players on the data market in terms of providing local channels are PeterStar (32 per cent), Metrocom (54 per cent) and Neva Line (6 per cent). In 2003, the number of local data channels of these companies increased by 64 per cent, 117 per cent and 25 per cent respectively from their 2002 figures. The total number of channels grew by 92 per cent during one year. Other operators possessing transport networks form the remaining 14 per cent.[4]

Most active on the St Petersburg market of Internet access over leased channels are Web Plus and ROL, who are sector leaders in ADSL (broadband access services) connections, catering for about 64 per cent of subscriber terminals. They are followed by

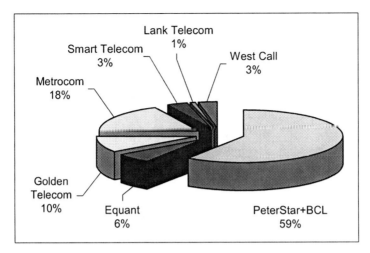

Figure 3.11.1 Market share of local lines

PeterStar, Quantum, and Golden Telecom (with 6 per cent, 5 per cent and 4 per cent respectively).

There is a separate group of operators in the telecommunications market who, based on their main activity, could be described as 'operators for operators'. Over 90 per cent of the traffic on their networks comes from the international traffic of other operators (including ISPs); the remaining traffic of less than 10 per cent (also mainly international) is provided by corporate customers. Amongst this group are ZAO LEIVO, ZAO Rascom, ZAO TeliaSonera, and OAO Rostelecom.

Progress trends of St Petersburg's telecommunications industry

Severe competition in the services market has led to a situation where operators are striving to diversify their business by providing new services. Web Plus, along with the provision of Internet access services via cards and using ADSL technology, has launched the provision of telephony services through IP-based telephone lines, and has acquired an operator, SPb Teleport.

Many companies are entering new market sectors. Those operators that were previously oriented mainly towards services to business customers are now seriously thinking about the individual sector. For instance, PeterStar initially concentrated on providing services to business customers, and generally served individuals only on Vassilievski Island, as agreed with PTN. At present, the company is launching projects constructing home networks on the basis of its MetroEthernet network.

As the St Petersburg telecommunications market is divided among several major operators that have been present for a long time, most major customers are already using the services one of these operators. Operators seeking new customers therefore have to look to small and medium-sized businesses. Due to the recent stabilization of the economic position, medium-sized businesses can now develop more actively, as they are more solvent and financially stable. They are gradually beginning to understand that in order to succeed in their objectives, they will need to employ high technology.

Operators have become increasingly interested in implementing integrated projects, for example arranging a full-service telecommunications infrastructure for customers rather than just providing them with several telephone lines. The organization of virtual private networks, as well as providing digital telephony and Internet access, is an important part of this process. This also forces communications operators to work in cooperation with system integrators, mobile operators and intellectual service providers.

The main players on the telecommunications market have set up broadband networks. Golden Telecom and PeterStar have constructed their own MetroEthernet networks. These allow them to avoid loss of quality and solve the problems of channel capacity that arise providing up-to-date services over copper cable by providing broadband access services (ADSL).

Service providers in both Moscow and St Petersburg are making efforts to fill their networks with content, including games, so as to attract extra income. Online games are among the areas increasing in popularity from year to year, according to the expert opinion of System Mass Media. Over 12–15 million users per month play online games in Russia. In March 2005, Web Plus launched an online game, 'Pentacor', into commercial operation. Operators are also planning to start the provision of new services such as 'video on demand' for the private individual.

It is now possible for alternative operators to obtain licences for national and international communication that previously were available only for Rostelecom. As a result, certain operators will change their status – local, zonal, long-distance operator – depending on the infrastructure they possess and in accordance with new rules on telecommunications networks interconnection and interaction. Golden Telecom was the first alternative operator to submit an application for a long-distance communication licence.

The above changes will reflect on the communication operators' revenues. According to a preliminary estimate of alternative operators, the revenues are expected to be split among local, zonal and long-distance operators as follows: local communication operators will get about 30 per cent of revenue from the provision of long-distance communication services, zonal operators 20 per cent, and long-distance communication operators 50 per cent.

St Petersburg plays an important role within the scope of the general programme of Russia's information communications development. This is the city in which the construction of pioneer technoparks is planned, a large investment flows concentration centre is located, and institutes of higher technical education are situated. Within the next few years, St Petersburg and the Northwest Region will become the largest zones of telecommunications development, guaranteeing rapid growth and investment return for operators.

Note

1. The term 'intellectual services' in this chapter refers to the broad range of communication and information access services provided by the Internet.

2. In this chapter, 'alternative operators' are the new entrants to the market, such as PeterStar, Golden Telecom, and Metrocom, in contrast to the longer established traditional companies. Their tariffs are not regulated by the government and they are not included in the monopolist list.

3. Backbone providers are those who own international and national channels.

4. Transport networks are networks of channels with all the equipment installed by an operator to be able to provide services.

Information sources

www.kondrashov.ru.
www.cnews.com.
www.comnews.ru.
www.miks.ru.
www.iksconsulting.ru.
www.gks.ru – an official site of the Federal Pubic Statistics Service.
Northwest Media Group's research 'St Petersburg Telecommunications Market in 2003'.
Encyclopedia of Communications – St Petersburg.

3.12

The Mobile Telecommunications Market

Anastassia Bogatikova, Senior Marketing Specialist, ZAO PeterStar

The mobile market in Russia

In the telecommunications industry, 2004 was marked by the legislative control that reformed the communications industry. The Federal Law 'About Communications' which took effect that year, was a key event for the industry, the main results of which will be evident in 2005. Despite these processes, revenue from communications services grew by 37 per cent, to 540 billion RUB, and foreign investments in the industry doubled to US$1.4 billion. According to analysts, mobile communication has played a large part in the industry's figures and has attracted most investments.

In 2004, the rate of growth of the Russian mobile communication market exceeded the most optimistic forecasts of analysts: the number of cellular subscribers again doubled and reached 72 million. Since the beginning of 2003 (18.5 million people), the subscriber base has grown more than 3.5 times over the two years. In comparison with the 2003 results, the total number of subscribers has doubled (an increase of 104 per cent), and at the end of 2004, the level of service penetration reached 51.2 per cent for the country as a whole. As estimated by iKS-Consulting, the revenue of cellular communications operators grew by 58 per cent in 2004, amounting to US$8 billion. The highest rate of growth was achieved by Megafon (96.6 per cent), followed by MTS (83.2 per cent) and Vympelcom (68.1 per cent). According to CNews analysts, in 2003 these three operators had 37 per cent of the entire telecommunications market in Russia (mobile, fixed and other services).

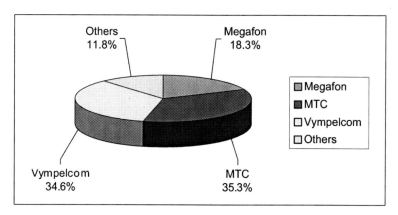

Note: MTC = mobile operators

Figure 3.12.1 Market share by operator, 2005

According to ACM-Consulting, in February 2005 the total subscriber base of all Russian cellular operators reached 81.7 million. At the end of February 2005, the level of penetration was 56 per cent – double that of February 2004, when the level was 27.5 per cent. In March 2005, the number of cellular subscribers in Russia increased to 86 million. The total level of penetration reached 58.7 per cent, more than double the figure for February 2004. During March 2005, the subscriber base grew by 3.8 million (100,000 less than in February), a reduction in the rate of growth of 2 per cent compared with the previous month. Growth in the regions amounted to 88 per cent of total growth, and the regions accounted for over 79 per cent of the total subscriber base in the country as a whole. As of February 2005, the total number of cellular commu- nications users in the regions was 57.7 million, and the level of pene- tration reached 47.3 per cent, 2.3 per cent more than in January 2005.

Figure 3.12.1 provides a breakdown of market shares by mobile communications operator in Russia.

In 2004, the largest Russian operators did much to saturate the market – the number of subscribers connected monthly was commen- surable with the population of a large city and even certain regions of Russia. For instance, in December 2004, MTS and Vympelcom between them sold seven million contracts, having thus provided mobile tele- phones to almost 5 per cent of the population of the country.

According to analysts, the decline in the growth rate was a result of a glut in the Russian mobile communications market. The glut at the beginning of 2005, compared to a similar period in 2004, can be explained by the excessive activity of mobile operators in terms of connecting subscribers. According to experts, the number of new con- nections will also reduce in the future. Increasing competition among mobile operators for individual customers leads to a decline in the cellular operators' average rate per unit (ARPU) and hence their average revenue per mobile user. Compared with the end of the second quarter of 2004, this indicator fell by 25 per cent to US$15. As a result of the approaching glut on the market, the operators' priorities will gradually change. They will seek to retain a high level of profitability, rather than expanding SIM card sales at any price. In particular, they will seek to increase their share of revenue from the provision of additional services.

The mobile market in St Petersburg

History and the main market players

The information and telecommunications industry plays an important role in economic development. Its development has an influence on the growth of business and intellectual activity of society. The development of telecommunications services is a necessary precondition for creating business infrastructure and a favourable investment climate, increasing employment and developing modern information technology.

The Northwest Federal Okrug (region) of the Russian Federation is one of the largest industrial regions (with over 10 per cent of GDP) and one of the most developed telecommunications markets in Russia (with about 16 per cent of total revenue from Russia's telecommunications services).

The telecommunications services market is one of the most profitable economic sectors of St Petersburg. The city's mobile communications market began developing in 1991, when ZAO Delta Telecom launched the provision of services, including local, national and international communications on the analogue NMT-450i standard. In 1993, Northwest GSM entered the market (in 2001 it was legally reorganized as a Northwest affiliate of OAO Megafon). In 1994, OAO St Petersburg Telecom appeared on the market (the company operates under the trademarks FORA Communications and, from the summer of 2003, Tele2).

In 2003, the St Petersburg mobile market became second in terms of market size. That year was marked by three new cellular operators appearing and actively promoting themselves in the St Petersburg market: BeeLine and Tele2, both operating the GSM standard, and SkyLink, applying the CDMA 450 standard. These three new operators (the 'big three') succeeded in gaining 10 per cent of users in St Petersburg.

At present, there are seven cellular operators working in the territory of St Petersburg. Four of them operate the GSM standard: OAO Mobile TeleSystems (MTS), Vympelcom (through the BeeLine trademark), Megafon and Tele2. One network uses the CDMA-450 standard (SkyLink), and there are two operating old NMT and N-AMPS standard networks: Delta Telecom and FORA respectively. Competition in St Petersburg began with five operators: MTS, Megafon, Vympelcom, Tele2, and SkyLink, and only a few local subscribers use the services of the other operators.

OAO Megafon provides local, national and international cellular communications on the GSM digital standard. Services in the Northwest Region are rendered by the Northwest affiliate of OAO Megafon. The company provides the direct city and federal mobile numbers of the 921 code. In addition to St Petersburg and the Leningrad Oblast, Megafon provides services in the northwest of Russia in the Arkhangeslk, Vologda, Kaliningrad, Musmansk, Novgorod and Pskov Oblasts, the Republic of Karelia and Nenets Autonomous Okrug. In 2001, Megafon completed its legal reorganization and started rebranding. By the end of 2002, the Northwest GSM trademark had been entirely replaced by the Megafon trademark.

MTS is one of the largest cellular communications operators in Russia and the CIS countries. In the northwest, it provides both direct city and federal numbers of code 911. MTS's licence portfolio includes 87 out of 89 regions of Russia, Ukraine and the Republic of Belarus. In St Petersburg and in the northwest, a 100 per cent subsidiary of MTS operates – OAO Telecom XXI. MTS has constructed its network in all regions of the Northwest Federal Okrug, including St Petersburg, the Leningrad, Vologda, Kaliningrad, Murmansk, Novgorod, Pskov and Arkhangelsk Oblasts, the Nenets Autonomous Okrug, and the Republics of Katrelia and Komi. In 2004, MTS announced the creation of a northwest macro-region that covered the above regions.

Vympelcom provides GSM standard services for local, national and international communications. The company provides both city and federal numbers of codes 903 and 905. It covers over 66 regions of Russia. In addition to St Petersburg, Vympelcom also possesses licences to provide communications services in the northwest in the Arkhangelsk Vologda, Kaliningrad, Murmansk, Novgorod and Pskov Oblasts, the Republic of Karelia and Nenets Autonomous Okrug. By July 2004, its BeeLine GSM services were available to the residents of all northwest regions covered by the company's licence portfolio. Due to its unified business structure, the subscribers of each region are granted access to a set of additional services, including those based on GPRS technology: GPRS WAP, GPRS Internet, Multimedia Message Sending (MMS) and a universal payment system. The operator's network is being intensively extended in St Petersburg and the Leningrad Oblast.

OAO St Petersburg Telecom has operated on the cellular communications market since 1994, providing services on the N-AMPS standard under the FORA Communications trademark. In April 2002, the company obtained a GSM-1800 licence. During the same year, a GSM network project was established. The project was managed and financed by the Tele2 AB Holding. Since July 2003, a new GSM-1800 network has been in commercial operation, the services of which are promoted under the Tele2 trademark. Tele2's digital network in St Petersburg is part of the national project 'Tele2 Russia'.

ZAO Delta Telecom provides services for local, national and international communication on the analogue NMT-450i standard. In addition, from December 2002, it has operated another cellular network on the digital CDMA-450 standard under the SkyLink trademark. The company provides both direct city and federal numbers of code 901. At present the company is still operating an NMT-450i network, launched in 1991, servicing about 50,000 subscribers; however, it is planning to close this as the licence period expires in 2005.

Since different operators arrived in St Petersburg at different times there was little competition at the initial development stage. This, together with slow economic progress, has resulted in a non-uniform and rather belated (compared with other countries) formation of the cellular communications market. Only in recent years have subscribers been able to appreciate and use the whole range of services offered by operators, due to increased purchasing capacity resulting from the upsurge in the economy.

The year 2003 was marked by the development of new additional services based on high-speed data technology. According to iKS-Consulting, in 2003 revenue from additional mobile services amounted to US$370 million in Russia, or approximately 8 per cent of the overall revenue of cellular operators. In April 2003, a GPRS-based service accessing the Internet and WAP resources first became available for Megafon subscribers in the northwest. The MMS service also became available. The launch of GPRS and MMS allowed the operators to put into commercial operation various additional hi-tech services, and to establish appropriate tariffs. MTS offered its subscribers a similar service in June 2004. In December 2004, Megafon offered its corporate customers a service called 'GPRS – Corporate Network'. This enabled Megafon to access the corporate networks of customers such as banks, filling stations and other multi-affiliate structured firms.

In 2003, services were also available on the St Petersburg market for high-speed data transmission and Internet access. Previously, a high-speed Internet access service was available to the residents of St Petersburg from the SkyLink cellular operator. The CDMA-450 standard that SkyLink's network operates in is noted for its high data speed: up to 153 Kbps. Now GSM network subscribers are also able to take advantage of this service. From 2003, Megafon Northwest provided such data services based on EDGE technology, not just in the territory of St Petersburg but also in the Leningrad Oblast, in places where there is high demand for such services. At present, EDGE technology is supported by 60 base stations. Their number is constantly increasing and, as early as the first half of 2005, there will be 500 base stations. This was available to Vympelcom's subscribers from December 2004. EDGE technology makes it possible to transmit data at a speed of up to 473 Kbps, thus extending the capabilities of the existing services at no extra cost to subscribers. EDGE, as well as GPRS, is a technology that accesses data services, such as Internet access ('Mobile Internet'), WAP resources access ('WAP Access'), multimedia message exchange ('MMS Text', 'MMS Postcard') and VPN. In the spring of 2004, Megafon launched an Internet access service based on wireless data network technology (Wi-Fi) in St Petersburg.

Intense rivalry amongst mobile operators, in their scramble for subscribers, forces them to create additional attractive services. This is reflected in the mass appearance of additional enquiry, information and entertainment services that, together with data and Internet services, contribute to maintaining the level of subscriber average rate per unit (ARPU).

In an attempt to satisfy the need for additional services, content providers have found their niche. The Russian market for mobile content is currently being developed at a rate surpassing even that of cellular communications industry development. The highest profits – 71 per cent of total profits of content providers – are currently derived from the sale of music, logos and JAVA games. Online games bring in 22 per cent for content providers. Within the revenue structure, 1 per cent is brought in by information projects, and 6 per cent by media projects. This is now the most rapidly developing sector. In 2004, revenue from the Russian mobile content market amounted to about US$300 million. According to J'son & Partners' research, in 2005 users of mobile telephones will pay over US$550 million for the use of mobile content. While at present the ARPU from additional mobile communications services is about US$12 per month, in the near future this figure could increase to US$20. In St Petersburg, the companies cooperating with mobile operators include Audiotele, Solvo International, Infon, I-Free and Nikita.

At present, there are practically no areas in St Petersburg where cellular services are not available for subscribers. According to research, Megafon is the leader in terms of coverage in St Petersburg and the Leningrad Oblast. MTS has the best voice transmission quality. The Vympelcom network has the best coverage amongst all operators, ensuring good voice transmission quality. All networks in the large settlements of the Leningrad Oblast demonstrate almost equal quality of coverage, with a difference that can be merely determined by the principle of construction (the network topology). The overall coverage in the city provided by Tele2 remains less than that of the 'big three' operators, and Tele2 is hardly present in the Leningrad Oblast, except in some regional centres adjacent to the city.

At the same time, operators are trying to extend their networks to the maximum number of St Petersburg's metro terminals. In 2003–2004, Megafon, MTS and Vympelcom continued extending their networks in the St Petersburg Metro. At the end of 2004, cellular communications services were available to subscribers at over 54 metro terminals (from MTS and Megafon), while Tele2 subscribers have been able to take advantage of the service at main metro terminals only since April 2005.

Industry performance

The general trends in mobile communications development have not passed St Petersburg by. In 2004, the local market demonstrated a subscriber base growth of more than 50 per cent. At of the end of 2003, penetration of cellular communications services in the city amounted to 55.7 per cent, and at of the end of 2004, 89 per cent of all residents used mobile phones. The number of subscribers grew from 3.5 to 5.6 million during one year (see Table 3.12.1).

Table 3.12.1 Subscriber levels of all mobile operators in St Petersburg (December 2001 to February 2005)

	Dec 2001	Dec 2002	31 Dec 2003	31 Dec 2004	31 Jan 2005	28 Feb 2005
Mobile users	2,030,000	2,840,000	3,500,000	5,644,000	5,797,703	5,911,085
Penetration level (%)	–	–	55.7	89.0	91.4	93.2

In January 2005, the total number of subscribers in St Petersburg increased from 5.644 million to 5.798 million. The level of cellular communications penetration in St Petersburg reached 91.4 per cent (up from 89.0 per cent in December 2004). At the end of February 2005, the penetration level had increased to 93.2 per cent.

According to ACM-Consulting, in January 2005 the St Petersburg cellular market breakdown by subscriber numbers was as follows: Megafon, 42.6 per cent (Megafon's subscriber base has now increased and has currently reached a level of four million subscribers); MTS, 32.5 per cent; Vympelcom, 17.9 per cent; SkyLink (Delta Telecom),

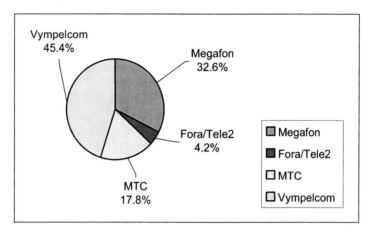

Note: MTC = mobile operators

Figure 3.12.2 Net growth in St Petersburg, February 2005

1.7 per cent; and Tele2, 5.3 per cent. Their share of the total growth in the number of St Petersburg subscribers in January 2005 was: MTS, 37.6 per cent; Megafon, 14.2 per cent; Vympelcom, 45 per cent; and Tele2, 3.2 per cent. Both operators and analysts suspect that this was the heyday of the cellular market in the northern capital.

Economic growth and consequent rises in individual incomes have led to the growth in the telecommunications market. In 2001, GDP increased in Russia by 5.1 per cent, in 2002 by 4.7 per cent, and in 2003 by 7 per cent, remaining at 7 per cent in 2004. Such continuous GDP growth over several years has resulted in an increased purchasing capacity. Some other economic events, however, have no effect on the mobile communications market. When the rouble strengthened in 2004, there was no increase in the revenues of mobile operators because their tariffs are fixed in US dollars.

The provision of cellular telephony in the regions is still at a low level, because a growth in the subscriber base is possible only if operators start to provide services in regions as well. However, this depends on the development of the regional economies, and in particular on the development of small and medium-sized businesses. The deficiency in fixed communication services in the regions is also a significant factor for the development of cellular communications. Due to Russia's rapid rate of economic development and to the high demand for communication services in the regions, the low level of telephone installations in 2003 appeared to be offer advantages to the cellular companies. In 2003, the cellular market grew by 31 per cent over 2002, while GDP growth was only 7 per cent. Such impressive development was the result of 'hypercompetition' among operators during 2003–2004. Cellular operators' proceeds increased in those years and improvements

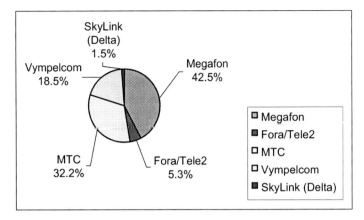

Note: MTC = mobile operators

Figure 3.12.3 Market share in St Petersburg, February 2005

in cost management and regional business efficiency enabled them to improve their financial positions.

As the corporate customer sector is still rather limited, the cellular operators, chasing subscriber base, have been scrambling for mass customers. This was encouraged by the introduction of prepaid technology on GSM-standard cellular services on their networks. In 2003, the number of prepaid subscribers increased by more than 180 per cent. Their share in the all-Russian base mobile market approached 50 per cent. The target audience expanded as operators offered low tariffs based on prepayment, so returns per customer are low. This has led to a decline in ARPU, which in 2003 was on average US$15 in Russia. The Northwest Region is third in the ratings in terms of revenue per subscriber per month (US$15.5) and has a 14.6 per cent share of the all-Russian cellular communication revenues. In order to increase earnings from this category of subscribers, operators offer additional services, Internet access and data services.

The geographical expansion of business and the improvements in communications quality and the level of basic services have surpassed the growth of the subscriber base and resulted in an expansion of marketing activity. The gradual saturation of the market has resulted in a slow shrinkage in the growth rate of the subscriber base. Operators compete with each other by means of different tariff plan revisions, coverage zones, communication quality, service levels and various additional services. Nevertheless, the main factors that influence the choice of operator for subscribers are still tariffs and having an operator in the immediate vicinity.

Because the operators entering the St Petersburg market in 2003 tried to offer different attractive tariffs to win a larger market share, migration of subscribers from one operator to another increased rapidly, along with intranet movements (where subscribers move from one tariff to another within the network of the same operator). This migration was partially the result of the absence of connection charges, which allowed subscribers to switch from one operator to another without loss. This movement of subscribers reduces the period of active use of operator services, and the operator has to spend more on connecting a subscriber than it receives from the subscription. In the light of this, mobile operators are striving to ensure customer loyalty, particularly from corporate and high-spending customers, offering them bonus plans and VIP services, and introducing additional enquiry, information and entertainment services (Solvo International, Audiotele, Infon and the like).

However, although the marketing activities of cellular operators might have increased subscribers' disloyalty, a positive tendency is being observed on the market; whreas in February 2004, 82 per cent of those polled had one SIM card and 69 per cent were not going to change their operator, in September 2004, the figures were 75.2 per cent and 69 per cent. The number of migrating subscribers is gradually decreasing for subjective reasons (sooner or later a customer will decide on a preferred operator) and the improvement in service provision quality.

During 2004, mobile operators were excessively active in their scramble for subscribers. Although the activities of these companies were outwardly similar under intense competition, the operators were engaging in different tasks. For instance, Megafon and MTS were focusing on holding their leading positions. Megafon strove to hold its position as leader, and MTS struggled to retain its current position; although in December 2003 the operator had 34 per cent of the market, by the end of 2004, MTS's market share was 32.4 per cent.

In contrast to MTS and Megafon, whose market strategies in 2004 could be described as entirely 'defensive', Vympelcom, another 'big three' operator and the third to appear in St Petersburg, was attacking the market all year long with the purpose of consolidating its grip. In the spring and summer of 2004, the operator initiated new marketing campaigns practically every month and this resulted in a noticeable increase in its subscriber base. According to ACM-Consulting, while at the beginning of 2004 Vympelcom's share in St Petersburg was only 9 per cent, by the beginning of 2005 it had increased to 17.2 per cent. However, its active marketing policy resulted in the company's ARPU being reduced to US$14.3.

During 2004, St Petersburg Telecom (belonging to the Swedish Tele2 holding) made no marketing efforts to attract subscribers to the FORA network, but concentrated on developing its GSM operator. The fourth GSM operator in Petersburg, Tele2, tried to convince subscribers that its services were always cheaper than those of its competitors. The company chose unusual marketing campaigns and tariff offers to hit the target and, during 2004, it remained a rather stingy provider of information services. In spite of positioning its services as the cheapest in the city, according to ACM-Consulting, Tele2 failed to increase its market share noticeably in 2004. At the beginning of the year, the company served only 3 per cent of the total number of subscribers, and only slightly expanded its presence in the market over the year, to 5.4 per cent. The main result of the company's activity was the launch of its network.

Until recently, GSM companies were not inclined to regard SkyLink as a competitor. However this operator's rather aggressive marketing during 2004 has played its part, and in the autumn all GSM players almost simultaneously cut prices considerably for unlimited tariffs. According to ACM-Consulting, based on the 2004 results, SkyLink's share is not large (1.7 per cent). However the operator's revenue per subscriber is US$60–70 per month, while the figure for GSM networks is much less – about US$14.

Analysts have called 2004 'a golden fall' for the mobile communications market.

Mobile market development trends

According to the experts, the attractiveness of the industry in 2005 will be primarily determined by its cellular sector. Troika Dialog's analysts forecast a growth of about 40 per cent.

Cellular companies develop rapidly as they start to offer their services to non-corporate clients – individual customers – and so expand their subscriber bases. Cellular tariffs for intranet (ie within the network of the same operator) roaming within Russia will reduce rapidly, and for certain destinations this service is now cheaper than fixed-line international communications.

According to the analysts of ACM-Consulting, penetration of cellular services in St Petersburg is likely to reach 100 per cent by the middle of 2005, and the operators will have to scramble for other operators' subscribers rather than for new ones. The analysts are inclined to believe that the focus of interest under existing conditions will be the leaders' confrontation with other market players. While the federal operators' shares on the St Petersburg market have been redistributed in 2004, Vympelcom, focusing mainly on the mass market, succeeded in increasing its share by 8 per cent; Megafon's position became slightly weaker; and MTS retained its share. The market redistribution trend will continue in 2005.

The revival of business activity will also contribute to the growth in demand for corporate cellular communications services. The corporate market is growing at 20 per cent per year, and cellular operators are developing programmes aimed at corporate customers. In the near future, the St Petersburg SkyLink company is planning to revise its programmes oriented towards business customers. Megafon has also expanded its tariff scale for corporate customers. Thus, operators are becoming more active in the corporate market, which at the end of 2004 was undermined by unlimited tariffs (offers that let subscribers call as much as they want for a fixed monthly payment) of GSM operators.

Dealer bonuses for connection were abruptly reduced by the opera-tors and resulted in a situation, at the beginning of April 2004, where most St Petersburg dealer networks started a process of removing the discounts they had given on phones bought when connecting to a network through their shops. This may lead to a reduction in the num-ber of campaigns aimed at stimulating connection to this or that cellular communication network. Then the operators themselves will be burdened with this task.

Approval of new rules in the provision of local, zonal and interna-tional communications will give rise to a situation where mobile operators will be forced to revise agreements with those subscribers using direct city numbers. According to a preliminary estimate by ACM-Consulting, costs per subscriber will be about US$1. This will force subscribers to sign an additional agreement for the provision of redirecting calls from a direct city number to a federal number with a fixed operator (or a mobile one that will operate on behalf of the fixed operator), and the mutual settlement system that exists amongst operators of different networks will be ended. Payments to them will be in 'live' money, so the operators' proceeds will increase and hence they will be liable to pay greater contributions to the universal service fund (USF). (As there is not enough money in some regional budgets to provide basic telephone services to people in remote regions, the government is taking steps to compel operators to allocate a proportion their revenue to the USF to fund services.) This innovation will affect subscribers in the form of a redirection charge, the tariff for which will be established by the Federal Tariffing Service. Deductions to the USF will reduce the revenues of cellular operators, as the reserve will be replenished from their proceeds.

Cellular communications will continue expanding to the regions for the purpose of increasing subscriber base through mass-market sub-scribers, at the same time decreasing the market share of traditional operators. The low level of telephone installations in the regions, as well as an underdeveloped cable network, can explain this. At the same time, increased competition for subscribers has forced mobile and fixed communications operators to look for ways of cooperating. Thus, Vympelcom, jointly with Golden Telecom, furnishes a service called 'Fixed Mobile Communication'. Intensive development of the regional market will demand huge investment; therefore, as estimated by the Finance Company NICOIL, the operators' cashflows will not become positive before 2006.

According to an ACM-Consulting forecast, if the current rate of growth continues, as of the end of 2005 the total number of all Russian cellular subscribers will be 119 million; in other words, the cellular communication penetration threshold will be exceeded by 80 per cent.

Sources

Information from the J'Son and Partners company.
www.cnews.com.
www.comnews.ru.
Information from ACM-Consulting.
Information from iKS-Consulting.
Encyclopedia of Communications – St Petersburg.
Newspaper 'КоммерсантЪ' – St Petersburg.

3.13

The IT Sector in Russia and St Petersburg

Legal and tax problems for investing

Victor Naumov, PhD in Law, Head of Intellectual Property and Information Technology Protection Group, Ernst and Young (CIS)

The development of the IT market in Russia and St Petersburg

In early 2005 the Russian Government adopted a policy to support the innovation sector. By mid-year, it is expected that a special law to stimulate new technologies will be adopted, and a programme will be put forward to promote special economic zones.

According to Leonid Reyman, Ministry of Information Technologies,[1] by 2010 the government plans to establish between six and 10 industrial parks, of which one will be located in St Petersburg.[2] The St Petersburg industrial park is expected to be one of the first to be launched.[3]

Currently, the Russian IT market is worth just over US$9 billion, and, provided that the proposed governmental measures are implemented, will rise to US$40 billion by 2010.[4]

In 2003 export software development, one of the most dynamic sectors of the IT market in Russia, totalled US$546 million, and is expected to reach US$944 million by the end of 2005 (see Figure 3.13.1).

It is no coincidence that St Petersburg has been chosen as a pilot area for IT business development. The city and the region have a well developed IT sector and all necessary preconditions for further

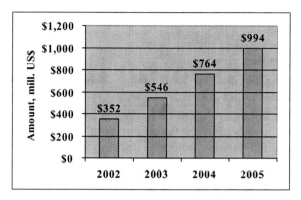

Source: Russian export software market survey, Cnews Analytics, Fort-Ross
(http://www.cnews.ru/reviews/free/offshore/russia/).

Figure 3.13.1 Software exports from Russia: realities and forecasts

successful development: a geographical location near to Finland and the Baltic states, educational and intellectual strengths, IT business associations and appropriate enabling regional legislation.

The northern capital has accumulated huge scientific potential. As reported by *CRN/Re (IT-business) Magazine*, St Petersburg accounts for 15 per cent of Russia's R&D institutions, which employ around 7 per cent of the working population of the city. According to the RF Statistical Committee, as of the beginning of the 2003/2004 academic year, there were 763 students (of all disciplines) per 10,000 people in the population, twice as many as the Russian average.[5]

St Petersburg is home to the head office of RUSSOFT,[6] an association of the most important and powerful software developers in Russia, Ukraine and Belarus. RUSSOFT comprises over 70 IT companies, together employing over 6,000 highly qualified personnel.

It is in St Petersburg that representative offices and research centres have recently been opened by many world IT market leaders. The most recent opening took place in mid-2004, when Intel Corporation launched a software development laboratory in the city. Motorola, which has been present on the St Petersburg software market since 1993, intends to increase its staff to 500.[7]

It is logical that the Russian IT industry leaders are concentrated in Moscow, the financial and administrative centre of the country. However, St Petersburg-based companies have a strong potential to compete.

Table 3.13.1 provides a list based on CNews Analytics data, outlining the position of St Petersburg in the top Russian IT companies' rating as of the beginning of 2005, featuring eight St Petersburg companies.[8] Two St Petersburg companies – Nienshantz and Berkut – were ranked fourth and ninth, respectively, in the Cnews Fastest Growing Companies Rating in 2004.

Table 3.13.1 St Petersburg IT companies in the all-Russia IT Business Rating

No.	Company	Core business	Rating	Sales, 2004, kRUR (1)	Sales, 2003, kRUR (2)	Number of staff	Growth, %
1	Merlion (LC Group), Moscow	Hardware distribution	1	22,160,398	19,322,100	1,500	14.7
2	NKK, Moscow	Group of companies	2	17,671,235	14,384,230	1,485	22.9
3	IBS, Moscow	Group of companies	3	17,167,297	14,414,900	3,419	19.1
4	BCC	Integration	23	2,520,875	1,580,020	520	59.5
5	Nienshantz	Integration	26	2,230,255	962,138	310	131.8
6	OLLY	Integration	38	1,054,122	586,128	64	79.8
7	RAMEC-BC	Hardware production	40	959,373	843,700	140	13.7
8	Berkut	Software development	58	577,582	314,838	330	83.5
9	Polycom Pro	Integration	84	201,670	168,740	87	19.5
10	Reksoft	Software development	93	137,423	100,937	220	36.1
11	Digital Design	Software development	99	115,000	138,800	160	-17.1

Note: Column (1) corresponds to average US$ exchange rate for 2004 (28.81 RUB), and Column (2) to the rate for 2003 (30.68 RUB).

Source: Cnews, March 2005.

The IT business of the region is actively promoting international cooperation. This year, in addition to RUSSOFT, 16 St Petersburg-based companies took part in CeBit; altogether the St Petersburg offshore software development market in 2004 is estimated at US$200 million.[9] Along with the expansion of foreign companies, the market has been experiencing a growing number of mergers and acquisitions. For example, the Russian company Epam Systems (established in 1993; staff in 2004, about 1,200; turnover in 2003, US$18 million) acquired a St Petersburg-based company, Star Software. The deal will result in Epam Systems' turnover increasing to over US$30 million, making the company a major player in the Russian offshore software development market.[10]

Regulation of the IT sector in Russia and St Petersburg: legal and tax problems for investing

Development of the IT-sector is clearly influenced by many economic, social and political factors. It is interesting to see how business agents appraise the factors influencing sectoral development, taking software export development as an example. In the 'Russian export software market survey' conducted by CNews Analytics and Fort-Ross in 2004 they assessed the success rates of solving the various issues in Russia (Table 3.13.2).

Table 3.13.2 Rating success in solving export software development market issues

Issue	At present	In 10 years
State support	Very poor	Satisfactory
Labour force	Good	Good
Infrastructure	Good	Good
Legislation	Poor	Satisfactory
Education	Good	Good
Cost of services	Good	Satisfactory
Service quality	Good	Good
Cultural consistency	Good	Good
Political situation	Good	Good
Integration of Russia in the global economy	Satisfactory	Good

Source: CNews Analytics, Fort-Ross, 2004.

As Table 3.13.2 shows, the most problematic spheres for business are legislation and lack of state support. Let us briefly describe the established practices for regulating the main legal issues of the sector in Russia as a whole, and in St Petersburg in particular. The main standard legal regulations for development of IT-technologies in Russia are adopted at the Federal level; only an insignificant amount of authority is delegated to the constituent entities of the Federation and the regions. Due to the specific character of Russian legislation, the activities of IT-sector companies are regulated under the following areas:

- civil legislation;

- intellectual property legislation;

- information and media legislation;

- telecommunication legislation;

- electronic document control and electronic commerce legislation;

- tax legislation;

- customs legislation;

- export control legislation;

- currency control legislation;

- accounting legislation;

- other areas of legislation.

Civil legislation forms the basis for all economic sectors in Russia, and for the IT sector in particular. The special information and media legislation (or information legislation) controls information relations, and the creation and development of information resources and systems; parallel to it is telecommunications legislation. The primary subject matter of the two last is information and communication technologies. In theory, electronic document control and electronic commerce legislation should operate alongside them; however, this sector in Russia is underdeveloped and is regulated by a limited number of state legal standards.[11]

The IT sector is particularly influenced by intellectual property legislation. In theory Russia's intellectual property laws are good and follow modern international practice, but in practice efficiency is low because owners fail to pay proper attention to protecting their IP rights. For the law to work effectively, copyright holders, the state and society all have to pay constant attention to intellectual property protection issues. These difficulties are a brake on the development of the

IT industry, since its main products, which are the results of intellectual labour, can only be protected at considerable cost.

According to the statistics of the Supreme Arbitration court of the Russian Federation, in 2004 the arbitration courts considered only 750 civil cases pertaining to infringement of intellectual property rights (including computer software, databases and other IT issues). Set alongside almost a million other lawsuits, this figure shows that Russian law enforcement practice in this field is still only embryonic.

The greatest number of obstacles to the sector's development are found in tax, customs and export control legislation. The laws of these sectors include the main administrative barriers, and there are internal flaws and discrepancies in the various legal texts that lead to gaps in law enforcement and reduce legal clarity for the business. This unnecessarily increases the legal and tax risks.

Another serious drawback of the IT legislation is the low convergence level among legislation of various kinds. Almost every legal area uses a separate terminology in its laws, and so it is very difficult to bring together the systems and principles used in different fields. This further complicates the tasks of businesses that have to operate in an uncertain legal environment.

Aware of this range of problematic issues, the Russian state and the business sector have started to develop approaches to overcome the current situation. The most recent initiative in the area of IT development incentives has been a package of draft laws on the creation of special economic zones (SEZ). These are based on the draft of the Federal law 'On special economic zones', submitted to the RF State Duma on 28 April 2005, which is currently being prepared for its first reading. This was accompanied by draft amendments to customs and tax legislation. Parliament is expected to start considering the draft law before the summer vacation period.

For IT, the draft proposes to create special technical incorporation zones of up to 2 km^2 for the manufacture of scientific and technical products, and to provide them with the infrastructure for industrial use, including computer software and databases. The proposed zone creation concept states that the RF Government is to identify the types of activities permitted on the SEZ territory. Tenders will then be applied for by the constituent entities of the Russian Federation together with municipalities on the territories of which it is proposed to create the SEZ.

The overall state zone development policy will be defined by an authorized federal executive authority, while the direct management and supervision of the zones (except for tax and customs matters), and registration of SEZ residents, shall be the responsibility of the territorial authority.

To be eligible to become a member of a technical and incorporation SEZ, a company must be registered in the SEZ's municipal territory. It must also conclude an agreement on technical and incorporation activities with the territorial authority, submitting the necessary documents, including its business plan, to the authority. Under the current version of the draft law, the business plan is a core document that will be considered by a special body – the Expert Council for Technical and Incorporation Zones – formed by the federal executive authority appointed to manage the SEZ. Following approval by the Expert Council, the territorial authority will conclude an agreement with the applicant. In theory, this procedure will not take more than 53 business days.

Two aspects of the proposed concept immediately strike the observer: the low level of involvement of local authorities in SEZ management, and the way the whole system depends on bylaws that specify important elements such as the business plan contents and the sequence of the consideration process.

In addition, the model described in the law imposes serious restrictions on businesses. For instance, an SEZ may be created only on sites owned by the state or municipalities; at the time a technical SEZ is created and incorporated, no land in the zone should be owned or used by citizens or legal entities (apart from educational or scientific and research organizations). Moreover, no SEZ resident is permitted to own affiliates or separate units outside the economic zone.

It is hard to tell when and in what final version the SEZ draft laws will be adopted; however, they will by no means resolve all practical legal issues faced by the IT industry. Among other problems:

- Labour relations are affected by issues related to the protection of the intellectual property rights, commercial secrets and staff secondment (a popular method to achieve the benefits of intellectual labour).

- Taxation, including unified social tax (UST), issues are relevant to labour relations, and there are questions of how to define tax liabilities when transferring IT rights, and a range of other tax issues.

- Customs controls cause difficulties when software and IT are exported or imported. There are also export controls designed to limit the flow of items that may be used to the detriment of the state and society.

There are other topical business issues related to currency control and accounting, the creation and acquisition of IT-sector items and appraisal of the copyright to IT.

In labour relations issues, Russian legislation on intellectual property protects the employer, who has exclusive rights to intellectual property items created by an employee. In the case of copyright (computer software, databases, integral chip topology, etc), the title to products emerges at the moment of creation. One important aspect of the national legislation should be noted: it is considered impossible to assign rights to products that have not yet been created; thus, the creation of each important item should be officially established by the parties. Though this is optional, failure to do so may cause problems for the company.[12]

It should be noted that many details of Russian intellectual property legislation differ from the Western model. For instance, whereas in the United States software can be patented as an invention, this is not the case in Russia, where it is rather a copyright object. If an employee creates an item that may be patented as industrial property, the employer may apply to be registered as the patent owner (ie assert the company's right to the invention, utility model or industrial device) within a four-month period. If the employer does not do so within this period, the right to register the patent for this item shall be regarded as passing to the employee (as creator of the item).

It may be concluded that, as far as IT is concerned in the sphere of intellectual property, the main problems and responsibility fall upon the company. Companies must have effective internal systems of accounting and of asserting rights to any complex, high-value items they produce (for instance, software), as well as for protecting their commercial secrets. Lack of such systems will expose the company to serious legal risks, while efficiency in this area will minimize them.

In the IT sector, there are often agreements for the secondment of employees. The legal aspect of secondment has long been an issue for Russian law. When a researcher is an employee of a Russian company but is participating in a secondment scheme, the secondment could be qualified as labour relations between him/her and a foreign company. For the foreign company it means, in particular, a whole range of tax issues, including establishing the permanent representation of a foreign company in Russia and payment of UST to the Russian budget.

UST is extremely important in the science-driven IT sector. Wages are generally the main cost item in this field, and the RF Tax Code establishes payments and other considerations paid for the benefit of individuals under labour and civil law agreements as the tax base in terms of UST. The existing tax rate of 26 per cent (on a descending tax scale) is a heavy burden for Russian IT businesses, and a brake on their competitiveness. The rate is expected to be reduced to 14 per cent for SEZ residents when the SEZ draft laws are adopted.

It should be noted that under the planned SEZ regime, the resident companies may apply to come under a simplified taxation system prescribed in the tax legislation. This gives some businesses the option to voluntarily substitute a special tax calculated on the basis of revenue or of profits for the profits tax, the property tax, UST and VAT (except in the case of the import of goods to the RF territory).

Customs and export controls are of great importance for foreign economic relations. Customs controls in Russia do apply to the relocation of goods such as software media, though they do not cover the assignment of title to intellectual property items or regulate areas such as data transmission through the Internet. All export/import customs clearance procedures in respect of IT products are time consuming and require submission of many documents.

Considerably more time is required in respect of goods, services and the products of intellectual activity (such as software) that may be used to create weapons of mass destruction or the means of their delivery, or other types of armament and military technology. In such cases, the procedures are governed by customs control legislation requirements. Foreign economic transactions involving IT and specially listed software are controlled in legally established forms through transaction licensing and permits to execute transactions, and by state inspection and registration of transactions.

SEZ draft laws provide for a special customs regime for importing foreign goods to an SEZ, and their further processing without the need to pay duties and VAT (the base rate of which currently amounts to 18 per cent); when goods are exported, only the export duties for foreign and Russian goods exported outside the RF are imposed.

Russian legislation in the IT sphere in question uses particular terms: intellectual property, exclusive rights, intellectual activity results and intangible assets. Tax legislation, however, expresses its regulations in a different set of terms: works, goods, services and property rights. This difference of terminology causes great difficulty in legal enforcement. There are a great many practical problems, for example, over identifying elements: for instance, whether software can be identified as a type of service that may be exported. Another problem is in demonstrating to the state authorities that software has indeed been exported, which must be proved in order to qualify for zero per cent VAT; unfortunately in Russia nobody is sure what is the optimal procedure for exporting source codes in electronic form and dealing with nonmaterial rights.

Unlike traditional exporters in other industrial sectors, Russian IT companies face the complicated procedure of refunding VAT to the exporters of goods and IT services. The export VAT problem is complicated. When exporting the goods, the exporter has the right to a refund of VAT; however, in the IT sector the contractual subject matter is often not so much the physical medium but the intellectual property rights to, for example, the programmes installed on that medium. Thus, if an exported Russian software programme is classified as taxable at the zero per cent rate, yet the exporter has the right to claim a refund of VAT, then in a question of the assignment of the intellectual property title the relations may not be clearly defined.

This is due to the poor wording of the RF Tax Code, which is open to various interpretations of whether VAT needs to be applied and whether tax refunds can be claimed.[13] As a result, the tax authorities need to clarify the law in order to enforce it, while the courts have different approaches to resolving the legality of this tax application and refund. There are thus serious tax risks, which can only be reduced by legislative changes and the creation of a uniform law enforcement practice. Unfortunately, this may take a long time to happen.

The profits tax is also critically important for each sector of the economy. In Russia this tax is made up of both Federal and regional rates, and may amount to 24 per cent. St Petersburg is one of the few Federation constituent entities that have recently established special tax benefits for the IT sector: a reduction of the regional profits tax rate from 17.5 per cent to 13.5 per cent will come into effect from 1 January 2006. The overall tax rate will thus be 20 per cent.[14]

This concession will be granted to entities paying the profits tax to the budget of St Petersburg, provided they have invested at least 50 million RUB (about US$1.8 million) in fixed assets for industrial purposes in any calendar year, starting 1 January 2005, and receive revenue from, in particular:

- selling their own production goods, in particular, computers, fibre-optic cables, liquid-crystalline devices and semiconductor elements;

- developing system software and applications.[15]

St Petersburg has established a benefit validity period of three years for the taxpayer; compared with future SEZs; this innovation may significantly reduce the heavy tax burden currently applied to IT companies.

Concluding comments

Concluding this brief analysis of the main legal and tax problems of the industry, it should be noted that new laws concerning the support of informational and communication technologies are currently being prepared for adoption in Russia, together with gradual coordination of the regulations of various sectors of the existing legislation. However, this does not eliminate the risks for the industry and investors, most of which are related to tax legislation. Moreover, in Russia it is necessary to take into account the complicated administrative procedures relating to foreign economic relations, and the obvious need to invest in measures to protect intellectual property, which is still important for IT businesses in Russia.

In general, St Petersburg experiences problems similar to those in other regions of Russia in terms of the IT industry. However, apart from its tax benefits, the city is a centre of intellectual capital and enjoys a favourable geographic position, further helping to facilitate success and create characteristic advantages in respect of developing the city's IT sector and attracting investments.

Notes

1. The site of the RF Ministry of Information Technologies and Communications can be found at: http://www.minsvyaz.ru.

2. Julia Belous, 'The Ministry of Information Technologies and Communications suggests that the government support industrial parks with money.' *Vedomosti*, 21 April 2005.

3. The first industrial park is likely to be based on the St Petersburg State Telecommunications University named after Prof. Bonch-Bruevich.

4. Prime-TACC, *Telecom News*. 8 April 2005.

5. Diana Wainber. Northwest IT Business Overview. 'Who wants to be 'closer to the centre'.' *CRN/Re (IT-business) Magazine*, special issue No 3/2004, IT Business in Russian Regions.

6. Official web-site: http://www.russoft.com.

7. Robin Munro. 'City vies for position as high-tech centre.' *Saint Petersburg Times*, 16 April 2004.

8. See. http://cna.cnews.ru.

9. 'CeBit Encourages IT Business.' *Delovoy Petersburg*, 15 March 2005.

10. Julia Belous, Gleb Krampez. 'Programmers uniting.' *Delovoy Petersburg*, 16 September 2004.

11. The core document in this sphere is the Federal law 'On electronic digital signatures' of 2002, which has been criticized from the date of its adoption and is seldom implemented.

12. In Russia there have been several lawsuits between software developing companies and their employees, and lawsuits concerning

the companies where groups of programmers migrated, over the title to the created software. For instance, in cases A56-582/00 and A56-8603/99, heard by the Court of Arbitration of St Petersburg in 1999–2000, the claimant unsuccessfully claimed that the disputed computer software had been created by his employees when employed by the company and, accordingly, he had the title to obtain the copyright that had been unlawfully used by the defendant. However, the latter objected, pointing to the civil agreements concluded with the software authors (who had worked with the claimant before the lawsuit and then left his company) on the copyright assignment. These two cases demonstrate the importance of formally establishing the status of company inventions in Russia.

13. Article 148 of the RF Tax Code.

14. St Petersburg Law of December 16, 2004 No. 620-88 'On incorporation of an addition to the St Petersburg law'.

15. The revenue share should equal at least 80 per cent of the taxable proceeds.

3.14

Sophisticated Communications Services within Different Spheres of St Petersburg's Economy

Gilbert Doctorow, General Manager, Eurologos St Petersburg

Knowledge of foreign languages in Russia

Knowledge of foreign languages was considered a sign of heterodox thinking and possible disloyalty rather than a praiseworthy attribute under the Soviet Union, and for this reason the managerial and governing classes seldom spoke or read anything other than Russian. Business visitors were expected to take official interpreters to their meetings and tourists relied on their group chaperones to help with translations.

Like much else, these Soviet traditions have been largely swept away over the past dozen years. Private and public foreign language courses have proliferated in St Petersburg just as elsewhere in Russia. And even if St Petersburg's movers and shakers may not necessarily be comfortable conversing in English, it is most likely that their wives and certainly their children will be able to hold their own in the language and possibly also in another European language as well.

In recent years there has been a massive infusion of foreign terms into Russian parlance. It is not merely separate words or abbreviations, but whole concepts that are being taken from English. This is especially true in such new fields as computer programming and telecommunications, where texts may at first glance look and sound like Russian but on closer inspection reveal themselves to be a string of neologisms. The words may not even decline by cases, and the result is something as semantically confusing as the current tendency in English to use nouns as adjectives in series.

In St Petersburg's large companies and state institutions there are external affairs departments where the best communicators in foreign languages are concentrated, just as in the past. However, unlike in the Soviet period, nowadays people proficient in English will also be found throughout the organization: certainly at the level of secretaries and personal assistants, and very likely among junior staff whatever their functional specialty. You need only open one of the local English-language newspapers and look at the help wanted notices in the classifieds to be persuaded that Russian organizations as well as foreign multinationals operating in St Petersburg place a premium on language skills when recruiting.

St Petersburg is a major educational centre with a national significance, and its universities and higher technical schools have been turning out a steady stream of professionals trained in English and other languages as well as in their chosen field of learning in response to the needs of industry and government.

The English that is written and spoken by locally trained Russian linguists certainly has its peculiarities. To our ears it can sound stilted, fussy, even Dickensian. It struggles with, and generally never masters, the use of our definite and indefinite articles. It fumbles with our prepositions. Its word order is often the reverse of English, with subjects situated where we put our predicates. And it makes overly heavy use of the passive voice. However it is entirely intelligible to native English speakers from America and Britain.

The market for language services within different sectors of St Petersburg's economy

In light of the above comments, we may ask: what is the St Petersburg market for language services, and what does this tell us about the city in terms of its attractiveness for outside investment?

We can confirm that St Petersburg's leading industries and government sectors have passed the first test of sophisticated consumers: they know the limitations of their in-house language capabilities and skills, and are prepared to buy on the open market the expertise they require to communicate effectively and achieve their business objectives. They are ready to open their wallets and to pay the market price for superior quality translations, and given the high rate of inflation and the appreciating value of the rouble in line with high oil prices over the past several years, the Russian market price for translations has moved ever closer to Western European price levels, to the point where today the rate is only about 25–30 per cent lower.

Cultural tourism

In a city where cultural tourism enjoys a high profile in the local economy, it should come as no surprise that St Petersburg's museums and musical establishments have been making great efforts to provide language amenities to foreign visitors. In part they satisfy their needs by engaging expatriates directly, either on salary or as freelancers; in part they purchase language services from translation agencies such as Eurologos, which make the translations abroad in countries where the target language is spoken.

Thus it is that visitors to the Mariinsky Theatre will find entirely competent English-language programmes offered for sale by seating attendants and an English translation of the opera libretto projected on a screen over the stage. Similarly, the State Hermitage operates a dynamic, fully bilingual English–Russian website that is among the most sophisticated of all the world's major museums and is updated several times a week. To a greater or lesser extent, such institutions as the Russian Museum, the Historical Museum (Peter and Paul Fortress) and the suburban palaces all offer high-quality English and other foreign language materials, in writing and audio guides, to assist overseas guests to understand and enjoy their visit.

The hospitality industry

As may be expected, St Petersburg's hospitality industry is also a consumer of professional language services purchased on the open market. Hotel and restaurant menus, promotional literature and house journals are nearly always in English as well as Russian, and sometimes are also available in other European languages.

One may say there is a close correlation between the sectors of St Petersburg's economy most actively engaged in export and the demand for professional language services. Moreover, the given sectors are coincidentally the fastest growing and most vital. These include the food processing industry, telecoms, and IT.

The food processing industry

St Petersburg is a major centre of the Russian food processing industry, with a number of key national players headquartered in the city and surrounding region. And while much of this production is strictly domestic in orientation, the brewing subsector has a distinct international orientation. Baltika is not only Russia's most widely consumed beer brand; it is the second-largest selling brand in Europe as a whole, and year after year the company, which is foreign-owned, receives top official honours as one of the most important exporters in the Russian Federation. Baltika now exports its various products to more than 30 countries around the world, and its export department has to prepare advertising and promotional copy in a number of world languages. They are therefore a regular consumer of language services bought on the open market. The company's major competitors in St Petersburg are also foreign-owned and have all passed through phases of investment in imported plant and equipment which required translation of service brochures and training materials for their staff from German, Dutch and other foreign languages.

Translations into Russian at large domestic companies as well as government offices are commonly performed in-house, since there is no shortage of 'native speakers' among the staff. However, foreign companies entering the market regularly use the services of professional translation bureaus on the ground in Russia, such as our own, to produce promotional and technical service literature for use at trade fairs, or merely in support of their domestic distribution partners. While much of this is contracted for in Moscow, where most foreign as well as Russian companies have their national headquarters, some goes to St Petersburg offices like ours due to more favourable cost and pricing considerations.

The IT sector

Compared with Moscow and the couple of other key IT centres in the Russian Federation, St Petersburg stands out not so much because of the size of its programming operations as because of its clear export orientation. Whereas the Moscow-based software development houses grew as integrators and installers of foreign products to serve the needs of domestic government and industry, the St Petersburg programming community, consisting of many small and medium-sized entrepreneurial firms, has largely implemented the Indian model of export-based on-demand services, with the United States and Western Europe as the predominant markets. Accordingly, their promotional materials are nearly all in English and they make use of professional outside copywriters and editors to ensure high levels of professionalism in their marketing efforts. They also quite often run permanent in-house language training courses to continually raise staff qualifications in communications.

Besides the Russian-based programming companies, St Petersburg has become one of the country's main centres for research and development by leading worldwide IT industry players such as Motorola. These foreign-owned labs work closely with their overseas colleagues on major projects and are a magnet for local engineering talent. They provide ample incentives for young Russians to hone their English language skills.

Telecommunications

Although Moscow is the headquarters city for the Russian national telecommunications operators, St Petersburg is a big production centre for the industry, with such international suppliers as Alcatel and Siemens having a long-established presence in the city. These manufacturers have very large and ongoing requirements for translation of their technical literature into Russian, and commonly contract out the work to local translation houses.

Given the vast volume of work and the iterative nature of the vocabulary used by the telecoms industry, this particular work lends itself to machine-translation and is often so delivered. In that regard, it is worth mentioning that St Petersburg is a world centre of mathematical linguistics, which is the base area of knowledge driving the design of translation algorithms. This explains the existence in St Petersburg of a company like Promt, a worldwide competitor in the niche market of machine-translation software, as well as the presence in the city of the research and production facilities of Russian suppliers of electronic dictionaries and language-training software.

Concluding comments

The conclusion one reaches from this short survey of the multilingual services consumed by the St Petersburg economy is that these services are appreciated by an increasingly sophisticated clientele, which in certain areas is well integrated into the world economy. The level of sophistication in this area is a positive factor for foreign investors.

In closing, I wish to add some personal observations on the positive business environment for suppliers in the service sector such as Eurologos. Within certain thresholds of turnover, the so-called simplified tax regime, with its 6 per cent tax on turnover effectively replacing a profit tax, reduces tax reporting and documentary record keeping to a bare minimum. The liberal rules on money transfers abroad make it wholly practicable to sell foreign-based services such as our translations on the Russian domestic market profitably. And the rising price levels on the Russian market make it ever more attractive for international firms like ours.

Company Profiles and
Investor Experiences

3.15

The Business Experience of Private (Foreign and Domestic) Investors in St Petersburg

Sergei V. Ochkivsky, Director of Development, Association of Joint Ventures of St Petersburg

Introduction

The business experience of companies either partially or wholly financed by foreign capital which have been operating in St Petersburg can be traced through the recent history of the city's Association of Joint Ventures (JVA), a business-lobby organization that has been working with both foreign and domestic private firms for some one-and-a-half decades. This chapter provides a summative overview of the work of the JVA in the 1990s and 2000s, its relationships with both private entrepreneurs and the organs of the state, and four brief profiles of the business experience of its member companies in St Petersburg.

The St Petersburg Joint Venture Association

There were only a few dozen joint ventures in Leningrad at the end of the 1980s. Forming a joint venture was the only legal format that allowed foreign entrepreneurs to do business inside the Soviet Union. A hybrid of private capital and Soviet governmental red tape was not particularly conducive to private initiative, and yet this misshapen version of quasi-private enterprise did much good for the country, and for the foreign businesses involved.

Even in the early days, however, it was clear that joint businesses needed a non-governmental association to lobby for the joint venture sector, still very much the black sheep of the Soviet economy. The free market, slowly but surely gestating in the entrails of a top-down economy, required much lobbying to make its voice heard. In 1990, four joint ventures – LenWest (with Germany), Filco (Finland), Dialog (United States), and Tschaika (Germany) – founded the Leningrad Joint Venture Association. Very soon dozens more businesses co-owned by foreign investors joined the club.

The early phases of the development of the JVA

In its evolution, JVA has, roughly speaking, undergone four phases and shifts of focus in a bid to stay abreast of the changing economic, social and political environment in which its member companies operated day to day. Phase one may be code-named 'informational'. This covered the period when the Soviet Union and then Russia went from having no legislation on private enterprise and investment to having very many laws that were constantly changing, sometimes very abruptly. The political crisis that followed the Soviet Union's collapse was of catastrophic proportions. In this precarious environment, the leaders of the group, by now renamed the St Petersburg JVA (referred to here as SPb JVA), had to dedicate their effort almost entirely to deterring or palliating the adverse effects of ill-conceived laws and executive decisions issued at both federal and regional level. At that juncture, the price of inaccurate or belated information could have been a spate of bankruptcies. One can judge the Association's work by the fact that not a single one of its member companies went out of business.

The enactment of the Russian Civil Code

The enactment of the Civil Code of the Russian Federation spelled the end of one epoch, and the beginning of another, which would become a period of legislative lobbying. By 1996, when phase two began, Russia already had a package of legislation setting the 'rules of the game' for foreign investors.

The Civil Code finalized the formation of a legal framework necessary for foreign investors to come to Russia. The Civil Code, which may be rightfully described as an 'Enterprise Constitution', cemented seven fundamental precepts:

1. Inalienability of private property.

2. Equal opportunities for all players governed by civil law.

3. Freedom to make contracts.

4. A ban on arbitrary interference in private affairs.

5. Free and unrestricted exercise of civil rights.

6. The right of a wronged entity to seek redress.

7. Judicial protection.

From 1995 on, Russia and St Petersburg would see a fast-growing influx of foreign investment money. Better laws minimized investment risk, while rapid if turbulent market growth guaranteed attractive returns. All these developments inspired the SPb JVA to shift its focus towards legislative lobbying. During the preceding years, this would not have been possible due to an enormous number of laws being made and changed all the time.

In Russia, foreign nationals and foreign investment dollars were zealously kept away from politics, so trying to shape federal legislation was out of the question. Instead, JVA focused on local laws, which at the time were allowed to go a long way in 'customizing' federal laws to local conditions.

But the change in priorities did not prevent the JVA from continued exercise of its imposing arsenal of tools designed to lobby and protect the rights of its members at all levels of government. One such tool was the Cross-Agency Commission on Foreign-Owned Companies, established under St Petersburg City Hall on the JVA's initiative in 1994. The commission, headed by then vice mayor and would-be President of Russia, Vladimir Putin, played a large part in resolving a complex impasse, when Otis St Petersburg and Rothmans Neva were retroactively made liable for value added tax (VAT) and huge penalties. Co-hosted by the Association, a roundtable with Russian government officials resulted in the repeal of the charge for the use of the word 'Russia' in a company name. The charge had affected many joint ventures that were compelled to use the word 'Russia' in their names under previous legislation.

A launch pad for civilized interaction between business and the state

Over the course of time, SPb JVA has become a launch pad for civilized interaction between authorities and the city's most dynamic economy sector. But foreign co-owned businesses themselves set a good example of such civilized interaction. Unlike their Russian counterparts, they dutifully abide by Russian law, paying all taxes, never paying their employees off the books, and providing fringe benefits for their staff. Of the city's top 10 taxpayers, six are partially or fully foreign-owned companies. With this much clout, the JVA Executive Directorate has been able to negotiate successfully with federal and regional authorities, securing appropriate decisions, overturning many bureaucratic hurdles, and thwarting counterproductive ordinances. An additional argument in favour of joint ventures is that, in the industries where they operate, such joint ventures shape and promote better business ethics and best practice in the Russian business community, bringing it closer to internationally accepted standards. But foreign investment is not an abstract notion. It means that Russia's economy is being refurbished and revitalized with cutting-edge technology, equipment and management practices. The result is that domestic products have become more competitive internationally.

Many former Association executives have been very successful in their subsequent careers, and some have become prominent statesmen. V. I. Kozhin, who stood at the helm of SPb JVA in 1993 through 1994, currently manages the Office of the President of Russia. Former Executive Board member V. I. Yakunin was first appointed senior deputy to the Railways Minister, and then senior deputy to the President of Russian Railways OAO. Of the other former Executive Board members, A. N. Niago currently heads the state-run nuclear power company TVEL; A. N. Gendelev works for the Office of Overseas Properties of the President of Russia; and A. I. Vakhmistrov is Vice-Governor of St Petersburg.

In 1998, the St Petersburg Legislative Assembly passed three ordinances that became definitive for foreign investment, all proposed by the JVA and drafted in collaboration with its consultants. After this, St Petersburg briefly became one of Russia's most attractive destinations for foreign investment dollars.

Two federal ordinances, enacted in 1999 and 2000 respectively, hobbled the investment incentives provided by the local laws. These counterproductive ordinances were: the Federal Act Re: Foreign Investment in the Russian Federation and Part Two of the Russian Fiscal Code. Both deprived foreign investors of incentives in the name of giving domestic and foreign investors equal opportunity, and severely curtailed regional governments' discretion in regulating the investment process.

In 1998, the Association's effort resulted in first a suspension and then repeal of the Russian Central Bank Directive Re: Delegating Foreign Currency Settlement in Export and Import Transactions, which had had considerable adverse implications for business. The second operating phase of SPb JVA ended by 2000, when Vladimir

Putin was elected President of Russia. By that time, Russia's economy had substantially recovered from the 1998 currency crisis, and in 2000 steady economic growth began, driven by both a depreciated rouble, and the government's consistent effort in revitalizing Russia's statehood and consolidating political stability.

In this more favourable environment, SPb JVA changed its main focus once again, this time in favour of helping its member companies develop their businesses. This called for a new strategy and a new arsenal of tools to influence authorities at all levels. SPb JVA drafted and adopted its new medium-term strategy at its general meeting in early 2003.

A more favourable business environment

A more favourable business environment is only possible where businesses can efficiently interact with authorities and the latter have a vested interest in making the ideas of the business community work. In other words, authorities and businesses need to strike a mutually acceptable compromise. In this context, a non-governmental association like SPb JVA plays a much stronger role, being in an exclusive position to pave the way for businesses and authorities to meet each other halfway. But once the parties have found an equilibrium that both are happy with, the association must look out for the government as well as the private sector. To be an effective watchdog and lobbyist for private businesses, it is essential to find a way to meet their needs by balancing them with the interests of the state and society.

Having learned this lesson, SPb JVA focused on precisely that task. In view of the failure of the then incumbent of St Petersburg City Hall to formulate a cohesive investment policy, it was decided to help authorities address that priority. After a sizable amount of research, Association consultants came up with an Investment Policy Concept for St Petersburg, drawing on both the Association's own vast experience and the success stories of those Russian regions that had been most successful in wooing investors. The Concept analysed the legal framework for investment in St Petersburg and Russia, identified the main problems facing investors, and set forth recommendations for federal and regional executive authorities and lawmakers.

In the autumn of 2003, copies of the Concept were issued to all key economic decision makers in the new municipal government, including the new governor, Valentina Matvienko. Some of the JVA's recommendations are already being put into action. The city now has a vice-governor in charge of investment, a new Committee for Investment and Strategic Projects, and two investment agencies.

The Investment Code of St Petersburg

On 27 October 2004, the St Petersburg Legislative Assembly passed the first draft of the Law Re: Investment Code of St Petersburg, drafted by the Legislation Committee in collaboration with JVA consultants, drawing on the guidelines set out in the Concept. Both the Concept and the Code were drafted with important contributions from international and Russian consulting firms, including PricewaterhouseCoopers, Duvernois Consulting, EPAM Law Offices, Hedman Osborne Clarke Alliance, the Institute of Enterprise Studies, Consult, and Baker and McKenzie. Investors are looking forward to the enactment of the Code, scheduled for summer 2005, which will make St Petersburg the first region in Russia to have adopted a codified ordinance, blazing the trail for a new area of jurisprudence – investment law – in Russia.

The Code is like no other existing investment ordinance, federal or regional, in that it is a 'package' bill covering all agendas at once. So far, the greatest difficulties for investors have arisen out of their relationship with regional authorities. Responding to this problem, the Code is heavy on processes, procedures, timelines and accountability of officials responsible for implementation over the entire spectrum of issues pertaining to the relationship between authorities and investors. The key points of the Code are:

- conservation of the tax environment existing as of the date financing begins to flow into an investment project, for the duration of the payback period but no longer than seven years;

- survivorship of investment agreements when officials are replaced or changes are made to how the investment process is regulated;

- that no investment may be nationalized without prior, equitable compensation by the state for all and any loss thus caused to the investor and/or other project stakeholders;

- an equal footing for authorities and investors when it comes to complying with investment law and any applicable agreements, as well as any restrictions, procedures and policies therein stipulated.

The Investment Code text is available in the Regional Investment Law section at www.spbasp.ru.

The promotion of legislative lobbying

In addition, legislative lobbying has continued along the lines of ideas and proposed amendments to existing federal and St Petersburg ordinances.

One notable problem arose over Constitutional Court Ruling No. 169-0, which empowered internal revenue bodies to disregard the existing practice of VAT deductions. Law-abiding taxpayers woke up one day as suspected criminals. The situation was fraught with positively catastrophic implications for both businesses and the entire economy. The active stance taken by the Association alongside other NGOs helped defuse the conflict.

In order to maximize sales for Association members, SPb JVA consultants have teamed up with municipal government officials to form work groups addressing the following issues:

- a better purchasing system for St Petersburg government contracts, worth around US$2.5 billion a year;

- increasing the number of manufacturing companies supplying Russian Railways OAO to the tune of around US$8 billion annually.

This effort will continue, but in due course SPb JVA plans to get other 'natural' monopolies involved, such as UES RAO and Gazprom RAO.

Having looked into the business of Association members, SPb JVA consultants have identified a problem stemming from an insufficient number of domestic turn-key component suppliers serving the manufacturing and high-tech industries. To address this weakness, Interkos-VI, an Association member, teamed up with the JVA Executive Directorate to draft and submit to the St Petersburg government a list of proposals on how to manage the restructuring and development of local component-manufacturing companies. The resultant cluster of manufacturers will be able to meet the subcontracting needs of other industries as well.

More recently, the Association has submitted to the St Petersburg government a set of proposals, drafted by St Petersburg Oil Terminal, on how to reengineer the way the city's transportation and transit industry is managed. A new specialized committee has been established by City Hall to oversee this project.

Over the course of handling all these priorities, the Executive Directorate became aware of an information problem or, in other words, a lack of information infrastructure for business. To fill the information gap, SPb JVA has taken steps to establish an information system to keep entrepreneurs fully updated on market status and developments. A prototype has been identified for such a system, but it needs some more work. The Association is currently negotiating with prospective investors for this project, both private and municipal.

As a problem-solver for Association members, the Executive Directorate has had to address an extensive cross-spectrum of issues, including:

- allotment of land plots for new construction, and real estate properties;

- infrastructure support for business development;

- helping Association members enter other regional markets in Russia;

- many other problems Association members run into when dealing with federal and regional government bodies.

Problem-solving for the business community

As a helpful problem-solver for the business community, the Association has matured and grown stronger, assuming a range of new responsibilities as an investment guide, expert, and support network for investment projects. The high professional level of our services is assured by top-notch specialists working for our member companies and/or sitting on the Directorate. Association member companies do business across the entire range of fields essential to making any investment project – no matter how challenging – a success.

The state could not help noticing, and its top decision-makers could not have failed to appreciate, the achievements of the SPb JVA. Association head, N. V. Sivach, has been awarded an Order for Service to the Homeland, Class II, for his contribution to improving the city's foreign investor appeal, implementing new technology and creating new jobs. The President of Russia, Vladimir Putin, has praised the Association for its time-honoured commitment to the success and prosperity of joint business. Putin has issued a series of decrees giving national awards to SPb JVA members. Overall, more than 100 company CEOs and executives, including foreign nationals, have received awards for their commitment to promoting better international ties. These include H. Guffers (Philip Morris Izhora), V. O. Suomalainen (Neste St Petersburg), Z. Sethi (PricewaterhouseCoopers), M. Bason (Petro JTI), J. Wanderplatze and D. Jeger (Alcatel), M. H. Gerd (Astoria), V. Deseny, H. Halem and B. Knauf (Pobeda), J. T. Koskinen (Mantsinen) and O. Staas (Radisson SAS).

The St Petersburg Joint Venture Association, which will be marking its 15th anniversary this year, has over the years matured as a powerful network uniting the front-tier foreign-owned companies operating in St Petersburg and the Leningrad Region, and has built up a solid reputation as an efficient problem-solver in the service of the business community.

JVA address:

58 Moika River nab., Suite 316,
St Petersburg 190000, Russia
Tel.: +7(812) 312-7954
Fax: +7(812) 315-9470
e-mail: association@jv.spb.ru
http: www.spbasp.ru

Executive Directorate:
Nikolai V. Sivach, President
Sergei V. Ochkivsky, Director of Development

Profile 1: Pulkovo Holding and Pulkovo Management Company

The industrial and constructing corporation Pulkovo was founded in 2004 as the managing company for Pulkovo Holdings, which includes several consolidated enterprises operating together from the one location and drawn together by joint capital and the implementation of mutual projects. The companies acting under Pulkovo Holdings are in essence one commercial structure. The core business of the Pulkovo Group is centred on the construction industry, and the group is heavily involved in the design, production and assembly of industrial, administrative, commercial and sports complexes and buildings. Other areas of business include the marketing and sale of buildings materials such as sandwich-panels, metalware and fireproof doors in the Russian and ex-Soviet markets.

The enterprises in Pulkovo Holdings include several firms, namely:

- OAO Aeroportstroy (founded in 1941), which designs and produces metalware and undertakes building and assembling jobs. The company built the airports of Leningrad, Murmansk, Riga and several other cities.

- ZAO Petropanel (founded in 1999), which produces wall and roof sandwich-panels, shaped elements and profiles. The shaped elements can be assembled in practically any configuration according to the requirements of specific projects.

- OAO Petropanel (founded in 2001), which produces modern fireproof doors, under licence, using the technology and equipment of the Finnish company, Saajos Oy. The possibility of launching a joint venture with this company with the purpose of manufacturing marine and anti-burglar doors is being contemplated at present.

- OOO Monolitstroyinvest (founded in 2004), which manufactures high-quality ready-mixed concrete.

- OOO Riburg (founded in 2004), which designs and produces window and door assemblies in association with the German firm Shuko metal-based laminate.

All of the enterprises comprising Pulkovo Holdings are private and have no state equity. OAO Aeroportstroy, which was privatized in 1995, is the only former state enterprise in the group. OOO Riburg is a joint venture company with foreign investors, as 50 per cent of the enterprise is owned by private individuals from Latvia.

It is difficult to estimate the market share of the Pulkovo Group in St Petersburg's market for the construction of industrial buildings, or of the market of metal frames and sandwich-panels, since both have been growing rapidly in recent years, with dozens of new suppliers and producers appearing. However, it is not unreasonable to suggest that Pulkovo holds around 8–12 per cent of these markets in St Petersburg and northwestern Russia. The company also has a presence in the market for construction and building materials in the remainder of Russia, though this could be as small as 1 per cent.

Pulkovo is a strong player with regards to both domestic and foreign competitors for the quality level of its products, production technologies and output. The company employs an operating system whereby design technology is united in a single chain with production (the application suite of the three-dimensional design 'Hyper Style' makes this possible). The company's designers have received training in Sweden and the United States, which gives a further guarantee of high quality. A number of European customers, including Rockwool (Denmark), KPA Unicon (Finland), Estconde (Estonia) have agreed contracts with Pulkovo even without asking for tenders, since they seem to realize that quality must come first and this largely determines the price. Unfortunately, the majority of Russian customers and general contractors prefer minimal price and minimal quality.

Pulkovo differs markedly from the overwhelming majority of both Russian and foreign construction firms since it owns its own manufacturing facilities, which allows the company to increase its competitive capacity in terms of prices, quality of work and timing of orders. The company is thus the pre-eminent leader in the northwestern Russian market for construction and building materials. The company's exports are at present minimal due to the dynamically expanding needs of the domestic market.

The Russian construction market suffers from a lack of quality raw materials, and Pulkovo has to currently import mineral wool from Rockwool (Poland) and Paroc (Finland). However, the high demand for their products is forcing these producers to move some of their production to Russia: Rockwool is currently building a plant in the Russian city of Vyborg (with the assistance of Pulkovo), while Paroc plans to build a plant in northwest Russia. In order to accommodate its production of sandwich panels, Pulkovo imports further production units from the Ruukki (Finland), SSAB (Sweden), Corus (England) and Thyssen Krupp (Germany). The company sources its metal from Russian producers due to the relatively high quality and low price. The equipment and range of production technologies used by Pulkovo comes from the United Kingdom, Germany, Holland and Finland and includes such well known brands as Kaltenbach, Hyperterm, Gietart, Isowall, Finn-Power, Elba, Stahl, Kemppi and Geka, among many others.

Although the current Russian business climate and legal framework for the development of business is far from perfect, the fact that the volume of business in the construction market is so high at the moment more than compensates for these legal and institutional disadvantages, in the view of Pulkovo's management. More and more foreign companies are establishing themselves in Russia, and Pulkovo's management believes that in due course the legal and institutional environment will also improve. Having reliable partners in the current Russian construction market will help foreign companies realize the fact that delays in entering the market now will result in lost opportunities later. Pulkovo is therefore interested in making contact with foreign partners to undertake large industrial projects both in Russia and abroad.

Basic company data

Pulkovo conforms to international standards of quality (certified by the standard ISO 9001:2000), but does not use international accounting standards at the present moment.

Contact details and address
196210, Russia, Saint-Petersburg, Ulitsa Shtyrmanskaya, 11
Tel. +7 (812) 104-14-96, 104-14-59
Fax +7 (812) 104-12-85
marketing@pulkovo.biz
www.pulkovo.biz

Pulkovo Holdings has representative offices in several Russian cities including:

- Moscow;

- Magnitigorsk;

- Syktyvkar;

- Krasnoyarsk;

- Tula;

- Voronezh.

Plant capacity:

- Design and production of weld structural units: 1,000 tons a month.

- Production of wall and roof 'sandwich'-panels: 50,000 m² per month.

- Production of fireproof doors EI-30 and EI-60 under licence from Saajos OY, Finland: 500 items per month.

- Production of metal-plastic windows: 1,000 m² per month.

- Production of formed section: 30,000 running metres per month.

- Assembling of industrial buildings, hangars, warehouses: 7,000–8,000 m² per month.

- Production of pre-mixed concrete: up to 20,000 m³ per month.

Management of ICC PULKOVO
General Director: Valeryi Klimov.
Chief Engineer: Anatoly Grigoriev.
Developing Director: Nikolay Pokidko.

Profile 2: INTERCOS-IV

INTERCOS-IV was established in 1992 by four mechanical engineers who were previously employed in the machine-building sector of the Russian military-industrial establishment. During the early 1990s there was a lack of large-sized manufacturers of tooling for the Russian automotive industry and the majority of enterprises were compelled to order machine-tools from abroad. The economic reforms of the 1990s changed this situation, and the automobile plants started to purchase the necessary machine-tools independently from the Ministry of Automotive Industry, which previously regulated the manner in which

Russian firms sourced their tooling needs. It was in this changing economic environment in the automobile components sector that INTERCOS-IV was founded, and subsequently became one of the first Russian enterprises that offered the automotive industry such services as design and manufacturing of machine-tools. The company's first major order was secured in 1992, when the Latvian bus plant, RAF, ordered a set of dies from INTERCOS-IV. The next important stage of the company's development was a significant order from Daewoo Motor Polska.

INTERCOS-IV's next major project was to manufacture dies for car body panels for the Lublin car company (Poland). In the course of developing this project, INTERCOS-IV used 3D engineering technology for the first time and developed stamp manufacturing (there was a lack of high-quality stampings in the Russian market and INTERCOS-IV took advantage of the opportunity to use the experience of die manufacturing and also the availability of large-sized presses used for testing and trialling of dies). As the company's business developed, it established a strong network of contracts and cooperation in business development with leading machine-building and metallurgical plants in northwestern Russia, the Russian Republic of Tatarastan and Ukraine. All these plants within the INTERCOS-IV network have high technical potential and serious business development opportunities. As the company's business has developed further, its number of employees has expanded and now stands at 160, among whom are some of the most skilful die designers in Russia.

INTERCOS-IV is currently one of the best technologically equipped Russian enterprises and has the capability to react quickly to all innovations. Use of the right marketing policy, together with continuous renovation and modernization of resources, has enabled the company to widen its field of activity and helped to attract a new and diverse customer base.

INTERCOS-IV is a reliable partner for different machine-building enterprises, and the company today is capable of providing for the whole production cycle: from machine-tool design and manufacturing up to mass serial production of details at its press line.

INTERCOS-IV is one of the leading large-scale tooling manufacturers for the automobile industry both in Russia and abroad. INTERCOS-IV has worked with almost all Russian and CIS automobile plants, including GAZ, AvtoVAZ, ZIL, MAZ, AZLK and UAZ, as well as with the major foreign companies including VW, Ford Motor Company, Kirchhoff, Renault, Daewoo Motor, Hayes Wheels and Caterpillar.

The company has recently concluded contracts with VW, OAO GAZ, OAO UAZ, Avtoframos, Ford, Electrolux and Kirchhoff, and has further contracts with Nothelfer, Merloni, OAO GAZ, Scania, TRW,

Delphi, Benteler and Johnson Controls. INTERCOS-IV is presently involved in a project with ZAO Ford (the new C307 project), which involves traditional design and development of dies, welding fixtures and serial stamping of body parts. INTERCOS-IV has also nearly completed negotiations with Scania for machine-tool manufacturing, pressed parts production, welding and painting of assemblies for trucks made by this company in Europe. Further contracts for the development of new technologies with OAO Severstal and AFK System have also been concluded. INTERCOS-IV's agreement with Electrolux relates to the production of pressed parts after the manufacturing of dies, and the company is also presently exploring opportunities for cooperation with Merloni (Ariston).

Overall, it can be said that INTERCOS-IV offers a wide range of products that include the manufacturing of steel and iron casting, moulds for plastic, dies of up to 40 tons, welding fixtures, special devices and production of sheet-metal parts. The company also offers a full range of engineering services, including design and process development with use of up-to-date CAD/CAM technologies. INTERCOS-IV management has viewed the Russian economic growth of recent years positively, and foresaw the interest of foreign investors in the Russian market, which helped INTERCOS-IV reach its goals in terms of enlargement of its customer base and product/services diversification.

Die development is a quite creative process that requires taking into account such factors as degree of complexity, material features, minimal die dimensions, type of panel, accuracy and the customer's press line. The design department of INTERCOS-IV is equipped with up-to-date computers using software such as Pro/ENGINEER, Pro/DESIGNER of Parametric Technology Corporation and T-flex CAD. CAD/CAM specialists have experience of use of CATIA, AUTOCAD, UNIGRAPHICS, and EUCLID. To simulate stamping processes, the company's specialists use the CAE AUTOFORM product. Large-sized machining of dies is done on 5-axis machines (RAMBAUDI and FIDIA) and 3-axis machines (WALDRICH COBURG and WALDRICH SIEGEN). Use of modern cutting tools such as SANDVIC, WALTER, SGS, INGERSOLL, GARRYSON allows company specialists to use the optimal cutting modes with requested quality. The company's experimental division is equipped with ERFURT presses that can also be used for testing

A quality management system based on ISO 9000 standards has been introduced by INTERCOS-IV management and allows the company to carry out the following tasks:

- to carry out its activities according to the customers' requirements and expectations;

- to be confident of the quality of the systems implemented and of finished goods;

- to compete in the global market;

- to carry out scheduled activity;

- to reduce production costs and constantly improve its activity.

The quality system of the company is certificated according to GOST R ISO-9001- 96 standards at the certification authority of Quality Systems 'Test-St Petersburg' (QS#00171). In the near future INTERCOS-IV plans to certify the Management Quality System according to the requirements of international standards ISO 9001-2000, and improve it in order to get the certificate of compliance with ISO 16949 – 2002 (QS for the automotive industry).

Skilled controllers carry out monitoring and measurement activities inside the company at every stage of production, from the analysis requested by the customer up to the testing and/or finishing measurement of the product. In this industry at present, the measurement of spatial complex forms geometry as the basic requirement for all modern manufacturers of tooling. At INTERCOS-IV this is carried out with the help of the portable multi-axis measurement machine FAROArm. The measuring methods give us the capacity to compare the physical surfaces with the original part specifications with an accuracy of +0.05 mm.

The company's manufacturing premises include storage and stamping areas, the CNC machine zone, assembly and try-out zones and Quality Assurance. The storage area contains two cutting machines. The stamping area is equipped with 18 pieces of equipment, including 16 presses (100–800 tons). The CNC machine area is equipped with four machines: two Coburgs, a Fidia and a Rambaudi. The Coburg machines are 3-axial, and the Fidia and Rambaudi are 5-axial. The mechanical area includes five lathe machines, 17 polishing machines, seven milling machines and 10 drilling/boring machines. Quality assurance uses Faro (United States) measuring machines to take precise dimensions.

The company's main export markets are Germany (majority), the Czech Republic and Poland. It imports materials from Germany and Sweden; standard parts from Germany, Japan, the United States, Sweden, Finland and Poland; and equipment from Germany, Italy and Finland.

INTERCOS-IV invests heavily in training programmes in all company departments, including courses for design-process and quality service. Representatives of the company's planning, production management departments, CNC-programmers and try-out teams are currently participating in courses in the United Kingdom and at VW in Germany.

Basic company data

Company address
Head Office: Bolshoy pr.P.S., 25A,
St Petersburg, Russia, 197198
Phone +7 812 232 1476; +7 812 233 7352
Fax +7 812 232 4679
info@intercos-iv.ru
www.intercos-iv.ru

Manufacturing premises
Volkhonskoye shosse, 4,
Lomonosovsky region,
Leningradskaya oblast' 198323
Phone +7 812 336 2658; +7 812 336 2659; +7 812 149 6621

Head of Board
Strategic Development Director: Boris Lazebnik
Managing Director: Timur Shoshtaev
Deputy Managing Director: Pavel Olkhov
Plant Manager: Leonid Alexandrov

Profile 3: ZAO Elcoteq

Founded in 1991, Elcoteq Network Corporation is a leading electronics manufacturing services company (EMS). Elcoteq Network provides globally end-to-end solutions consisting of design, manufacturing, supply chain management and after-sales services for the whole lifecycle of its customers' products. The company operates in 15 countries worldwide and employs approximately 19,480 people. Elcoteq's consolidated net sales for 2004 totalled 2,953,700 million euros and the company is listed on the Helsinki stock exchanges.

In 2004 Elcoteq Network Corporation continued with the globalization of its business and the company offers its portfolio of services to clients in the core markets of Europe, Asia and America. The company has unified its work methods and operational systems across all of its plants internationally, allowing for the production of identical products and standards of work at the many different factories the corporation operates worldwide. Elcoteq Network Corporation has plants in Finland, Estonia, Russia, Hungary, Germany, Mexico, China, and most recently India, where it opened a factory in Bangalore employing over 1,000 people in autumn of 2004. The corporation also has service centres in Sweden, Germany, the United States, Japan and Hong Kong, and after-sales service centres in Hungary and China. Elcoteq NPI centres are located in Finland, Estonia, Russia, Germany and the United States.

ZAO Elcoteq, located and registered in St Petersburg, is a branch of Elcoteq Network Corporation. ZAO Elcoteq provides electronic manufacturing services and engineering services for several Russian and international companies, including Sony-Ericsson, Nokia, SchmidTelecom, Lucent Technologies, VSM and several others. ZAO Elcoteq is notable as the only Russian enterprise on the domestic Russian market for electronic services that offers a full range of services in the field of electronic manufacture at a high technological level and at world standards of quality.

ZAO Elcoteq commenced operations in St Petersburg in 1997, and in the first year the company invested heavily in personnel training, development of the newest technologies (some of them unknown in Russia at that time) and debugging of productions. The company's first customers were Husqvarna Sewing Machines and Ericsson. By 1998 the company was employing 86 people, commenced its export-oriented and mainstream assembling business activities, and obtained a licence for 'processing under customs control'. Within a short period of time, the company's staff expanded noticeably: 100 in 1999, 194 in 2002 and 238 by 2004. The spectrum of services provided to customers was extended, new technologies were deployed, and the settlement of customs procedures duly commenced. In 1999, ZAO Elcoteq passed a System of Quality audit and received the certificate ISO 9002 from the DNV Company. Also in that year, the company joined the Euro-Russia project, the purpose of which was to increase the degree of integration between Russia and the EU through the development of business networks of the enterprises. Participants in the project included hi-tech Russian enterprises such as Petrel, and well-known Scandinavian companies such as Electrolux, SturaEnso, Skanska and Nokia.

In 2000 Elcoteq extended its production further and began to manufacture mobile accessories, doubling its overall production capacity in June of that year. It also participated in the TEDIM project (Telematics in Foreign Trade Logistics and Delivery Management) and obtained ISO14001 certification. In 2002, the company adjusted its business strategy, introducing new engineering product services thanks to which the company was able not only to develop new products for its customers, but also to offer services in design and introduce new manufactured products.

One of the highlights of the public relations side of Elcoteq's corporate activities during 2003 was the Motocross MCRace2003, which was held on 22–26 May and celebrated the 300th anniversary of the founding of the city of St Petersburg. The driving force behind this event was Anttii Piippo, Chairman of the Board of Directors, and founder and main shareholder of Elcoteq Network Corporation, who acknowledged the participation of the heads of several large Finnish corporations in the event. Back on the business front, 2004 saw the opening of the second Elcoteq plant in St Petersburg, in a ceremony attended by representatives from the city's government, Elcoteq management and the general contractor, Lemcon. Production at the plant will commence in the autumn of 2005.

Profile 4: Closed Joint-Stock Company Rascom

CJSC Rascom provides up-to-date high-quality telecommunications services targeted at telecom carriers and corporate customers in accordance with the Law 'On communications' of the Russian Federation and other normative documents of the State Committee of Russian Federation for telecommunications and the IT sector. Rascom's licences and technical facilities allow the company to offer the following telecommunications services:

- leasing private digital channels for local, intra-zone, long-distance national and international communications;

- providing telematic services and Internet access;

- connecting to public telephone networks.

The company has 100 employees, and its offices are located in St Petersburg (headquarters) and Moscow. Rascom operates on the territory running along its own fibre-optic network between Moscow, St Petersburg and the Finnish–Russian border. The company was founded in June 1993 and built its first fibre-optic communications line (FOCL) (670 km, 2 × STM-1) running between Moscow and St Petersburg during the winter of 1993–94. Rascom's first commercial contract came in June 1994, and the company soon extended its FOCL network, building further fibre-optic lines between Chudovo and Novgorord (80 km, December 1995), and Vyborg, Buslovskaya and the Russian–Finnish border (August 1996).

In 1997 the transmission system of the Moscow–St Petersburg FOCL was upgraded from STM-1 up to STM-16, increasing transmission capacity up to 2.4 Gbps, while in September 1998 the section of the FOCL from St Petersburg to the Finnish–Russian Border was upgraded from STM-4 up to STM-16. In the same year, Rascom built a further 130 km FOCL STM-1and STM-4 between St Petersburg,

Zelenogorsk and the Finnish–Russian Border, as well as a Moscow regional STM-1 ring to connect the Moscow-Electrosviaz nodes in Solnechnogorsk and Klin with Rascom's network in Moscow and Zelenograd – a project completed in 1998. By late 2000 Rascom was providing full physical protection for the whole FOCL network length from Moscow to the Finnish–Russian Border.

In 2001 Rascom launched a Giganet high-speed Internet backbone route featuring full support for the MPLS technology at all connection points. In the following year, the company launched an STM-64 transmission system and DWDM linear-path equipment on the section of the FOCL between St Petersburg and the Finnish–Russian Border (the total potential transmission capacity of the backbone network increased up to 15 Tbps). In September 2002, Rascom built the second Moscow city STM-16 ring to connect with the networks of the companies Rostelecom (M-9, 12th flour), MTS (M9, 2nd flour) and CandW with Rascom's own network. This connection linked Rascom's backbone communications network to the Basic synchronization network of the Russian Federation.

Later in 2002, Rascom's telephone network was commissioned, having a transit switch in St Petersburg. In March 2003, within the GTS-CE space, an IP-network node was installed in Frankfurt and the GIGANET network connected to the networks of the central European telecom carriers of the ANTEL (GTS-CE) group. In May 2004, Rascom's communications node in Velikiy Novgorod was upgraded, while in December of the same year the construction and commercial commissioning of Rascom's new communications nodes in Stockholm and Frankfurt were completed.

Launching the nodes in Stockholm and Frankfurt has become the first step in the long-term strategy for Rascom's development over the next five years. In keeping to this strategy, Rascom is permanently extending the geographical market for its services in the central European region and in Scandinavia. The most popular routes for ordering international capacities from Moscow and St Petersburg have been chosen as directions for further strategic development. The second stage of the long-term network extension programme will be the creation of SDH nodes in London and Helsinki, which are scheduled to be commissioned by mid-2006.

3.16

PeterStar Company Profile

Anastassia Bogatikova, Senior Marketing Specialist, ZAO PeterStar

Mission

PeterStar aims:

- to create and improve telecommunications systems equipped with the most advanced technology;
- to satisfy telecommunication service users and fully meet the most demanding customer requests;
- to develop a business based on values such as teamwork, professionalism, innovation and openness in providing information on the trend of affairs of the company.

Introduction

ZAO PeterStar is at present a leading alternative operator in the Northwestern Region and one of the largest in Russia (after Golden Telecom and Sistema Telecom).[1] It is a leader in the corporate telephony and data services market, and the second biggest Internet access services provider in the St Petersburg telecommunications market. The company and its affiliates employ over 850 staff. In 2004 the company's turnover amounted to about US$80 million. PeterStar controls all stages of its service provision process. According to a number of industry sources, in 2004 the company was officially recognized as one of the top 10 Russian Internet providers. Research conducted by J'son and Partners shows that PeterStar is ranked as the third Wi-Fi operator in Russia. The company has been awarded an RF Goscomsvyaz prize in the field of quality, and is rated among the 30 largest telecommunications companies of Russia by *Expert* magazine. PeterStar's 2003 results earned it a laureate in the VII all-Russian competition for 'The Best Russian Enterprises', in which it was nominated for the category 'For the Highest Financial Efficiency'. The company's 2004 results won it the title 'The Best Taxpayer of St Petersburg'.

PeterStar is not only known for its achievements in the field of telecommunications; its takes an active part in charitable activities in St Petersburg and sponsors well-known cultural and sports events, such as the International St Petersburg Open Tennis Tournament, as well as giving support to the Hermitage State Museum. PeterStar is entered in 'The Golden Book of the Nation' and has received awards from the International Fund of the 'Patrons of Art of Russia' for its services in the field of charity.

In 2003 the company extended its operations beyond the bounds of St Petersburg, and it now offers telecommunication services not only there but also in the markets of other regions. The company has affiliates in Moscow, Kaliningrad, Vyborg, Pskov, Veliky Novgorod, Petrozavodsk and Murmansk. PeterStar furnishes services on the basis of licences to provide local and national telephone communication services, telematics services and data services; to lease communication channels; to provide videoconferencing services; to design buildings and structures (licensed at the I and II levels of responsibility); and to construct buildings and structures.

Organizational history and technical background

ZAO PeterStar – an integrated network operator – was founded in 1992, and has become one of the most competitive alternative operators in St Petersburg. Since 1992 the company has invested about US$150 million in the development of its network.

Brief chronology of major corporate achievements

In 1992 a digital switch made by the British manufacturer GPT was selected as the basis for the PeterStar network, and our first client – the Grand Hotel Europe – was connected.

In 1994 PeterStar constructed a telephone node for 100,000 numbers based on the 5ESS equipment manufactured by AT&T (now Lucent Technologies). The node was launched as a fibre-optic network, and its first stage was completed in 1994. From the very beginning, the PeterStar telephone network was fully integrated in the existing Petersburg telephone network and formed an important part of the city telecommunications infrastructure. The network includes three digital

Lucent 5ESS switches and two Ericsson AXE-10 switches. By using equipment from several vendors the company is able to maintain its independence, as well as to optimize network maintenance costs. At present the company possesses the largest fibre-optic network in the city, with a total extent of more than 2,000 km. The capacity of the PeterStar fibre transport network core corresponds to the STM-64 level (10 Gbps).

PeterStar established a card payphone network in St Petersburg in 1994, which it sold three years later to BCL.

The company has been providing data services since 1995. The PeterStar data network is built on the basis of a wide range of the most advanced multiplexing equipment and ATM switches, manufactured by General DataComm and Alcatel.

In 1996 PeterStar obtained a full licensing coverage for the North-west Region and Moscow, with licences for the provision of national telephone, telematics and videoconferencing communication services.

The company entered the regulated telephony market in 1997. As agreed with the incumbent carrier – Petersburg Telephone Network (PTN) – and the Administration of the Vassilievski Island District of St Petersburg the company implemented a large-scale project of city telephone network retrofitting in Vassilievski Island. Under this project, 37,000 telephone lines were switched from obsolete analogue telephone exchanges of PTN over to the PeterStar digital network. All this work was carried out at the expense of PeterStar. As agreed with PTN, PeterStar serves all residents of Vassilievski Island under the regulated PTN fixed tariffs. In the middle of 2002 PeterStar additionally took over services for 24,000 telephone numbers. Many of St Petersburg's communication carriers use PeterStar's numbering capacity.

In 1998 a public videoconferencing hall was opened, using Picture-Tel equipment, and a call centre was launched. Prepaid calling card services, including international roaming, were provided. In that year, PeterStar was named as 'The Winner of Competition in the Field of Communication Service Provision Quality' in the category 'Communication carriers'.

PeterStar is eager to take up opportunities to provides services on the basis of wireless technology. Since 1998 it has used the MultiGain wireless equipment made by ECI Telecom, operating on a 2.4-2.8 GHz frequency band. As well as Saint Petersburg itself, the PeterStar wireless network covers the city's suburbs and various settlements of the Leningrad Oblast, including Olgino, Lisy Nos, Strelna, Pargolovo, Shushary, Krasnoe Selo, Vsevolozhsk and Vyborg. In 2003 PeterStar retrofitted the existing wireless network, thus allowing the company to offer not only telephony services but also Internet access services at a speed of up to 512 Kbps.

Internet services were launched in 1998. ZAO PeterStar, the largest alternative operator of Petersburg, provides Internet access services over dial-up and leased channels, as well as hosting and web design services.

In 1999 PeterStar obtained certificates from the State Technical Committee of Russia in the field of network management system security. PeterStar possesses one of the most advanced data centres in St Petersburg, equipped with efficient servers, up-to-date software, and a guaranteed uninterrupted power supply system. The PeterStar data centre ensures 24×7 monitoring of channels and equipment. In 1999 the company held the first virtual Internet auction in cooperation with Lufthansa and Comstar. It also launched Internet dial-up access services jointly with Web Plus. Services over the PeterStar data network were provided on accessing exchange bid systems, including the Moscow Interbank Monetary Exchange (MIME) bid system. A licence was obtained to work with information containing state secrets.

2000 was marked by PeterStar's own TV project, when it put out a programme called 'The Telephone and Me'. The company was an Official Partner at the 2000 World Ice Hockey Championship. In its commercial and technical work, PeterStar started constructing wireless access base stations in Vyborg and Vsevolozhsk, and provided voice transmission services over the PeterStar data network. It also succeeded in solving the 'Y2K Problem' on the PeterStar network.

2001 saw the opening of the PeterStar Network Management Centre, providing for 24/7 monitoring of transport and data networks. PeterStar began constructing an Internet access node that by 2005 had been connected to the network by channels with aggregate capacity of 500 Mbps.

In 2002 the company started expanding and retrofitting its switches. A PeterStar node was put into operation in Moscow, and ADSL services were launched in Vassilievski Island. Construction work began on the multi-service MetroEthernet (high speed data transmission) network, based on Cisco Systems equipment; this network's services were promoted under the trademark 'IP Backbone'. A network was constructed using VPN/MPLS technology to provide high-speed data exchange (up to 100 Mbps) and the option of creating protected corporate networks. The IP Backbone network has a ring structure and provides for use of a high-capacity (up to 10 Gbps) core. Based on the IP Backbone network, PeterStar began to offer broadband Internet access and data services. According to PeterStar, services such as 'video on demand' and multimedia conferencing were promising prospects at that time.

The new MetroEthernet network solved two problems: establishing a backbone network capable of handling large volumes of traffic, and providing high-speed access to this network to ensure the provision of a wide range of modern services. In the second quarter of 2004

PeterStar completed its IP backbone construction project in St Petersburg. In the course of construction, it had used DPT (Dynamic Packet Technology) technology, combining the advantages of SDH and Gigabit Ethernet technologies. The network's architecture provided for a wide range of services to both corporate and private users, including broadband Internet access, integrating LANs with high data exchange speeds and constructing virtual corporate networks. It was also possible to provide VoIP services, integrate PBXs on a 'point-to-point' basis or with operator intranet switching, create virtual private networks (VPN), and construct office IP telephony networks based on the Cisco Call Manager platform, as well as arranging additional office telephone lines.

In January 2003 PeterStar put into operation a broadband wireless access network (WBA) that made it possible to use high-speed Internet access channels to construct corporate networks and connect customers to the telephone network by 2 Mbps channels. The WBA network was based on the Ericsson Mini-Link BAS equipment (with an operating frequency band of 26 GHz). One important WBA advantage is its speedy service provision. In this respect, the quality of services furnished by this technology is at least the same as that of services provided over fibre-optic cable (for instance, an IP-based data speed can reach 10 Mbps). The WBA network is also used for arranging communication for symposiums, conferences and exhibitions.

In 2003 PeterStar began construction of Internet hot spots (Internet access points, usually in public places such as cafes, airports or hotel lounges) using Wi-Fi technology (IEEE 802.11b, 802.11a). PeterStar used the most advanced equipment, thus ensuring the required speed, reliability and security of the Wi-Fi networks. The MetroEthernet network infrastructure that can handle large volumes of traffic is an ideal one for quickly implementing wireless networks for both corporate customers and public Internet access. Base stations are connected to the existing PeterStar broadband access network by 100 Mbps channels. By the summer of 2004 PeterStar had established 30 hot spots using Wi-Fi technology in St Petersburg. The company installed touchscreen Internet terminals at various public sites: cafes, airports and passenger terminals (at Pulkovo Airport, the Grand Hotel Europe and Grand Hotel Emerald). In the same year, in order to attract small-sized companies, PeterStar revised its tariffs for data services and established a single price for services within the entire speed range irrespective of the technology applied.

In 2003–04 PeterStar constructed Internet nodes in London and New York. At present PeterStar is connected to Internet traffic exchange points such as SPB-IX (Petersburg), MSK-IX (Moscow), XchangePoint (New York) and LINX (London).

In 2004 PeterStar started to develop a communication network using up-to-date PON (Passive Optical Networking) technology that ensures the most efficient and economical method of constructing large multi-service access systems.

Product lines

ZAO PeterStar provides local, national and international telephone communication services, as well as ISDN services. Its telephone communication services are based on the most advanced technology and provided with 24/7 technical support. At the beginning of 2004, PeterStar was serving about 100,000 telephone lines (including 37,000 lines in Vassilievski Island). Telephone lines are provided not only via copper and fibre-optic cable but also using wireless technology.

The PeterStar digital telephone network ensures the highest quality and reliability of connections by making use of the most advanced technology. It is based on efficient 5ESS exchanges (made by Lucent Technologies) and AXE exchanges (Ericsson). The network makes it possible to digitally connect modern PBXs supplied by different manufacturers.

The digital telephone network provides subscribers with services such as analogue telephony, ISDN services and digital trunks (E1). The 'last mile' can be arranged using a copper pair, optics or modern wireless access technology.

PeterStar offers its customers unique wireless connection capabilities. Customers are given a chance to connect several traditional telephone lines under Wireless Local Loop (WLL technology, as well as connecting to a digital trunk and obtaining high-speed Internet access by means of WBA technology.

ZAO PeterStar also provides data services. The PeterStar network structure makes it possible to arrange both high-speed digital leased channels connected to subscribers by optics (2 Mbps–2.4 Gbps trunks) and slower data speed channels (up to 2 Mbps) that can be organized over copper or fibre-optics cable, or under WBA technology as requested by the subscriber. The structure of the PeterStar transport fibre-optic network provides for a 100-per-cent redundancy by means of automatically routed channels, making it possible to choose an alternative data exchange route in case a network segment is damaged. PeterStar data services ensure quality and reliable communication at a flexible price, offering a flexible discount scale.

PeterStar offers a wide range of Internet access capabilities depending on customer needs. Large and medium-sized businesses are offered leased circuit Internet access services. Customers are connected by a leased circuit arranged on the basis of different access technologies: copper wires, fibre-optic cable and wireless technology (xDSL, LRE, Frame Relay, EoF (Ethernet over Fibre), WBA (wireless broadband access), Wi-Fi). PeterStar uses the most advanced technology and transmission system equipment, thus ensuring the highest access quality, high speeds and stability.

Small business and private customers are offered dial-up Internet access services. PeterStar possesses the largest modem pool (quantity of numbers used for dial-up access to the Internet) in St Petersburg of over 5,000 lines; the company uses its own telephone lines. The modem pool is used to provide the company's customers not only with dial-up Internet access services but also with VPDN (Virtual Private Dialup Network) services. Dial-up access services are provided to the PeterStar telephone network customers either on the basis of prepaid cards or on a credit basis, not only in Saint Petersburg but also in the regions: in Moscow, Pskov, Veliky Novgorod. Of the client base of those using dial-up access services, 80 per cent are individuals, while 20 per cent are corporate users. PeterStar provides Internet leased channel access over copper wires, fibre-optic cable and by means of wireless technology. The operator makes use of the following technologies: xDSL, Long Reach Ethernet, Frame Relay, EOF (Ethernet over Fibre) and WBA (wireless broadband access). The development of broadband access services began in 2002, the same year that the company started its cooperation with cable TV providers to provide customers with Internet access.

In addition to telephony, data and Internet access services, the company provides videoconferencing, hosting and web design services, constructs home networks and supplies telecommunications equipment, as well as providing inquiry and information services.

The company puts a high priority on dealing with business customers in various fields: high-tech companies, medical institutions, commercial facilities, factories, banks, construction firms and so on. PeterStar does a great deal of business with business centres: at present the company provides services at more than 200 business centres of category A, B and C. It also cooperates with organizations constructing top-class and standard dwelling houses, to which PeterStar provides telephony and Internet access services. The company actively cooperates with state structures.

The company also deals with individuals. As agreed with PTN and the Administration of Vassileostrovski District, PeterStar serves the Vassilievski Island residents under regulated tariffs. By the beginning of 2003 the backlog of demand for telephone installation within the PeterStar service zone in Vassilievski Island had been met in full. In spite of the provision of telephony services to the residents at the tariffs regulated by the state, revenue from this segment is continuously growing because of the provision of Internet access services and premium rate services. At present the company is giving priority to a promising business of constructing Home Networks on the basis of its own MetroEthernet network, as well as jointly with cable TV providers (a Katrina company).

PeterStar does not only interact with end users. The company works with communication carriers who purchase its numbering capacity and channels. The company deals with ISPs in terms of IP traffic sales and VPDN services provided.

Labour

Highly skilled and motivated personnel play a vital role in establishing an efficient company. PeterStar, as a company determined to achieve long-term success, puts great effort into achieving a high-quality of staff. Today the company counts over 850 employees, including affiliates. During 2004 over 100 employees were trained at various skill improvement courses. There is a standing training system in the company; on these training courses, skilled employees share with young specialists their experience and knowledge gained over a number of years.

A personnel certification process allows the company to better understand the quality of the workforce and the potential of the employees. Special attention is paid to the training and development of groups of key employees.

In general, high-quality work in the field of human resources management enables PeterStar to avoid any risk of deterioration in the quality of its personnel.

Business development

PeterStar is a dynamically developed company that aims for high-quality approaches to satisfy the needs for telecommunication services by means of applying up-to-date technological solutions.

In 2001 the company went through the change of leadership. This led to certain changes in the company's tariff policy and structure that benefited its subsequent activities. The company focused on servicing large customers, trying to reduce the number of less remunerative clients by transferring them to new tariff plans. It also decided to increase the number of digital connections. Even though in 2001 mobile operators bringing in a considerable income transferred their traffic to the network of Petersburg Transit Telecom, PeterStar continued its development in the other segments, as is shown by its current position in the telecommunications market of St Petersburg.

PeterStar is a traditional leader in the telephony market among alternative operators in St Petersburg. It has 60 per cent of the corporate telephony market in both quantitative (numbers) and money (US$) terms.

By the end of 2004, PeterStar occupied the No 1 position in the data service market, with a share of 40 per cent of the data market (leaving behind its closest competitor – Metrocom).

On the Internet access market, the breakdown by market share is somewhat different. PeterStar is one of the three operators occupying leading positions. According to the results of 2003, the leader in terms of the number of Internet channels is Web Plus with 52 per cent. This is because it is practically the only company that is capable of providing ADSL services outside the Vassilievski Island territory.

In terms of general service provision figures, PeterStar has demonstrated a steady growth during past four years. In comparison with 2001, the company's revenue in 2002 increased 17 per cent. In 2003 revenue increased 18 per cent. And based on the 2004 results revenue grew 21 per cent during one year.

During recent years the company has intensively built up its infrastructure. Thus, in 2002 the volume of investments grew 66 per cent compared with 2001, and increased a further 63 percent in 2003 vs 2002. In 2004 the company spent about US$15 million on its development.

According to the PeterStar General Director, the company has a strong potential to simultaneously improve the well-being of the company and continue its regional development.

Note

1. In this chapter, 'alternative operators' are the new entrants to the market, such as PeterStar, Golden Telecom, and Metrocom, in contrast to the longer established traditional companies. Their tariffs are not regulated by the government and they are not included in the monopolist list.

Part Four

Commercial Legislation for St Petersburg – The Taxation and Legal Environment

4.1

The Regulatory Environment for International Business in the Russian Federation

CMS Cameron McKenna

Russia is in the midst of economic and legislative reforms. Since 1990 the Russian government has put a statutory framework into place to bring the country up to modern standards and harmonize legislation. Although Russia does not yet have a stable and established legislative system, this issue remains one of the key priorities of the present Russian government.

The legal structure developed at a rapid pace during the 1990s, with significant reforms being attempted in almost every sphere of law. The process of consolidating and rationalizing the legal framework of Russia's market economy remains ongoing, with major changes anticipated in a number of key areas.

Constitutional structure

Constitution

The Constitution of the Russian Federation ('the Constitution') was adopted by a national referendum on 12 December 1993. The Constitution defines the sovereign power of the Russian Federation, and describes its federal structure, governing system and the principle human rights enjoyed by the citizens of Russia. The Russian Federation is governed by a political system modelled after many currently existing in Western Europe. The governing system is composed of three branches: the executive, legislature and judiciary.

Federal structure: local and federal government

The Russian Federation consists of 89 'subjects', including regions, ethnically based autonomous republics, territories and the federal cities of Moscow and St Petersburg. The Constitution granted these 'subjects' certain autonomy over their own internal economic and political affairs. Heads of the executive branches of 'subjects' are appointed by the legislative body of such 'subject', at the recommendation of the President of the Russian Federation.

The Constitution sets out a general list of powers reserved to the federal authorities. Other powers are expressed as jointly exercisable by the federal and local authorities. The regional authorities are then allocated all other powers not specifically reserved by the federal government or exercised jointly. These include powers to manage municipal property, establish regional budgets, collect regional taxes, and maintain law and order. Bilateral power-sharing treaties between the central government and the 'subjects' of the Russian Federation have become an important means by which the boundaries of their respective power and authority are defined and clarified. The Constitution gives regional bodies the authority to pass laws, provided they do not contradict the Constitution and existing federal laws. Many 'subjects', however, have adopted their own constitutions, which in several cases allocate powers to the regional government that are inconsistent with the provisions of the Constitution.

The president

Under the Constitution, the president, who is elected for a four-year term, is the head of the state. The Constitution does not provide for a vice-president. The president has the right to choose the chairman of the government, with the approval of the State Duma (the lower house of the Russian parliament). The president, upon the recommendation of the prime minister, appoints ministers, who are responsible for the introduction of primary and secondary legislation in their respective fields.

Russia's president determines the basic direction of Russia's domestic and foreign policy and represents the Russian state in both domestic and foreign affairs. As commander-in-chief of the Russian armed forces, the president approves defence policy, appoints and removes commanders of the armed forces, and confers higher military ranks and awards.

The president has broad authority to issue decrees and directives that have the force of law, although the Constitution states that they must not contradict other federal laws or the Constitution. In certain circumstances, the president has the right to dissolve the Duma.

The executive branch and its structure

The executive branch of the Russian Federation is headed by the government of the Russian Federation (*pravitelstvo*), which comprises the chairman of the government, vice-chairman and 17 ministers. Although formally the president is the head of the state and not the head of the executive branch, in actuality the government is subordinate to the president. For example, the key ministries and federal services (such as the Ministry of Foreign Affairs, the Ministry of Internal Affairs and the Federal Security Service) report directly to the president and not the government.

Following the major reform of the executive branch, which was carried out in 2004 (aimed at setting out a clearer and more efficient structure of the branch, in addition to reducing the amount of bureaucracy), the current structure of the executive branch is as follows: 1) the government; 2) federal ministries (mainly responsible for legislative activity in their spheres and the coordination of subordinate agencies and services); 3) federal agencies (mainly responsible for licensing, permits, etc in their established spheres); and 4) federal services (controlling functions). Federal agencies and services may be subordinate either directly to the president (as is the Federal Security Service), to the government (like the Federal Anti-monopoly Service) or to a particular ministry.

Parliament and the basics of the legislative process

The legislative branch of the Russian Federation is the chamber of the Federal Assembly (*federalnoye sobraniye*), which consists of the Federation Council (*sovet federatsii*) (178 seats, filled by representatives of the executive and legislative branches of each of the 89 federal administrative units) and the State Duma (*gosudarstvennaya duma*) (450 seats, half elected by proportional representation from party lists, with the remaining half elected from single-member constituencies. Members are elected by direct popular vote to serve four-year terms). The two chambers of the Federal Assembly possess different powers and responsibilities, although the State Duma is the more significant.

The Federal Assembly is a permanent functioning body, in that it is in continuous session, except in the regular break between the spring and autumn sessions. Deputies of the State Duma work full-time on their legislative duties; they are not allowed to serve simultaneously in local government or to hold federal government positions.

Each legislative chamber elects a chairman who controls procedure. The chambers also form committees and commissions to deal with particular issues. These prepare and evaluate bills, report on bills to their chambers, conduct hearings and oversee the implementation of laws.

Bills may originate in either legislative chamber, or may be submitted by the president, the government, local legislatures, the Supreme Court, the Constitutional Court, or the High Arbitration Court. Bills are first considered by the State Duma and must pass three readings before being passed to the Federation Council. After adoption by a majority of State Duma members, a bill is considered by the Federation Council. If it is rejected by the Federation Council, a Conciliation Commission may be established, comprising representatives of the Duma and Federation Council, to review and amend the bill before it is presented again to the Federation Council. The establishment of a Conciliation Commission is the prescribed procedure by which differences in bills are considered by both chambers.

When a bill is adopted by the Federation Council, it must be signed (and therefore made law) by the president. The president has a final veto, which if exercised can be overridden by a resolution passed by two-thirds of the members of the Duma and Federation Council.

The judicial system

The judicial system in the Russian Federation is divided into three branches: the courts of general jurisdiction (of which the federal Supreme Court is the court of last resort), the *arbitrazhniy* or commercial court system with the High *Arbitrazhniy* Court as the supreme body, and the Constitutional Court. The judicial system is also divided into a federal system and a system of local courts of the various 'subjects' of the Russian Federation.

The Constitutional Court has jurisdiction to decide whether federal and local legislation and regulations comply with the Constitution. This court will also resolve jurisdictional disputes between the federal or local authorities, and may interpret and clarify provisions of the Constitution.

Criminal, civil and administrative cases involving individuals not engaged in business activity are dealt with by the courts of general jurisdiction. The initial stage in this system is the magistrates court. Magistrates serve each city and rural district. The entire system consists of the magistrates, district courts of general jurisdiction, Supreme Courts of the constituent 'subjects' of the Russian Federation, and the Supreme Court of the Russian Federation. Decisions of the lower courts of general jurisdiction can be appealed through the intermediate district courts and the Supreme Courts of the 'subject' of the Russian Federation, up to the Federal Supreme Court.

As established by the Arbitration Procedure Code, which came into force on 1 September 2002, economic disputes involving legal entities, individuals engaged in business activity and disputes between legal entities and its participants (shareholders) are dealt with by the *arbitrazhniy* or commercial arbitration courts. These are sometimes referred to, rather misleadingly, as 'arbitration courts'. The *arbitrazhniy* court system consists of the *arbitrazhniy* courts of the 'subjects' of the Russian Federation, *arbitrazhniy* courts of appeal, federal *arbitrazhniy* courts and the High *Arbitrazhniy* Court of the Russian Federation. The High *Arbitrazhniy* Court is the highest court for the resolution of economic disputes.

The Ministry of Justice administers Russia's judicial system. The Ministry's responsibilities include administering the court system and supervising court activity and organization, in addition to a number of other supervisory, administrative and systematic functions.

Law enforcement functions are performed by the Procurator General's Office (*procuratura*), which has local offices in cities and provinces, by the Ministry of Internal Affairs and by the Federal Security Service. The Procurator General's Office supervises the law enforcement agencies, investigates crime and prosecutes offenders. The Ministry of Internal Affairs controls all the various police agencies and supervises the prisons and fire service. The Federal Security Service (formerly the KGB) is responsible for counterintelligence and also investigates organized crime and terrorism.

Basics of the civil law system

Legal system and legislative subordination

The constitutional laws, federal laws and laws of the Russian Federation form the foundation of its legal system. Presidential Decrees, Orders of Government and decisions of various ministries support and describe the provisions of primary legislation and, as a matter of constitutional theory, should not contradict them.

The Russian legal system is a civil law system in the continental European tradition. Various codes govern all major spheres of business activity, the principal ones being:

- Civil Code of the Russian Federation (*grazhdanskiy kodeks*);

- Tax Code of the Russian Federation (*nalogovyi kodeks*);

- Customs Code of the Russian Federation (*tamozhennyi kodeks*);

- Labour Code of the Russian Federation (*trudovoi kodeks*).

Civil legislation

The civil legislation of the Russian Federation is based on the Civil Code (Parts I, II and III) (Part IV should be adopted soon) 1994. Pending adoption of Part IV, some parts of the Civil Code of the Russian Soviet Federal Republic of 1964 and Civil Code of the USSR of 1991 remain in force.

Tax legislation

Russia is currently in the midst of significant tax reform. In August 2000, Part II of the Tax Code was made law and became effective in January 2001. However, many tax regulations are in transition. The main taxes currently are:

- *Profit tax.* Profit tax is levied on an enterprise's gross profit. The general tax rate is 24 per cent of gross profit, although this is subject to various exceptions.

- *Value added tax* (VAT). VAT is calculated on the sale value of goods, services or works at a general rate of 18 per cent, subject to certain exceptions. Imported goods are also subject to VAT.

- *Excise tax.* Excise tax is levied on the sale or importation of certain goods (alcohol, tobacco, jewellery, cars, oil, gas, etc). The tax rate varies for each product.

- *Land and property taxes.* Land and property taxes are levied by the local or regional authorities at a rate dependent on the property's location.

- *Personal income tax.* Personal income tax is calculated at a flat rate of 13 per cent.

Property, currency, customs and international legislation

The Constitution gives Russian citizens general rights to own, inherit, lease, mortgage and sell property; however, there are many gaps and ambiguities in the relevant legislation. The Land Code, which came into force on 29 October 2001, purports to regulate the use and ownership of municipal and industrial land. Agricultural land is specifically excluded from the jurisdiction of the Land Code and is regulated by a separate federal law on agricultural land, which came into force on 27 January 2003. This law provides that agricultural land cannot be owned by foreign legal entities or individuals, or by Russian legal entities if more than 50 per cent of their charter capital is owned by foreigners.

Russia has extensive and complex currency control legislation. In the year 2003 the President signed the new federal law, 'On Currency Regulation and Currency Control', which replaced the existing and more restrictive version. Most of the provisions of this law came into effect in June 2004.

This law contains an exhaustive closed list of currency operations, the performance of which may be regulated by the Russian Government or the Central Bank. Reversing the previous situation, the law changes the main principle of Russian currency control from 'everything that is not allowed is prohibited' to the opposite position of 'everything that is not prohibited is allowed'. Instead of requiring specific permission for certain types of 'capital operations', as in the previous version of the law, the new law establishes a liberalized approach to such operations. Currently, the requirement to obtain a special licence from the Central Bank for performance of a currency operation is abolished. Instead, capital currency operations may be subject to the requirement to provide special accounts (depending on the type of the operation) and a mandatory reserve requirement, which may vary from 3 to 50 per cent of the amount of the operation, for a period of between 15 and 365 days.

The mandatory conversion requirement in relation to foreign currency export proceeds is set at a maximum level of 30 per cent, with the Central Bank having the right to establish a lower percentage. In November 2004 the Central Bank reduced the mandatory conversion requirement to 10 per cent.

Many of the currency control restrictions established by the new law are due to be abolished as of 1 January 2007.

The main legislative act governing Russian customs legislation is the Customs Code of the Russian Federation, of 28 May 2003, which has been in force since 1 January 2004. Additionally, the customs sphere is regulated by other federal laws and legislatives acts of the president, the government and the Federal Customs Service (formerly the State Customs Committee). Russian import tariff rates vary from 0 to 100 per cent, depending on the imported item. For example, the tariff rate for cars depends on their year of production and varies from 1.4 to 3.2 euros per cubic centimetre of engine capacity. The import tariff rates for tobacco vary from 5 to 30 per cent. In addition to import tariffs, VAT and selective excise taxes are also applied to imports. Import licences are also required for certain types of goods (for example, alcohol).

The Constitution states that general principles of international law and international treaties are part of the legal system of the Russian Federation. If Russia is a party to an international treaty that contains provisions contradictory to the provisions of any domestic legislation, the provisions of the international treaty will prevail.

Foreign investment legislation

While the encouragement of foreign investment is a stated Russian government priority, there have been difficulties in creating a stable, attractive investment climate. Foreign investors' concerns about the legal system, corruption and taxation are key factors affecting foreign investment, rather than any explicit express restrictions imposed by the government.

Foreign investment law

The main legislative act governing the sphere of foreign investments is the law of the Russian Federation, 'On Foreign Investment in the Russian Federation', of 9 July 1999 ('Foreign Investment Law'). The Foreign Investment Law provides the statutory basis for the treatment of foreign investment. This law states that foreign investors and investments shall be treated no less favourably than domestic investors and investments, subject to certain exceptions. Such exceptions may be introduced to protect the Russian constitutional system, the morality, health and rights of third persons, or in order to ensure state security and/or defence.

Russian legislation may also introduce special rights promoting foreign investment. The Foreign Investment Law permits foreign investment in most sectors of and in all forms available in the Russian economy: portfolios of government securities, stocks and bonds, and direct investment in new businesses, in the acquisition of existing Russian-owned enterprises, in joint ventures and so on. Foreign investors are protected against nationalization or expropriation unless this is provided for by federal law. In such cases, foreign investors are entitled to receive compensation for their investment and other losses.

Restrictions on foreign investment

Currently, there are some explicit restrictions on foreign direct investment, although relatively few. For example, foreign ownership in the natural gas monopoly, Gazprom, is limited to 14 per cent. Legislation also limits foreign investment in the electric power company, Unified Energy Systems (UES), to 25 per cent.

The 'Russian Law on Insurance', of 27 November 1992 (as amended) currently sets a ceiling of 25 per cent on the total amount of foreign investment in the domestic insurance industry, as a percentage of the total insurance capital in Russia. Insurance companies in which foreigners own more than 49 per cent of the charter capital may not engage in certain types of insurance business, including life assurance.

The Central Bank has the right to use reciprocity as a criterion to specify the types of business that foreign banks may be licensed to operate in Russia, and is permitted to impose a ceiling on the total amount of foreign bank capital, as a percentage of the total bank capital in Russia. At present, foreign banks' share of the total capital is well below the 12 per cent ceiling set by the Central Bank.

International treaties

Russia is party to a number of international treaties, which are aimed at the protection of foreign investments:

- *Bilateral investment treaties.* These treaties generally guarantee non-discriminatory treatment for foreign investments and investors in Russia. They provide for compensation to be paid for expropriation or nationalization, and allow disputes to be referred to international arbitration. Russia holds such agreements with the United Kingdom, Germany, Italy, Spain, the Netherlands, Finland, France, Switzerland and others. The treaty entered into with the United States is awaiting ratification.

- *Treaties for the avoidance of double taxation.* These treaties generally provide relief from double taxation, guarantee non-discriminatory tax treatment and provide for cooperation between the tax authorities of the respective signatory countries. Russia has such agreements with Austria, the United Kingdom, Greece, Denmark, Ireland, Spain, Italy, Canada, Cyprus, the Netherlands, the United States, Germany, France, Switzerland and many other countries.

4.2

Corporate Structures

*Stanislav Denisenko, Head of KPMG
St Petersburg Legal Group*

Under the Soviet system, enterprises were owned by the state and were subject to centralized control. The only way a foreign legal entity could represent its interests in the former Soviet Union was by opening a representative office.

Legislation passed in the 1990s in connection with Russia's transition to a market economy allowed foreign investors to create business entities in Russia and to select from a range of legal ways of doing business the one that was most favourable for them.

At present, there are several possible options for starting to do business in Russia that a foreign investor may consider when structuring its investments. The main options are as follows:

- opening a representative office or a branch of a foreign legal entity;

- creating a business entity solely or jointly with a Russian or foreign legal entity or individual;

- acquiring assets of and shares in Russian companies.

In this chapter, we will consider the issues related to representative offices and branches of foreign legal entities in Russia, as well as the legal forms of business entities that are most commonly used in Russia.

Representative offices and branches of foreign legal entities

A foreign company may choose to establish a presence in Russia through a representative office or a branch. As both representative offices and branches are subject to more flexible foreign currency control regulations than Russian business entities, both of these legal avenues for creating a subdivision in Russia are quite common.

The activities carried out by branches and representative offices have a lot in common. In addition to representing the interests of a foreign legal entity, representative offices and branches in Russia often perform the same commercial activities as the foreign legal entity.

However, current legislation works against the practice of doing business via representative offices and branches. The legislation may be interpreted as ruling that the functions of a representative office only include representation and the protection of interests of a foreign legal entity (such as obtaining contacts, carrying out market research and advertising its activity) and that a representative office is not entitled to conduct the full-scope commercial activities carried out by the foreign legal entity. No such restrictions are set with regard to branches.

Consequently, taking into consideration the fact that the creation of a branch and its subsequent functioning do not differ significantly from the creation and functioning of a representative office (see Chapter 4.3, 'Practical steps for establishing a corporate presence'), it is more flexible for a foreign legal entity to have branches rather than representative offices in Russia.

The management structure and the related corporate documents of representative offices and branches are not complicated. In both cases, management is performed by the head of the separate subdivision (a representative office or a branch). Both representative offices and branches operate in accordance with corporate documents and regulations approved by the founding company, and the head of the separate subdivision is appointed by the founding company and acts on the basis of a power of attorney.

Please note that a number of types of activity in Russia are only permitted on the basis of an appropriate licence (permit) issued by an authorized state body. Obtaining these licences can cause problems. Many Russian state bodies are reluctant to issue them to branches and representative offices of foreign legal entities on the grounds that they may only be issued to Russian legal entities. Moreover, a number of statutory regulations stipulate directly that only Russian legal entities may engage in certain types of activity (eg insurance).

In addition, foreign employees of the representative offices and branches of foreign legal entities may face certain problems when obtaining work permits to work in Russia (see Chapter 4.9 'Employment law and work permits for expatriates'). For example, the Russian Federal Migration Service has recently unexpectedly stopped issuing work permits for such employees and only issues them for foreign employees hired by Russian legal entities.

Finally, neither a representative office nor a branch is a legal entity separate from its founding company, meaning that the assets and liabilities of a representative office or branch are considered to be those of the founding company itself. However, when a foreign investor sets up a Russian legal entity, the responsibility of the foreign investor for the activity of that legal entity, including its debts, is normally limited to the foreign investor's contribution to the legal entity's share capital.

Russian business entities

Legislation governing the creation and activity of business entities in Russia is well developed and allows business entities to be established in various legal forms. The Russian Civil Code, which is the key regulatory act in this area, stipulates a significant range of legal forms of business entities. These are: a general partnership, a limited partnership, a limited liability company, a company with extended liability, a joint stock company, a production cooperative and a unitary enterprise.

However, please note that the most common legal forms of commercial entities created by both Russian and foreign investors are limited liability companies (the Russian abbreviation is 'OOO') and joint stock companies ('AO'). A joint stock company may be either 'open' ('OAO') or 'closed' ('ZAO'). Foreign investors usually select a specific legal form depending on the purpose for which the business entity is established, the number of founders, the proposed amount of share capital and other factors.

Both OOOs and AOs possess a universal legal capacity; in other words, they can perform any type of activity which is not forbidden by legislation. Some types of activity may only be performed if an appropriate licence (permit) is obtained from an authorized state body.

The above business entities are established for an unlimited period and may be reorganized into certain other legal forms. In order to carry out their commercial operations, OOOs and AOs may establish branches and representative offices in Russia and abroad, as well as subsidiary legal entities.

It is worth noting that neither an OOO nor an AO may be founded by a foreign legal entity acting as the sole founder if the latter, in turn, has another legal entity as its sole founder.

OOOs and ZAOs

The majority of business entities in Russia are established in the legal forms of OOOs and ZAOs. These legal entities are quite simple and have a lot in common. For example, the following characteristics apply to both forms:

• They may have no more than 50 shareholders.

- A statutory minimum amount of share capital must be paid by the founder(s), currently set at 10,000 Russian roubles (RUB) (currently approximately US$370). The share capital may be increased or decreased at any time, provided that it is not less than the statutory minimum amount of share capital set forth by legislation in force at the time of such a decrease.

- Contributions to the share capital may be made in monetary form or in kind.

- They have a quite simple management structure providing for two compulsory management bodies: the general shareholders' meeting and the sole executive body (general director or director).

- They enjoy the same rights and obligations in relation to the Russian state authorities (tax, customs, licensing bodies).

Despite the many similar features of OOOs and ZAOs, each of these forms has its own advantages and disadvantages which should be taken into account by a foreign investor when choosing the legal form for doing business in St Petersburg.

Advantages of an OOO

- Shares in an OOO belonging to its shareholders are not classified as securities, whereas shares in a ZAO are securities and their issue has to be registered with the Federal Financial Markets Service (the FFMS). Therefore, the incorporation of an OOO can be faster and less expensive than that of a ZAO.

- An OOO has greater flexibility than a ZAO in terms of structuring corporate governance: it has a more streamlined decision-making process. The shareholders of an OOO have more flexibility to amend the statutory provisions when drafting the OOO's constituent documents.

- The shareholders of an OOO may agree to prohibit the sale of their shares to third parties without the consent of other shareholders.

- The process for increasing the share capital of an OOO is faster and less expensive than for a ZAO.

Disadvantages of an OOO

- An OOO shareholder is allowed to withdraw from the OOO at any time without the consent of other shareholders, and to receive a portion of the OOO's net assets in proportion to his or her share in the OOO's share capital. Since such a withdrawal can disrupt the OOO's business activity, this should be taken into account, particularly for a joint venture and especially if the intended partner is not well-known.

Advantages of a ZAO

- A ZAO shareholder cannot withdraw and demand a portion of the net assets in proportion to his or her share in the ZAO's share capital. Although the shareholder may sell shares to third parties, this does not lead to the withdrawal of assets from the business.

- A ZAO is required to create and maintain a register of shareholders, which is the primary evidence of the shareholders' rights to shares. The ZAO may keep the register itself. However, in order to avoid manipulation of the rights of shareholders to shares, they may assign maintenance of the shareholders' register to an independent professional register holder.

Disadvantages of a ZAO

- Incorporation of a ZAO and its subsequent operation are more expensive due to the need to register issuances of shares at each increase in the share capital (please also note that, as a general rule, registration of each additional share issue is subject to a state fee of 0.2 per cent of the nominal value of shares issued, although the fee may not exceed 100,000 RUB – currently approximately US$3,700).

- If a ZAO's shares are acquired by a foreign investor, a currency regulation requirement may be established by the Central Bank of Russia to place a reserve amount on deposit with an authorized bank in an amount not exceeding 20 per cent of the funds used to pay for the shares for a period of up to one year (see Chapter 2.4 'Currency regulation').

- A ZAO must observe rather complex legislation on securities in the course of its business activity, and is subject to the control of the FFMS. (Each application for registration of additional issues of shares is accompanied by a quite thorough audit of the ZAO by the FFMS, which may lead to registration being refused. For instance, if a ZAO has negative net assets and applies for registration of an additional share issue in order to increase its share capital, the FFMS normally refuses registration).

Taking into account the advantages and disadvantages of both types of entity, in cases where 100 per cent foreign shareholdings or closed-held joint ventures are planned,[1] it is usually advisable to establish an OOO rather than a ZAO, since an OOO is more flexible and less expensive and bureaucratic to create and operate.

OAO

As mentioned above, a joint stock company may also be created in the form of an 'open' joint stock company (OAO). An OAO has a lot in common with a ZAO, in particular, shares in an OAO are classified as securities and their issuance is subject to registration with the FFMS, like those in a ZAO. The management structures are similar in both types of companies: the general shareholders' meeting is the supreme management body in an OAO, while the sole executive body (the general director or director) carries out the day-to-day management of the company. An OAO may also establish a board of directors, which is compulsory if the number of shareholders exceeds 50.

However, an OAO has a number of differences from a ZAO, the most significant of which are listed below:

- The number of shareholders in an OAO is unlimited. Accordingly, if it is intended to create a business entity that has more than 50 shareholders, and therefore may not be incorporated as a ZAO or an OOO, it may be incorporated in the form of an OAO.

- A larger minimum statutory share capital amount is established by legislation for an OAO (100,000 RUB, currently approximately US$3,700).

- An OAO is entitled not only to place its shares to a predefined group of persons, as is the case with a ZAO, but also to offer its shares publicly and sell them on the free market.

- The shareholders of an OAO do not have a pre-emptive right to purchase the OAO's shares when they are sold by other shareholders. Therefore, when a shareholder withdraws from an OAO by selling shares to a third party, other shareholders will be unable to hinder such a sale and prevent this third party from becoming a part of the business.

- An OAO's annual financial statements must be audited by an independent professional auditor (audit firm).

- An OAO must issue an annual report on its activities, annual financial statements and other information subject to disclosure in accordance with current legislation.

It is worth noting that Russian legislation establishes stricter requirements with regard to the disclosure of information by OAOs that place shares by both public offering and private placement among a pre-defined group of persons whose number exceeds 500. Among other requirements, legislation requires OAOs to publicly disclose (via the Internet) a wide range of information about the OAO's activities in the form of quarterly reports that also have to be submitted to the FFMS. The quarterly reports must contain, for example, details of the OAO's shareholders and management bodies, indicating the particular persons involved, details of bank accounts, the financial and economic activities of the OAO (including future plans, investments, sources of materials, suppliers and accounts payable, as well as the content, structure and cost of the OAO's fixed assets), and certain transactions performed by the OAO, indicating the subject of the transaction, price, parties involved and other significant aspects.

The list of information to be contained in the quarterly reports is very extensive, and we have only provided certain examples to demonstrate that, first, the systematization and publication of such information is rather time-consuming, and second, that disclosure of some of the required information may be undesirable for the OAO's shareholders if they want to keep the OAO's business transactions secret (eg from competitors).

Moreover, in the event of a public offering or private placement among a pre-defined group of persons whose number exceeds 500, an OAO is also obliged to disclose information (via the mass media and the Internet) in the form of public announcements of significant facts affecting the financial and economic activities of the OAO (eg details of reorganization, details of facts entailing a one-off increase or decrease in the cost of assets by more than 10 per cent). The information is to be disclosed within a few days of the occurrence of the relevant fact.

Therefore, a public offering of an OAO's shares or private placement among a pre-defined group of persons whose number exceeds 500 entails the need for the OAO to comply with a large number of requirements with regard to public disclosure of the OAO's activities.

Note

1. A 'closed-held joint venture' should be understood as a company where shares are held by a small number of persons (individuals or legal entities), who are closely linked to each other and have similar interests and, thus, there is no risk of conflict among such shareholders.

4.3

Practical Steps for Establishing a Corporate Presence

Stanislav Denisenko, Head of KPMG St Petersburg Legal Group

Having decided to do business in St Petersburg (by opening a separate subdivision – a representative office or a branch of a foreign company, or by establishing a Russian legal entity), a foreign investor approaches the next stage: the legalization of its presence in the St Petersburg market.

A foreign investor should note that when opening a separate subdivision of a foreign company, or setting up a Russian legal entity with foreign investment, it is impossible to limit oneself to the preparation of documents governing the activity of a newly established separate subdivision or legal entity. Statutory legislation stipulates a requirement to perform a number of registration procedures with the appropriate state authorities in order to legalize the activity of a foreign investor in Russia and St Petersburg. In practice, such pre-registration and registration procedures may take several months, although typically the timescale is of the order of one to three months.

Since registration procedures for separate subdivisions of foreign companies and Russian legal entities differ significantly, we will describe them separately below.

Opening a separate subdivision of a foreign company

The process of setting up a separate subdivision in St Petersburg consists of two stages: its accreditation in Moscow, and the registration of the foreign legal entity with the appropriate state authorities at the subdivision's location in St Petersburg.

Preparation of documents

To accredit a separate subdivision in Russia, a foreign investor should first of all prepare the documents related to that subdivision. These are: the decision of the authorized body of the foreign legal entity on opening a separate subdivision; the regulations on the separate subdivision;[1] and a general power of attorney granting its head the necessary authority. Russian legislation stipulates certain requirements as to the content of such documents.

The foreign investor will also need to collect a set of documents related to the foreign company opening the separate subdivision, including its constituent documents, an extract from the trade register of the country where it is incorporated (or a similar document) and a solvency letter from the bank servicing the company in the country of incorporation.

To accredit a representative office of a foreign company, the above documents should be supplemented by at least two reference letters from Russian business partners of the foreign company, confirming the expediency of its future operations in Russia and the fact that it has business connections there.

For the accreditation of the representative office, the foreign company will also need a document about the prospective location of the representative office in St Petersburg, either in the form of a guarantee letter issued by the prospective lessor confirming that certain premises will be leased out to the representative office upon its accreditation, or a lease contract with a copy of the certificate of the lessor's title to the respective premises.

It is worth noting that the state authorities of the Russian Federation (including those of St Petersburg) set special requirements with regard to documents issued abroad. The general rule is that all official documents issued outside the Russian Federation are only accepted by the Russian state authorities on official headed paper of the issuing authority with a consular legalization stamp. However, documents issued in a signatory country of the Hague Convention Abolishing the Requirement of Legalization for Foreign Public Documents of 5 October 1961 do not need consular legalization. In this case, a copy with an apostille is sufficient. The Russian Federation also has a number of international bilateral treaties that negate the requirement for legalization of foreign documents and stipulate that properly prepared documents should have an official stamp and the signature of an authorized person of the body issuing the respective documents.

Any document issued in a foreign language must be submitted to the state authorities with a translation into Russian certified by a Russian notary or consul.

In addition, the various state authorities set different requirements regarding the period for which foreign documents are considered to be valid.

Preparation and collection of the documents listed above will definitely take a considerable amount of time, which needs to be taken into account when making a decision on establishing a separate subdivision and planning the commencement of activity in St Petersburg.

Accreditation

Unlike other regions of the Russian Federation, in St Petersburg no preliminary approval by the local authorities is required to establish a separate subdivision. This is an advantage, as obtaining such approval would take additional time.

As mentioned above, wherever in Russia a separate subdivision is established it must be accredited in Moscow, which may be inconvenient for a foreign investor. However, a number of consulting companies in the St Petersburg market offer services to assist in the accreditation of separate subdivisions and can facilitate the procedure.

Accreditation of branches and representative offices of foreign legal entities is performed by the State Registration Chamber of the Ministry of Justice of the Russian Federation ('the State Registration Chamber'). A number of other authorized institutions, including the Chamber of Commerce and Industry of the Russian Federation and the Federal Aviation Agency, are also entitled to accredit representative offices in certain instances. However, it should be noted that the State Registration Chamber is solely responsible for maintaining the official Unified State Register of representative offices of foreign legal entities accredited in the Russian Federation. A certificate that the representative office has been entered into the Unified State Register, issued by the State Registration Chamber, confirms the official status of a representative office and is required when opening bank accounts, registering with the tax authorities, obtaining Russian visas and undergoing customs procedures. Therefore, if a representative office has been accredited with any authorized body other than the State Registration Chamber, the relevant documents must still be submitted to the State Registration Chamber in order for the information on the representative office to be entered into the Unified State Register.

The accreditation procedure entails the necessary documents being submitted to and considered by the relevant authorized body, and a certificate of accreditation of the separate subdivision being issued. A foreign company should also be aware that accreditation of a separate subdivision may be denied if an incomplete set of documents is submitted, as well as in some other exceptional cases stipulated by statutory legislation, including when the activity of a foreign legal entity opening a separate subdivision violates statutory legislation of the Russian Federation.

A foreign investor intending to enter the Russian market should take into account the fact that the accreditation fee differs, depending on the type of separate subdivision and the period for which it is being established. The accreditation fees may be up to US$4,200.

The period for which separate subdivisions of foreign legal entities are accredited – that is, the period within which they are entitled to operate in the Russian Federation – is up to three years for a representative office and up to five years for a branch. However, both a representative office and a branch may then extend the period of their accreditation by submitting a certain set of documents to the accreditation body and paying a fee of US$500 to extend the period of accreditation. A separate subdivision may extend its accreditation period an unlimited number of times.

The process of accreditation with the State Registration Chamber takes no longer than one month from the date the full set of documents is submitted. It is possible to accelerate the accreditation process (to seven working days) for an additional fee of US$500 charged by the State Registration Chamber.

A separate subdivision of a foreign legal entity is considered to have been established as of the date of its accreditation. However, upon accreditation in Moscow, the foreign legal entity that has set up a separate subdivision in St Petersburg must register with the appropriate state authorities in St Petersburg.

Registration of foreign companies at the location of their representative offices and branches in St Petersburg

Upon accreditation of its separate subdivision, a foreign legal entity must register with the tax authorities at the location of its separate subdivision in St Petersburg, as well as with the state statistics authorities and regional departments of state non-budgetary funds (the Social Insurance Fund, Pension Fund and Obligatory Medical Insurance Fund) that are the recipients of contributions and other mandatory payments due in relation to carrying out activity in Russia.

Statutory legislation also stipulates certain requirements with regard to the set of documents to be submitted to the above authorities. In general, the procedure for registration with all of these authorities takes approximately two weeks.

In summarizing the issues related to opening separate subdivisions of foreign legal entities in St Petersburg, it should be noted that in practice this is a rather bureaucratic process that requires a significant number of documents to be submitted to various authorities (both in Moscow and in St Petersburg). In practice, the entire process may take up to two months, including the time required to prepare documents.

Incorporation of legal entities

From the perspective of registration, the procedure for incorporating a legal entity in St Petersburg in certain instances (eg in the case of creating a limited liability company) is less bureaucratic and time consuming than the establishing of a separate subdivision of a foreign company.

The registration of legal entities is primarily regulated at the federal level by the Federal Law on State Registration of Legal Entities and Individual Entrepreneurs No 129-FZ of 8 August 2001. Under current legislation, the state registration of legal entities incorporated in Russia is primarily performed by the Russian Federal Tax Service through its territorial divisions. However, there are certain exceptions, and some types of newly incorporated legal entities (eg credit organizations) are subject to state registration with other authorized institutions.

Preparation of documents

Irrespective of the legal form selected for the entity incorporated by a foreign company, the entity's registration in St Petersburg will require the submission of documents regulating the entity's business, such as the decision on incorporating the legal entity, and the entity's constituent documents. Due to the fact that current legislation establishes certain requirements for the content of the incorporation documents, special attention should be given to the relevant legal regulations when preparing such documents.

In addition, the registration authorities will require an extract from the register of foreign legal entities (or another similar document) with regard to the foreign company incorporating the Russian legal entity, issued by a competent authority in the country of incorporation of the foreign company. It should be noted that the state authorities that register legal entities impose certain requirements with regard to the format of documents (as in the case of the accreditation of separate subdivisions).

Before applying to the state authority that registers legal entities, the relevant state duty should be paid. At present the state duty for the registration of a legal entity amounts to 2,000 Russian roubles (RUB) (currently approximately US$70).

Payment of share capital

A foreign founder should also take into account that the incorporation of a legal entity in Russia implies that the entity's share capital should be paid in accordance with the procedure and timeframe established by legislation. The payment may be made either in monetary form (by opening a bank account and transferring funds to it) or in kind (by contributing property to the share capital, including property rights).

Registration of a legal entity

With regard to the state registration procedure in St Petersburg, the most important innovation is the existence since April 2004 of the Unified Registration Centre of Legal Entities (located at the Inter-regional Tax Inspectorate of the Federal Tax Service of Russia No 15 of St Petersburg). This is a practical implementation of the so-called 'one-window' idea, by means of which legislators aimed to simplify the procedure for incorporating legal entities in Russia.

It is now no longer necessary to spend time and effort applying to numerous district and city agencies when registering a legal entity incorporated in St Petersburg. Instead it is registered in the Unified Registration Centre, which then transfers the details of the incorporated legal entity directly to the statistics authorities and the appropriate state non-budgetary funds (the Social Insurance Fund, Pension Fund and Obligatory Medical Insurance Fund) for registration. The Centre processes between 200 and 350 applications a day.

Thanks to the simplified registration procedure in St Petersburg, five days after the documents are submitted to the Unified Registration Centre a legal entity receives a state registration certificate accompanied by a complete package of documents confirming registration with the tax authorities, state statistics authorities and state non-budgetary funds.

The entire procedure of state registration and registration with the appropriate authorities, including the compilation of documents, will not normally take more than three to five weeks, which is quicker than the accreditation and registration of a separate subdivision.

Registration of the issuance of shares

A significant feature of the incorporation process for joint stock companies of any type (both open and closed) is the need for an additional step: the registration of the issuance of shares of the joint stock company as securities. This is carried out by the Federal Financial Markets Service (FFMS). It should be noted that, under Russian legislation, shares cannot be traded without such registration.

The registration of the issuance of shares is a rather complicated procedure, requiring the compilation of a number of documents that must be submitted to the FFMS within one month of the state registration of a joint stock company. The registration of the issuance of shares normally takes 30 days from the date all necessary documents are submitted but, in certain instances, legislation allows this timeframe to be extended by the FFMS. In addition, the registration of the issuance of shares requires payment of a state duty of 11,000 RUB (currently approximately US$400).

Anti-monopoly arrangements

In addition to the above, a foreign company doing business in St Petersburg should take into account that Russian legislation contains a number of regulations aimed at preventing or restricting monopoly activity and unfair competition in the markets of Russia.

Under this legislation, if the total assets owned by all founders of a newly-incorporated legal entity as per their latest balance sheets exceed 2 million minimum statutory monthly wages (at present, this amounts to 200 million RUB, which is currently approximately US$7.3 million), the Federal Antimonopoly Service should be informed of the incorporation of such a company within 45 days of its state registration.

In the case of a failure to notify the antimonopoly authority, the founders of the newly created legal entity and its managers may be held administratively liable, and in certain cases the legal entity may even be liquidated on the basis of a court decision.

Licensing

As already mentioned in Chapter 4.2 ('Corporate structures'), certain types of business may only be undertaken by a legal entity if it obtains a special licence (permit). A list of such types of activity is established by the Federal Law on the Licensing of Certain Types of Activities No 128-FZ of 8 August 2001, and other federal laws regulating the licensing of certain types of activity. Such activities include, among others, transportation of passengers and cargo; medical, pharmaceutical and appraisal activity; tour operating; auditing; investment funds and credit activity. It should be noted, however, that in the near future a new law may be adopted that will reduce the number of activities subject to licensing.

The right to carry out such an activity starts from the date the relevant licence is obtained (or within the timeframe stipulated in the licence). Licences are normally issued for a period of five years or more.

The newly incorporated Russian legal entity should apply to the appropriate state bodies authorized to issue licences for the kind of activity it intends to undertake. The list of documents to be prepared and submitted to obtain a licence is quite extensive, and varies depending on the type of licensed activity. In addition, an applicant has to pay a state duty for the consideration of a licence application and the issuing of a licence, which may range from an amount equivalent to several US dollars to several thousand US dollars, depending on the type of licensed activity.

As a rule, the decision on granting a licence should be taken by the authorized state authorities within 60 days of the date when all necessary documents are submitted. It should be noted that in certain instances established by the law (eg if the legal entity does not meet the licensing requirements and conditions), the licensing bodies may refuse to issue the licence.

For performance of a licensable activity without a licence, an administrative and (in certain instances) criminal liability may be imposed. In addition, a legal entity performing such activity may be liquidated upon a decision of the court.

Conclusion

We have described the registration procedures for incorporating a Russian legal entity and a separate subdivision of a foreign legal entity in St Petersburg. It should be noted, however, that the list of procedures described above is not exhaustive. In certain instances, the incorporation of a Russian subdivision of a foreign investor may have specific procedures, and the appropriate registration procedure may differ from that stated above. For example, a more complicated, costly and lengthy process would be required for the incorporation of credit institutions in Russia.

When incorporating a subdivision in St Petersburg, therefore, a foreign investor should check whether special requirements are established by Russian legislation for the incorporation of such a subdivision.

Note

1. The 'regulations on the separate subdivision' should be understood in the current context as the document aimed at regulating the separate subdivision for its own management. However, Russian legislation establishes certain requirements to such regulations that should be taken into account while preparing that document.

4.4

Business Taxation

Peter Arnell, Head of KPMG St Petersburg Tax Department, and Alisa Melkonian, Tax Manager

Introduction

Russia, which has traditionally been associated with high tax rates and a non-transparent tax system, has made significant progress towards reforming the system and decreasing the burden on companies and individuals. The principal changes were made within a comparatively short period of time and resulted in the abolition of turnover taxes, the elimination of many small taxes and a significant reduction in tax rates for the main taxes. The changes include:

- abolition of road users' tax, sales tax and advertising tax;

- reduction of the general corporate income tax rate from 35 to 24 per cent (from 2002);

- reduction of the standard value added tax (VAT) rate from 20 per cent to 18 per cent (from 2004);

- reduction of the unified social tax rate (UST) from 35.6 per cent to 26 per cent (from 2005), and the earlier introduction of a regressive scale of rates down to a marginal UST rate of 2 per cent for those on the highest salaries;

- reduction of the general personal income tax rate to 13 per cent (from 2001).

Another important change was the introduction of the Tax Code in order to create a single document regulating all aspects of taxation, to clarify taxation rules and to make them understandable for both Russian companies and foreign investors.

The extensive treaty network that Russia has developed with the majority of European countries also plays a significant role in making the Russian tax system attractive. Although Russia is not a member of the Organization for Economic Cooperation and Development (OECD), the provisions of the OECD Model Convention on income and capital are widely used in practice when concluding bilateral tax agreements. In addition, tax legislation stipulates that the provisions of these bilateral tax agreements prevail over domestic legislation.

There is no advance rulings system in Russia. The taxpayer is entitled to receive free information from the local tax authorities on taxes, legislation and other provisions, as well as written explanations of the application of tax legislation. However, this information is not binding on either taxpayers or the tax authorities. Furthermore, the explanations received from the tax authorities are often ambiguous, rendering them of little practical use in such cases.

The Russian tax structure conforms to the federal nature of Russia in that the various regions that comprise the Russian Federation have certain rights as regards levying taxes, although the extent of these rights has in recent years been reduced in favour of the central, federal authorities. The regions also have their own tax authority structures (local tax authorities, supervised by regional tax authorities, which are in turn supervised by the federal tax authorities).

Within the scope of the rights granted by federal legislation, the St Petersburg authorities are attempting to maintain and seeking to increase the city's attractiveness in terms of taxation, both for Russian companies operating in the region and for foreign investors. For example, for a number of years St Petersburg has been granting concessions to companies making capital investments.

One of the advantages of the current St Petersburg legislation is that companies do not need to conclude special investment agreements with the city in order to enjoy tax concessions (which is the case in certain other regions of Russia).

Despite the recent positive trends in the Russian tax environment, there remain a number of less desirable features for investors and the business community. Russian tax legislation is subject to frequent changes, which also influence St Petersburg legislation as the latter is required to conform to federal legislation. Russian tax legislation is also subject to inconsistent or inaccurate interpretation by the tax authorities (unfortunately St Petersburg legislation is no exception in this regard). As a rule, in cases where ambiguity exists in relation to interpretation, tax law generally follows civil law. However, the tax authorities often interpret the provisions of civil law very broadly, making a presumption of tax avoidance, and the courts have followed this approach in several cases.

Taxation of companies

Under current tax legislation, taxes and levies can be categorized as follows:

- *Federal (1)*: applied throughout Russia in accordance with uniform rules and rates (eg VAT, excise tax, UST and personal income tax).

- *Federal (2)*: applied throughout Russia in accordance with uniform rules, but the rate for the locally collected portion of this tax may be determined locally (eg corporate income tax).

- *Regional / local*: listed in the Tax Code and enacted by the regional or local authorities. These taxes are collected entirely regionally or locally (eg corporate property tax and land tax). The general attributes of these taxes (eg taxable base, taxpayers and maximum level of tax rates) are established by federal legislation, but the regional/local authorities are entitled to determine the tax rate within the established limits, the payment procedures, due dates and reporting formats. The regional authorities may also grant tax concessions at their discretion.

The Tax Code also stipulates a number of special tax regimes for certain groups of taxpayers such as small businesses.

Corporate income tax

General issues
Under current tax legislation, corporate income tax is to be paid by Russian legal entities and foreign legal entities whose activities create a permanent establishment (PE) for corporate income tax purposes or which receive certain types of income from a Russian source (eg interest, royalties).

The Russian definition of the term 'permanent establishment' broadly follows the concept of the OECD Model Convention on income and capital.

The tax period is a calendar year. In general, the accruals method is used to identify income and expenses. Since some of the rules for calculating the corporate income tax base differ from financial accounting rules, tax legislation requires that taxpayers maintain separate accounts for corporate income tax purposes.

Under the general rule, the corporate income tax base is determined as income gained less those expenses that are properly documented, economically justified and incurred for income-generating purposes.

The deductibility of some specific expenses is limited, for example:

- certain advertising expenses;

- entertainment expenses;

- certain employee insurance;

- per diem allowances.

The tax authorities have recently started to pay close attention to deductibility, and they challenge the deductibility of expenses that do not meet all the criteria stipulated by the legislation.

Corporate income tax is currently levied at a general rate of 24 per cent, which makes it competitive with Europe. Withholding tax is levied on the income of foreign legal entities without a PE in Russia at a rate of 20 per cent. Where dividends are paid to non-residents, the domestic withholding tax rate is 15 per cent. Freight income is taxed at 10 per cent. Interest income on state securities is taxed at either 15 per cent or zero per cent.

The regional tax authorities are entitled to reduce the general corporate income tax rate by up to 4 per cent. The rates with regard to certain types of income of foreign legal entities can be reduced by an applicable double tax treaty.

Capital gains are taxable as normal business income.

Corporate income tax incentives
The Tax Code stipulates a certain number of investment incentives with regard to corporate income tax that are widely used by companies. For example:

- Investments made by foreign investors (irrespective of their share in the ownership of the relevant entity) with the purpose of financing capital expenditures for production are exempt from corporate income tax if:

    - they are used within one year of receipt;

    - the taxpayer accounts separately for income and expenses in connection with such financing.

- In practice, the use of this benefit is subject to close control by the tax authorities. If any of the conditions are not met, the corporate income tax exemption will be lost.

- The gratuitous receipt of assets (including monetary funds) by a Russian legal entity is not subject to corporate income tax on the recipient in cases where the contributing organization owns more than 50 per cent of the share capital of the recipient. Such assets (except for monetary funds) are only exempt from corporate income tax if they are not transferred to third parties within one year from the date of their receipt.

- Losses incurred for corporate income tax purposes may be carried forward for up to 10 years. Loss relief may not reduce subsequent taxable profits by more than 30 per cent per year.

For corporate tax incentives granted by St Petersburg legislation, see the 'Investment incentives granted by St Petersburg legislation' section below.

Value added tax

General issues
VAT is designed as a 'cascade' tax to be borne ultimately by consumers but collected through taxable persons, on a basis similar to the EU model.

As a general rule, VAT is levied on the sale of goods, work or services in Russia, construction and assembly work performed for a company's own purposes, and the importation of goods into Russia.

Specific rules exist to determine the place of supply of goods, work and services.

VAT taxpayers are legal entities (Russian and foreign companies involved in the sale of goods, work or services in Russia) and individual entrepreneurs and entities that import goods into Russia. If a supplier of goods or services subject to Russian VAT is not registered with the Russian tax authorities, VAT should be collected by the Russian payer from the amount paid to the supplier.

VAT is levied at a general rate of 18 per cent, except on certain medical goods, foodstuffs and children's clothes, which are taxed at 10 per cent, and certain supplies that are exempt from VAT (eg certain financial services, pharmaceuticals). A zero per cent tax rate applies to most exports. Goods imported into Russia are generally subject to import VAT.

VAT payable to the budget is determined as the sum of output VAT (received from customers) less input VAT (paid to suppliers/contractors or to the customs authorities). The tax period is one month. Output VAT can be calculated on a cash or accruals basis at the taxpayer's discretion. It should be noted that it is planned to introduce an important amendment to VAT legislation, under which VAT shall be recognized on an accruals basis only.

Input VAT is recoverable if certain conditions stipulated by legislation are met. For example, under current tax legislation, VAT on capital construction and materials used therein can only be recovered after the assets completed by capital construction have been put into operation and booked as fixed assets. This deduction is made in the month in which the taxpayer begins to depreciate the corresponding assets for tax purposes.

In practice, the current mechanism for recovering input VAT related to capital construction entails a significant temporary negative cashflow. For many companies performing construction this has become a painful issue. However, it is planned to introduce measures for the immediate recovery of VAT paid during capital construction in the foreseeable future.

The recoverability of input VAT, which reduces the amount of VAT due, is subject to tight control by the tax authorities and requires exacting accounting procedures and the existence of proper tax invoices.

VAT incentives
The Tax Code stipulates an investment incentive with regard to VAT. Fixed assets that qualify as 'technological equipment' imported into Russia as a contribution in kind by a foreign shareholder to the charter capital of a Russian legal entity may be exempt from VAT if certain conditions are met.

Excise tax

In accordance with Russian tax legislation, excisable goods include alcohol and alcoholic drinks, tobacco goods and oil products. As a general rule, excise tax is levied on excisable goods produced by companies and sold in Russia, as well as those imported into Russia.

A special taxation procedure is established for oil products, which requires that the taxpayer obtain a certificate of registration of parties that perform operations with oil products, issued to companies and individual entrepreneurs by the tax authorities.

The payers of excise tax are legal entities, individual entrepreneurs and entities that import goods to Russia, if they perform excisable transactions.

An excise tax rate may be set either as a percentage or as a fixed amount in relation to a set volume of excisable goods. For certain types of excisable goods, combined rates can be applied.

In practice excise tax rates are high. Moreover, since excise tax represents a significant portion of inflow to the Russian budget, these rates are usually subject to increase on an annual basis.

Payroll taxes

Unified social tax

The UST is levied on companies and individual entrepreneurs making payments to individuals. The cost is borne and paid for by companies, with no contribution from employees.

In general, UST is levied on payments, whether in cash or in kind, made by employers to their employees, including remuneration under civil law contracts. Certain payments are exempt from UST, including all types of compensation payment and per diem allowances within the established statutory limits.

An annual regressive scale of tax rates is applied for UST, from a maximum rate of 26 per cent to a minimum rate of 2 per cent. The 2 per cent rate applies to earnings in excess of 600,000 RUB (approximately 17,000 euros). The tax period is a calendar year. However, monthly advance payment is required.

In addition to UST, there are obligatory contributions for injury and professional illness to be paid to the Social Insurance Fund at a flat rate. This cost is borne by companies, with no contributions from employees. The rate varies, depending on the risk category that the employing company falls into, as determined by the Fund. The current minimum contribution is 0.2 per cent of payroll and the maximum is 8.5 per cent.

Personal income tax

Personal income tax (PIT) is levied on the income of individuals who are tax residents in Russia (that is, who reside in Russia for at least 183 days per annum), and on non-residents receiving income from sources in Russia.

The PIT cost is borne by individuals. Employer companies withhold PIT at the time of payment and transfer it to the budget as tax agents. The tax period is a calendar year.

In general, Russia is considered to have one of the lowest PIT rates in Europe. PIT is levied at a general 13 per cent rate except for: income received by non-residents, which is taxed at 30 per cent; dividends, which are taxed at 9 per cent; and certain limited types of income taxed at 35 per cent (eg prizes). Russian tax legislation provides for a number of deductions and allowances, which are only available in relation to income taxable at the 13 per cent rate.

Under Russian tax legislation and double tax treaties, which prevail over domestic legislation, double taxation relief can be granted by means of credit for foreign tax.

Taxes on capital

Taxes on capital levied at the corporate level consist of corporate property tax and land tax. Both taxes are regional, which means that general attributes of these taxes (eg taxable base, taxpayers and maximum levels of tax rates) are established by federal legislation, but the regional or local authorities are entitled to determine the tax rate within the established limits, as well as the payment procedures, due dates and reporting formats.

Corporate property tax

Corporate property tax applies to both Russian and foreign legal entities with property in Russia. For Russian legal entities and foreign legal entities whose activities create a permanent establishment in Russia, taxable property consists of fixed assets recorded as such in financial accounting. For foreign legal entities, whose activities do not create a permanent establishment in Russia, only immovable property located in Russia to which the foreign legal entity has property rights is subject to corporate property tax in Russia.

Land is not subject to corporate property tax.

In St Petersburg, corporate property tax is levied at the maximum rate of 2.2 per cent. The tax period is a calendar year and advance payments are required on a quarterly basis.

However, specific exemptions from corporate property tax have been granted by the Tax Code on the federal level (eg for railways and power lines). For corporate property tax concessions granted by St Petersburg legislation see the 'Investment incentives granted by St Petersburg legislation' section below.

Land tax

Land tax is levied on the land plot area, and in general, the payers of land tax are companies or individuals owning land. The basic tax rates are established at the federal level and adjusted for inflation on an irregular basis. The specific rates are set by the regional authorities. The land tax rate in St Petersburg ranges from 0.775 RUB (approximately 0.02 euros) to 25.105 RUB (approximately 0.7 euros) per m^2 per year, depending on the town-planning value of the area. The laws on the St Petersburg budget for each particular year establish the tax rate increase coefficient applicable in the year. In 2005, for example, a factor of 9.504 is applied to the above rates.

Land rent is often paid instead of land tax, since the majority of land is owned by state and is rented out to companies. The rent rate is linked to the land tax rate and has the same structure: a basic rate, annual multiplying coefficients, and further adjustments depending on various features of the land plot.

For land tax concessions granted by St Petersburg legislation see the 'Investment incentives granted by St Petersburg legislation' section below.

Other taxes

Current tax legislation also stipulates other taxes, including a mineral-extraction tax (levied on minerals extracted from an underground plot provided to the taxpayer for use under licence), water tax (for the use of water resources), transportation tax (on registered vehicles), inheritance and gift tax, and tax on gambling activities. In addition, the Tax Code stipulates state duties (in instances of requests to the state authorities) and duties for the usage of biological resources.

The Tax Code also stipulates a number of special tax regimes for certain groups of taxpayers, which are primarily intended for small businesses (eg the simplified taxation system and unified tax on imputed income for certain types of activity).

Anti-avoidance

Transfer pricing

Under current legislation, the tax authorities are entitled to monitor the completeness of taxes paid in the following instances:

- transactions between related parties;
- barter transactions;
- cross-border transactions;
- when prices used by taxpayers for identical goods, work or services fluctuate by more than 20 per cent in either direction within a short period of time.

Using this legislation, the tax authorities may decide to calculate additional taxes for a company if it is proved that the prices established by this company for its services have resulted in the prices being considerably lower than the market price.

An analysis of current Russian arbitration court practice related to transfer pricing shows that cases are commonly resolved in favour of taxpayers, due to the lack of information on market prices and, accordingly, the inability of the tax inspectorates to demonstrate the similarity of services and transaction circumstances used to substantiate the tax adjustments. However, we believe that the risks related to transfer pricing cannot be disregarded, particularly as amendments could be introduced to current legislation that may provide improved mechanisms for tax base adjustment.

Thin capitalization rules

In accordance with tax legislation, interest paid by a Russian company to a foreign legal entity that directly or indirectly holds more than 20 per cent of the Russian company is subject to thin capitalization rules, under which interest is only partially deductible where the debt to equity ratio exceeds 3:1 (12.5:1 for companies engaged in banking or leasing activities). The remainder is considered as dividends and subject to the relevant taxation in accordance with Russian legislation, as modified by any applicable double tax treaty.

Controlled foreign company

Currently there is no CFC legislation in Russia.

Investment incentives granted by St Petersburg legislation

Corporate income tax concessions

Recently approved St Petersburg investment legislation stipulates a reduction of the corporate income tax and corporate property tax rates for companies that invest over 150 million RUB (approximately 4 million euros) in fixed assets during one calendar year starting from 1 January 2005 (hereinafter, the 'qualifying year'), provided that these companies meet certain criteria.

In addition, a reduction of the corporate income tax rate is granted for companies with sales income from certain types of activities (including the production of electronic devices and the development of software) that exceeds 80 per cent of the total sales income accounted for corporate income tax purposes ('development companies') and which invest over 50 million RUB (approximately 1.3 million euros) in fixed assets during the qualifying year.

One of the main criteria that should be met in order to obtain these concessions is that the investments should be made for production purposes in the territory of St Petersburg, and are intended to produce sales to third parties for the purposes of earning profits.

In addition, St Petersburg investment legislation prescribes that the minimum amount of taxes payable to the St Petersburg budget should not be less than the corresponding amount paid in the qualifying year. If this condition is not met in any year following the qualifying year, the taxpayer automatically loses the right to these concessions.

The corporate income tax concessions can be applied for a period of three years following the qualifying year.

A reduced corporate income tax rate (if the companies meet the above-mentioned conditions) is established for legal entities that invest in the qualifying year:

- from 150 to 300 million RUB (approximately 4–8 million euros); for these companies the reduced corporate income tax rate will be 22 per cent;

- over 300 million RUB (approximately 8 million euros); for these companies the reduced corporate income tax rate will be 20 per cent.

For 'development companies' investing over 50 million RUB (approximately 1.3 million euros), the reduced corporate income tax rate will be 20 per cent.

Corporate property tax

There are concessions for payers of corporate property tax who invest over 150 million RUB (approximately 4 million euros) in fixed assets during the qualifying year starting from 1 January 2005. Provided that these companies meet other criteria discussed above with regard to corporate income tax, they can pay corporate property tax at a reduced rate of 1.1 per cent (the basic tax rate stipulated by current legislation is 2.2 per cent).

Land tax

Under St Petersburg legislation, companies that own land and invest in the construction or reconstruction of real estate located on it, irrespective the amount of the investment, are exempt from land tax for the standard construction or reconstruction period for the relevant approved project, and for two years after the expiry of this period.

Summary

Russia's tax regime has improved significantly in recent years and the headline rates of corporate income tax, VAT, UST and personal income tax are now competitive in an international context. St Petersburg maintains its attractiveness in terms of taxation, which assists the general increase in the number of companies operating in the region and the new investors attracted to it.

4.5

Auditing and Accounting

Alisa Melkonian, Tax Manager, and Nina Goulis, Tax Consultant, KPMG St Petersburg

Introduction

In recent years Russia has made significant progress towards the modernization and unification of its auditing and accounting rules. The reform of the accounting and financial reporting system started with the adoption of the Federal Law on Accounting in 1996 and the revision of the Regulation on Accounting and Financial Reporting in 1998. It continued with the introduction of the new Chart of Accounts in 2000 and a series of accounting regulations, also sometimes referred to as Russian Accounting Standards (RAS). The reform of the regulation of audit activities resulted in the introduction of the Federal Law on Auditing Activities in 2001 and on Auditing Standards in 2002, as well as the introduction of the Code of Ethics of Russian Auditors in 2003.

The auditing and accounting rules are established centrally at a federal level and do not vary from region to region.

Although Russia has not yet officially introduced International Financial Reporting Standards (IFRS) and International Standards on Auditing (ISA), it is moving towards their adoption in the foreseeable future. For example, the Russian accounting and auditing standards that currently exist are based on IFRS and ISA respectively. The recently approved Conceptual Approach to the Development of Accounting and Reporting in the Russian Federation in the Medium Term outlines the Russian government's plan in relation to the adoption in Russia of IFRS. According to this plan, over the next five years it is expected that all Russian groups of companies will be required to use IFRS in the preparation of their consolidated financial statements and that statutory financial statements for other companies will be prepared in accordance with Russian accounting standards, which will become increasingly based on IFRS.

It should be noted that companies currently operating in Russia and those that enter the Russian market could face problems with the adoption of IFRS. For example, they may experience a shortage of qualified staff with sufficient knowledge of IFRS. If so, international audit and consulting companies working in Russia (for example, the so-called 'Big Four' – one of which is KPMG) will be able to provide the best assistance since they have extensive experience in consulting and auditing under IFRS.

Another important planned change relates to the abolition of obligatory licensing of auditing activities. Instead of obtaining a state licence, audit companies will be obliged to become members of a self-regulating association.

Despite recent reforms, many administrative provisions and reporting characteristics of the former Soviet system remain. Thus current Russian accounting practice can be characterized by the following:

- The state, represented by the government, remains responsible for the overall administration of accounting in Russia and for elaborating general approaches to its development.

- Although accounting principles often appear very similar to IFRS, in many cases they are applied differently in practice.

- While, according to Russian legislation, the main function of accounting is to provide the users of financial statements with complete and reliable information on an entity's performance and financial position, accounting is still seen as a tool to ensure that entities comply with tax legislation.

- While 'substance over form' is stated as the principle for the preparation of financial statements, in practice form often takes priority over substance.

- Financial accounting has become to a large extent separate from tax accounting, which has greatly increased the amount of accounting work required by companies.

Auditing

General issues

Russian audit activities are regulated by the following:

- the Federal Law on Auditing Activities;

- auditing standards;

- the Code of Ethics of Russian Auditors;

- methodological guidelines, including explanatory letters from the Ministry of Finance and other authorities.

Compulsory audit

Under Russian legislation, an annual audit of financial statements is compulsory for the following entities:

- open joint-stock companies;

- credit or insurance companies, commodity and stock exchanges, investment funds and non-budgetary state funds;

- organizations or individual entrepreneurs whose annual earnings from goods sold, work performed or services rendered exceed 500,000 minimum monthly wages (as at 1 April 2005, 50 million RUB or 1.4 million euros), or whose total assets exceed 200,000 minimum monthly wages as at the end of the reporting period (as at 1 April 2005, 20 million RUB or 500,000 euros);

- state or municipal unitary enterprises whose financial results correspond to the conditions stipulated in the previous item (Russian regions may reduce the level of the financial performance indicators mentioned in the previous item for municipal unitary enterprises);

- organizations or individual entrepreneurs for which an audit is compulsory in accordance with other federal laws.

Moreover, in accordance with a decision of the internal audit committee, of the general shareholders' meeting or the board of directors, or upon the demand of a shareholder or a group of shareholders holding 10 per cent or more of the voting stock, all joint stock companies are subject to an audit.

Companies are normally entitled to select their own auditor. Currently an auditor may be a legal entity or a registered entrepreneur possessing an appropriate licence. However, amendments to current legislation are planned, by which licensing of audit activities will be abolished. Instead of obtaining a state licence, audit companies will be obliged to become members of self-regulating associations.

In addition to a compulsory annual audit of financial statements prepared in accordance with RAS, companies may, on their own initiative, engage international audit companies (for example, the so-called 'Big Four') to perform an annual audit in accordance with IFRS in order to ensure that the attestation of the financial statements is in line with the expectations of international investors and financiers.

Auditing standards

As at 1 April 2005, there are 16 auditing standards. These standards regulate areas such as the documentation of audit work, issues related to significance and audit evidence. In addition, seven new auditing standards will be introduced in the foreseeable future, which will cover topics related to audit evidence in specific cases, analytical procedures, and management representations and explanations, among others. These auditing standards broadly follow the corresponding ISA.

Accounting

General issues

The Russian accounting system is regulated by a number of legal acts, and consists of different levels of documentation, including:

First level: Federal laws regulating the way accounting is set up and maintained by companies
The most important document within this level is the Federal Law on Accounting, which contains basic accounting and reporting requirements.

In addition, civil legislation provides the overall framework for business activities and applies to both legal entities and individuals in Russia; it consolidates many accounting issues. For example, the Civil Code of Russia defines a legal entity as having its own balance sheet, establishes the obligatory approval of annual financial statements, provides definitions of subsidiary and associated companies, and determines procedures for reorganization and liquidation of different kinds of legal entities.

The Federal Law on Consolidated Financial Statements is planned to be introduced in the foreseeable future.

Second level: Accounting Regulations (Standards)
At present there are 20 Accounting Regulations (Standards) for commercial entities (apart from credit institutions, whose activities are regulated by special standards), which regulate the issues related to accounting policies, compilation and presentation of financial statements, accounting for fixed and intangible assets, inventory, loans, income, expenses, financial investments and profits tax, among others.

In total, 30 Russian Accounting Standards are intended to be adopted. In particular, it is intended to adopt regulations governing the accounting for investments in joint activity and dependent organizations.

In practice, the existing regulations contain similar provisions to the relevant IFRS. However, significant technical differences exist. For example, in accordance with RAS, deferred income tax is calculated using the Profit and Loss method rather than Balance Sheet approach applied under IFRS.

Third level: methodological regulations and instructions
This level of documentation consists of methodological instructions on accounting issued by the Ministry of Finance with regard to particular issues.

One of the most important documents at this level is the Chart of Accounts and related instructions.

Fourth level: accounting policy developed by companies themselves
The fourth level of documentation includes documents belonging to the company itself, which determine its accounting policies in all systematic, technical and organizational aspects and are established by order of the company. If there are any specific accounting methods used by companies that are not described in the relevant RAS, companies have the right to develop them independently and adopt them by describing them in the accounting policy.

Branches and representative offices of foreign legal entities located in Russia are allowed to maintain their accounting on the basis of regulations established in the country in which the foreign company resides, unless these regulations contradict IFRS.

General accounting principles

The key accounting principles in Russia are as follows:

- The matching principle. In accordance with this principle, business transactions are recorded in the reporting period in which they occur, regardless of when receipts or payments relating to these transactions are actually made.

- The going-concern principle. In accordance with this principle, it is assumed that a company will continue operating in the foreseeable future.

Companies should use a working chart of accounts developed on the basis of the centrally-established Chart of Accounts.

All business operations performed by companies should be supported by relevant confirmation documents, which constitute primary accounting documents that form the basis for the preparation of financial statements.

Accounting records should be maintained in Russian. If some of the documents are prepared in a foreign language, the tax and other authorities may require a notarized translation into Russian.

Business transactions should be accounted for in the currency of Russia (roubles). Assets and liabilities expressed in foreign currency should be converted into roubles at the exchange rate set by the Central Bank of Russia as at the date of the transaction, as well as at each reporting date.

Statutory financial reporting requirements

In accordance with current legislation the statutory financial reporting package shall include:

- the balance sheet;

- the income statement;

- supplements to the balance sheet and income statement (eg cashflow statement, statement on changes in equity);

- audit opinion, if required by legislation;

- notes to the financial statements.

Under Russian accounting legislation, the reporting year runs from 1 January to 31 December. The annual reporting package should be filed within 90 days of the end of a reporting year. Interim filings are also required, although on these occasions only the balance sheet and income statement are necessary. Interim filings are to be submitted on a quarterly basis and the deadline is established as the 30th day of the month following the reporting quarter.

Tax reporting is not included in the accounting financial statements.

The information in the financial statements for the reporting year and the previous year must be presented in comparable formats. A company's financial statements must include the results of the activities of the company's branches, representative offices and other subdivisions.

Financial statements should be available for the users thereof, namely the founders (shareholders), investors, credit institutions and creditors, among others.

Copies of financial statements are to be submitted to the tax authorities, statistics authorities and other authorities on request where prescribed by legislation. In certain cases (eg for open joint-stock companies) the financial statements and a final part of the auditor's report must be published. The publication of financial statements should take place not later than 1 June of the year following the reporting one.

As financial statements in Russia are prepared in accordance with statutory legislation, which differs from international standards, in order to present the financial statements to foreign founders or investors the statutory financial statements are normally brought into compliance with IFRS. This entails additional conversion costs.

In practice, the general Russian statutory accounting reporting requirements applied to Russian companies do not apply to a branch (or representative office) of a foreign legal entity. The latter is obliged to file tax returns with respect to the taxes payable by its branch (or representative office) and an annual report on its activities in Russia.

Summary

Russia's accounting and auditing standards have developed significantly over the last several years. The tendency towards the adoption of IFRS into Russian practice is very significant, as it shows not only Russia's intention to adopt international accounting standards, but also its desire to improve the presentation of financial reporting in order to give all users of financial statements a clearer understanding of the relevant company's financial position. However, applying these standards in practice may cause significant difficulties for Russian companies, since the IFRS principles are completely new to most accounting staff within Russian entities. Managing the transition for such people will be a challenge for the audit and accounting firms with relevant experience within Russia.

4.6

Let's Move Production to Russia

Customs clearance

Alexander Bespalov, Customs Expert, Pepeliaev, Goltsblat and Partners

Given the current rapid growth of production and the increasing inflow of foreign investment into Russia, the managements of big foreign corporations are deciding more and more frequently to move their existing productive capacity and industrial technology to the Russian Federation. Customs clearance of equipment imported as a contribution to authorized capital is an important stage in the implementation of an investment project, and the future of any production depends on this.

The legislation of the Russian Federation provides a favourable climate for attracting foreign investment into the Russian economy. A number of regulatory acts establish a preferential regime in relation to payment of customs import duties and VAT on imported production equipment, components and spare parts (hereafter the 'goods') brought in as a contribution by the foreign investor (founder) to the authorized capital of Russian enterprises with foreign participation. It is worth noting that:

- Import tariffs for production equipment classified in accordance with the commodity items of the Commodity Classification for Foreign Trade (hereafter the TN VED RF – analogous to the Harmonized System), fluctuate between 5 and 10 per cent of the customs value of the imported equipment.

- The flat rate for VAT in Russia is 18 per cent,

Thus, the amount saved (23–28 per cent of the customs value of the equipment) makes such projects – involving the import of equipment as a contribution to authorized capital by a foreign founder – quite attractive from the economic point of view.

At the same time, it should be noted that the above tariff benefits are granted subject to a number of quite strict requirements:

- The imported goods should not be excisable.

- The imported goods should be fixed productive assets.

- The goods should be imported during the period of the formation of the authorized capital of the Russian enterprise with foreign participation.

The goods imported should also fall under the category of production equipment, components or spare parts, and be classified in accordance with the commodity groups of the TN VED RF, which are given in the list of production equipment presented in the Appendix to Order No 131 of the State Customs Committee, dated 7 February 2001.

Import duty benefits are granted for all goods that are fixed productive assets as defined in the All-Russian Classifier of Fixed Assets (OK 013-94 (OKOF)) (approved by resolution No 359 of Gosstandart (State Standards Commission), dated 16 December 1994).

Where goods that have benefited from reduced customs duties and VAT are released into free circulation, they have the status of conditionally cleared goods. They are considered as foreign goods, and for a virtually unlimited period they can be checked and audited by the customs authorities, which are required to confirm that the enterprises with foreign participation that registered the given goods under the preferential regime are using the goods for their designated purpose.

The project manager faces a considerable volume of work in preparing for and implementing the procedure for importing an entire complex of production equipment into Russia in the form of main production lines, auxiliary equipment and devices, as well as all the constituent parts. Four main stages may be identified.

Stage 1: preliminary definitions

This stage entails: drawing up the list of equipment; questions of classification and determination of the country of origin of the goods; determining the customs value; defining the concept of import (as discussed later); drafting amendments to the foundation documents of the Russian company.

Russian customs legislation imposes on the equipment importer (the Russian enterprise with foreign participation) a specific obligation in relation to the classification of the goods, identification of their country of origin, and establishing their customs value. These issues are directly connected with the formation of the tax base and subsequent calculation of the customs duties due for payment (even in the event that preferential treatment is granted).

This stage may be broken down into several operations, entailing:

- determination of the list of equipment and the concept of its import, proceeding from the principle of minimization of customs commodity codes and in accordance with the rules for interpreting the TN VED RF;

- checking that, under the customs commodity codes, the goods may be classified as fixed assets and production equipment;

- identifying the country of origin of the goods;

- establishing the customs value of the production complex in accordance with the selected terms of delivery INCOTERMS 2000;

- ensuring that the list of equipment comprising the production complex intended for importation is included as an in-kind contribution among the amendments to the foundation documents of the Russian enterprise with foreign participation;

- state registration of amendments to the foundation documents;

- independent appraisal of the production complex;

- application to the Federal Customs Service of the Russian Federation (hereafter – FCS RF) for VAT payment benefits to be applied to the imported equipment when customs formalities begin;

- registration of the package of foundation documents and receipt by the relevant customs authority of a decision by the FCS RF concerning VAT payment benefits;

- receipt by the relevant customs authority of a positive decision about applying customs duty and VAT payment benefits to the imported equipment when customs formalities begin.

After the list of equipment has been drawn up, the concept of the import of the equipment and the formation of goods batches need to be determined. There are two concepts of the import. These are customs clearance and GOST R (state standards) certification of a production equipment complex:

- one-off deliveries of functionally complete machines and/or production lines, using the standard (usual) declaration method;

- individual components of machines and/or production lines, applying an FCS RF classification decision and a special declaration method.

When drawing up the list of equipment for inclusion in the amended foundation documents of the Russian company with foreign participation, account should be taken of the fact that this list should contain:

- the name of the equipment, indicating the quantity, type, brand or model thereof;

- the name of the producing company;

- the country of origin;

- the value of the components of the equipment and the overall value in foreign currency (indicating which currency) and its equivalent in Russian roubles.

In addition, the foundation documents must give information about:

- the period of the formation of the authorized capital from the time the decision is made to increase it through an in-kind contribution;

- the time schedule for the import of the equipment into Russia;

- the date on which the exchange rate of the Central Bank of Russia is used to establish the rouble value in relation to the foreign currency in which the value of the imported equipment is declared;

- the delivery terms of the equipment to Russia, determined by one of the international trade terms INCOTERMS 2000.

Amendments to the foundation documents of the Russian enterprise with foreign participation, drawn up, duly registered and reflecting an increase in the authorized capital through an in-kind contribution by the foreign investor, shall be handed over to the territorial division of the Russian tax authorities for state registration.

The next step is to apply in writing to the FCS RF for VAT payment benefits to be applied to the production equipment imported as a contribution to the authorized capital.

Stage 2: organization and resolution of issues pertaining to transportation logistics

The choice of an appropriate transportation company is a factor of some importance for the successful implementation of the project as a whole, as is the subsequent development of the relationship and agreement about procedures. The company should have with a good reputation on the transport and logistics services market, experience of implementing such projects and a substantial transport fleet of various types and sizes. It will also need the capacity to organize multi-modal (mixed) shipments and arrange for convoy escort of road deliveries by customs authorities (for cargos with a high customs value) and the road traffic inspectorate (for wide and heavy loads, requiring special permits, drawing up of a route and time schedule, and organization of an escort).

The chosen transportation company must confirm and ensure precise observance of the project manager's instructions about both the formation and the movement of commodity batches. The governing principle in these operations must be: 'one commodity batch – one functionally complete machine (production line) – one commodity code'.

When deciding on and organizing details relating to questions of transport logistics, special control must be exercised over:

- the formation of commodity batches;

- the packaging, labelling and loading of the equipment;

- liaison procedures with the transportation company and transportation of the equipment to Russia;

- customs border crossing points into the Russian Federation;

- arrival times at the bonded warehouse and presentation of the goods for customs clearance.

In addition, the route to be followed by the various means of transport should be drawn up and agreed with the transport company, governed by the principle of minimizing both the number of load transfers en route, and the number of sea and land customs borders crossed.

The transport company must ensure performance of all the necessary customs procedures when crossing the customs frontier of Russia (arranging for a customs escort for expensive loads, declaring and organizing the procedure for internal customs transit, and making provision for customs inspections). The transport company must also ensure that the designated transport (whether lorry, barge or other mode) arrives at the delivery and customs clearance destination within the time limits set by the Russian frontier customs authorities for delivery of both the goods and the means of transport, and that the goods and transport are presented to the customs authority ready to undergo the customs clearance and control procedures.

Stage 3: organization of customs formalities

The most important stage in implementing the project as a whole is probably that of undergoing customs formalities in Russia, since it is at this stage that the imported goods have to be cleared by customs so as to qualify for the import duty and VAT payment benefits. The fees for the customs clearance of imported equipment are calculated at a fixed rate on the customs value, in the same way as the duty and the VAT, and must be paid in the same manner and at the same times as other types of customs payment. They do not constitute a component in the customs payments subject to preferential treatment (unless otherwise established by special legislative acts of the Russian government).

The fees may be paid into the bank accounts of the customs authority at the time of customs clearance (on the day on which the customs declaration for the load is submitted). They may also be paid earlier, as an advance payment, but it should be noted that article 329 of the Customs Code of Russia establishes that all customs payments should be made within 15 days of the date on which either the goods are presented to the customs authority on arrival in the customs territory of Russia, or the internal customs transit is completed.

A factor of particular importance for the success of the project is the choice of an appropriate customs broker to undertake all operations associated with the customs clearance of the production equipment imported under the preferential regime.

Stage 4: obtaining permits

The complex of documents required to import production equipment, subject to mandatory certification, into the customs territory of Russia includes:

- a certificate of compliance from Gosstandart of Russia (the 'GOST R certificate');

- a sanitary and epidemiological report from the Chief Sanitary Inspector of Russia (hereafter the 'health and environmental safety certificate').

Moreover, the importer should be aware of the need to receive written permission from the Ministry for Natural Resources of Russia to import any equipment containing refrigerants that are not ozone-depleting agents, the circulation of which is subject to regulation (licensing) in accordance with the provisions of the Vienna Convention of 22 March 1985 on protection of the ozone layer, and of the Montreal Protocol of 16 September 1987 on substances depleting the ozone layer.

At the same time, to avoid possible difficulties and delays, it is advisable for health and environmental safety certification of both the equipment and the finished output ultimately produced to be performed by the local territorial division of the sanitary and epidemiological inspectorate.

The import of production equipment (both used and new) involves a complex of interconnected measures to fulfil legal, transport and logistical, customs and certification tasks.

Competent co-ordination of the corresponding services and subdivisions, both state-controlled and those of commercial organizations, as well as fulfilment of the given tasks to a high standard by the project team, will result in timely and due performance of the work on the project to import, certify and gain customs clearance under a preferential tax regime for the complex of production equipment.

It should be noted that, during the last decade, dozens of foreign enterprises have been set up and commissioned in Russia and have made use of this preferential tax regime. This, in turn, has led to a steady demand for the implementation of such projects on the customs services market.

4.7

Intellectual Property

*Tom Stansmore, Head of St Petersburg
Representation for Pepeliaev, Goltsblat
& Partners*

Russians learn at an early age that the radio, television, the steam engine and the light bulb were invented in Russia. Whether or not these facts are historically true, one thing is acknowledged: these inventions were first patented in other countries.

The debate is interesting, not only from an historical perspective, but because it illustrates a couple of interesting points regarding the lack of confidence in the laws protecting intellectual property (IP). Namely, the lack of confidence in Russian IP laws is not a new phenomenon and may have deprived the country of technical and intellectual resources (not to mention historical recognition).

These negative consequences have not gone unnoticed by the Russian government. Since the fall of communism, Russia has introduced new laws for patent, copyright and trademark protection modelled after those in the West, and has been fine tuning them through amendments ever since (even the Criminal Code has been amended to include IP violations and the Customs Code to provide for trademark registration to assist in seizing unauthorized imports). Russia has also ratified many international treaties concerning IP protection (including the Paris Convention and the Madrid Agreement). Even manufacturers' associations and government commissions have been established to effectively coordinate the system.

First impressions, however, are always the most difficult to change and the new laws on the books will only go so far in solving the problem. Stories about counterfeit products on the Russian market (jeans, soaps and detergents, cigarettes, sneakers, food products, automobile parts and anything else one can imagine) are well known, and indeed true. Counterfeit products do indeed all too often make it to the shelves of Russian stores and kiosks and the consequences are also far too familiar: consumers suffer from the poor quality of the goods, rights holders lose their reputation and profits, and the State loses tax revenue.

Simply put, Russia has made great progress in harmonizing its IP laws to conform with those of the West and has created the beginnings of an internal enforcement system to make those laws work efficiently, but the problem has not gone away. The issue is not only important to trademark owners; the Russian government also has much at stake. Intellectual property enforcement has been raised repeatedly during talks about Russia's entry to the World Trade Organization (which has been going on for the past 10 years now), with industries from both the United States and Europe lobbying their governments to push for changes in Russia.

The Russian government is taking the issue seriously. The body tasked with the responsibility for enforcing intellectual property rights is the Interior Ministry's Federal Service for Economic and Tax Crimes. The Ministry has formed a division devoted exclusively to combating intellectual property violations, with corresponding units located throughout the country. Last year alone, it was reported that 500 underground factories had been uncovered and 3,500 criminal cases had been brought.

These figures may indeed represent a good beginning, but they should be recognized as only that, a beginning. Those who have worked in Russia will testify to the fact, that if you want something done right, you have to do it yourself (or at least be involved in the process). Part of Russia's problem with IP rights enforcement stems not from the laws themselves, but the lack of confidence in those laws. Indeed, it is a common misconception that the Russian legal system provides victims with little means of taking the offensive against counterfeit products, but it is this feeling of helplessness that contributes to the problem. Simply put, if the holder of a Russian trademark is suffering from counterfeit goods on the market, it is very unlikely that anything will be done to stop those sales without the holders of the trademark blowing the whistle themselves.

Trademark owners can typically find out about infringement through their distributors (these may be either dependent or independent agents, but in either case counterfeits are eating into their sales). To combat counterfeit goods effectively, accurate information is essential. Russia is the largest country in the world, and having people on the ground in far-flung areas who have a vested interest in protecting the brand is probably the most valuable asset to any trademark holder other than the mark itself.

To the Russian trademark owner, distributors become the key source of information not only in identifying the problem, but also in measuring the extent of the damage (size of market share). The decision to take the next step and bring legal action is usually based on this information, and competent professional advice is critical at this stage.

Russian legislation provides procedures that the victims of trademark infringement can use to shut down producers or distributors of counterfeit goods. As stated earlier, however, victims are often not aware of these remedies or are dissuaded from using them because they mistakenly believe that the system is too complicated or corrupt to provide trademark owners with an effective remedy.

It should always be kept in mind, however that the trademark owners are not completely alone in their fight to assert their IP rights, as the Russian government is under international pressure to combat illegal goods. Granted, this pressure does not automatically manifest itself on a local level (especially in many far-flung areas throughout the country). Very often, in fact, when the local divisions of the Ministry of Economic Crimes are contacted directly (especially in areas far from Moscow), those requesting action quickly become frustrated by what often appears to be a never-ending series of bureaucratic hurdles. It is often here that Russia's poor reputation and lack of confidence in IP legislation gains credence.

When enforcing a trademark, one needs to be cognizant of the fact that, by definition, one is entering into Russia's legal system. And like legal systems everywhere else in the world, Russia's has rules and procedures that can appear ambiguous and confusing to those not familiar with them. Just like in any other situation when legal action is brought, professional advice and assistance is crucial.

We work closely with Russia's Interior Ministry to combat illegal production and have found that trademark owners are far from helpless in protecting their brands. On the contrary, once a working relationship is developed and the procedures understood, the Russian government's own innate desire to combat illegal production works to the advantage of the trademark owner. Navigating the system requires resolve, determination and knowledge, but perseverance gets results. Russians are very brand conscious and the market is too big to ignore. Given the amount of money trademark owners invest to promote and market their brands, it makes good economic sense to procure professional assistance when needed to combat illegal production, and has left many trademark owners with a sense of empowerment.

4.8

Arbitration and Dispute Resolution

Stanislav Denisenko, Head of KPMG
St Petersburg Legal Group

Introduction

At present Russia has a developed judicial system. Under the Russian Constitution, the judicial authorities are independent of the legislative and executive authorities, which do not have judicial functions and are not entitled to interfere with the decision-making process in court.

The Russian judicial system consists of several branches. Depending on the subject and nature of a particular dispute, as well as on the parties involved, disputes in Russia may be considered by: 1) state arbitration courts; 2) federal courts of general jurisdiction and justices of the peace; 3) the Russian Constitutional Court and regional constitutional courts.

Unlike certain European countries, Russia does not have special courts dealing exclusively with cases of one single category (for example, tax disputes, bankruptcy cases or investment disputes).

Since the Russian judicial system is unified throughout the Russian Federation and is subject to federal regulations, what we consider below are the fundamentals of 'arbitration and dispute resolution' as provided for by federal legislation with specific features related to St Petersburg (where applicable).

Consideration of cases by federal courts of general jurisdiction and justices of the peace

Cases in which at least one party is a physical person and which are not related to entrepreneurial activity but involve disputes arising out of civil, family, labour, housing or other legal relationships are considered in Russia by federal courts of general jurisdiction and justices of the peace. The latter consider cases of the lowest importance (in particular, property disputes, which generally involve relatively low claims) and their decisions may be appealed against in the superior federal courts of general jurisdiction (except the Russian Supreme Court).

The system of courts of general jurisdiction in St Petersburg includes district courts functioning throughout its entire territory. Some administrative districts of St Petersburg have more than one district court. Like district courts in other Russian regions, the district courts in St Petersburg suffer from inadequate financing and poor office facilities. There are too few judges for the number of disputes submitted to the courts for consideration, especially during the past few years when this latter number has grown by several times.

Decisions taken by district courts in St Petersburg may be appealed against in the City Court of St Petersburg. Decisions taken by district courts (under certain circumstances) and those taken by the City Court of St Petersburg may in turn be appealed against in the Russian Supreme Court in Moscow.

The procedure for the consideration of cases by federal courts of general jurisdiction and justices of the peace is established by the Russian Civil Procedural Code of 14 November 2002 ('the Civil Procedural Code'), which establishes specific timeframes for the consideration of cases by courts of each instance. As a rule, this is one to two months from the date when an application or a complaint is received by the court. In practice however, due to the heavy workload of judges in St Petersburg, the consideration of cases may take up to several years.

Consideration of cases by the Russian Constitutional Court and regional constitutional courts

The Russian Constitutional Court and regional constitutional courts, including that of St Petersburg, only consider a limited range of cases. These are primarily ones related to the interpretation of the Russian Constitution and constitutions (fundamental laws) of the relevant Russian regions, or the review of certain regulations with lesser legal force with regard to their compliance with the Russian Constitution and regional constitutions.

For example, in instances stipulated by statutory legislation, a complaint may be filed with the St Petersburg Charter Court, which is the constitutional court of St Petersburg, in relation to the violation of the

St Petersburg Charter (the fundamental law of St Petersburg) by a particular law or regulation of the city or municipal authorities. If the law or regulation is deemed by the St Petersburg Charter Court not to comply with the St Petersburg Charter, it will be declared invalid. The St Petersburg Charter Court has recently considered a number of issues, including those related to authorities of the St Petersburg City Administration in the sphere of privatization, land tax rates in St Petersburg and the authority of the St Petersburg City Administration's subdivision in the provision of real estate objects on investment terms.

Consideration of cases by arbitration courts

Cases related to the performance of entrepreneurial and other economic operations are considered in Russia by arbitration courts, which are permanent state courts and are separate from courts of private arbitration. In practice, these courts consider the majority of disputes involving foreign legal persons, as well as Russian companies with foreign investment.

In particular, arbitration courts consider the following types of cases:

- economic disputes between companies (individual entrepreneurs);

- cases relating to collection of fines from companies (individual entrepreneurs) for violating statutory legislation;

- cases related to administrative offences, if a business entity or an individual entrepreneur is held liable;

- insolvency cases.

Arbitration courts also consider cases concerning disputes between shareholders and joint stock companies, or between participants in other business entities and such entities, arising out of the companies' or entities' activities. Therefore, disputes that may arise between foreign investors acting as shareholders or participants of Russian business entities and such business entities are resolved in arbitration courts.

Arbitration courts are better equipped than courts of general jurisdiction and are supplied with the necessary resources. The judges of arbitration courts are more experienced in consideration of complicated legal issues than those of the courts of general jurisdiction. Judges of arbitration courts in St Petersburg are traditionally considered to possess high professional capacities. This is due to a number of

factors, including a solid educational background obtained in the
St Petersburg Law School, which is one of the leading law schools in
Russia, and their involvement in a significant number of complicated
commercial disputes that arise frequently because of the concentration
of large-scale international and Russian businesses in St Petersburg.
Since judges of arbitration courts in St Petersburg are quite experienced in settling complicated disputes and usually express independent and well-grounded opinions, their decisions and legal approaches
are widely studied and sometimes serve as guidelines for lawyers and
judges in other regions.

Arbitration court system

The arbitration court system includes courts at the following four
levels:

- regional arbitration courts (the first, lowest level);

- arbitration courts of appeal, in which decisions taken by subordinate
  arbitration courts may be appealed against;

- arbitration courts of cassation, in which decisions taken by subordinate arbitration courts may be appealed against;

- the Russian Supreme Arbitration Court, in which decisions taken
  by any subordinate arbitration court may be appealed against in the
  cases stipulated by legislation.

The majority of cases within the jurisdiction of arbitration courts are
considered by regional arbitration courts, which act as courts of first
instance, although a very limited number of disputes may only be considered by the Russian Supreme Arbitration Court in the first instance.

The arbitration court hearing procedure

General provisions
The arbitration court hearing procedure is stipulated in the Russian
Arbitration Procedural Code of 24 July 2002 ('the Arbitration Proce-
dural Code'); foreign procedural law does not apply.

However, the arbitration courts may apply foreign substantive law
if this is stipulated either by an international treaty entered into by
Russia, or by Russian law, or by an agreement of the parties. When
applying foreign law, the arbitration courts treat the content of the
applicable provisions in accordance with their official interpretation,
practical application and doctrine in the respective foreign state. In

certain instances, foreign law does not apply. For example, only Russian law is applicable to contracts related to land plots, subsoil zones and isolated water bodies and other real estate property located in Russia, as well as to contracts on setting up Russian legal entities with foreign participation.

Litigation in the arbitration courts is based on the principle of competitiveness and equality of the parties in terms of their procedural rights. Foreign legal entities, companies with foreign investment, international institutions, foreign citizens and stateless persons have rights equal to those of Russian physical and legal persons. However, Russia may impose retaliatory restrictions on the procedural rights of foreign persons of countries that have introduced restrictions with regard to Russian individuals and legal entities. At present no such restrictions exist in Russia.

Representation in an arbitration court
Individuals are entitled to litigate in an arbitration court either in person or via their representatives. The fact that an individual litigates personally does not deprive him or her of the right to representation.

Individuals, including individual entrepreneurs, may be represented in an arbitration court by attorneys-at-law (professional lawyers, members of the bar association who have obtained the status of attorney-at-law upon passing the relevant bar exams), as well as by other persons rendering legal support.

Companies may be represented by:

- their heads or other staff;

- attorneys-at-law;

- other persons rendering legal support, including employees of consulting and law firms, which often represent their clients in the arbitration courts.

Litigation fees for the consideration of cases by an arbitration court
Court proceedings in Russia are performed on a chargeable basis, and the exact amounts of court fees are clearly defined by Russian legislation. Litigation fees are normally paid before the claim or appeal is filed.

The fees currently charged for the consideration of cases by the arbitration courts are quite low. When filing a claim for money or property, depending on the amount claimed, the litigation fees may vary from 500 Russian roubles ('RUB') (currently approximately US$20) to 100,000 RUB (currently approximately US$3,700).

The scale of litigation fees with regard to a claim for money or property is regressive (ie the percentage of the claimed amount payable as the fee decreases and the claimed amount increases). The maximum percentage (4 per cent but no less than 500 RUB) is charged when the amount claimed is less than 50,000 RUB (currently approximately US$1,850).

A positive aspect is that when an appeal or cassation appeal is filed with the appropriate superior arbitration court, the litigation fee is fixed at only 1,000 RUB (currently approximately US$40).

As a general rule, the litigation fees incurred by the party who wins a case are imposed by the arbitration court on the loser. However, expenditure related to employing a representative (an attorney-at-law or other person rendering legal assistance) incurred by the winning party are only imposed by the arbitration court on the losing party within a 'reasonable amount'. This is established subjectively by the arbitration court, taking into account the specific circumstances of the representative's involvement in the dispute.

Consideration of cases by an arbitration court of the first instance
The Arbitration Court of St Petersburg and the Leningrad Region serves as the arbitration court of the first instance. As a general rule, this Court must consider a case and take a decision within three months of a claim being filed therewith. Unlike the general jurisdiction courts, the arbitration court normally meets the established deadlines for court proceedings, and cases are rarely delayed.

A decision taken by the Arbitration Court of St Petersburg and the Leningrad Region may be appealed against in the Thirteenth Arbitration Court of Appeal serving as the arbitration court of appeal, or the Federal Arbitration Court of the Northwest Area serving as the arbitration court of cassation (both located in St Petersburg), or the Russian Supreme Arbitration Court in Moscow within the timeframes established in the Arbitration Procedural Code.

Consideration of cases by an arbitration court of appeal
During the appeal proceedings, the Thirteenth Arbitration Court of Appeal may reconsider the case and has the right to reassess the available evidence and to assess additional evidence that may be presented at this stage in the cases, as established by the Arbitration Procedural Code.

Consideration of cases by an arbitration court of cassation
The Federal Arbitration Court of the Northwest Area only reviews the legitimacy of disputed court decisions from the perspective of whether legislation has been correctly applied. It may not reassess the available evidence and no additional evidence may be presented.

Consideration of cases by the Russian Supreme Arbitration Court
Court decisions of Russian arbitration courts that have entered into force may be reconsidered within the framework of judicial supervision by the Russian Supreme Arbitration Court, on the basis of an application submitted by one of the parties participating in the case or by other parties whose rights and obligations are affected by the court decision.

However, the list of reasons for the Russian Supreme Arbitration Court to reconsider the case is limited, and in practice this court very rarely agrees to reconsider cases.

Conclusion of an amicable agreement
At any stage of the arbitration process, the parties have the right to conclude an amicable agreement in written form that defines their rights and obligations and serves as the basis for terminating the proceedings, provided that the said agreement is approved by the arbitration court.

Execution of decisions of the arbitration courts

Decisions of the arbitration courts are enforced in Russia by special state officials called 'bailiffs', within the framework of special execution proceedings.

Such proceedings are carried out by bailiffs on the basis of an application by the party in whose favour the court decision was taken and an attached writ of execution issued by the arbitration court on the basis of the court decision, confirming the winning party's right to obtain money, property or other compensation from the party that lost the case (the debtor).

If the debtor or any third parties prevent the bailiffs from performing execution, the bailiffs may be assisted by the police.

Transfer of disputes lying within the competence of arbitration courts to courts of private arbitration

As a general rule, with the agreement of the parties, civil law disputes (which fall under the jurisdiction of arbitration courts) may be transferred to courts of private arbitration.

The functions of courts of private arbitration may be performed both by a permanent court of private arbitration – such as the International Commercial Arbitration Court of the Chamber of Commerce and Industry of the Russian Federation, or the Private Arbitration Court of the St Petersburg Chamber of Commerce and Industry – or by an 'ad hoc' court of private arbitration formed by the parties to settle a single dispute.

The parties have the right to transfer a case to a court of private arbitration formed either inside or outside Russia.

It should be noted that, in practice, the option of appealing to a court of private arbitration is not used very often in Russia. This is due to the lack of trust in non-governmental arbitrators by Russian participants in disputes, as well as to the necessity of appealing to an arbitration court in order to enforce a decision taken by a court of private arbitration (if the debtor refuses to execute or attempts to evade voluntary execution of the arbitration award). However, foreign courts of private arbitration, such as those at the Arbitration Institute of the Stockholm Chamber of Commerce, are often utilized to settle material disputes with the involvement of foreign companies.

Execution of decisions taken outside Russia and awards made by Russian courts of private arbitration

Decisions of foreign courts and awards of foreign courts of private arbitration and international commercial arbitration courts made outside Russia are only recognized and enforced in Russia if the recognition and enforcement of such decisions are mandated by an international treaty.

For example, the Convention on the Recognition and Enforcement of Foreign Arbitral Awards (New York, 1958), to which Russia is a party, serves as the basis for the recognition and enforcement of the relevant foreign arbitral awards in Russia.

In any case, if the decision on a dispute emerging in the course of business activities has been taken by a court of private arbitration in Russia, or by a foreign court, court of private arbitration or international commercial arbitration court outside Russia, the writ of execution for the purpose of enforcing the decision is issued by an arbitration court after separate court proceedings initiated by the party requesting execution.

In the course of such proceedings, the arbitration court does not reconsider the case, but only reviews the existence or non-existence of the basis for issuing a writ of execution. In particular, an arbitration court may refuse to issue a writ of execution if a party was not duly informed of the time and place of consideration of the case, or if the decision violates either 'the basic principles of Russian law' (for decisions of Russian courts of private arbitration) or the 'public policy of the Russian Federation' (for decisions taken outside Russia). Since the concepts of 'the basic principles of the Russian law' and 'the public policy of the Russian Federation' are not specifically described by Russian legislation, they are subjectively defined by arbitration courts within the framework of each specific case. Of course, such wide definitions may provide in practice a significant level of discretion for the arbitration courts to influence the successful recognition and enforcement in Russia of awards of courts of private arbitration.

Employment Law and Work Permits for Expatriates

Stanislav Denisenko, Head of KPMG St Petersburg Legal Group

Labour legislation

Russian labour legislation is one of the most developed areas of Russian law. Many of its provisions were worked out in Soviet times and are still reflected in the legislation in effect today. The key document of labour legislation is the new Russian Labour Code of 30 December 2001 ('the Labour Code') which applies to both Russian and foreign legal and physical persons throughout the entire territory of Russia, and regulates labour relations between employers and employees in detail.

As labour legislation is primarily aimed at protecting the employee as the weaker party in labour relations, the employer may not make rules on working practices that might imply worse conditions for the employee than those established by law, even with the employee's consent.

Employment contract

Labour relations between an employee and the employer in Russia must be documented by a written employment contract. If, for any reason, a company fails to conclude a written contract with an employee who has started work, an employment contract shall be considered to have been concluded and the employee shall be subject to all guarantees stipulated by Russian labour legislation.

The drawing up of an employment contract with an employee in written form has advantages for the employer, who can use it to detail specific conditions of labour relations that are not directly stipulated by legislation in order to avoid possible disputes with the employee in the future, as well as stipulate provisions aimed at protecting its interests. For example, when hiring staff, the employer may set a trial period for an employee, which in general may not exceed three months. This is only possible if a trial period clause is included in the employment contract; otherwise, the employee will be considered to have been hired without provision for a trial period.

Duration of the employment contract

The general rule in Russia is that employment contracts with employees should be concluded for an indefinite period of time.

However, legislation stipulates a number of instances (for example, appointing a general director or chief accountant, or hiring employees for seasonal work) where an employment contract may be concluded for a specific period of time.

Generally a fixed-term employment contract expires at the end of the period for which it has been concluded. However, if neither the employer nor the employee has requested that the contract be terminated at that time, and if the employee continues to fulfil his/her job responsibilities after the expiry of the contract, the latter shall thereafter be considered to have been concluded for an indefinite period of time. Thus, if the employer does not wish to continue labour relations with the employee after the expiry of the fixed-term employment contract, it should notify the employee of this in writing in advance.

Working hours and leisure time

Under Russian labour legislation, an employee's working hours should not exceed 40 per week. The legislation does allow the possibility of working overtime, but this may not exceed four hours within two successive days, or 120 hours per annum.

Pursuant to labour legislation, employees are entitled to an uninterrupted weekly rest of no less than 42 hours. Furthermore, the employer shall provide the employee with an annual paid vacation of 28 days. For employees performing certain types of work (for example, those employed under dangerous or harsh working conditions), legislation stipulates a longer vacation.

In addition to weekly rest and annual vacation, employees are also entitled to the 12 public holidays established by statutory legislation.

These include the New Year's holidays that were introduced by Russian legislators at the end of 2004. Therefore, when planning business in Russia, foreign companies should now take into consideration the fact that the governmental authorities and many Russian companies suspend their business operations at the beginning of January for at least one week.

Remuneration

Remuneration is normally paid in monetary form in roubles.

Legislation stipulates the statutory minimum wage and an employer may not set a salary or a wage for an employee below that amount. At present, the statutory minimum wage is set at 720 Russian roubles (RUB) (currently approximately US$25) per month. As the minimum wage is currently below the cost of living (for example, the minimum cost of living in St Petersburg is about 3,000 RUB, or currently approximately US$110), in practice salaries and wages paid by employers to their employees exceed the statutory minimum by several times.

The legislation lays down that salaries and wages should be paid at least every two weeks on the date stipulated by the employer's internal labour regulations, a collective agreement (if such exists) and an employment contract. However, we envisage that the law will be revised in the near future and that employers will be permitted to pay salaries and wages to employees once a month.

Termination of the employment contract

An employment contract may be terminated by agreement of the parties thereto, as well as on the initiative of either the employee or the employer.

An employee is entitled to terminate the employment contract on his or her own initiative at any time by giving notice to the employer two weeks in advance. The employer may not prevent the employee from terminating the contract, even if the parties have signed a fixed-term employment contract.

On the employer's initiative, an employment contract may only be terminated in instances expressly stipulated by legislation, such as:

- company liquidation or job redundancies;

- an employee's unsuitability for the position occupied or job performed;

- repeated failure to fulfil job responsibilities by the employee without a valid reason if disciplinary action has already been taken against him or her;

- a single serious violation by the employee of his or her duties (unauthorized absence from work, attendance under the influence of alcohol, drugs or other toxic substances, and certain other instances stipulated by the Labour Code);

- a single serious violation by the head or deputy head of the company (or branch or representative office) of his/her duties;

- misconduct of an accountable employee that gives the employer reason to lose confidence in the employee.

However, the employer may not freely use the right to dismiss an employee in all of the above instances. For example, should the employer decide to dismiss an employee due to his/her unsuitability for the position occupied or job performed, the employer's opinion alone will not be sufficient. The unsuitability must be properly documented and supported by sufficient evidence. It is noteworthy that in most cases where employees who are unhappy about their dismissal on such grounds go to court, the courts tend to rule in favour of the employees rather than the employers.

When taking a decision to dismiss an employee, the employer should take into consideration the fact that staff may not be dismissed (unless the company is liquidated or an employer who is an individual entrepreneur terminates his or her activity) while they are temporarily unable to work or on vacation. It should also be considered that for certain categories of staff (eg pregnant women and mothers with children under the age of three years old), the general list of grounds for dismissal is significantly reduced.

Labour relations with company management

Taking into account the specific nature of the activity of such officers as the general director and the members of the management board, labour legislation establishes special regulations for labour relations between these officers and the employer.

In many respects such regulations are aimed at protecting the employer's interests, and take into account the regulations established with regard to such officers by corporate legislation. For example, the employment contract of a general director may establish a trial period of up to six months. As a general rule, an employment contract concluded with the general director may be terminated at any time by the employer (regardless of when it is due to expire), through a decision to dismiss that person and the appointment of a different general director, provided that the employer has paid appropriate compensation to the dismissed general director.

In order to protect the employer's interests, legislation also establishes that the company's general director may only occupy paid positions with other entities with the written permission of the appropriate company management body (the general shareholders' meeting or board of directors).

The company's general director acts not only as the company's employee but also as its management body. Therefore, when drawing up the contract of employment the employer should observe the established corporate and registration procedures, in addition to the normal requirements established by labour legislation. For example, when appointing a new general director, the company's superior management bodies should take an appropriate decision on his or her appointment, and the company must submit an application to the state registration authorities and enter the details of the new general director in the unified Russian state register of legal entities.

For any employer, especially companies whose shareholders are unable to constantly control the activities of the head of the company, the issue of the authority of the general director is of great importance. He or she traditionally has extensive authority to take independent decisions on a large number of issues, including financial issues arising in the course of the company's business activity; such decisions may be binding on the company, even if they are detrimental to the shareholders' interests). In order to protect the interests of the company's shareholders, the general director's authority may be restricted in the company's incorporation documents and in the employment contract concluded between the company and the general director.

Work permits for foreigners

Under Russian legislation, a foreign citizen ('the foreign employee') temporarily staying in Russia only has the right to work in Russia if s/he has a work permit (except for certain legally defined categories of employees who may work without permits, such as diplomatic representatives or employees of foreign companies involved in the production or supply of technological equipment to Russia who perform installation work, after-sales service and subsequent repair of such equipment).

In order to employ a foreign employee, the employer has to undertake a series of actions, which in practice may involve extensive time and effort.

First, the future employer applies to the appropriate state authorities (the state employment bodies and the Russian Federal Migration Service) for permission to employ foreign personnel. This permission confers the right to employ a certain number of foreign staff and serves as the basis for a foreign employee to obtain a work permit in the future. The permit is normally valid for not longer than one year.

Before a foreign employee can start working in Russia, the employer must also obtain a work permit in the employee's name and arrange for an invitation to enter Russia. On the basis of this invitation, the foreign employee will be able to obtain a visa to enter Russia with the intent to work.

After entering Russia, the foreign employee must register with the Russian internal affairs authorities within three days of arrival at the place of his/her temporary residence.

In St Petersburg these procedures normally take from two to four months, and undoubtedly complicate both the operations of companies employing foreign staff and the lives of the employees themselves.

The number of foreign employees is limited by quotas that the central government sets annually for each region of Russia on the number of invitations to enter Russia with the intent to work. Work permits may be only issued within the limits of these quotas. The 2004 the quota for St Petersburg was set at 5,000 permits.

Consideration of labour disputes

The Labour Code provides for the possibility of labour disputes between employers and employees being resolved out of court by forming a commission on labour disputes that operates on a permanent basis. Such a commission may be created in the employing company, and should include an equal number of representatives of employees and the employer. Decisions taken by the commission are enforceable. If one of the parties disagrees with the decision taken, it may be challenged in court.

To resolve an issue resulting from labour relations, the employee and the employer may also appeal to the court of general jurisdiction rather than taking the issue to the commission on labour disputes. The consideration of such disputes can be a lengthy process, which sometimes lasts for years. Moreover, a review of court practice in this category of cases shows that most decisions are in favour of employees, as the weakest and most unprotected party to labour relations. Proof of even one procedural non-compliance with labour regulations by the employer (eg violation of the deadline for applying disciplinary action to the employee) has been enough for a decision to be taken in favour of the employee.

Liability for violating labour legislation

Russian law establishes liability for failure to observe labour legislation. For example, employers who delay payment of salaries must pay salaries with interest of not less than 1/300 of the refinancing rate of the Central Bank of Russia (currently 13 per cent per annum) for each day of delay.

If legislation has been violated when dismissing an employee or transferring him/her to a different job, the employee has the right to appeal in court for 'moral compensation'. This may also be claimed from the employer in other instances when moral damage has been caused to the employee through an illegal action or inaction of the employer.

For violations of labour legislation, a company officer may be subject to an administrative penalty, up to a maximum of 5,000 RUB (currently approximately US$180). If such an officer has already been subject to an administrative penalty for a similar administrative violation, he or she may be barred from certain positions in companies for as long as three years.

For violations of the rules on employing foreign employees, a penalty may also be imposed on the company, a company officer or the foreign employee, and the latter may be deported from the Russian Federation.

If violations of labour safety regulations result in severe damage to a person's health, the company officer responsible for observing these regulations can be held criminally liable. The punishment for such an offence may be imprisonment for up to one year.

In the present section, we have not aimed to list all kinds of liability for violating labour legislation but have simply provided some examples to show how important is the issue of compliance with labour law in Russia.

Trade union activities in Russia

Foreign investors intending to start doing business in Russia may be interested to know about the role of trade unions in Russia, and whether their influence on the regulation of labour relations is as strong as in many Western countries.

In Soviet times, trade unions played an enormous role in the regulation of labour relations between employers and employees. Most decisions could only be taken by an employer with the trade union's approval.

However, although the employees' right to associate in trade unions is established by law, in practice trade unions are concentrated in large companies founded in the Soviet era. They are generally not set up in most new, fast-developing companies.

Part Five

Appendices

Appendix I

Service Companies

1.

Baltic Travel Company – destination services Russia

Baltic Travel Company is a destination-management company that delivers world-class service performance, maintains and develops a strong management team, has top level contacts with all suppliers and state governing authorities, and has a technical and operational infrastructure in St Petersburg and Moscow. Baltic Travel Company currently enjoys a long-standing partnership with a number of international clients and always looks forward to expanding and developing relationships with new and existing clients. The success of Baltic Travel Company lies in listening to our clients' requirements and expectations, prompt responses to inquiries, and delivering an unparalleled level of service and quality. It is our policy to show a strong degree of creativity and flexibility in the programmes and events we propose and can customize to meet budgets. Baltic Travel Company stands for reliable, prompt, sound, punctual and attentive service, and we pride ourselves on delivering on our promises.

Services

- programmes tailored to your requirements;
- flexible programme budgeting;
- full scope of sightseeing tours in St Petersburg and Moscow;
- conference and meeting management;
- finding venues;
- the best group transportation in St Petersburg and Moscow;
- professional interpreters and guides;

- project teams providing full operational support;
- visa support.

Products

- unique tours in St Petersburg and Moscow;
- special events and theme parties;
- private visits to museums and places of interest;
- private receptions at palaces and museums;
- full range of classical and Russian folklore entertainment;
- complete database of venues;
- negotiated rates at selected hotels, restaurants and venues.

Baltic Travel Company Structure

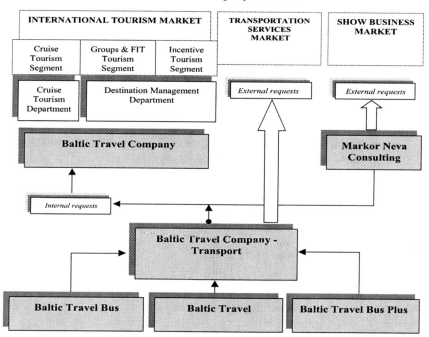

Figure 1 Baltic Travel Company structure

Baltic Travel Company team

Baltic Travel Company can assure you that only the most experienced staff will work with your guests. BTC arranges a project team (PT) consisting of a project manager, programme manager and an assistant programme manager who will be in charge of programme tours, activities and events development and implementation. The PT is responsible for all areas of planning, operation and finance It has the following responsibilities:

- making all arrangements, programme activities and tours in accordance with the requirements of a client;

- maintaining daily contact with a client;

- arranging all bookings with suppliers required for operation of the tours and programme activities and events;

- providing clients with visa support letters for obtaining Russian visas;

- operating all on-site activities, including but not limited to arrivals/departures, tours loading and dispatching; museums/places of interest visits, special events coordinating;

- responding to additional requests of a client;

- providing adequate, clear invoices in accordance with the terms, conditions, procedures and requirements to be agreed between a client and BTC.

The project manager will be a focal point of contact as the person who creates a proposal that offers different venues, tours and activities, noting all the requirements of the client. He or she will also have direct responsibility for operation of all tours and activities arranged.

A specialist appointed as a programme manager handles operational correspondence, arranges all necessary bookings for tours and activities and prepares invoicing information for the Finance Department.

The assistant programme manager arranges the bookings with museums and venues covered by the programme tours and activities. He or she will assist the programme manager in running tours, activities and events, and issues visa application letters if needed.

If the programme requires additional staff, the General Director will assign the required number of programme managers and assistants to cover all items of each activity.

Every six months, all members of the project team participate in training programmes that are specially created by our training managers based on 'follow-ups' of the most complicated and successful programmes and on new experience from annual world travel markets and exhibitions.

BTC transport

All transportation for groups will be arranged in 49-seat Volvo buses. These vehicles are owned and operated by Baltic Travel Company and have valid licenses and insurance. At present, Baltic Travel Company owns 21 Volvo deluxe buses. The buses are air-conditioned and equipped with appropriate audio-visual devices and WC. The buses have been produced with the use of advanced safety technology and are ergonomically designed for the passengers' comfort.

Folklore group

BTC set up the 'Highlights of St Petersburg' in 1995 as a professional music, singing and dancing ensemble. It consists of a choir, orchestra and dancing group, who perform either together or independently in accordance with the venue size and clients' requirements. All the artists have special training and experience of performing at the different stages. They consist of:

- choir: 12 people;

- orchestra of folk instruments: 10 people;

- dance group: 16 people.

Since its foundation, the 'Highlights of St Petersburg' has been successfully performing in the best concert halls of St Petersburg and Russia. Germany, China, Spain, Thailand have been captivated by the high professionalism of the group.

The concert will take the audience on a fascinating spiritual journey through different regions of Russia, with acrobatic Don Cossack dancers, Russian and Ukrainian choral singing, flamboyant dances and nostalgic songs of the gypsies. The Web site address is www.russianfolklore.com

Contact information

Visiting address: 7, Pirogovskaya Embankment
194044, St Petersburg, Russia
Mailing address: PO Box 109, SF 53101,
Lappeenranta, Finland

Tel: +7 812 118 47 69; 118 66 10
Fax: +7 812 118 66 11; 327 40 70
E-mail: info@baltic.spb.ru
www.baltictravel.com

2.

Inpredervice

The St Petersburg state unitary enterprise Inpredservice was founded in 1992 and is an official representative of the St Petersburg City Administration (government) in serving the increasing number of diplomatic missions, international bodies, foreign companies and their representatives. The establishment of a unified, large, specialized enterprise allows higher-quality and more effective organization of work to ensure close interaction and business cooperation between the city administration, diplomatic corps and entrepreneurs who are developing major investment projects in St Petersburg and the Leningrad Region. In order to pursue its objectives in serving St Petersburg's international community, Inpredservice exercises the right of economic management and owns a significant amount of urban property, including a large volume of comfortable housing premises. In order to maintain and service these facilities to a high level, the company has its own modern production and economic base.

The main assets at the company's disposal and the services which it can therefore provide to its clients include:

- A range of leased buildings, offices and apartments.

- A hotel complex with modern serviced apartments ranging in size from 50 to 200 m^2 in the central parts of the city. It also has a restaurant and secure car parks, and outside the city (including the Karelian Isthmus and in the town of Zelenogorsk) has country cottages and country houses.

- The security of leased premises, living quarters and car parks is ensured by state-of-the-art modern video surveillance facilities. The security services that the company offers are conducted jointly with the city's law enforcement agencies.

- Transport services for business partners are provided by a fleet of modern cars and minibuses.

- For personnel work: recruiting and employment registration of skilled specialists to foreign agencies and companies.

- Consultancy and legal services: consultancy on matters of corporate and tax law, real estate transactions, registration of enterprises at the Registration Chamber of St Petersburg and the Leningrad Region.

Inpredservice's wide range of services are offered at a competitive price, since the company takes into account the overall importance of state objectives with regards to the development of investment projects in St Petersburg and Leningrad Region.

One of the company's advantages is that it can offer its clients the use of high-quality facilities within close proximity of their enterprises and firms. As a reliable business partner, Inpredservice is capable of providing the working conditions, accommodation and recreation facilities required by foreign businesspeople, and has already met the needs of many well known corporate clients including Henkel, Nestlé, Petroteknip, Hauni, Zepter, Philip Morris, Izhora and many others.

Contact information

34 Kutuzov Embankment, 191187,
Saint-Petersburg, Russia
Phones: + 7(812) 272-15-00, 279-50-24
Fax: +-7(812) 275-85-72
E-Mail: info@inpredservice.ru
www.inpredservice.ru

Company management

General Director: Morozov Boris Veniaminovich

Chief Engineer: Ganin Aleksandr Viktorovich

Deputy Director of Finance: Shevchenko Alla Viktorovna

Appendix II

Useful Web Site Links and Web Site Reviews for St Petersburg

1. Committee for Investment and Strategic Projects of the Government of St Petersburg (http://www.gov.spb.ru/gov/admin/otrasl/invest)

2. Internet-portal 'Investments into the hotel infrastructure of St Petersburg' (www.hotelinvest.ru)

3. 'Webplan portal on the regions of the Russian Federation' (http://region.investportal.ru/)

4. Committee on the Economic Development, Industrial Policy and Trade of the Government of St Petersburg (http://www.cedipt.spb.ru/)

5. Public department 'Department of Investments' of the Government of St Petersburg (http://stateinvest.spb.ru/rus/)

6. The North-West of Russia in Figures – 2004 (http://www.brcinfo.ru/files/download/Stat-NWRussia.pdf)

7. Federal State Statistics Service (http://www.gks.ru/)

8. Committee on State Statistics for St Petersburg and Leningrad Region (http://www.gostat.spb.ru/)

9. Russian Union of Industrialists and Entrepreneurs (Web: www.rspp.ru or Email: volsky@mksnet.ru)

Appendix III

Contributor Contact Details

Adaptec Company, Russia

Bolshaya Semenovskaya 49
Moscow 105023, Russia
Tel/Fax: +7(095) 369 1762/1877
Email: adapteccom@mail.ru
Contact: Alexander Krivtsov

Association of Joint Ventures of St Petersburg

58 Moika River nab, Suite 316
St Petersburg 190000, Russia
Tel: +7(812) 312 7954
Fax: +7(812) 315 9470
Email: association@jv.spb.ru
Web site: www.spbasp.ru
Executive Directorate:
Nikolai V. Sivach, President
Sergei V. Ochkivsky, Director of Development

Baker & McKenzie

St Petersburg Office
57 Bolshaya Morskaya Street
St Petersburg 190000, Russia
Tel: +7(812) 303 9000 / 325 8308
Fax: +7(812) 325 6013
Email: spb.office@bakernet.com
Contact: Maxim Kalinin

Moscow Office
Sadovaya Plaza, 11th Floor
7 Dolgorukovskaya Street
Moscow 127006, Russia
Tel: +7(095) 787 2700
Fax: +7(095) 787 2701
Email: moscow.office@bakernet.com
Contact: Paul Melling

Beiten Burkhardt, St Petersburg

Nevsky Prospect, 30
191011 St Petersburg, Russia
Tel: + 7(812) 327 76 36
Fax: + 7(812) 327 76 37
Web site: www.bblaw.ru
Contacts:
Denis Martyushev
Email: DMartyushev@bblaw.de
Dr Thomas Heidemann
Email: THeidemann@bblaw.de

BISNIS

Igor Yegorov
BISNIS Representative for Northwest Russia
US Consulate General St Petersburg
Tel: +7(812) 326 2585
Fax: +7(812) 326 2561
Email: Igor.Yegorov@mail.doc.gov

City Realty Ltd

35 Bolshaya Morskaya ul., 1st Floor
St Petersburg 190000, Russia
Tel: +7(812) 312 7842 / 710 6305
Fax: +7(812)710 6457
Email: info@cityrealtyrussia.com
Web site: www.cityrealtyrussia.com
Contact: Paul May, General Manager

CMS Cameron McKenna

Pavaletskaya Square 2/3
Moscow 115054 Russia
Contact: David Griston
Tel: +7(501) 258 5000 (office)
Tel: + 7 095 108 7106 (mobile)
Email: David.Griston@cmck.com

DLA Piper Rudnick Gray Cary

Malaya Morskaya street, 23
190000 St Petersburg, Russia
Tel: +7(812) 703 7801
Fax: +7(812) 703 7802
Web site: www.dlapiper.com
Contact: Victor Naumov
Email: victor.naumov@dlapiper.com

Ernst & Young (CIS) B.V.

St Petersburg Branch
Malaya Morskaya Street, 23
St Petersburg 190000, Russia
Tel: +7(812) 703 7800
Fax: +7(812) 703 7810
Web site: www.ey.com/russia
Contact: Anna Gavrilova, Marketing Coordinator
Email: Anna.Gavrilova@ru.ey.com

Eurologos

Rue Paul Spaak, 24
1050 Brussels, Belgium
Tel: +322 640 8241
Email: info@eurologos-spb.com
Contact: Gilbert Doctorow, Executive Director
Email: gdoctorow@yahoo.com

Government of St Petersburg
Committee for Investments and Strategic Projects

Smolney, Entrance 6, Office 477
191060 St Petersburg, Russia
Tel: +7(812) 576 7106 / 576 6067
Fax: +7(812) 576 7045
Contact: Pavel A. Brusser
Head of Investment Appraisal Department
Email: brusser@cisp.gov.spb.ru

Institute for Entrepreneurial Issues

Marat Street, 92
191119 St Petersburg, Russia
Tel: +7(812) 703 4091 / 703 4090
Fax: +7(812) 703 3008
Web site: www.ipp.spb.ru
Contact: Alexei Shaskolsky, Ph. D
Email: a.shaskolsky@ipp.spb.ru

KPMG

19 Moskovsky pr., Level 4
St Petersburg 198005, Russia
Tel: +7(812) 325 8348
Fax: +7(812) 325 8347
Contacts:
Peter Arnett, Partner, Head of Tax
Email: PArnett@kpmg.ru
Stanislav Denisenko
Senior Legal Manager, Head of the Legal Group
E-mail: SDenisenko@kpmg.ru
Alisa Melkonian, Tax Manager
Email: AMelkonian@kpmg.ru

Lenenergo

Marsovo Pole, 1
191186 St Petersburg, Russia
Tel: +7(812) 318 3974

Fax: +7(812) 318 3747
Contact: Gregory Kharenko, PhD
Deputy-Head of Investor Relations
Email: kharenko@upr.energo.ru

Pepeliaev, Goltsblat & Partners

St Petersburg Office
54 Shpalernaya str.
St Petersburg 197136, Russia
Tel: +7(812) 333 0717
Fax: +7(812) 333 0716
Web site: www.pgplaw.ru
Contact: Tom Stansmore
Head of Representative office
Email: t.stansmore@pgplaw.ru

Moscow Office
Krasnopresnenskaya nab. 12,
Entrance 7, World Trade Center-II
Moscow 123610, Russia
Tel: +7 (095) 967 0007
Fax: +7 (095) 967 0008
Web site: www.pgplaw.ru
Contact: Ekaterina Kleimenova
Marketing and Business Development Manager
Email: e.kleimenova@pgplaw.ru

PeterStar

Bld. 31, Line 16, Vassilyevsky Island
199178 St Petersburg, Russia
Tel: +7(812) 324 5807
Fax: +7(812) 329 9007
Contact: Anastassia Bogatikova
Senior Marketing Specialist
Email: bogatikova@office.peterstar.com

Raiffeisenbank Austria

Severnaya Stolitsa Branch, St Petersburg
Moika Embankment, 36

191186 St Petersburg, Russia
Tel: +7 (812) 718 6800 / 331 9194
Fax: +7 (812) 718 6801 / 331 9194
Contact: Pavel Sivak, Marketing Manager
Email: psivak@raiffeisen.ru

Research and Design Institute of Regional Development and Transportation

36 Chugunnaya Street
194044 St Petersburg, Russia
Tel: +7(812) 333 3172
Fax +7(812) 333 3190
Contact: Svetlana Vorontsova
Email: investpro@ipr.ru

Sebastian FitzLyon F.R.I.C.S., S. Zinovieff & Co. Chartered Valuation Surveyors

Australian Honorary Consul
Northwest Russian Consular District
Italianskaya Street, 1
191011 St Petersburg, Russia
Tel & fax: +7(812) 325 7333
Email: sf@zinovieff.ru
Web site: www.Zinovieff.ru

Web-invest Bank

Nevsky Prospect, 38
191011 St Petersburg, Russia
Tel: +7(812) 326 1305 (ext. 1751)
Fax +(812) 332 2323
Web site: www.web-invest.ru
Contact: Alla Petrova
Head of Department for Equities Analysis
Email: A.Petrova@web-invest.ru

Printed in the United States
120194LV00003B/1/A